Father Chaucer

Samantha Katz Seal is an Associate Professor of English and the Pamela Shulman Professor of European and Holocaust Studies at the University of New Hampshire. She has been an American Council of Learned Societies Fellow and a Visiting Scholar in Harvard University's Medieval Studies Program.

T0355324

Father Chaucer

Generating Authority in
The Canterbury Tales

SAMANTHA KATZ SEAL

OXFORD
UNIVERSITY PRESS

Great Clarendon Street, Oxford, OX2 6DP,
United Kingdom

Oxford University Press is a department of the University of Oxford.
It furthers the University's objective of excellence in research, scholarship,
and education by publishing worldwide. Oxford is a registered trade mark of
Oxford University Press in the UK and in certain other countries

First published 2019
First published in paperback 2023

Published in the United States of America by Oxford University Press
198 Madison Avenue, New York, NY 10016, United States of America

British Library Cataloguing in Publication Data
Data available

Library of Congress Cataloging in Publication Data
Data available

ISBN 978–0–19–883238–6 (Hbk.)
ISBN 978–0–19–890488–5 (Pbk.)

DOI: 10.1093/oso/9780198832386.001.0001

OXFORD STUDIES IN MEDIEVAL
LITERATURE AND CULTURE

General Editors
Ardis Butterfield and Christopher Cannon

The monograph series Oxford Studies in Medieval Literature and Culture showcases the plurilingual and multicultural quality of medieval literature and actively seeks to promote research that not only focuses on the array of subjects medievalists now pursue – in literature, theology, and philosophy, in social, political, jurisprudential, and intellectual history, the history of art, and the history of science – but also that combines these subjects productively. It offers innovative studies on topics that may include, but are not limited to, manuscript and book history; languages and literatures of the global Middle Ages; race and the post-colonial; the digital humanities, media and performance; music; medicine; the history of affect and the emotions; the literature and practices of devotion; the theory and history of gender and sexuality, ecocriticism and the environment; theories of aesthetics; medievalism.

For Andrew

"*This ecstasy doth unperplex,*
        We said, and tell us what we love..."

Acknowledgements

I have nine years worth of acknowledgements to make for this book, from its distant origins as a dissertation prospectus in 2010 to its current incarnation. My time at Yale was replete with guidance, generosity, and friendship, and my first thanks must go to my doctoral advisor, Alastair Minnis. Alastair allowed me to follow the threads of my interest in reproductive metaphor from medical texts to Chaucer, and, more than anyone else, inspired my deep fascination with *The Canterbury Tales*. I am truly grateful to him, and to my other professors—Jessica Brantley, Roberta Frank, Anders Winroth, Ian Cornelius, Robert Nelson, and Margot Fassler—for the models of scholarship and mentorship that they set, and for the years of kindness and support with which they gifted me. I owe significant thanks to my Yale medievalist community more broadly, especially to Katherine Hindley, Andrew Kraebel, Lauren Mancia, Greg Roberts, Madeleine Saraceni, Anne Schindel, Joe Stadolnik, Aaron Vanides, Elizabeth Walgenbach, Eric Weiskott, and Jordan Zweck. Laura Saetveit Miles and Mary Kate Hurley both read chapters of this manuscript, and have given me their brilliant advice and their wonderful friendship.

I have also benefitted immeasurably from the unending energy, and passion of the medievalist feminist community. When, in 2012, I presented part of this work at the Medieval Academy meeting, I never expected the two other panelists to become such incredible mentors and friends. Holly Crocker and Nicole Nolan Sidhu have written recommendations, read my work, and collaborated on conference panels and journal issues. Most recently, Nicole has been my co-editor for two special journal issues on feminism. They have given me so much of their time, and truly set a standard for feminist practice. I would like to thank the Society of Medieval Feminist Studies as well for giving me an opportunity to serve on the advisory board and participate in some of the crucial research and advocacy being done to craft a more just and inclusive Medieval Studies. I would like to thank Angie Bennett, Suzanne Edwards, Carissa Harris, Dorothy Kim, Emma Lipton, Roberta Magnani, Julie Orlemanski, Elizabeth Robertson, Leah Schwebel, Emily Steiner, Diane Watt, Tara Williams, and Barbara Zimbalist for how their work has inspired and invigorated my own, in addition to reshaping the field in absolutely essential ways. Carolyn Dinshaw's *Chaucer's Sexual Poetics* has been the text that I have returned to again and again, and that gave me first the courage to reimagine Chaucer and, eventually, to write this book; I offer my heartfelt gratitude to its author.

At Weber State University, I would like to thank Hal Crimmel, Sian Griffiths, Janine Joseph, Julia Panko, Scott Rogers, Sally Shigley, Shelley Thomas, and especially Jennifer Mitchell for all the camaraderie, advice, and support that they gave to me. I would also like to thank Diane and Steve (Z"L) Mitchell for their boundless kindness to my family.

The English department at the University of New Hampshire has nurtured my career, and given me profound resources to develop this book. I would like to thank my department chair, Rachel Trubowitz, for the time and advice that she has given me, and to thank my other fellow medieval/early modern faculty—Dennis Britton, Doug Lanier, Sean Moore, and Reginald Wilburn—for their mentorship and camaraderie. I would also like to thank Kabria Baumgartner, Cris Beemer, Rachel Steindel Burdin, Monica Chiu, Jaed Coffin, Diane Freedman, Robin Hackett, Tom Haines, Marcos del Hiero, Soo Hyon Kim, James Krasner, Alecia Magnifico, and Laura Smith for their friendship over the past four years. My writing of this book was supported by a summer stipend from the UNH Graduate School, and by my time as a faculty fellow in the 2016 UNH Writing Academy. For the latter experience, I would like to thank Dean Michele Dillon, Eleanor Abrams, Jo Daniel, Julie Williams, and especially my Writing Academy mentor, the late Burt Feintuch.

Ardis Butterfield and Chris Cannon have been instrumental in helping the book reach its current shape. Their thoughtful, perceptive critiques have challenged me to refine my arguments, and their unflagging enthusiasm for this project has buoyed it throughout the move to publication. I am deeply honored for my book to be included in their new series at OUP, and am so very thankful for their support. Brendan O'Neill first expressed interest in publishing the book for OUP, and I am grateful to him and to Jacqueline Norton as well for moving the book forward through the review process. Catherine Owen and Aimee Wright have been fabulous editors, and I appreciate their work very much! Thanks go as well to Markcus Sandanraj, who has shepherded my book through production. My anonymous readers offered invaluable criticism and brilliant recommendations for revision; thank you. An earlier version of part of chapter 3 was published in the *Open Access Companion to the Canterbury Tales* in 2017, and I appreciate the permissions of the editors—Candace Barrington, Brantley Bryant, Richard Godden, Dan Kline, and Myra Seaman—to have it reprinted here.

And finally, I must thank my family. My parents, Phyllis and Steven Katz, nurtured my passion for medieval literature and history since I was a young child. Their support, love, and encouragement—and that of my brothers, Nick, Ted, and Andrew Katz, and sister-in-law, Jenn Katz—has been everything to me. I'd like to thank my in-laws as well, Tina and Bob Cook, Tom and Nancy Seal, and Marianne Seal and Sean Smithberger for their love and kindness.

I walked across the stage at Yale to receive my doctorate while pregnant with my son, Fredric; my daughter, Judith, was born just as this book was going to press. Freddy and Diti are the delights of my life. Chaucer may have concluded that procreation was an unsteady source of authority, but for me, it has been only a joy and an honor to raise and cherish them within this world. Still, without the women who work at Creative Times Academy in Ogden, Utah, and Growing Places in Durham, New Hampshire, this book would never have been written. Their labor with our children was not only performed with love, it has been received by us that way as well.

My husband, Andrew, has been my partner for the last eleven years. He heard the ideas that would become this book when they were just some notes I had jotted down while studying for orals; he was my sounding board for all the twists and turns that this book has taken. When I wanted to give it up, he talked me through it, and when I wasn't sure that anyone would want to read it, he talked me through that too. He is my best editor, best indexer (thank you again!), and best friend. This book- and all the books I could ever write—is for him.

Contents

Introduction

The Dream of "Father Chaucer"

The lak of [Fortune's] favour
Ne may nat don me singen, though I dye,
'Iay tout perdu mon temps et mon labour:'
For fynally, Fortune, I thee defye!
Geoffrey Chaucer, "Fortune"[1]

In life and in death, Geoffrey Chaucer was a fortunate man. In 1349, when the Black Death annihilated 50% of London's population, it simultaneously brought great wealth and new social opportunities to the surviving members of the Chaucer family. John Chaucer, father of Geoffrey, accumulated property from his deceased relatives, consolidating wealth that would otherwise have been beyond the reach of a city vintner, and then used that new affluence to win a position in the royal household for his son.[2] John Chaucer's wealth also facilitated an advantageous marriage for his son; the union of Geoffrey with Philippa de Roet not only offered the Chaucers an air of gentility (Philippa's father had been knighted), but strengthened the Chaucer connection with the royal household and, eventually, would turn John of Gaunt, the Duke of Lancaster, from Chaucer's noble patron to his brother-by-marriage.[3] In the span of a single generation, the Chaucers rose from merchants to members of the court.

More fortunate still, Geoffrey became the father of two sons, Thomas and Lewis Chaucer.[4] The new patrilineal generation likewise saw a rapid accumulation of

---

[1] All quotations from *The Canterbury Tales* are from *The Riverside Chaucer*, ed. Larry D. Benson (Oxford: Oxford University Press, 1986).

[2] Derek Brewer, *Chaucer and His World* (Cambridge: D. S. Brewer, 1978): 17–25; Derek Pearsall, *The Life of Geoffrey Chaucer: A Critical Biography* (Oxford: Blackwell, 1992): 27–8. For a detailed survey of Chaucer's male-line ancestry, see Lister M. Matheson, "Chaucer's Ancestry: Historical and Philological Re-Assessments," *The Chaucer Review* 25.3 (Winter 1991): 171–89.

[3] The evidence (though not fully conclusive) points to Sir Payne de Roet, a knight of Hainault, as the father of Philippa Chaucer and Katherine Swynford. De Roet had come with Queen Philippa from Hainault to England in 1327, and remained affiliated with her court before eventually moving to that of her sister, Margaret of Hainault, the Holy Roman Empress. Accordingly, both Queens, but especially Queen Philippa of England, remained active in advancing the interests of de Roet children. For an overview of opinions on Philippa Chaucer's family identity, see Margaret Galway, "Philippa Pan, Philippa Chaucer," *The Modern Language Review* 55.4 (October 1960): 481–7, at 485–6.

[4] For the biography of Thomas Chaucer, see Martin B. Ruud, *Thomas Chaucer* (Minneapolis, MN: University of Minnesota Press, 1926); J. S. Roskell, Linda Clark and Carole Rawcliffe (ed.), *The House*

Father Chaucer: Generating Authority in The Canterbury Tales. Samantha Katz Seal, Oxford University Press (2019).
© Samantha Seal.
DOI: 10.1093/oso/9780198832386.001.0001

wealth, property, and *gentil* connections, culminating in the marriage of Geoffrey's granddaughter, Alice Chaucer, to the Earl of Salisbury and then to the future Duke of Suffolk. In testament to this remarkable social climbing, Alice Chaucer commissioned a grand tomb for her parents, Thomas and Matilda Chaucer, paying homage to the fortunes of her family with the display of a full twenty-four heraldic shields (including that of the Plantagenets) whose human possessors she could claim as kin.[5] Chaucer denounced Fortune as "a fals dissimulour" in the poem that serves as this introduction's epigraph, but the evidence of his own life proved her capacity for bounteous good will.[6]

And yet this is only half the story of "Father Chaucer," the poet whom John Dryden dubbed the progenitor of English poetry, and whom G. K. Chesterton and others credited (erroneously) with "tossing off a little trifle called The English Language."[7] For Fortune's gifts, even when granted, were insufficient, incapable of bestowing upon man or poet alike that far more valuable attribute: authority. Fortune's spinning wheel, "whirling up and doun" (Fort 11), is inherently opposed in its geometry to the visions of literary authority and poetic descent that Chaucer crafts in his invocations of the classic poets. When Chaucer thinks of the fathering of poetry, he pictures it in a line of ascension. Thus, for example in *Troilus and Criseyde*, he charges his "litel book" to "kis the steppes, wher-as thou seest pace/Virgile, Ovyde, Omer, Lucan, and Stace" (TC 1786, 1791-2), in other words to participate in a progression of literate authority defined by its linearity.[8] It is this same line of poetic descent that gives such

of Commons 1386-1421, Vol. II (Stroud: Alan Sutton Publishing, 1992): 524-32. For both Thomas and Lewis Chaucer, see Donald R. Howard, *Chaucer: His Life, His Works, His World* (New York: E. P. Dutton, 1987): 93-4; Seth Lerer, "Chaucer's Sons," *University of Toronto Quarterly* 73.3 (Summer 2004): 906-16. References to both of Chaucer's sons are also contained within *Chaucer Life-Records*, ed. Martin M. Crow and Claire C. Olson from materials compiled by John M. Manly and Edith Rickert, with the assistance of Lilian J. Redstone and others (Oxford: Clarendon Press, 1966): 541-6. Kittredge questioned the existence of Lewis Chaucer, postulating that the *Treatise on the Astrolabe* might instead have been intended for Lewis Clifford, but the more recent discovery of a 1403 listing of a Ludovicus Chaucer as a soldier in Wales has established both Lewis Chaucer's birth and his attainment of adulthood. G. L. Kittredge, "Lewis Chaucer or Lewis Clifford?" *Modern Philology* 14.9 (January 1917): 129-34. For the evidence on the life of Lewis Chaucer, see Lerer, "Chaucer's Sons," 907.

⁵ E. A. Greening Lanborn, "The Arms on the Chaucer Tomb at Ewelme," *Oxoniensia* (1940): 1-16; Joel T. Rosenthal, *Patriarchy and Families of Privilege in Fifteenth-Century England* (Philadelphia, PA: University of Pennsylvania Press, 1991): 26; John Goodall, *God's House at Ewelme: Life, Devotion, and Architecture in a Fifteenth-Century Almshouse* (Aldershot, UK and Burlington, VT: Ashgate, 2001): 169-75.

⁶ Geoffrey Chaucer, "Fortune," *The Riverside Chaucer*.

⁷ John Dryden, *Fables Ancient and Modern; Translated into Verse, from Homer, Ovid, Boccace, and Chaucer: With Original Poems* (London: Jacob Tonson, 1721); G. K. Chesterton, *Chaucer* (New York: Sheed and Ward, 1956). For the history and analysis of the idea that Chaucer "invented" the English language, see Christopher Cannon, *The Making of Chaucer's English: A Study of Words* (Cambridge: Cambridge University Press, 1998): 48-90.

⁸ For Chaucer's grouping of classical authors, see Elizaveta Strakhov, "'And kis the steppes where as thow seest pace:' Reconstructing the Spectral Canon in Statius and Chaucer," *Chaucer and Fame: Reputation and Reception*, ed. Isabel Davis and Catherine Nall (Woodbridge: Boydell and Brewer, 2015): 57-74. A. C. Spearing notes that this may be the first time a writer in English refers "to his own

meaning to Dryden's imaginings of Spenser as Chaucer's "poetical son," and, as Helen Cooper notes, to the motif of poetic fatherhood more generally.[9] To think of paternity (whether biological or poetic) as a stable staircase leading one up and down across the varied flights of history was to imagine a mode of human authority capable of overcoming Fortune's wheel, of transcending the arbitrary judgments of the Divine. The motif of the medieval father is a bulwark of patriarchy and male power set against the spinning vagaries of female whim. It is a stone foundation that stops the wheel, allowing man to endow his own time and labor with meaning and authority, and to impose a male linearity upon time itself.[10] Carolyn Dinshaw identifies the essential divide between medieval temporalities as between the "straight time of patriarchal reproduction" and the "queer" modes of non-linearity, but here "queer" and "female" are symbolically inseparable: they are the terms for the temporal chaos that man must control with his authority.[11]

The *auctoritas* of the medieval father is recognizable to a contemporary reader despite, or rather perhaps because, of its supposed transhistoricity. The reproductions of patriarchy across time self-mythologize a single paternal authority for which all men yearn and have always yearned, unmoved by death or time. This is the mode of paternal authority that Harold Bloom, for example, in his classic text on poetic authority, *The Anxiety of Influence*, visualizes as the institutional and domestic antithesis from which the modern poets have fought and rebelled.[12] Likewise, it is this image of paternal authority to which, as Seth Lerer and Stephanie Trigg have established, the late medieval and early modern poets turned as a source of legitimation and intellectual identity.[13] Yet as I will argue in this book, that contemporary picture of paternal authority is one hopelessly flawed, and we must critique it both at a macrocosmic level and at an acutely specific one in its applications for Geoffrey Chaucer. In general terms, paternal authority has for far

work by either of the grand titles of tragedye or comedye; indeed, except for Chaucer's own use of the word tragedye a little earlier in his translation of Boethius, perhaps neither word had previously been used in English at all." A. C. Spearing, *Medieval to Renaissance in English Poetry* (Cambridge: Cambridge University Press, 1985): 32.

---

[9] Helen Cooper, "Choosing Poetic Fathers: The English Problem," *Medieval and Early Modern Authorship*, ed. Guillemette Bolens and Lukas Erne (Tubingen: Narr, 2011): 29–50.

[10] As Patricia Skinner has argued, we can see medieval women inverting this model to impose the cyclicality of a feminine mode of time (often based upon the repetitive movement through marital states) in the place of a linear, masculine one. Patricia Skinner, "The Pitfalls of Linear Time: Using the Medieval Female Life Cycle as an Organizing Strategy," *Reconsidering Gender, Time, and Memory in Medieval Culture*, ed. Elizabeth Cox, Liz Herbert McAvoy, and Roberta Magnani (Cambridge: D. S. Brewer, 2015): 13–28.

[11] Carolyn Dinshaw, *How Soon Is Now?: Medieval Texts, Amateur Readers, and the Queerness of Medieval Time* (Durham, NC: Duke University Press, 2012): 54.

[12] Harold Bloom, *The Anxiety of Influence: A Theory of Poetry*, 2nd Edition (Oxford: Oxford University Press, 1997).

[13] Seth Lerer, *Chaucer and His Readers: Imagining the Author in Late Medieval England* (Princeton, NJ: Princeton University Press, 1993); Stephanie Trigg, *Congenial Souls: Reading Chaucer from Medieval to Postmodern* (Minneapolis, MN: University of Minnesota Press, 2002).

too long been assumed to be a static mode of representation against which variations of individual filiation may become more sharply defined; in other words, we have consistently looked to the "sons" to characterize their "fathers." The first and fundamental question that this book asks is what if paternity is not the stable bulwark of systemic patriarchy and literary authority, but rather the shakiest of stones in each respective artifice?

The Canterbury Tales is a poem about male authority in the midst of patriarchal crisis and of secular ambition in the face of renewed lay devotion, and most of all it is a poem of a poet uncertain in his posterity. Reproduction is its anxiety and its critique, the metaphorical (or, sometimes, not-so-metaphorical) manifestation of the human desire to claim something more for its humanity than what God has allowed. It is through images of reproduction that Chaucer reflects upon his own multifaceted embodiment of authority—as a man, a father, and a poet. Masculine authority codifies his present status, but the limitations of poetic and paternal authority throw his future into contest. Where later poets and scholars saw paternity as a stable, and indeed stultifying, force, Chaucer saw it as fundamentally destructive, the destabilizing emblem of all that man wanted and could not have upon the earth. Paternity was the physiological embodiment of human doubt and human inadequacy. Even the most successful of fathers (and Chaucer, with only two sons and apparently no grandchildren at the time of his death, was far from such) were reminded of the sharpness of the *rota fortuna*'s turns, the brutal upheavals of their world. And yet reproduction was the closest that man could get to playing God, to writing his own future into the world, and seeing a newly vital self before his eyes. It was a mechanism of production whose promise to men was as undeniable as its results were too often unreliable.

Therefore, while Chaucer recognizes a (highly specific) version of paternal authority, he qualifies its grandeur according to its unattainability. For Chaucer, fatherhood was a highly recognizable motif, deployed often by classical authors and poets, and yet it was one that no medieval Christian could fully embody. For the dream of the stable father was a dream of a purely human authority, of a triumph as mortal as it was male, expressed through an overt antagonism to women, time, and the harsh decrees of their God. In *The Canterbury Tales*, Chaucer positions himself as one caught between man's desire for such authority and the recognition of that desire as sacrilegious as well as doomed. He has his Knight preach through the character of Theseus to those assembled at Athens, and on pilgrimage:

> Wel may men knowe, but it be a fool,
> That every part dirryveth from his hool,
> For nature hath nat taken his bigynnyng
> Of no partie or cantel of a thyng,
> But of a thyng that parfit is and stable,
> Descendynge so til it be corrumpable.
> And therfore, of his wise purveiaunce,

He hath so wel biset his ordinaunce
That speces of thynges and progessiouns
Shullen enduren by successiouns
And nat eterne, withouten any lye.

(KnT 3005–15)

There is no true progeny, no posterity, no authority for mortal man. All things break down with time. The very act of reproduction results in loss, and in degradation. In this way, the production of offspring is little different from the production of texts, although the degradation of the progenitive object that Chaucer describes in *Adam Scriveyn*, for example, is precipitated by Adam's "negligence and rape"—in other words, by a negative human intervention. Adam is an unworthy vehicle for Chaucer's "offspring," and so his poems are ruined by degree and by transmission. In the Knight's oration above, on the contrary, there is no negative human intervention, but only the callous, unfeeling witness of the mortal world. It is Nature herself, driven by God's "ordinaunce," who destroys the original through its replications; it is the human body that is conditioned to decay.

Time controls men, fathers and sons alike, and they move to its tune, against their will if necessary. Moreover, there is no escape from loss in modes of poetic descent. The same steps of poetry on which, in *Troilus and Criseyde,* Chaucer wishes one day to stand will crumble in turn as all things must, as all flesh does before men's eyes. The successions and authorities, through which men dream of living after death, cannot bear the faith men put in them. Time seeks its prey, text and flesh alike. There is no alternative image, no staircase of authoritative men ascending up to heaven; there is only woman's wheel, bringing all men and their works back to the dust from which they were born.[14]

And yet the miracle of *The Canterbury Tales* is that, despite the foregrounding of human futility at the very beginning of the poem, the pilgrims keep traveling, keep joyfully reaching for those ambitious modes of authority that they *know,* that they have just been *told,* will remain always out of human grasp. "Wel may men knowe, but it be a fool…" the Knight begins his description of human deterioration, but despite the risk of being called a fool, he does not end his speech there. The Knight tells us that nothing made by humans lasts nor truly matters, even as he himself makes something out of words. As A. C. Spearing argues, Chaucer used his "pagan worlds in order to gain the courage and impetus to question his own God."[15] He writes his stories, some pagan, some not, in order to give himself and his readers room to interrogate the world, to struggle with the

---

[14] Andrew Galloway reads the section about "successiouns" here as an "affirmation of sexuality" that "expel[s] the tone of clerical bookishness, and even of high politics," but I tend to read both the sexuality and the high politics of aristocratic diplomacy as inextricable within a single philosophy of how to reproduce within the world. Andrew Galloway, "Authority," *A Companion to Chaucer,* ed. Peter Brown (Oxford: Blackwell Publishers, 2000): 23–40, at 33.

[15] Spearing, *Medieval to Renaissance,* 57.

restrictions imposed upon human generation by his faith. Chaucer and his pilgrims tell their company of readers again and again that creation is impossible for man, and yet they still create, one story after another, one linked narration following the last. Indeed, the speech by Theseus within the context of the *Knight's Tale* is not meant to urge men and women to death nor to despair; it is meant to inspire them to marry and to procreate. As he continues, for "thanne is it wisdom, as it thynketh me,/To maken vertu of necessitee" (KnT 3041–2). Man will derive only loss from his reproductions, but that is no reason and no excuse not to reproduce.

Fortunate Fathers

Fortune is an achievement of the moment, the mutable bounty that fills the hand or flees the clutch of fingers as it wishes. But authority is reinforced by the claim of antiquity.[16] Authority makes manifest not only the human capacity to produce, but, more importantly, the capacity to *reproduce* in turn, in perpetuity. As Chaucer's Dame Prudence quotes Cicero to her husband, Melibee, "Tullius seith that 'grete thynges ne been nat accompliced by strengthe, ne by delivernesse of body, but/by good conseil, by auctoritee of persones, and by science;' the whiche thre thynges been nat fieble by age" (MelT 65–65A). Authority, like wise advice and science, may wield its influence across the bounds of time; it does not fade with the flesh. And so, while each man may judge his own fortunes from looking at the offspring of his form, his authority will be known only after his death. As Larry Scanlon writes of the *Pardoner's Tale*, "in the narrative's exploration of death's liminality, it will find the source of its own discursive authority, an authority which consists precisely of the inescapability of the divine."[17] Man's authority is realized through his acquiescence to divine authority; by allowing the self to be annihilated through death, man offers his moral, humble stance as a foundation for posthumous memorialization.

That ambivalent withdrawal from dynastic aspiration was a wise one according to the demographics of Chaucer's time. While the Chaucer family had been deeply indebted to the social upheaval of the Black Death, they were not immune from the trauma of its aftermath or the overall high rates of male line extinction. As K. B. McFarlane calculated, "on the average during the period 1300–1500, a

---

[16] Alastair Minnis quotes Walter Map on this point, as Map argued that his own work would only gain true authority through the legitimization of his death. Minnis notes that Map was correct in attributing authority to historical remove, but that he underestimated the decree of remove required, since his work became commonly attributed in the Middle Ages to a Roman historian. A. J. Minnis, *Medieval Theory of Authorship: Scholastic Literary Attitudes in the Late Middle Ages*, 2nd Ed. (Philadelphia, PA: University of Pennsylvania Press, 2010): 11–12.

[17] Larry Scanlon, *Narrative, Authority, and Power: The Medieval Exemplum and the Chaucerian Tradition* (Cambridge: Cambridge University Press, 1994): 199.

quarter of the families contained in [the nobility] became extinct in the direct male line every twenty-five years; in fact just over 27%, and this wastage is spread pretty evenly over the whole period."[18] It is a highly controversial question whether this high rate of mortality and familial extinction was associated with the plague and its habitual recurrences, or was simply the result of an insufficient birth rate and consistent level of infant mortality.[19] Yet whatever its origin, families struggled to find male heirs to maintain their property. Likewise, in the political upheaval of the 1380s, Chaucer witnessed the abrupt fall from power (and often demise) of both aristocrats and men of the mercantile class, like Chaucer's colleague on the wool custom, Sir Nicholas Brembre, Mayor of London. Royal favor could be withdrawn or overruled, and elevation to the courtly ranks came with its own pressures of familial preservation. Patrilineality, as both a legal and social construct, ultimately had only a limited capacity to avert crisis for its devotees. As male heirs died and daughters inherited, old family lines died out or were absorbed into the lineages of new men.[20]

The rapidity with which men like Chaucer, Brembre, or their peer, Michael de la Pole, earl of Suffolk, advanced in their climb to gentility and noble rank, was thus intertwined with the tragedy of other, older families. Within this historical moment, the prerequisites of authority had shifted enough for certain already privileged men to set individual merit against the primacy of noble blood. And yet such men, lacking the authority of noble ancestry, were vulnerable in their ability to maintain their power and wealth, let alone to transmit their acquisitions to the next generation. The Merciless Parliament of 1388 not only executed many of Chaucer's friends (including Brembre and Sir Simon Burley), but it stripped their children of any further potential for advancement.[21] The success of a man like Chaucer was the result of decades of familial investment combined with the fortunes of post-plague inheritance and royal favor. But a political mistake could

[18] K. B. McFarlane, *The Nobility of Later Medieval England* (Oxford: Oxford University Press, 1973):146.

[19] McFarlane himself argued that the data on familial extinction during the major plague year of 1349 pointed to a low impact from that event, although he recorded a demographic reaction among the nobility to the plague of 1361. McFarlane, *Nobility of Later Medieval England*, 168–71. For more on the debates upon this question, see L. R. Poos, "Plague Mortality and Demographic Depression in Later Medieval England," *Yale Journal of Biology and Medicine* 54.3 (1981): 227–34; S. J. Payling, "Social Mobility, Demographic Change, and Landed Society in Late Medieval England," *The Economic History Review* 45.1 (1992): 51–73; Mark Bailey, "Demographic Decline in Late Medieval England: Some Thoughts on Recent Research," *The Economic History Review* 49.1 (1996): 1–19; David Herlihy, *The Black Death and the Transformation of the West* (Cambridge, MA: Harvard University Press, 1997): 39–58.

[20] Chaucer's own family had benefited from just such an inheritance in 1306 when a distant relative inherited a valuable business and changed his name to "Chaucer," but in that case the family name had been preserved through transfer to a new bloodline.

[21] However, the subsequent change in royal dynasty did allow Sir Simon Burley's son, Sir William Burley, eventually to regain royal favor and become a Speaker of the House of Commons under King Henry VI. James Alexander Manning, *The Lives of the Speakers of the House of Commons* (London: E. Churton, 1850): 86–91, at 89; Roskell, *House of Commons*, 432–5.

wipe that all out, leaving a man's children unprotected and in far worse straits than his parents had been. Merit was not a guarantee of continuity nor did it offer a refuge for posterity. Such men, in surpassing their fathers' influence and social status, had also surpassed the protections of their paternal line.[22] Furthermore, since so much of wealth was solidified through marriage to heiresses, there were rarely any surviving male affinal kin capable of exerting authority in defense of young offspring.[23] These "new men" of late medieval England therefore faced the dangerous volatilities of the royal court without the stabilizing counterweight of hereditary power and historical legitimacy.

For Chaucer, the late fourteenth century was a moment haunted by the memory and foreknowledge of death. No aristocratic family of fourteenth-century England was far from the precipice of catastrophe. As Chris Given-Wilson notes, "Forfeiture and bankruptcy played a relatively small part in thinning the ranks of the peerage; the great majority of extinctions occurred simply for lack of male heirs."[24] The Plantagenet kings themselves spent the latter half of the fourteenth century in one dynastic crisis after another, and one bitter critique of Richard II's reign was that he had deliberately aggravated the crisis by marrying a seven-year-old child instead of a woman of reproductive age.[25] In contrast, by the time of Richard II's forced abdication in 1399, Henry of Bolingbroke, father of four sons, promised a future for England in a way that childless Richard could not; he symbolized a form of male authority that had become more valuable as it had become

---

[22] In contrast, the accusations of treason that the five primary victims of the Merciless Parliament of 1388 made to counter against the Duke of Gloucester were immediately dismissed according to his lineage. In Thomas Favent's account of the Parliament, the speaker of the House of Commons supposedly addressed the Duke of Gloucester, saying "Lord duke, you have sprung from such a worthy royal stock, and you are so near to us, in a collateral line, that you cannot be suspected of devising such things." No comparable expression of faith was granted to Nicholas Brembre or Simon Burley. A. R. Myers, ed. *English Historical Documents: 1327–1485, Vol.4* (New York: Oxford University Press, 1969): 162.

[23] Sir Michael de la Pole, the son of the Michael de la Pole, Earl of Suffolk, who had been banished after the Merciless Parliament, rectified this vulnerability by marrying Katherine de Stafford (the niece of the Earl of Warwick) in order to solidify Warwick's investment in the repatriation of the Suffolk inheritance. Warwick had intervened for Sir Michael in 1388, and continued to do so throughout the 1390s. For Warwick's attempts to protect Sir Michael, see John Smith Roskell, *The Impeachment of Michael de la Pole, Earl of Suffolk in 1386* (Manchester: Manchester University Press, 1984): 200–1. On "great creations" of the nobility that failed in the next generation, see George Holmes, *The Estates of the Higher Nobility in Fourteenth-Century England* (Cambridge: Cambridge University Press, 1957): 39.

[24] Chris Given-Wilson, *The English Nobility in the Late Middle Ages: The Fourteenth-Century Political Community* (New York: Routledge, 1996): 65. Given-Wilson also observes that of the three hundred noble families summoned to parliament throughout the course of the fourteenth century, only around thirty families were summoned both at the beginning of the century and at the end. The rest of the families had either faded from prominence by the end of the century or rose into the ranks of the aristocracy during the period.

[25] Adam Usk, *The Chronicle of Adam Usk: 1377–1421*, ed. and trans. C. Given-Wilson (Oxford: Clarendon Press, 1997): 18–21. For a discussion of the political impacts of Richard's childlessness, see Katherine J. Lewis, "Becoming a Virgin King: Richard II and Edward the Confessor," *Gender and Holiness: Men, Women, and Saints in Late Medieval Europe*, ed. Samantha J. E. Riches and Sarah Salih (London and New York: Routledge 2002): 86–100.

more scarce.[26] Such a situation provided opportunities for men of all ranks, from Henry Bolingbroke, earl of Derby, to Geoffrey Chaucer, son of a London vintner. But it also pushed such men, the fortunate survivors of an overthrown world, to look to their own futures in turn, and to fear for their sons if Fortune spun her wheel again. Chaucer's generation had survived one of the worst epidemics in human history and had flourished in its aftermath. Yet as they moved ever closer to the inevitability of their own deaths, they confronted the harsh ramifications of the same human crisis that had enriched them.

A medieval man in want of an heir was a man in conflict with both his future and his past. As Andrew Cole and D. Vance Smith note, much of the critical legacy of medieval studies has emphasized the significance of human continuity as a defining aspect of the Middle Ages, for "to be medieval is to posit a future in the very act of self-recognition, to offer a memory or a memorial to a future that will be recognized at a time and place not yet known."[27] A legitimate male heir was time corporealized, a memorial to the self not yet extinct and yet a likeness of a younger self already gone. To be without a male heir, or to be in doubt as to the capacities of one's male heir, was thus to be severed from the material chain of human time, and from all its inherent promise of a yet-to-be-grasped authority.

This book is an account of Chaucer's struggle with the recognition of his own mortality and of the potential inadequacies of the heirs he would leave behind. It treats *The Canterbury Tales* as an extended poetic meditation on man's desire to sire and to determine his future, undercut by the shattering realization that as a weak, mortal man he must eventually acquiesce to the powerlessness and impotence of the human condition. Chaucer sketches out man's hope for posterity as a unifying condition across the social classes of the medieval world; neither aristocratic birth nor ecclesiastical office can ensure the longevity or quality of a man's remnants upon the earth. Reproduction thus operates as one of the symbolic languages of the poem, as well as the all-encompassing hermeneutic against which all such semiotics must be read. It is the motif of human hope and the rhetoric of its despair. Moreover, in a poem that is bookended by the authority of Christian orthodoxy through a holy martyr and a holy sermon, reproduction offers an alternative path to authority, one defined as natural and temporal rather than divine. As the pilgrims wend their way to Canterbury, they explore alternative technologies for the creation of personal authority—they reproduce through their words what they hope to have reproduced in the flesh. They turn to poetry and

---

[26] The Lancastrians were noted for their remarkable fecundity and the close bonds between John of Gaunt, Duke of Lancaster, and his son, Henry of Bolingbroke. In his biography of Henry IV, Ian Mortimer notes, for example, that in 1381–82, "father and son were now practically inseparable." Ian Mortimer, *Henry IV: The Righteous King* (London: Jonathan Cape, 2007): 42.

[27] Andrew Cole and D. Vance Smith, "Outside Modernity," *The Legitimacy of the Middle Ages: On the Unwritten History of Theory*, ed. Andrew Cole and D. Vance Smith (Durham, NC: Duke University Press, 2010): 1–38, at 19.

procreation in the insistence of their desire to leave something in the world, something ratified not by God, but by each man, and by a community of men.

There are female pilgrims too, of course, and female characters within the *Tales*. But Chaucer's investment in reproduction as a system of pre-existent meaning, a cultural site within which he can situate his own crisis, codifies and entrenches an active/passive system of sex division and sexual practice. Luce Irigaray describes the function of such a model:

> Man is the procreator, that sexual production–reproduction is his 'activity' alone. Woman is nothing but the receptacle that passively receives his product . . . Matrix—womb, earth, factory, bank—to which the seed capital is entrusted so that it may germinate, produce, grow fruitful, without woman being able to lay claim to either capital or interest since she has only submitted 'passively' to reproduction.[28]

As I will argue in this book, the model of reproductive perfection that Chaucer elevates as a source of male authority capable of competing with death is one that demands ultimate passivity from its women—and not from just the women themselves, as individuals, but from their wombs. Unruly women are barren women in *The Canterbury Tales*; they are the stumbling block in man's ambitions, the humbling tool with which God keeps man human. Chaucer chooses reproduction as the underpinning of his philosophical exploration because, while the desire to reproduce in the flesh represents man's ultimate uncertainty, it also enforces a stability of meaning upon the female bodies that operate as the mechanisms of its productivity. The functionality of the female body within this perspective grounds the ephemeralities of male interpretation, allowing men to negotiate the fluidity of their identity as men only insofar as female identity remains the static source of their self-discovery. Women thus become an essential part of *The Canterbury Tales* without ever truly *mattering* within the poem.[29] Their bodies are the tools with which men fight death, but their "voices" are only ventriloquized in the pursuit of male triumph. Chaucer was writing a poem about humanity, and, as Judith Butler writes, reproduction excludes women from that category: "the nurse-receptacle freezes the feminine as that which is necessary for the reproduction of the human, but which itself is not human."[30]

This book is therefore divided into three sections, according to the three most significant rhetorical motifs of medieval paternity: certainty, productivity, and likeness. Utilizing medieval medical and theological accounts of the human body, its mortality, its sex/gender designations, and its reproductive capacities, these

[28] Luce Irigaray, *Speculum of the Other Woman* (Ithaca, NY: Cornell University Press, 1985): 18.

[29] In contrast, for reproductive imagery used in medieval literature by, and for, medieval women themselves, see Jennifer Wynne Hellwarth, *The Reproductive Unconscious in Late Medieval and Early Modern England* (New York and London: Routledge, 2002).

[30] Judith Butler, *Bodies That Matter: On the Discursive Limits of "Sex"* (London and New York: Routledge, 1993): 42.

three sections (each containing two chapters) provide a detailed account of the centrality of reproductive theory to *The Canterbury Tales*. In the two chapters in Section I, "On Certainty," we witness the way in which Chaucer establishes a semiotics of doubt upon the reproductive female body, and limits both men's certainty in their own cognition and in their temporal connection to their lineage. Section II, "On Creation," documents Chaucer's depictions of alternative forms of reproductive technology and reproductive mating–male/male partnerings, human/ science partnerings, human/God partnerings, and male/male/female partnerings— as he asks, in the face of the female undermining of "traditional" heterosexual reproduction, what other possibilities might be available for modern man? Finally, Section III, "On Likeness," addresses the interaction of sex and likeness, as men grapple with the impossibility of ever achieving the self-referential perfection of Father and Son. God was able to sire an heir in his own undifferentiated likeness, but human men fail in this pursuit, siring those "monstrosities" of unlikeness: daughters, or inadequate sons.

All three sections of the book explore the painful medieval interweaving of faith and science with the anxieties of humanity, but Section III, "On Likeness", not only documents the stakes of human ambitions, but also humanity's ultimate acquiescence to the rigid restrictions upon its ambitions. Christianity waits, wherever men's pilgrimages may wend. And so Chaucer must leave behind the science and poetry with which he has played along the road, must turn once again to the Church that both offers, and restricts, man's hope for immortality. In this sense the pilgrimage ends as it began, with the holiness of Thomas Becket and the helplessness of those men who now have no choice left but to call upon him. The journey from Southwark is a brief wandering away from the sharpness of doctrine, but it is also always a wandering in awareness of its future retraction. And finally, since this is a book as much about the passing of time and human ambition as it is about sex and poetry, the conclusion brings all four themes to fruition in Chapter 6, "Father Chaucer's Heirs." This final chapter brings Chaucer's own vision of his future heirs directly up against the retrospective visions of those who claimed to succeed him—one "Father Chaucer" against another in a centuries-long struggle for the meaning of a single man's life.

Wandering along the road to Canterbury, all human institutions are lost, all structures undermined. And thus while it has been the practice of centuries to impose a specific order upon *The Canterbury Tales* (typically one that corresponds to the order within the Ellesmere manuscript), this book moves away from such rigidity, from the retrospective vision of a Chaucer with the authority to enforce the order of his text.[31] Such an approach accords well with the trends of modern

---

[31] Earlier scholars believed that even if the Ellesmere or Hengwrt manuscript orders were not the best structure for the *Tales*, that there nevertheless *existed* an ideal, author-contrived order. For an example of this kind of critical argument, see Robert A. Pratt, "The Order of *The Canterbury Tales*," *PMLA* 66.6 (December 1951): 1141–67. Pratt also provides an account of Walter Skeat and Frederick

textual scholarship, for Chaucerians have increasingly found themselves dissatisfied with the arbitrary structure that editions of *The Canterbury Tales* have given to the text.[32] As Arthur Bahr has argued, Chaucer's work "is not one fragmentary poem but a poem of fragments whose conventional capitalization (e.g., Fragment I or VII) implies a secure, stable integrity at odds with the meaning of the word fragment itself."[33] It is human to long for linearity, to wish to make sense of our texts, but ordering *The Canterbury Tales* can too easily become a practice of artificially constructed authenticity.

And so, this book approaches *The Canterbury Tales* with an eye to the fluidity of disorder, with an awareness of the inherent, deliberate messy nature of the text. Derek Pearsall perhaps most clearly advocated the adoption of such a flexible method of inquiry when he suggested, in 1985, that the text be read "partly as a bound book (with first and last fragments fixed) and partly as a set of fragments in folders."[34] The flexibility of this model is remarkable, for it imagines a *Canterbury Tales* always writ new for the reader, always reborn in the imagination of the person who encounters Chaucer's text. This book could perhaps be said to unite Pearsall's fluid model with the thematic, labyrinthine one emphasized by Donald Howard, who argued that Chaucer's work could be read as "an elaborate structure with many turnabouts in which the path clusters now on one side, now on another, sometimes sweeping past whole areas where it has been before, and yet which through its overall form and conception encompasses all of its design and arrives at its end."[35] For while this book embraces a freely moving compilation of textual parts, it also understands Chaucer's poem as inherently intertwined with a strong central concern with human authority. In whatever order one reads the text, those commonalities and anxieties remain and call out for attention; I have simply organized this book so as to analyze the subthemes inherent within this reproductive discourse.

And yet I do not wish to deny that an inherent aspect of linearity persists within the *Tales*, for Chaucer has set his pilgrims on the road to Canterbury, on a journey that the reader will never see them finish. Moreover, the pilgrims themselves express an awareness of time growing late, of day ending, and of lives drawing to a close. In this sense, the text enforces a linear temporality if not a

---

Furnivall's nineteenth-century conflict over what pattern to impose upon the text. Pratt, "Order of the Canterbury Tales," 1141–4.

[32] Even within the introduction to *The Riverside Chaucer*, probably the most famous and authoritative edition of *The Canterbury Tales*, Larry D. Benson acknowledges that "there are no explicit connections between the fragments…and consequently no explicit indication of the order in which Chaucer intended the fragments to be read. (Indeed, there is no explicit indication that he had made a final decision in the matter)." Benson, *Riverside Chaucer*, 5.

[33] Arthur Bahr, *Fragments and Assemblages: Forming Compilations of Medieval London* (Chicago, IL: University of Chicago Press, 2013): 157.

[34] Derek Pearsall, "Theory and Practice in Middle English Editing," *Text* 7 (1994): 107–26, at 114.

[35] Donald Howard, *The Idea of The Canterbury Tales* (Berkeley, CA: University of California Press, 1976): 331.

linear structure; its movement is driven not by the order of texts, but rather by the inherent progress of human life. Time moves forward, in all the *Tales*, in whatever order one reads them. From this perspective, even the "bookend" tales (that of Knight and Parson) transcend the stability of their fixed place. For Chaucer knows that the *Parson's Tale* awaits his Knight, that all romance and play upon the road will fall before mortality. And so this book concludes with Knight and Parson together, bound by the inherent similarities of their texts upon man's fate, reflecting upon the insufficiencies of their own authority. For, defying the order of editors and editions alike, Chaucer's tales are nevertheless tied together at last by their sense of human inadequacy, by their painful, insistent awareness of the ends that are yet to come.

Mortal Man and the Dream of Authority

The rest of this Introduction is devoted to discussing Chaucer's more general concern with mortality's impact upon human authority, and the opportunities offered by poetry for a balancing of individual and collective forms of memory. The question of authority in *The Canterbury Tales* can only be represented by a complex knot of interwoven adjectival modifiers, such as literary, moral, historic, Christian, and cultural. It is the interaction between these separate modes of authority, indeed, that has been the foundational argument of much Chaucerian scholarship. Larry Scanlon has argued against a "monolithic ideal of medieval authority" and demonstrated how Chaucer's use of the exemplum as a narrative form serves to reveal authority itself as mere discursive construction.[36] The question of etymological overlap between auctour and auctoritee makes the definition of authority a crucial question for understanding *The Canterbury Tales*.

Scholars and readers alike have tended to favor Chaucer the individual, Chaucer the poet whose words will be his progeny.[37] This is the Chaucer who seeks consolation in earthly reputation, who makes a distinction in *The House of Fame* between those whose names are untouched by glory and those whose names persevere in Fame's shadow. On one side of a "roche of ice" (HF 1130), Chaucer (the narrator) witnesses the unfortunate illegibility of the names of those people for whom "unfamous was wexe hir fame" (HF 1146).

---

[36] Scanlon, *Narrative, Authority, and Power*, 5.

[37] See, for example, Alastair Minnis's conclusion to his article on the relationship between Chaucer, Gower, and their Classical predecessors, in which he privileges poetic remove rather than lineage. "Chaucer and Gower had at least in common a refusal to play the role of dwarf, however clear-sighted, to the ancient giants. Above all else, they were their own men, respectful of their distance from the old men of great authority, and from each other." A. J. Minnis, *De vulgari auctoritate*: Chaucer, Gower and the Men of Great Authority," *Chaucer and Gower: Difference, Mutuality, Exchange*, ed. R. F. Yeager (Victoria: University of Victoria, 1991): 36–74, at 65–6.

> Tho saw I al the half y-grave
> With famous folkes names fele,
> That had y-been in mochel wele,
> And hir fames wyde y-blowe.
> But wel unethes coude I knowe
> Any lettres for to rede
> Hir names by…
> But men seyn, 'What may ever laste?"
>
> (HF 1136–42, 1147)

And yet on the other side of this rocky hill, Chaucer reads the still clear and shining names of those whose names were "conserved with the shade…of a castel" (HF 1160, 1162). Enough fame and enough luck so as to reside in fame's enduring grace, and a man can trust that his name will be known long after his own life.

This vision of poetic longevity testifies to the power of the individual, unlinked from the mechanisms of collective posterity.[38] The names are written next to each other, but each is the name of an individual; the relationships between such nomenclatural neighbors are left vague and undefined. Men's names are preserved according to their own specific merit and to the intervention of an external force. Moreover, as John McGavin notes, names within the poem mark not only a differentiation of identity between individuals, but also a "reputation [that] fixes a person's significance through time and society, and as a consequence, prescribes the uses which others will make of him and her."[39] The memory of each "name" (in McGavin's broad sense) marks a communication between the inscription and its reader (Chaucer), but not a communication between the names themselves. The recognition of meaning is depicted as a solitary pursuit for subject and object alike. The names are simultaneously clustered and isolated upon that rock, representing a vision of eternity predicated upon the embrace of the replication of subjectivity over the reproduction of community.

Such a system of memorialization and recognition privileges an immortality bought with the memorializations of the tongue, rather than those of the loins. As Ruth Evans observes about this passage, "the melting away of the names is not entirely arbitrary: it is also due to their being used within the traditions of *auctoritas*. Use or conservation: what exactly is the function of the (memorial) archive, and how will the methods of archiving affect knowledge in the future?"[40] Evans

---

[38] It is these kinds of individual relationships with Chaucer's poetic progenitors that are explored, for example, in William T. Rossiter, "Chaucer Joins the *Schiera*: *The House of Fame*, Italy and the Determination of Posterity," *Chaucer and Fame: Reputation and Reception*, ed. Isabel Davis and Catherine Nall (Woodbridge: Boydell and Brewer, 2015): 21–42.

[39] John J. McGavin, *Chaucer and Dissimilarity: Literary Comparisons in Chaucer and Other Late-Medieval Writing* (Madison and Teaneck, NJ: Fairleigh Dickinson University Press, 2000): 59–60.

[40] Ruth Evans, "Chaucer in Cyberspace: Medieval Technologies of Memory in *The House of Fame*," *Studies in the Age of Chaucer* 23 (2001): 43–69, at 62.

postulates this as a problem of the "writing self," but it is as equally a dilemma for the male, reproductive self.[41] Chaucer's narrator is impacted by the dual nature of the threatened erasure; his identity as a poet thus serves as an augmentation of his identity as a man. Moreover, this scene demonstrates the limitations of poetic reproduction, poetic archiving, compared to the technologies of seminal reproduction and memorialization. For, one's name might still be spoken within this imposing castle, but those who will speak it will not be *of* one's name. There is no part derived from progenitor here. Instead, even if one is remembered, those who invoke that memory will exist outside it. Their investment in the posthumous reputation of famous men is ephemeral, immaterial, and cold. And indeed, that is the only the optimal scenario. For just as easily, the sun might shift, the shadows move, and the safety of the cold turn to destructive heat. And the name will melt away, with no one bound by blood to look for it. Each man is entirely on his own within this paradigm of poetic memory, dependent upon the circumstances of situation rather than the firm foundations of kinship and lineage.

The precariousness of this non-biological strategy of remembrance and immortality is sharp within *The House of Fame*. Instability is its logic, deceit its semiotic code. "Thus saugh I fals and sooth compound/Togeder flee of oo tydinge" (HF 2108–9). Those whose names are written in Fame's shadow may be remembered for posterity, but the authenticity of what is thereby reproduced in their names is nonetheless tainted by falsehood. Moreover, the fate of such men rests uneasily in the hands of a fickle goddess. "She [Fame] gan yeven eche his name/After hir disposicioun/And yaf hem eek duracioun" (HF 2112–4). Men cannot write themselves into perpetuity. All they can do is write for a woman's favor, to win arbitrary praise according to her whims. It is Fame herself who will decide whether they will be remembered, and her judgment will be rendered as she pleases. This is the harsh conclusion of Chaucer's poem. The dream with which he opened, as the narrator stood and heard the trumpets of Messenus, of Job, and of Theodomas, "and [of] other mo.../That in hir tyme famous were/To lerne" (HF 1243–50), was just a dream. Men might read each other's words across the centuries, but what they hear is fundamentally shaped by the distortions, perversions, and arbitrary whims of the passage of time.[42] As Lara Ruffalo wisely posits, the series of lists within the poem serve to alienate their objects

---

[41] Evans, "Chaucer in Cyberspace," 63.

[42] Gayle Margherita sees a similar concern within *Troilus and Criseyde*, where "the paternal figure of Lollius stands in for the narrator's anxieties about literary history. His name is a morphological paradox that represents the poet's own troubled relation to the literary past: its ending evokes the nobility of a lost classical tradition while its stem brings to mind a contemporary heterodox movement. As a "front" for the poet himself, Lollius at once commemorates the classical fathers of vernacular poetry and heretically violates their legacy." Gayle Margherita, *The Romance of Origins: Language and Sexual Difference in Middle English Literature* (Philadelphia, PA: University of Pennsylvania Press, 1994): 85. From Margherita's reading, Lollius's example accords well with the names upon the icy rock of the House of Fame; the challenge for the father is not just being remembered, but being remembered *in the right way*.

(and Chaucer, their observer) from time itself. "These things all exist at once, "now," in the list; they need the injection of time ... to make coherent stories of all this matter."[43] This dislocation of men and objects from their origins destroys the very nature of lineage and reproduction. And, as Ruffalo eventually concludes, the "absence of unity allows the *House of Fame* to portray a burgeoning multiplicity of literary authority, a veritable verbal hydra."[44] To create, and to trust in his creation and in those of others, man needs to understand the order of the generations. Otherwise, devoid of temporality or systems of heredity, man is all things, and no things, all at once.

Chaucer hears the trumpets of Messenus "Of whom that speketh Virgilius" (HF 1244) mediated through a mode of literary paternity, but it is rife with the arbitrariness of its own happenstance. For Chaucer depends on chance to have read Virgil, and on chance for Virgil to have read Messenus. Literary contact happens across such great spans of time that the contact becomes dislocated from causality, as author and reader find each other without knowing the meaning of their own encounter. Where biological paternity writes meaning into the very process of inheritance, literary paternity, blind to its own modes of perpetuation, can claim authority only from its object alone. Chaucer has read Virgil and thus he knows Messenus only through what Virgil himself has chosen to tell him, and what Virgil himself has chosen to read. Death, in such a model, is truly destructive, consuming not only human beings, but also the humanity of the ties between them. And poetry can pass on only a pale shadow of its progenitor, reproduced randomly and at the mercy of arbitrary time.

> Of whiche I nil as now not ryme,
> For ese of yow, and losse of tyme,
> For tyme y-lost, this knowen ye,
> By no way may recovered be.
>
> (HF 1255–8)

The immortality of verse is a flawed façade, one that passes on the names of men without preserving either flesh or spirit, or remembering the relationships between the men themselves. Time is lost, even when men rhyme, and the poem may well not be enough to bear witness to the poet. From this perspective, poetic creation becomes only a game of hazard, to attract the eye of Fame and pray that one passes gently through her hands.

The House of Fame ends abruptly, however, with the appearance of a "man of greet auctoritee" (HF 2158). The narrator's recognition of another man's presence within the dream cuts through the chaos of Fame's court and of the wildly

---

[43] Lara Ruffolo, "Literary Authority and the Lists of Chaucer's 'House of Fame:' Destruction and Definition through Proliferation," *The Chaucer Review* 27.4 (1993): 325–41, at 332.

[44] Ruffolo, "Literary Authority and the Lists," 338.

spinning wicker house that Chaucer has now entered. It offers the linkage of masculinity (even more significantly, a *material* masculinity) to replace the unstable vagaries of the feminine. "Atte laste I saw a man" (HF 2155), writes Chaucer, in an articulation of man's inchoate desire to be joined by another of his flesh. After all the importance placed upon names earlier in the poem, Chaucer cannot give a name to the man he sees before him (HF 2156). And yet the man's appearance of "greet auctorite" more than compensates for the ambiguity of his identity. Chaucer does not know who this man is, but he recognizes *what* he is when he recognizes him as a man. In the midst of spinning noise, the physical flesh of another man offers a point of solidity; it allows Chaucer to awake from his dream, to leave the petty promises of literary immortality behind so as to regain his own material form. In short, the man of great authority reminds Chaucer of the authority incumbent within masculinity itself: the weight of patrilineality, the stability of kinship, the unending reproduction of blood.[45] Lost in his ambitions as a poet, Chaucer is reoriented towards his ambitions as a man, ambitions that leave the poem unfinished, but the author whole.

In *The House of Fame* (completed 1379–80) we find an earlier Chaucer, a more hopeful Chaucer who still believes that male identity and its biological reproductions may compensate for the unknowability and instability of literary fame. In 1379, Chaucer was thirty-six years old, the father of young children, and the optimistic servant of a twelve-year-old king. The peasants had not yet imagined their revolt, the Lords Appellant had not yet presented their appeal, and the first barren queen was still a young girl in Bohemia, slightly older than the second queen's mother in Bavaria. In 1379 it still seemed as if men like Chaucer who had been accumulating power and wealth within the new regime would be able to pass it on to the next male generation and to the male generation after that. Patriarchy would be the stable form of their self-replication—poetry, its variable cousin, only their last resort. The construction of a hierarchy between poetry and patriarchy as modes of human perpetuation remains a consistent theme of late medieval/early modern poetry. Even when two centuries later Shakespeare imagines the older, defeated Richard II turning towards poetry as a means of self-memorialization ("For God's sake, let us sit upon the ground/And tell sad stories of the death of kings" [RII]), poetry has only become his chosen mechanism because patriarchy has already failed him. "For what can we bequeath/Save our deposed bodies to the ground?" (RII). The dissemination of property and the capacity to reproduce the self: these are supposed to be achieved through the legal, social, and biological triumphs of patrilineal descent. In short, in 1379

---

[45] Thus I do not see Chaucer realizing the "inevitable failure" of authority so much as giving up on one specific form of it, that based on the temporally chaotic, non-linear structures of poetic lineage, in favor of awaking as a man with all the authorities supposedly inherent to the sex. For a contrasting perspective, see Jacqueline T. Miller, "The Writing on the Wall: Authority and Authorship in Chaucer's 'House of Fame,'" *The Chaucer Review* 17.2 (Fall 1982): 95–115, esp. 112.

Chaucer could still imagine being rescued from the infelicities of Fame by a man of great authority; moreover, he could still imagine one day that he himself would become that man of great authority, producing an unending line of authoritative men in his image. The House of Fame could not hold him when he was young enough to be capable of immortality outside its walls.

But, by 1386 Geoffrey Chaucer had become a very different man, with a very different set of expectations and an entirely new understanding of what history was promising him (and of what it would ask for in return). Lee Patterson places the conflict between the collective pressures of social (and, moreover, historical) identity and the personal pressures of individual subjectivity at the very heart of Chaucer's poetic strategy.

> *Anelida and Arcite* and the *Troilus* define the problematic of history in terms of the relation of the individual to an unfolding historical totality, a totality that both stands over against the self and is nonetheless an effect of it. And both, and especially the *Troilus*, explore with often astonishing perspicuity the complex dialectic— between the subject and history—that is at the heart of the *Canterbury Tales*.[46]

Within this reading, Chaucer straddles both the demands of history and of his own subjectivity, as he articulates the oxymoronic simultaneity of man's investment in, and individuation from, his community. Patterson's argument here marks a true critical advance in the study of Geoffrey Chaucer's intellectual history as a specific field. However, by approaching intellect and philosophy as decorporealized forms, Patterson fails to follow the implications of his analysis. Chaucer does not merely articulate this dialectic; he embodies it. Chaucer's subjectivity is bounded by the demands of his bloodline, the collectivity of his identity as part of a kin-based history is materialized in his flesh. He is at once both his own individual and the reshaped product of all those individuals who formed the chain of his historical being. Moreover, what Chaucer negotiates in *The Canterbury Tales* is not only the dialectic between subject and history, but also the inseparability of the self from the united demands of ancestral fathers and putative sons. The historical totality that Patterson identifies is not an externalized threat to Chaucer nor is it merely the rippling byproducts of the self's movement through time. Instead, history *is* the self. It is the matter and form given by biology in answer to mortality; it is the encoding of posterity and ancestry in the same single drop of human blood. Moreover, for Chaucer, history is understood as obligation—the debt owed to the progenitors of one's blood—and as opportunity. The only hope for the subjective self (a composite of mind and body, but not soul) to persevere past the earthly demise of its flesh lies within the collective reproduction of its heritage of kin-linked subjectivities.

---

[46] Lee Patterson, *Chaucer and the Subject of History* (Madison, WI: University of Wisconsin Press, 1991): 26.

The Geoffrey Chaucer who wrote *The Canterbury Tales* in the late 1380s through the mid/late 1390s was a man beginning to feel the weight of history and the burdens of masculinity; he writes himself and his fellow men into the poem as subjects taunted by the past promise of their own virility rather than consoled by its potentialities. Tonally, *The Canterbury Tales* therefore reads as if it is a much later text than *The House of Fame*, rather than one only six years its junior. Part of that effect is likely a result of Chaucer's ongoing strategy of revision and addition to the poem, with many *Tales* and verses contained within the modern editions of the poem perhaps as late as the second half of the 1390s.[47] But much of that effect should also be attributed to the rapid escalation of tensions and political catastrophe during Richard II's reign, an escalation that Chaucer would have experienced on a personal level.[48] By 1386 Chaucer was also aging quickly in a society still plagued by endemic disease, in which male life expectancy (even when calculated for those who had already reached the age of 21) peaked between 45 and 53 years.[49] Thus, if both *The Canterbury Tales* and *The House of Fame* are read as poems about the search for authority in an unstable world, they appear almost hostile in the inversion of their conclusions. *The Canterbury Tales*, after all, ends with Chaucer's abdication of his own authority as he begs Jesus to forgive him for the very poem his reader has just read.

While in *The House of Fame*, the authority of patriarchy was sufficient to redeem a poet's excesses, no such salvation appears on the road to Canterbury, regardless of how many stories and how many storytellers appear along the way. Instead, the pilgrimage becomes a systematic process of masculine undermining, and of the devaluation of the human desire to recreate the self. Those who might aspire to great authority—the Host, the knight, various clerics, even Chaucer himself as the narrating poet—see their authority (both as poets and as patriarchs) mocked and denigrated from their very entry into Chaucer's tale. Chaucer ties the holistic diminishment of these men's authority explicitly and specifically to their reproductive capacities. For example, the Knight's authority as man and narrator is undercut early within the *General Prologue* through the introduction of his son, the Squire. The "verray, parfit gentil knyght" (GP 72) may have fought at a dizzying array of Christendom's great battles against the Infidel, but he has been unable to sire a worthy successor. Instead his son represents a reproductive parody of masculine likeness, "a lovyere and lusty bachelor" (GP 80) notable only for his curled hair and floral-embroidered tunics. The Knight has produced male offspring, but his son represents a degradation of his bloodline, and thus

---

[47] For discussion of the difficulties in dating *The Canterbury Tales*, see: Derek Pearsall, *The Canterbury Tales* (New York: Routledge, 1985): 2–8.
[48] Paul Strohm, for example, calls 1386 Chaucer's "crisis, his time of troubles," citing Chaucer's marital, financial, and political challenges. Paul Strohm, *Chaucer's Tale: 1386 and the Road to Canterbury* (New York: Viking Penguin, 2014): 2.
[49] Joel T. Rosenthal, *Old Age in Late Medieval England* (Philadelphia, PA: University of Pennsylvania Press, 1996): 4.

signifies the Knight's inability to compensate the male ancestors whose flesh had come together to form the glory of the Knight himself.[50] Chapter 5 of this book explores the rhetoric of reproductive likeness in more depth, but it is important to note how crucial this concept of filial quality as the goal of masculine reproduction was during Richard II's reign. Indeed, the formal 1376 recognition of Richard II (then Richard of Bordeaux) as heir apparent to his grandfather, Edward III, had articulated the foundational principle of inheritance as one of masculine likeness.

> The Archbishop of Canterbury, who had been briefed by the king our lord to speak on his behalf, said that although the very noble and powerful prince my lord Edward, recently Prince of Wales, was departed and called to God, nevertheless the prince was as if present and not in any way absent because he had left behind him such a noble and fine son, who is his exact image or true likeness.[51]

One can feel some sympathy for the nine-year-old Richard's subjection to such scrutiny for his resemblance to his father, the Black Prince, the extremely violent and brutal "hero" of the early installments of the Hundred Years' War. But, more significantly, one can detect how substantially intergenerational masculine likeness was presupposed to substitute for mortality's harsh decrees.

Likewise, the example of young Richard and his deceased yet still present father, the Black Prince, indicates both the substantial investment that men had in siring sons who could be deemed to be "like" to them, and the equally substantial threat that men were under that they would be found "unalike" to their fathers. This remains one of the primary themes of late medieval romance, a genre within which young knights seem constantly to bump into their absent, unrecognized fathers, with a likeness in military (or sometimes courtly) prowess held out as the eventual key to paternal/filial recognition. But it is also one of the primary justifying fictions for the entire system of medieval primogeniture; a man's first son is judged legally to be the one most like him and thus the ideal recipient of his worldly goods and titles.

The logical irreconcilabilities of this system and its biological fictions appear constantly under critique within *The Canterbury Tales*, from the long discourse on the lack of likeness between fathers and sons within the *Clerk's Tale* (discussed in Chapter 1) to the similar mockery of supposedly hereditary gentility in the *Wife of Bath's Tale* (discussed in Chapter 2) to the disruptive plot of the *Man of Law's Tale* with its pattern of continuous vacillation between hereditary likeness

---

[50] This reading of the Squire corresponds to Patricia Ingham's analysis of the Squire and his *Tale* as signifying the ethical complexities of novelty and innovation. Patricia Clare Ingham, *The Medieval New: Ambivalence in an Age of Innovation* (Philadelphia, PA: University of Pennsylvania Press, 2015): 117–19.

[51] *English Historical Documents IV*, 122.

and dissimilitude. More broadly, this system of likeness was also profoundly undermined in late medieval England by the experience of plague and war, as well as that of political expediency. When Henry IV took the throne from Richard II in 1399, it became wise for the English people to recognize the superiority of his relationship with his grandfather, Edward III, in comparison to Richard's own likeness to that monarch.[52] Similarly, increasingly powerful and politically motivated polemics of "discovered" illegitimacy or legitimacy disrupted the social acquiescence to Hereditary male likeness as the primary mechanism for the distribution of property and power. Following Richard II's eventual deposition, for example, the Lancastrians spread rumors that he had been a bastard, since his actions had been so unlike those of his ancestors.[53]

The Knight's companionship with his son, the Squire, likewise testifies to the destabilization of these patriarchal sources of authority. The Squire is no more like his father than Richard II had proved by 1386 to be like his own respective parent. The Squire is flawed both in his attempt to recreate filial image of his father's military authority and in his poetic skill. The Knight tells the longest and most courtly tale in Chaucer's collection; the Squire tells one of the shortest and most inconsequential. The Knight has achieved glory in his own right, but his glory will fade with the waning of his life, a testament to his inability to create a worthy filial monument to his earthly existence.[54] Likewise he has told a beautiful story, but it is a story that ends with the death of a knight and the seemingly unproductive marriage of the other. The beauty of the Knight's world as both a father and a "poet" is characterized by its inherent transience. It can be grasped only by the man himself, and only for the brief moment of his earthly life.

Chaucer similarly destroys the ambitions of his other men who hope to find great authority within their powers of creation. One can characterize Chaucer's technique here as twofold: either he critiques "glorious" men like the Knight by depicting their inability to recreate that glory in their offspring, or he undermines the capacity of less glorious men like the Host or his own narratorial character to procreate at all. The Host therefore does not appear to have managed the creation of any heirs for his tavern, likely because his masculinity is repeatedly called into question by his wife with such attacks as, "By corpus bones, I wol have thy knyf/ And thou shalt have my distaff and go spynne" (MkT 1906-7). Likewise, Geoffrey Chaucer (the narrator) is critiqued as excessively feminine, a man who can neither sire strong male offspring nor tell a strong, engaging story. "What man artow? (Th 695)" charges the Host when considering the possibility of Chaucer

---

[52] Paul Strohm, *England's Empty Throne: Usurpation and the Language of Legitimation*, 1399–1422 (New Haven, CT: Yale University Press, 1998): 181–2, 249 n. 93.

[53] Adam Usk, *Chronicle*, 60–1.

[54] Stanley Kahrl argues that the Squire's failures to mimic his father are indeed intended to indict the entire courtly world of Chaucer's experience, documenting how far they have fallen from the chivalric ideal. Stanley J. Kahrl, "Chaucer's 'Squire's Tale' and the Decline of Chivalry," *The Chaucer Review* 7.3 (Winter 1973): 194–209.

telling the next tale. "This were a popet in an arm to embrace/For any womman, small and fair of face" (Th 701–2). Both the Host and Chaucer are imagined as sexually overmastered by their female partners, a situation that as we will see, was fundamentally detrimental to the conception of male offspring. It is also, the Host laughs, detrimental to the production of a virile story: "Now shul we heere/Som deyntee thyng, me thynketh by his cheere" (Th 710–11). On one hand, Chaucer will produce a story that is "like" to himself; such a production can only strengthen mechanisms of patriarchal likeness. However, Chaucer the narrator (at least as his author writes him) is a man whose masculine authority already appears somewhat flawed, a judgment born out by the humble, unprepossessing male characters of the tales that the narrator produces (*Sir Thopas* and *Melibee*).

In *The Canterbury Tales* the search for authority results only in the despair of encountering the inadequacies of its simulacrums. The man who embodies authority in his life cannot reproduce himself in the generation; the queered man finds himself able to create in his own image, but both progenitor and offspring are marked as sexual (and literary) abominations. Even more problematically, the doomed search for such an authority is not in itself a harmless pastime. Not only does it serve to reify and reinforce mankind's recognition of its own abasement, but it also serves to waste one of the only things that men do have at their disposal: time. When Chaucer finishes his *Tale of Sir Thopas* (or at least accedes to its interruption), the Host condemns Chaucer's literary offspring as both a biological and a poetic failure; more importantly, though, he condemns it as a waste of time. "Thy drasty rymyng is nat worth a toord!/Thou doost noght elles but despendest tyme" (Th 930–1). The comparison of Chaucer's tale with a turd links literary composition with the excretions of the body, resulting in a humorous image of Chaucer attempting to birth a story but only succeeding in bringing more shit to light. But this lack of productivity has its own victims. It leads Chaucer to waste not only his own time, but also the time of his fellow pilgrims. Time is the one commodity that the pilgrims share alike, and while the journey to Canterbury seems endless, the path (as constructed by the pilgrims' poetic competition) is fraught with reminders of how short their time on earth will be.

The task of tale-telling on the road to Canterbury, set to the company by the Host in the *General Prologue*, therefore represents a collective negotiation of medieval men and women's reproductive capacities and temporal limitations. Each pilgrim is asked to prove that the authority they have been granted within their world is equal to the measure of what they have contributed; both the material aspects of their bodies (and of the bodies that they have produced in turn) and the words that they have birthed are given equal weight in this evaluation. The process of storytelling thus becomes a competition of production, for which the winner will be rewarded with an experience of consumption, a *gratis* meal at the Tabard Inn. Moreover, it is a competition for authority to prove that one "bereth hym best of alle" (GP 796) and is therefore deserving of public respect.

The pilgrim who creates "tales of best sentence and moost solas" (GP 798) will be the pilgrim who has proved their worth by producing something of authority and value among all the noise of the world. He or she will have brought into being a story whose existence is enough to justify the author's time on earth, an object that will guarantee for the author a posterity worthy of the name.

This is the existential crisis at the heart of *The Canterbury Tales*: how can a man live authoritatively, reproduce authoritatively, in a world whose only purpose seems to be to demonstrate to him his own inconsequentiality? Are there secular alternatives (poetry or patriarchy, science or semiotics) that can compensate man for his own mortality, without Christian precepts of abnegation as prerequisite for salvation? That Chaucer closes the text by invoking the authority of religion in the *Parson's Tale*, even as he initiated the journey with the authority of "the hooly blisful martir" (GP), St Thomas Becket, has answered this question for some critics, who read the text as a whole as a consistently orthodox Christian allegory.[55] In contrast, this book argues that Chaucer depicts the acceptance of Christianity as an ongoing struggle, and that the *Parson's Tale* and the *Retraction* may thus be read as an ultimate, yet uneasy acquiescence to religious doctrine. Christian eschatology may be the only form of power and authority that Chaucer's pilgrims do not manage to disprove with their stories; as Chaucer notes in the *Prologue* to the *Legend of Good Women*, "ther nis noon dwelling in this contree/That either hath in heven or helle y-be" (LGW 5–6), and thus claims about the afterlife must be believed without challenge or empirical inquiry.[56] That is not necessarily a point in the Church's favor for Chaucer. He recognizes its authoritative demands upon his person, its imposition of epistemological structure upon his mind, and declares his devotion to its precepts… except when he is called away by the temptations of the world. "Ther is game noon/That fro my bokes maketh me to goon" (LGW 33–4), he boasts, until the month of May comes with its joyful flowers and fowls. Then, "Farwel my book and my devocioun!" (LGW 39). In May, Chaucer left behind the rigidities of doctrine to meet the divinities of Love; in April, he left behind the authoritative structures of London life to explore what else might exist in the world.

The search for alternative modes of authority, for creative and reproductive powers inherent within the human self rather than imposed upon it through divine grace, thus marks a detour rather than a departure from the doctrines of Christian faith. It is an indulgence to be engaged in upon the road, even though one's destination will demand a return to orthodoxy. If one must eventually

---

[55] The most famous example of such a perspective is that presented by D. W. Robertson in his *A Preface to Chaucer: Studies in Medieval Perspectives* (Princeton, NJ: Princeton University Press, 1962).

[56] Norman Klassen reads these lines as an example of Chaucer's tendency towards self-reflection within the dream visions, and in particular of Chaucer's interest in internalizing a debate between experience and authority. Norman Klassen, *Chaucer on Love, Knowledge, and Sight* (Woodbridge: D. S. Brewer, 1995): 195.

allow the Parson to speak because "the sonne wole adoun" (ParsT 69–70), one may nevertheless, earlier in the day, rebuke the beginning of another pilgrim's tale, "What amounteth al this wit?/What shul we speke alday of hooly writ?" (RT 3901–2). Christian salvation is the certainty to which all men, even Chaucer and Chaucer's Host, may return, repentant and begging for aid. And yet *The Canterbury Tales*, like *The House of Fame* and the *Legend of Good Women*, represents a fantasy of what it would be like to look *within* oneself and one's fellowship for salvation, rather than outwards to an unproven God. What is radical in Chaucer's poems are therefore not his conclusions (for all will end in affirmations of human inadequacy and retractions of human pride), but rather the daring provocations of his inquiry. Chaucer offers his medieval audience a chance to wonder at their own authority, to speculate upon their own creative power as human beings, before repenting to God for such hubristic usurpations of his (great) authority.

Paternity was the semiotic union of human doubt and human desire at the end of the fourteenth century. It was the hope for an heir that never materialized, the terror that a wife had presented one with a lover's son, the anguish when a prized heir was cut down in battle or by plague. But it was also the recognition of one's own face in younger flesh, the endowment of one's acquisitions into beloved hands, the connection of the self with the immortal chain of life that ran through one's body. To be a father was to claim a uniquely masculine and uniquely human form of power, privilege, and authority, and to be a father was to know that all such power could be taken away at Fortune's whim. To be a poet was similarly to make a material testament to uncertainty and to hope to create an offspring that would be at the whims of scribes and the mercies of readers.

The Canterbury Tales is Chaucer's confrontation with his desire to be that very father of poetry and father of sons that Dryden hailed him, although it is also his movement away from the impossibility of such a hope. It is a poetic assemblage designed to ruminate upon the passing of time, the instability of contemporary life, the joy and sorrow incumbent upon men who dream of obtaining any certainty or longevity here on earth. And, moreover, it is designed to mock Chaucer himself as much as any of his fellow men. For who shows more hubris, more foolish pride: the cousin-knights who fought to the death for the chance to procreate with a single lady, the oft-married yet barren Wife still looking for a husband; or indeed, the poet who has fought tradition to create in his own tongue only to query what remnants will persist from his enterprise and from his life? For all the positioning of Geoffrey Chaucer within the genealogies of English literature, Chaucer writes himself as a man deprived of his paternal bonds, uncertain of his poetic kin. He grapples with his Latinate forebears; he searches for fertile sons and reliable scribes. And, most significantly, he confronts his own most perverse ambition, his desire to find a path for man to claim immortality from his own humanity—from his body, mind, and loins—rather than from the cruel hands of his God.

SECTION I
ON CERTAINTY

1
Sexual Exegetics and the Female Text

For Chaucer and his fellow medieval Christians, the archetype of human fatherhood was Joseph, the husband of the Virgin Mary and the human "father" of Christ.[1] While the cult of St Joseph was not yet as developed in the fourteenth century as it would become in the fifteenth, Joseph's paternal nurturing of the divinely sired boy nevertheless provided a model for medieval men of the correct deployment of male authority within the family. Thus, Chaucer's Parson, for example, inserts Joseph into his retelling of the naming of Jesus, emphasizing that while Jesus was not of Joseph's direct bloodline, Joseph still fashioned the child's genealogy. The Parson preaches, "seyde the aungel to Joseph, 'Thou shalt clepen his name Jhesus, that shal saven his peple of hir synnes'" (ParsT 286). The angel here passes on Jesus's intended name from his divine father to his earthly one, in recognition of the male authority incumbent within the naming process.[2] Moreover, the Parson preaches that by giving his "son" the name Jesus, Joseph is also participating in an inimitable moment of semiotic perfection. "Jhesus is to seyn 'saveour' or 'salvacioun.' And hererof seith Seint Peter: 'Ther is noon oother name that is yeve to any man, by which a man may be saved, but oonly Jhesus'" (ParsT 287–287A). There is no gap between word and meaning here; all is perfection, all is reciprocal, all is authoritative.

For Chaucer's Parson, father Joseph offers a commentary on the capacity of human language to be perfected by the divine, and for an earthly paternity to be reinforced by its divine counterpart. And yet the Parson's authoritative Joseph must compete with the resonances of his far more common medieval incarnation: the foolish, doubting Joseph of religious drama. The Parson thus situates linguistic perfection in the mouth of one who was known for his inability to read or understand the signs of his own wife's pregnant flesh.[3] In the *N-Town Play*, for example, Joseph comically cries out:

---

[1] Cf. Paul Payan, *Joseph: Une image de la paternite dans l'Occident medieval* (Paris: Aubier, Collection Historique, 2006).

[2] Another example of this authoritative father Joseph can be found in Cynthia Hahn's reading of the Joseph figure from the Merode altarpiece as an allegory for God the father. Cynthia Hahn, "Joseph Will Perfect, Mary Enlighten, and Jesus Save Thee: The Holy Family as Marriage Model in the Merode Triptych," *The Art Bulletin* 68.1 (1986): 54–66.

[3] As Gail McMurray Gibson points out, iconographic and probably also dramatic stagings of this scene played on the theme of Joseph, in his doubt, confronting Mary's certainty. For example, the Salzburg diptych that Gibson describes has Joseph with an outstretched finger pointing accusingly at Mary's womb, while Mary's own fingers wind thread from her distaff across her womb to a painted cross. The viewer can look at the correct sign, even as they look at Joseph looking at the wrong one.

Father Chaucer: Generating Authority in The Canterbury Tales. Samantha Katz Seal, Oxford University Press (2019).
© Samantha Seal.
DOI: 10.1093/oso/9780198832386.001.0001

That semyth evyl, I am afrayd:
Thi wombe to hyghe doth stonde!
... Ow, dame, what thinge menyth this?
With childe, thu gynnyst ryth gret to gon?[4]

Joseph is here the unsuspecting, comic father forced to confront his sexual and intellectual insufficiencies.[5] Cuckoldry is the joke here, but it is reinforced by cognition; Joseph's impotence extends both to the creation of a child and to understanding that a child has been created. He must ask his wife to explain the signs he sees, even as he has needed God to sire his son.[6] The author of the play recreates this scene when Joseph encounters Zacharias and Elizabeth. There, Elizabeth mocks Joseph as "wys fadyr Joseph," after Joseph questions Zacharias, who is engaged in a mystical trance, if he suffers from "the palsye."[7] In the Middle Ages, Joseph symbolized fatherhood, but he also symbolized intellectual failure, the human mind overwhelmed by God's miracles.[8]

In this sense, Joseph is an ideal place to start for a study of paternity as a source of authority in *The Canterbury Tales* because he embodies the inherent contradictions that medieval men faced in their desire to ground their personal power in their reproductive capacities. The ease with which a man's paternal (and spousal) claims might so easily be countered by deception mirrored the inevitable slippages of language, sign, and meaning within a fallen, sinful world. The fear of cuckoldry is overshadowed by the fear of being unable to *perceive* that cuckoldry, of having the source of one's hope for posterity not only perverted but, even worse, rendered

---

Gail McMurray Gibson, *The Theater of Devotion: East Anglian Drama and Society in the Late Middle Ages* (Chicago, IL: University of Chicago Press, 1989): 165–6.

---

[4] *The N-Town Play: Cotton MS Vespasian D.8*, Vol. 1, ed. Stephen Spector (Oxford: Oxford University Press for the Early English Text Society, 1991): 124–5.

[5] As Daisy Black notes, the figure of Joseph here can also be read as an allegory for Jewish doubt requiring the benevolent intervention of Christian faith. Daisy Black, "A Man Out of Time: Joseph, Time, and Space in the N-Town Marian Plays," *Reconsidering Gender, Time, and Memory in Medieval Culture*, ed. Elizabeth Cox, Liz Herbert McAvoy, and Roberta Magnani (Cambridge: D.S. Brewer, 2015): 147–62, at 155–62.

[6] The pear-tree scene of Chaucer's *Merchant's Tale*, in which the young wife, claiming pregnancy, tricks her husband into disbelieving his own visual witness of her adultery, can be seen as a satirical parody of the biblical source. Kenneth Bleeth, "Joseph's Doubting of Mary and the Conclusion of the *Merchant's Tale*," *The Chaucer Review* 21.1 (Summer, 1986): 58–66.

[7] *N-Town Play*, 136.

[8] It is significant that in Jean Gerson's fifteenth-century *Josephina*, written in support of the cult of St. Joseph, there are no scenes of "doubting Joseph," despite their simultaneous popularity; instead Gerson begins with Joseph in Egypt, writing the saint as authoritative father. Daniel Hobbins, *Authorship and Publicity Before Print: Jean Gerson and the Transformation of Late Medieval Learning* (Philadelphia, PA: University of Pennsylvania Press, 2009): 97–100. Miri Rubin also comments on the developments in the cult of St. Joseph as evident in Gerson's attempts to recuperate Joseph from the comic deployments of medieval drama. Miri Rubin, *Mother of God: A History of the Virgin Mary* (New Haven, CT: Yale University Press, 2009): 323–9.

incomprehensible.[9] The female womb becomes the weapon through which God reminds man of his own humble inefficacy, that he is no more able to know than he is to create. How can a man hope to generate with authority, if he cannot even know with authority? And, more importantly, how can he claim to be a father like the Parson's Joseph, naming his son with perfect power, if Nature has made him so much more closely resemble the comic Joseph, frightened by a womb?[10]

For Chaucer, certainty is thus one of the major attributes of paternal authority; a man must be certain of his wife and of his children before he can claim them as the source of his authority. And yet certainty is also one of the markers of the impossibility for human beings to ever achieve this type of fatherhood. For there are no mortal men capable of knowing their wives or sons with anything more than faith, no human mind that can claim this exhaustive intimacy. As Chaucer's Miller preaches on cuckoldry, "I wol bileve wel that I am noon./An housbonde shal nat been inquisitiyf/Of Goddes pryvetee, nor of his wyf" (MilT 3162–4). Men who wish to know with their minds rather than merely their faith risk losing even the limited authority they possess. Better, the Miller urges, to accept that human beings cannot wield a more holistic authority in the world, particularly since, by accepting his own cognitive limitation, a man may be lucky enough to "fynde Goddes foyson there" (MilT 3165). The Parson tells men of fatherhood in Heaven, but the Miller tells them of the habits of the earth, and of the compromises that men make in their search for their own legitimacy.

The Miller gives his speech near the beginning of *The Canterbury Tales*, while the Parson gives his at the end. Between these two poems, Chaucer plays with how profoundly human ways of knowing influence man's ambition to be a father, to sire his future and know it for his own. This chapter will particularly emphasize these themes within the *Manciple's Tale* and the *Clerk's Tale*, but the rest of the book will also return to certainty and cognition as foundational concepts for the establishment of the medieval dream of fatherhood. Both of these poems emphasize male anxiety over their own intellectual capacities and over the inadequacies of the female texts which God has provided them. Chaucer's husbands, realizing their cognitive limitation, turn against their wives, blaming the women for not signifying more clearly rather than their own flawed understanding. Furious at their own humanity, they savage their wives for being likewise human. If only a woman were a readable text, they reason, then her husband could become a wise father in truth, safe from cuckoldry and secure in the certainty reserved for Father God.

---

[9] Mark Breitenburg refers to this as "cuckoldry anxiety," a pre-modern phenomenon in which the fear of cuckoldry "exists prior to any definitive signs of its prospect." Mark Breitenburg, *Anxious Masculinity in Early Modern England* (Cambridge: Cambridge University Press, 1996): 5.

[10] Many of the Middle English poems about the childhood of Jesus also emphasized Joseph's inappropriate behavior in later years, such as using corporal punishment unreasonably against the young child Jesus, and perversely respecting and fearing the judgments of his Jewish neighbors. Mary Dzon, "Joseph and the Amazing Christ Child of Late-Medieval Legend," *Childhood in the Middle Ages and the Renaissance: The Results of a Paradigm Shift in the History of Mentality*, ed. Albrecht Classen (Berlin: Walter de Gruyter, 2005): 135–57, at 146–50.

The Manciple's Tale and the Erasure of Certainty

When, in the *Manciple's Tale*, the crow sings "'Cokkow! Cokkow! Cokkow!'" (MancT 243) at his owner, Phebus, "the mooste lusty bachiler" (MancT 107), we must understand the inseparability of the identification of Phebus as cuckold with the etymological and mythographic resonances of the potential bastard child perhaps growing within his wife's flesh. The word cuckold is predicated upon false paternity; the shame of the slur is explicitly reproductive.[11] Moreover, the mythographic contexts of the story are also specifically concerned with childbearing. Chaucer has removed one of the central aspects of the story of Phebus and his tattling bird as it was told by Ovid and by French poets (including Guillaume de Machaut), namely how the adultery plot serves as origin story for Asclepius, the Greek god of medicine.[12] In Ovid's *Metamorphoses*, the story of Phoebus Apollo, Coronis (the unnamed wife in Chaucer), and bird (whether raven or crow) is a familial one, with the unfaithful wife simultaneously adulterous and pregnant.

Indeed, Ovid's account is of two interlinked fatherings, since it contains an extended digression about the birth of Ericthonius, the half-serpent child raised by Athena. Scholars usually locate the connection between the two stories in a common theme of guarding speech, since the daw who tells the tale of Ericthonius has been punished for gossiping about his hybrid body. But we can also see how, in Ovid's hands, both the story of Ericthonius and that of Asclepius are tales of paternal certainty.[13] Ericthonius is conceived when, while attempting to rape her, Hephaestus allows his semen to fall upon Athena's thigh. When Athena knocks the semen off her skin and onto the earth, the earth nurtures it and generates Ericthonius. Thus, while there might be some ambiguity in the maternal aspect of

[11] Cuckoldry is a common slur in premodern historical and literary texts alike. Cf. Douglas Bruster, "The Horn of Plenty: Cuckoldry and Capital in the Drama of the Age of Shakespeare," *Studies in English Literature, 1500-1900*, Vol. 30.2 (Spring 1990): 195–215; David M. Turner, *Fashioning Adultery: Gender, Sex, and Civility in England, 1660-1740* (Cambridge: Cambridge University, 2002): 83–115; Sara F. Matthews-Grieco (ed.). *Cuckoldry, Impotence and Adultery in Europe (15th-17th Centuries)* (New York: Ashgate, 2014). However, Derek Neal has argued that while early modern scholarship has "taken up the cuckold as the signal figure of dishonored masculinity," in medieval contexts it should be identified as functioning primarily as part of a larger conversation about appropriate husbandry. Derek G. Neal, *The Masculine Self in Late Medieval England* (Chicago, IL: University of Chicago Press, 2009): 73–6.

[12] For the differences between Chaucer's version and that of Ovid, see Jamie Claire Fumo, "Thinking Upon the Crow: *The Manciple's Tale* and Ovidian Mythography," *The Chaucer Review* 38.4 (2004): 355–75; Kathryn L. McKinley, "Gower and Chaucer: Readings of Ovid in Late Medieval England," *Ovid in the Middle Ages*, by James G. Clark, Frank T. Coulson, and Kathryn L. McKinley (Cambridge: Cambridge University Press, 2011): 197–230.

[13] In fact, the certainty of his divine paternal origin (compared to the skepticism which met similar claims by other half-divine mortals in Greek narratives) enhanced Asclepius's cult in antiquity. Wendy C. S. J. Cotter, "Miracle Stories: The God Asclepius, the Pythagorean Philosophers, and the Roman Rulers," *The Historical Jesus in Context*, ed. Amy-Jill Levine, Dale C. Allison Jr, and John Dominic Crossan (Princeton, NJ: Princeton University Press, 2006): 166–78, at 168.

Ericthonius's conception, his origin in Hephaestus's seed is certain.[14] Likewise, although Coronis is accused of adultery and therefore the paternity of her unborn child would seem to be in doubt, neither Ovid nor Phoebus Apollo himself admits to the possibility that Asclepius is not Apollo's son. His divinity, however minor, indeed proves his father's identity, while Phoebus, as a god himself, is capable of knowing for certain that the child is his own. Here, in a story of divine beings, the uncertainty surrounding women's sexual fidelity can be separated out from questions about paternity.

This is the version of the story that was perpetuated in the medieval French poetic tradition, with which Chaucer would have been familiar. There are some slight alterations: for example, the *Ovide moralise'* slightly expands both Coronis and Apollo's speeches of parental love, while in *Le voir dit*, Guillaume de Mauchaut's Coronis makes her maternal plea for Apollo to save the baby if he must kill her without the simultaneous admission of sexual guilt found in the previous versions, thus heightening the pathos of her death and undermining the certainty of the accusations against her.[15] And yet overall these other tellings of Coronis's murder at the hands of quickly repentant Phoebus remain focused on that relationship as a procreative one and move quickly between the sexual triangle of Coronis, Phoebus, and Coronis's lover, and the familial triangle of Coronis, Phoebus, and their child. The birth of Asclepius is not a threat to Apollo or a reminder of his cuckolding, but rather some small measure of recompense for the loss of his lover, Coronis.

Thus, the writing out of Coronis's pregnancy and Asclepius's caesarean birth (not to mention Ericthonius's birth) within the works of John Gower and Geoffrey Chaucer marks an extremely significant change to the story. In the *Manciple's Tale*, Chaucer focuses exclusively on the dangers of "janglyng" (MancT 350) as moral allegory, whereas Gower in the *Confessio Amantis* reads this myth as a warning against intemperate and rash action. And yet the *Manciple's Tale*, in particular, seems haunted by what Chaucer has so aggressively erased. Part of this effect stems from the fact that it remains a relatively long poem, even with the elision of so much of its plot. In contrast, Gower has contracted the story to a mere thrity-four lines, and therefore far less feels as if it is missing from his narrative. Moreover, Chaucer (as he does elsewhere) deliberately plays with the absences in his poem. When describing Coronis's murder, for example, he cannot keep from reminding his reader of the ways in which he has foreshortened the original story. "In his ire his wyf thane hath he slayn. /This is th'effect; ther is

---

[14] Vigdis Songe-Moller reads this story, and Ericthonius's status as the founder of Athens, as a Greek endorsement of an "ideal of one-sex humanity, where all children are boys, and each child originates from the father alone." Vigdis Soane-Møller, *Philosophy Without Women: The Birth of Sexism in Western Thought* (London and New York: Continuum, 1999): 5.

[15] As William Calin points out, Machaut even has Phoebus speculate upon Coronis's potential innocence, further undermining the perception of her culpability. William Calin, *The French Tradition and the Literature of Medieval England* (Toronto: University of Toronto Press, 1994): 358.

namoore to sayn" (MancT 265–6). There is in fact quite a lot more to say, as anyone familiar with the Ovidian myth would know.[16] The resistance to further speech while nevertheless invoking the significance of its absence may be seen as a continuance of the linguistic play within a *Tale* that contains excessively long-winded admonitions against too much speech.

But why remove the pregnancy story? For Gower, it appears to be a matter of fit. In addition to the sheer brevity of his *Tale of Phebus and Cornide*, it is a text overtly determined by its inclusion within the morally didactic structure of the *Confessio Amantis*. Specifically, it is included within the section warning the lover against the sins of "Contention." Here Ovid's tale of sexual infidelity and paternal intervention becomes recentered around Phebus and his hasty violence. In his wrath, Phebus has committed an irreversible crime against a woman he loves, one which he immediately regrets. The redemptive component of the story, Asclepius's survival and illustrious future, therefore must be excised so as not to undermine the somber didacticism of Gower's text. His Phebus is a repentant sinner, confronting his love's corpse. To offer this Phebus a child would be to offer him a measure of absolution, and by doing so, to undermine the importance of his story as a means of teaching men to be less easily stirred to wrathful action.

The domestic elements of the story as a whole are thus compressed, as the text consistently privileges Phebus's internal struggle with morality over his external interactions. This move away from the romantic tragedy more commonly foregrounded in French analogues is perhaps most evident in how Gower writes Coronis's murder. The scene of Phebus shooting his beloved with his arrows, in an act of penetrative domination meant to remind the reader of the characters' previous sexual intimacy, is one of the most climactic and extended moments of the story in Ovid and Machaut. In contrast, Gower delivers only the terse "And he for wraththe his swerd outbreide, /With which Cornide anon he slowh."[17] The transition from arrow to sword may be seen as a de-escalation of the erotic undertones of the scene, but it is also a move away from the imagined spectacle of the tragedy. Instead, romance is replaced by man's "full gret repentance" (803) and the condemnation of that "fals bridd" (792) who stirred up strife. Coronis herself appears in the story as a peripheral figure; her life and death serve only as mechanisms for masculine transformation from lover to penitent. Her child, as a factor that would undermine this progression, is given no place at all in the poem.

In contrast, Chaucer's motivation for cutting Coronis's pregnancy from his poem is slightly murkier. Certainly, brevity does not appear to be the precipitating

---

[16] As David Raybin notes, in Chaucer's hands, Coronis's death is reduced merely to a turning point in the plot. David Raybin, "The Death of a Silent Woman: Voice and Power in Chaucer's *Manciple's Tale*," *The Chaucer Review* 95.1 (January 1996): 19.

[17] John Gower, "Confessio Amantis," *The English Works of John Gower*, Vol. 1, ed. G.C. Macaulay (London, New York, and Toronto: Published for the Early English Text Society by the Oxford University Press, 1969): 247.

factor. The *Manciple's Tale* contains several narrative tangents and rhetorical effusions, including a 129-line excursus in praise of Phebus, "the mooste lusty bachlier/in al this world" [MancT 107–8]. It is possible that, like Gower, Chaucer has erased the explicitly reproductive elements of the story in order to eliminate a potential distraction from the moral lesson that his Manciple offers to the other pilgrims. And yet this didactic component of the text, arguing against unguarded speech, is itself unstable. Chaucer's investment in the work as a moral text is perhaps too mutable therefore to support alone such a radical choice of narrative excision. Instead, I would argue that Chaucer's removal of the reproductive material from his *Tale* is meant to be noticed by the reader, in a moment that sets the terms for the *Tale's* discourse on knowing and knowledge. Most scholars accept this text as one preoccupied with the unreliability of language, whether those verbal signs be employed for gossip or for poetry.[18] And yet it is crucial to conceptualize language as but one half of a larger semiotic process for Chaucer. Speech disseminates the signs that the eyes and brain have perceived. From such a perspective, the *Manciple's Tale* becomes as much as story about what one may know as about what one may say, as Phebus negotiates the conflicting semiotic data from his wife and his bird. The choice to remove the birth of Asclepius is thus a deliberate strategy to avoid the interference of the additional semiotic implications of medieval reproduction into this structure, as I will discuss subsequently.

The famous lines about the necessity of reciprocity between a linguistic sign and its meaning come as part of the narrator's denunciation of Coronis (unnamed throughout the poem), and her adultery.

> Hir lemman? certes, this is a knavyssh speche!
> Foryeveth it me, and that I yow biseche.
> The wise plato seith, as ye may rede,
> The word moot nede accorde with the dede.
> If men shal telle proprely a thyng,
> The word moot cosyn be to the werkyng.
>
> (MancT 205–10)

The Manciple frames his semiotic frustration in terms of female nomenclature, a feat no less remarkable in that it begins with a digression upon the misnaming of Coronis's male lover (or "lemman"), rather than of Coronis herself. As he continues to complain that social class should not allow one woman to receive the title "his lady, as in love" while another guilty of the same lechery is called "his wenche or his lemman" (MancT 218, 220). As Peter Travis notes, it is in the labeling of women (and thus the potential *mis*labeling of women) that the Manciple

---

[18] For example, see Britton J. Harwood, "Language and the Real: Chaucer's Manciple," *The Chaucer Review* 6.4 (Spring 1972): 268–79.

first grounds his concerns about duplicity and the unreliability of human signs, particularly linguistic ones.[19]

The fear of deception runs throughout the *Tale*. The Manciple indeed concludes his discourse on uncertain signs with a paradox: he repudiates literate activity so that he might return to his engagement with his literary tale.

> But, for I am a man noght textueel,
> I wold noght telle of textes never a deel;
> I wol go to my tale, as I bigan.
>
> (MancT 235–7)

He repeats the disclaimer of not being a textual man again within the poem (MancT 316), thus underscoring the importance of his rejection of this linguistically invested identity. And yet words are not the only signs that fail within the *Tale*. It is with "sadde tokenes" as well as "words bold" that the crow provides his witness to Phebus (MancT 258). Phebus in turn claims to be in "confusioun" as a result not of the crow's words alone, but rather from the contrast between the crow's words and signs and the corporeal semiotics of his now-murdered wife. He moves from the crow's testimony to the silent witness of Coronis's pale face, unable to reconcile the signs which he is forced to interpret with one another, and thus forced into profound uncertainty.

This moment does not last long, of course, as Phebus quickly chooses which signs, and which interpretation, to believe. However, this realization of his own fallible intelligence and flawed capacity to understand grounds the *Tale*, an effect which is only enhanced by the narrator's assurance that Phebus has made the wrong choice, that with certainty the reader may know which signs to believe and which to reject. In his uncertainty, Phebus rejects that about which we ourselves might be certain, in a narrational move that grants the reader an almost divine omnipotence while simultaneously highlighting Phebus's interpretative failures. It is no wonder, therefore, that Chaucer has rendered Ovid's divine being into a mere mortal, albeit a very pretty and noble one. It is Phebus's humanity, his restricted cognition, with which the reader sympathizes from the privileged position of knowledge granted by the Manciple and Chaucer to those encountering their text.

Thus, while Gower's decision to remove the pregnancy storyline from the text was likely motivated by moralist objectives, Chaucer's similar removal of that plot appears connected to his rejection of certainty as an obtainable human goal.

---

[19]   Peter Travis also concludes that the tale itself becomes "an utterance that cannot be trusted by any wary reader: whatever its narrator says is said only so that it can be gainsaid." Peter W. Travis, "The Manciple's Phallic Matrix," *Studies in the Age of Chaucer* 25 (2003): 317–24, at 319. And yet I would argue that for both women and the *Tale* the problem is not so much one of trust as one of certainty; linguistic semiotics may be trustworthy insofar as they operate according to a system of probability, *as long as* one recognizes the interpretative system itself as essentially uncertain and capable of rapid retractions.

In the *Metamorphoses*, Phoebus Apollo is misled about the character of his lover, and confused about the testimony of his bird. However, he is never uncertain about Asclepius's paternity. He knows that the child within Coronis's womb was sired by himself, an enviable piece of knowledge considering her apparent adultery. In fact, he does not even engage with any corporeal signs to ascertain the child's parentage. He has the power to know, without the necessity of interpretation or the possibility of doubt. There is no room for such certainty within the *Manciple's Tale*. Indeed, the crow taunts Phebus with precisely that point, singing "cokkow! cokkow! cokkow!" (MancT 243) as his initial revelation of Coronis's infidelity. Cokkow means not only cuckold here, but also cuckoo, the baby bird famed for being put in other birds' nests. It is specifically with paternal uncertainty that the crow assaults Phebus's faith in his wife. For, if Chaucer's Phebus is only a man and not a god, then he has no way to verify with any certainty that a pregnancy in his marriage was sired by himself.[20]

This corresponds well with one of Chaucer's other changes to the story, namely the alteration from Coronis as Phebus's lover to the status Chaucer grants her as Phebus's (anonymous) wife. Peter C. Herman has noted the significance of this change, arguing that "by transforming Phebus's mistress into his wife, Chaucer introduces politics into the tale, for in fourteenth-century England the implicit threat to male hegemony made adultery a politically destabilizing act."[21] Herman notes that Chaucer has also demoted the status of Coronis's lover, making him her social inferior by far, and thus furthering the outrage a reader should feel at the treasonous betrayal of Phebus by two who should respect his authority over them.[22] Herman's argument is a strong one, but it would be significantly enhanced by consideration of the reproductive underpinnings of medieval adultery law. The extramarital threat which wife and lover pose to Phebus's authority is grounded on the possibility that the wife might become pregnant by her lover, and pass the infant off as her husband's heir, thus completing the theft of his patrimony. In other words, Phebus has been granted a limited, but highly significant, reprieve from the "true stakes" of medieval sexual politics. For Chaucer to have transformed Phebus into a mortal man without removing the story of Asclepius's birth would be for him to have cast explicit doubt on Asclepius's paternity. To leave Phebus with not only a murdered wife but a false heir would be to render him the victim and moral object of the *Tale*. Chaucer must therefore mitigate Phebus's

---

[20] Similarly, as Eve Salisbury points out, there is no way for a human Apollo to kill his wife but save her unborn child; Salisbury attributes the removal of the Asclepius story from the Ovidian source as attributable to the desire to maintain sympathy for Apollo—impossible if the reader were to witness his murder of his innocent unborn child. Eve Salisbury, "Murdering Fiction: The Case of *The Manciple's Tale*," *Studies in the Age of Chaucer* 25 (2003): 309–16, at 314.

[21] Peter C. Herman, "Treason in the 'Manciple's Tale,'" *The Chaucer Review* 25.4 (Spring 1991): 318–28, at 319.

[22] Herman, "Treason in the 'Manciple's Tale,'" 319–21.

suffering, removing the son entirely from the story, if he wishes to maintain the crow instead as the exemplum of punishment and regret.

The crow's curse is however a somewhat paradoxical proposition when contextualized within this reproductive perspective. For, while condemned to lose both his white appearance and his sweet song, the crow is nevertheless promised a perpetuity of offspring. Even more significantly, his offspring will be marked with an indelible sign of his own paternity, granting him true certainty in his children and guaranteeing that he, unlike Phebus, will be preserved from the highest stakes of cuckoldry.

> Thou and thyn ofspryng evere shul be blake,
> Ne nevere sweete noyse shul ye make,
> But evere crie agayn tempest and rayn,
> In tokenynge that thurgh thee my wyf is slayn.
>
> (MancT 299–302)

Chaucer's Phebus, denied his son and his divine certainty, gifts his verbal tormenter with both these assets. It is a gift of knowledge to be envied and aspired to by medieval men, as subsequent chapters in this book will attest.

The ending of the *Manciple's Tale* may thus appear to possess a rather appalling message for its mortal male listeners. Despite the Manciple's multiple injunctions to "thenk on the crowe" (MancT 362), surely many of Chaucer's audience thought instead upon the human misery of Phebus and his "trouble wit" (MancT 279). His dilemma of whom to trust, his wife or the witness against her, and his subsequent panic that he has made the wrong choice, are symptomatic of the restricted cognition that defined mortal man. And yet if the moral of the crow's story is for one to stay silent, then the moral of Phebus's own story seems to be to hold back from the desire to know, in recognition of one's own inability to know with any kind of surety. Here we see perhaps a repetition of the theme of the Miller's famous adjunction that "An housbonde shal nat been inquisityf/Of Goddes pryvetee or of his wyf" (MilT 3164). In the absence of a perfection of knowledge, the flawed seeking after truth is far worse than ignorance.

It is this air of acquiescence, of a willingness to live with faith rather than certainty, which the Manciple conveys as a narrator. One consequence is to render the *Tale* such an appropriate predecessor to the Pardoner's sermon. However, it also serves to reassure the men unnerved by Phebus's plight, pointing them away from the familial relationship most likely to provoke uncertainty (the father/son bond of descent) to that which is most stable (the relationship between mother and son). The model of pedagogy which the Manciple performs as he lectures the pilgrims on how best to interpret his story is one defined by the understanding of the mother as tender constancy, fully invested in the welfare of the child in whom her biological contribution goes unquestioned. Indeed, the Manciple's mother addresses him exclusively as either "my sone" (ten times) or "my deere sone" (once). It is important not to discount the emphasis on possession here, nor to overlook the possessive pronoun that appears yet again in the Manciple's own reference to her as "my dame" (MancT 317). If we again think of the Manciple as a prophet of the "good enough" theory of knowing, then perhaps we can read these maternal intrusions as a form of putative resolution within the narrative. The pilgrims who listen to these final lines may receive advice on judicious silence, but they also have received instruction on the fallen contexts of human cognition, on what can be known and what cannot. The Manciple, as in his earlier encounter with the Cook and his semiotic probabilities, turns to the symbolic contrast of knowable maternity and uncertain paternity to urge his audience towards faith, and away from the doomed pursuit of a knowledge beyond their grasp.

"For by assay ther may no man hit preve…"

If the *Manciple's Tale* serves Chaucer as a proscriptive negotiation of the intellectual and semiotic challenges faced by fallen man, then the *Clerk's Tale* may be seen as Chaucer's sharp denunciation of those fathers who rebel and struggle against acquiescence to the divine will. Walter, the story's paternal protagonist, is seen as continually at odds with the natural structure of his world. The Clerk begins his story with Walter's refusal to participate in the perpetuation of his own lineage, a fault harshly condemned within a society so consumed by patrilineal inheritance. We receive no fewer than three references to Walter's "fadres olde" (ClT 61), "eldres hym bifore" (ClT 65), and "linage" (ClT 71) in the first fourteen lines of the poem; indeed, it will be another six lines before we learn Walter's own name. This opening privileges the family as communal unit over the individual protagonist, noting the extent to which earlier fathers have already invested in Walter. There are generations of fathers who depend for their future "generation" upon Walter joining them in their joint lineage.

Walter distinguishes himself through his unwillingness to accept his own place in this masculine chain by marrying and siring heirs.

> I blame hym thus: that he considered noght
> In tyme comynge what myght hym betide
> But on his lust present was al his thoght.
>
> (ClT 78–80)

On one hand, these lines reflect a common medieval devotional motif centered upon man's awareness of his own mortality. To be unmindful of one's own death was to be inadequately concerned with the question of salvation, and therefore easy prey to the lusts of the world; the Clerk's condemnation of Walter for such sins is thus to some extent rote, and comparable to admonishments found in the fourteenth-century *Prik of Conscience*, for example, to men that "at morowe when thou seest lyght,/Thenke that thowe shal dyghe er nyght."[23] Medieval Christians were expected to live under an omnipresent awareness of their own imminent death, and maintain it in their thoughts.

However, the Clerk's complaint that Walter failed to think about "in tyme comynge what myght hym betide" is also an articulation of Walter's poor memorialization of the deaths of his male ancestors. Walter's forefathers represent a pattern of linear, predictable temporality; they are the steps of authority that Walter might one day wish to join. In turning away from them and from their example, Walter not only betrays the heritage of masculinity and bloodline, he also rejects participation in that mode of male time reinforced by reproduction. When the leader of Walter's subjects reminds him that, "deeth manaceth every age" (ClT 122), he therefore articulates not only a devotional philosophy about mortality, but also a secular strategy of temporal marking. The vision of "every age" is a vision of successive time, of repetition, and of reciprocity.

Moreover, it is a vision of certainty. Death, unlike human language or human women, is a knowable category, predictable in its inevitability. The anxieties and slippages of human life and semiotics are resolved in the eventual annihilation of the earthly form, perfected in the salvation of the soul. Walter has before him that very certainty for which he will search endlessly throughout the *Tale*. Death and his forefathers, the stable patterns of his own ancient flesh, proffer the authoritative structure, the balancing of subjectivity and interpersonal intimacy, that Walter so often complains does not exist. He hardly heeds the warning that, "thurgh youre deeth, youre lyne sholde slake" (ClT 137). The only threat to the certainty of death and its patterns of reliable primogeniture (at least as imagined in the *Tale*) is Walter's own refusal to participate through imitation.[24] A single abdication of authority in the present can destroy the stable transmissions of the past. Without an heir, Walter may die differently than his ancestors, ending both the "genetic" line and the very mechanism of reproducibility. He threatens not only their blood, but their conception of time as ever progressive, ever mobile.

The common speaker articulates this point even more clearly for Walter, calling upon the Marquis to reflect upon the cognitive implications of death's dual temporalities, the immediate and the eternal.

> And al so certain as we knowe echoon
> That we shul deye, as uncerteyn we alle
> Been of that day whan deeth shal on us falle.
>
> ClT 124–6

---

[23] The *Prik of Conscience*, Book III, Lines 904–5.

[24] This pragmatic attitude to death mirrors Takami Matsuda's characterization of death as a knowable, reliable phenomenon within the *Pardoner's Tale*. Matsuda writes, "It is important to note that here is no sign of the cupidity or impatience by which a dying man is often tempted in the *ars moriendi*. The Old Man knows that life in this world is to be held in contempt but also to be lived through without despair, and he is waiting for his death which can now come only naturally." Matsuda calls this attitude to death "worldly prudence." Takami Matsuda, "Death, Prudence, and Chaucer's 'Pardoner's Tale,'" *The Journal of English and Germanic Philology* 91.3 (July 1992): 313–24, at 316.

Man's mortality works to enforce upon humanity the scale of difference between its paltry intellect and that of the divine. In God's decree of death there is a cosmic, universal certainty; in the subjective experience there is only confusion.[25] If man wishes to calculate the earthly details of his life as if he might know himself with some authority, he is doomed to failure. All certainty belongs to God, reinforced by His fatal command.

The extent to which the poem appears as a didactic, pedagogical experience for Walter is predicated upon the assumptions of class structure built into the exchange between Walter and his subject, as it will be later in the poem between Walter and his peasant wife. The subject, by the very nature of his earthly subjection, is allowed an external perspective on these questions of authority and epistemology. Lacking earthly mastery, humility and acquiescence to God comes easily to such men, whom the Clerk describes alternatively as "meeke" and "pitous" (ClT 141). Their poverty of rank grants them the wisdom to perceive their poverty of power, whether cognitive or paternal. Indeed, the focus that these men put upon Walter's own paternal legacy and potential sirings serves to occlude the questions of their own respective paternities as a source of their individual authorities. In their pleas to Walter to consider his fathers and future sons, they do not refer to their own; they are imagined as dislocated, fully humble and humbled. Through the ancillary nature of their relationship to Walter and his paternal authority, they also provide a model for Walter to follow with his divine Father. Such humble men wish to serve, rather than to recreate, the magnificent perfection of the divine Paternity; they acknowledge their comparable contemptibility and express that individual limitation with reference to man's intellect. Therefore, their "as it oghte seme/ Honour to God and yow, *as we kan deme*" (ClT 132–3, emphasis mine) functions as a model of humility, linking the corporeal reality of human flesh with its cognitive insufficiencies. These lines also, however, indicate precisely how perverse we should judge Walter's pride to be. For, Walter's capacity to "deme" is as limited as that of his subjects, and it is God alone who determines how things "oghte seme," and who deserves the honour.

This is the crucial context for the *Clerk's Tale's* subsequent spousal interrogations. Walter has that certainty that he desires at his very fingertips, but it is one that necessitates man's surrender of his own authority to the will of God, and therefore Walter is dissatisfied with what it offers him. To trust in the knowledge of one's own impending death and the examples set by one's fathers' death, is to trade certainty for sovereignty. Far better, from Walter's perspective, to seek both at once, through the domination of one's wife. Listening to his subjects, he

---

[25] I thus find the traditional identification of this scene as the introduction of the theme of mutability into a longer discourse on order, such as articulated for example by S. K. Heninger, Jr, too imprecise. Death does not embody mutability here so much as it reminds Walter that the universal order of things—stable, unchanging—is reinforced in its progressions by mortal mechanisms. Mutability does not contrast with Order therefore, but is rather inseparable from it; it is that linkage that Walter has so problematically forgot. S. K. Heninger, Jr, "The Concept of Order in Chaucer's 'Clerk's Tale,'" *The Journal of English and Germanic Philology* 56.3 (July 1957): 382–95, at 387.

understands that reproduction will be the key to his reassertion of his own power, but he overestimates the mastery that even the production of an heir will grant him. For, while his male ancestors rest in the peaceful oblivion of having produced an heir and passed away, Walter questions the system of heredity itself. "For God it woot," says Walter, "that children ofte been/Unlyk hir worthy eldres hem bifore" (ClT 155–6). Walter, informed that his own flesh is the culmination of the compounding of male blood and time, refuses to recognize those paternal investments. Perhaps he is entirely unlike his "worthy eldes;" perhaps his sons will be entirely unlike himself. The entire system of male compensation for mortality might be a mere fiction, according to the evidence of his experience, and most importantly, Walter cannot be certain that it is not. The reproducibility of the subjective self through the creation of offspring is not empirical model to be examined. It must be known through faith or not at all.

For Walter, the failure of likeness between father and son is both a biological fracture and a semiotic one. In that pivotal exchange between Walter and his people's representative, the gap between sign and meaning becomes an inherent component of the negotiation. The spokesman pleads:

> Boweth youre nekke under that blisful yok
> Of soveraynetee, noght of servyse,
> Which that men clepe spousaille or wedlock.
>
> ClT 113–5

The oxymoron of the "sovereign yoke" is compounded by the imprecision of marital linguistics. Once a yoke is fastened around his neck, how will Walter know whether it is emblematic of his authority or servitude within his marriage, if he cannot even be certain of the word to call his state?[26] It is this multiplicity of terms for the same thing that Chaucer decried in *Troilus and Criseyde*, as evidence of the alienation between word and meaning common to the postlapsarian world.[27] If there are two words for the same thing, then one can never know which word is best, which word is more reciprocal to its meaning.

It is unfortunate, therefore, that Walter so profoundly misinterprets the wise advice provided to him about the restricted nature of human cognition in a world where the only certainty is death. While Walter acknowledges the lack of semiotic reciprocity upon the earth, he interprets that limitation as a challenge to be rectified rather than as a test of piety demanding acquiescence. Confronted with the natural inability of fallen man to be certain of anything except death, Walter

---

[26] Donald Green argues that in the distinction between sovereignty and service, the townspeople articulate the necessity of Walter submitting not to his wife (as a courtly lover), but to his proper role as an aristocratic man. Donald C. Green, "The Semantics of Power: 'Maistrie' and 'Soveraynetee' in 'The Canterbury Tales,'" *Modern Philology* 84.1 (August 1986): 18–23, at 20.

[27] Cf. Elaine Tuttle Hansen, *Chaucer and the Fictions of Gender* (Berkeley, CA: University of California Press 1992): 162–9.

begins to order his subjects to provide the kinds of reliable signs that have just been denounced as impossible to perceive. He commands them to treat his future wife with respect "in word and werk, both heere and everywheere" (ClT 167), or in other words, to make their linguistic and physical signs perfectly correspond. As if this is not enough to reassure him, he further issues an almost identical order that they "neither grucche or stryve" (ClT 170) against his choice of wife. The repetition of the command undercuts its authority, endowing the scene with a lack of trust between Walter and his subjects which is only augmented a few lines later when the subjects dread that Walter still might not wed, despite his vows to them (ClT 181–2). The suspicion that neither party will carry out their promises may be seen as an inevitable result of the linguistic unreliability to which the subjects had just testified.

Walter, however, seems to still believe in the possibility of enforcing a reciprocity between sign and meaning, whether through aristocratic or patriarchal privilege. It is Griselda's natural harmony between her reality and her appearance that first attracts him to her.

> Commendynge in his herte hir wommanhede
> And eek hir vertu, passynge any wight
> Of so yong age, *as wel in chiere as dede.*
>
> (ClT 239–41, emphasis mine)

Both Griselda's face and behavior speak of an extraordinary moral character, and that appears to be enough for Walter when he first beholds her. Her most visible and public signs correspond to one another, and therefore seem to indicate an internal state that matches perfectly. In fact, the reader has already been assured of the perfection of the relationship between Griselda's signs and self when the Clerk grants a privileged view inside Griselda's heart to note its freedom from "likerous lust" (ClT 214).

Walter, on the other hand, does not get to see inside Griselda's heart; nevertheless, he trusts that he knows its content, based on the external signs that she has presented to him. This is, in fact, all that he initially asks from Griselda as way of spousal assurance. It is Griselda's visible presentation that he seeks to control, according to their marital negotiations. He counsels her to disobey him "neither by word ne frownyng contenance" (ClT 356). On the contrary, Griselda offers him something far beyond that which he demands; she states "I swere that nevere willingly/ *In werk ne thought* I nyl yow disobeye" (ClT 362–3). This vow goes far beyond what Walter has asked, and indeed Tara Williams argues that, "by raising the demands on herself, Griselda exercises a certain degree of control in the exchange."[28] Griselda promises her future husband that she will remain consistent

---

[28] Tara Williams, "'T'assaye in thee thy wommanheede:' Griselda, Chosen, Translated, and Tried," *Studies in the Age of Chaucer* 27 (2005): 93–127, at 111.

in her external and her internal signs, a promise whose fulfillment he has no ability to assess. Such a vow presumes that Walter will be willing to accept on faith that which he cannot know with certainty. It is Griselda herself who first verbalizes the possibility of forbidden knowledge that will soon so obsess her husband.[29] Before, Walter was determined to live with the natural doubts characteristic of the human condition. But after Griselda promises him perfection, Walter cannot stop his strivings for that ideal.

It is also impossible to separate out the medieval association of men with the literal and women with the figurative from Walter's inability to believe Griselda's signs. Griselda's promise to Walter is magnified by the "evidence" of her sex, which provides testimony against her capacity to signify perfectly. As Catherine Cox writes, "Griselda is an ideal woman in part because she is an unwomanly woman—that is she exemplifies a masculine ideal that contradicts misogynistic stereotypes of the mutable, "slyding," and unstable feminine."[30] This does not go quite far enough, in my opinion. When one marital partner transgresses his or her gender role in *The Canterbury Tales*, it consistently seems to trigger a re-evaluation of the other partner's gender performance. The *Wife of Bath's Prologue* provides ample examples of this, as Chapter 3 will argue, but perhaps the most concise illustration of the point comes from the prologue to the *Monk's Tale*, when Harry Bailly recounts his wife's many challenges to his masculinity. Frustrated with her husband's lack of violence (in her defense), Goodelief Bailly declares, "By corpus bones, I wol have thy knyf,/And thou shalt have my distaff and go spynne!" (MkT 1906–7). Chaucer's pilgrims seem to imagine gender performance in marriage as a seesaw; gender transgression in one catalyzing the reverse gender transgression in the other.

It should be less of a surprise, therefore, that as Griselda promises (and appears to deliver) a more masculine form of literalism, that Walter begins to perform the feminine role of deception and of encouraging a deliberate misreading of his body's signs. Unable to tell if his wife's deeds and thoughts are indeed as inseparable as she claims, Walter manifests within his own flesh that very fracturing of sign and meaning which he so fears to perceive within Griselda. As Chaucer writes: "And forth he gooth with drery contenaunce,/But to his herte it was ful greet plesaunce" (ClT 671–2). For all the dramatic undeniability of Walter's "torture" of Griselda, it is worth noting that it is Walter himself who undergoes

---

[29] Gail Ashton sees Griselda's investment in establishing the existence of her own secret interiority as a deliberate attempt to create a female identity within her masculine-dominated world. Ashton reads Griselda as endowed with a "patience which not only marks [her] as holy but provides an opportunity for the secret nurturing of a hidden masked self." Gail Ashton, "Patient Mimesis: Griselda and the Clerk's Tale," *The Chaucer Review* 32.3 (1998): 232.

[30] Catherine S. Cox, *Gender and Language in Chaucer* (Gainesville, FL: University Press of Florida, 1997): 70.

the most brutal transformations in the course of the *Tale*.[31] Griselda moves rather complacently from one external manifestation to another; when her clothes match her interior virtue, she appears to be no more content than when the two sharply diverge.[32]

As he increasingly experiences the divergence between sign and meaning within his own body, Walter seems to become ever more certain that a similar break in signification must exist within his wife.

> "He waiteth if by word or contenance
> That she to him was changed of corage,
> But never coulde he finde variance:
> She was ay oon in herte and in visage"
>
> (ClT 708–11)

It is Griselda's heart that Walter wishes to read, that fundamentally inaccessible organ to which so many of her external signs refer. He engages in a similar reading process in the following passage:

> "For now goth he ful faste imagining
> If by his wyves chere he mighte see,
> Or by hire word aperceyve, that she
> Were changed; but he never hire coulde finde
> But ever in oon ylke sad and kinde"
>
> (ClT 598–602)

These lines stress Walter's sensory experience of semiotic observation and analysis, even as they document his frustration with his own cognitive limitations. He spends his intellectual abilities perusing the evidence before him, yet his frustration lies not in the paucity of signs, but rather in his own flawed capacity to assess them.

It is as a reader of female flesh that Walter finds fault with himself (and by extension, with Griselda), but it is as an overzealous reader that Chaucer finds fault with him. In his refusal to accept his wife as the flawed, unknowable text that she is (despite her superlative virtue), Walter rebels against the natural order of human cognition. Sarah Stanbury reads Walter's pursuit of a too comprehensive

---

[31] Jill Mann likewise argues that Walter is transformed by his interactions with Griselda; Mann believes that Walter's human desire for change is eventually taught self-sufficiency and contentment by Griselda's reliable "sameness." Mann, *Feminizing Chaucer*, 120.

[32] For more on Griselda's transformations of person via her clothing, see Roger Ramsey, "Clothing Makes a Queen in the *Clerk's Tale*," *The Journal of Narrative Technique* 7.2 (Spring 1977): 104–15; Kristine Gilmartin, "Array in the *Clerk's Tale*," *The Chaucer Review* 13.3 (Winter 1979): 234–346; Laura F. Hodges, "Reading Griselda's Smocks in the *Clerk's Tale*," *The Chaucer Review* 44.1 (2009): 84–109.

knowledge of Griselda as framed "by the [problematic] sacramentalizing of a human bond."[33] She continues:

> Griselda's translation into a sacred sign levies an extraordinary promise of revelation and sanctity even as that translation, contracted through the verbal promise of marriage, highlights the dilemma of ordinary knowledge of the other. In real time, bodies that give themselves to us by private consent in marriage cannot be kept or fully known.[34]

I agree with Stanbury that we should read Walter's attempts to know Griselda fully as religious in tone, but I disagree with the division she seems to make between secular knowledge/condemned curiosity and sacramental knowledge/legitimate inquiry. Walter does not merely model the inappropriate application of a sacramental cognitive system to a mundane, human object. Instead, his unceasing demand for perfect signification from his wife would be as illegitimate if the object whose meaning he sought was purely holy. It is the demand for certainty itself which is heterodox, representing, as it does, an empiricist turn away from faith.[35]

"To wrye the wombe…"

Although we can identify Walter's investigation of his wife as an act of "scientific" curiosity run amock, an overweening display of human intellectual pride, it is significant that he himself does not become the symbol of his own unmoderated excess. Instead, Griselda's womb functions as the powerful metaphor for the restrictions on human cognition. Walter's testing of his wife is fully contextualized within the functions of her womb, its pregnant swell and labored contractions. Before she brings forth their daughter into the world, Griselda is so well respected that her subjects suppose "that she from heven sente was" (ClT 440). When Walter is absent, she serves as an authority in his stead, mediating arguments and passing down judgments upon her subjects. "Ther nas discord, rancor, ne hevynesse/In al that land that she ne koude apese" (ClT 432–3). Griselda is not the instigator of obsession and unrest that she becomes later in the *Tale*, neither is she the emblem of submissive passivity with which her name is synonymous. Instead, as the consort of a powerful autocrat, Griselda herself acts as a considered, judicious ruler. Moreover, her moderate approach to authority stands in stark

---

[33] Sarah Stanbury, *The Visual Object of Desire in Late Medieval England* (Philadelphia, PA: University of Pennsylvania Press, 2008): 139.

[34] Stanbury, *Visual Object of Desire*, 139.

[35] For a history of Christian critiques of ungoverned intellect from late antiquity through the Middle Ages, see Edward M. Peters, "Transgressing the Limits Set by the Fathers: Authority and Impious Exegesis in Medieval Thought," *Christendom and its Discontents: Exclusion, Persecution, and Rebellion, 1000–1500*, ed. Scott L. Waugh and Peter Diehl (Cambridge: Cambridge University Press, 2002): 338–360, at 339.

contrast with the abuses carried out by Walter; Carol Falvo Heffernan argues that here Griselda "proves herself to be, in her husband's absence, the kind of ruler he must yet learn to be."[36]

And yet as soon as Griselda gives birth to a child, both husband and subjects immediately reverse their opinions of Griselda and begin to view her signs of goodness with suspicion. While Walter feigns the outcry of his people which he tells to Griselda as the rationale behind his supposed murder of their children, it is undeniable that after her experience of childbirth, Griselda rapidly becomes an object of public anxiety. We are told immediately after the birth of her unnamed daughter,

> Al had hire levere have born a knave child,
> Glad was this markis and the folk therfore;
> For though a mayde child come al before,
> She may unto a knave child atteyne
> By lyklihed, sin she nis nat bareyne.

(ClT 444–8)

Griselda has disappointed her husband and her people by presenting them with a daughter instead of a son, evidence of a reproductive inadequacy with which many other medieval women might have empathized.[37] In a sense, by bringing forth this unwished daughter, she has served to remind them all not only of the differentiation between the genders (and the original inferiority of woman's creation compared to that of man), but also of the postlapsarian stratification of men and women. As her husband and subjects must reconcile themselves to the birth of this little girl instead of the hoped-for boy, they must simultaneously confront Griselda as a woman (a descendent of Eve), rather than merely as a conjugal partner or authoritative ruler.[38]

Griselda's daughter is a reminder of the link between Griselda and the "realities" of female nature. Since Walter specifically married Griselda so that

[36] Carol Falvo Heffernan, "Tyranny and Commune Profit in the 'Clerk's Tale,'" *The Chaucer Review* 17.4 (Spring 1983): 332–40, at 336.

[37] Most medieval medical texts, for example, give multiple pieces of advice for how a woman may conceive a son, and how a pregnant woman may discern whether or not the child in her womb is male. The author of *The Knowing of Woman's Kind in Childing* writes that "For 'a' woman that will conceive a man child: let her dresse here in suche maner wise in the deede of hire naturall lykynge: let hire lefte hype lye hier than here right, for so she shal make the seed of man to falle on the right side where the male is conceived. And in the same maner do on the tother side for the female. *The Knowing of Woman's Kind in Childing: A Middle English Version of Material Derived from the* Trotula *and Other Sources*, ed. Alexandra Barratt (Turnhout, Belgium: Brepols, 2001): 47.

[38] This reading therefore breaks with Allyson Newton's interpretation of this passage as a denial of the maternal "in order to absorb it into illusory, autonomous male succession." Allyson Newton, "The Occlusion of Maternity in Chaucer's *Clerk's Tale*," *Medieval Mothering*, ed. John Carmi Parsons and Bonnie Wheeler (New York and London: Garland Publishing, 1996): 63–75, at 67. Unlike Newton, I do not believe medieval maternity can be separated or placed into opposition with patrilineal structures; instead, I read the medieval maternal role as one deeply embedded within the patriarchal construction of reproductive authority.

"a straunge successour sholde [not] take youre [his] heritage" (ClT 138–9), by producing a daughter instead of the male heir, Griselda's womb has publicly "deceived" her husband and his subjects; by extension, Griselda herself is now understood to be capable of deception. As the wife of an aristocrat heavily invested in the structures of primogeniture and male descent, Griselda's pregnancy would have been understood as signifying the promise of a male heir. Male babies were considered the ideal result of reproduction; the author of the *Trotula*, for example, elides the distinction between the desire to conceive and the desire to conceive a male, linking conceptive remedies unthinkingly and exclusively to the production of a son.[39] In a similar manner, the historical record offered by the diary of the royal French midwife, Louise Bourgeois, denotes extreme differences between the quality of reproductive care and exultation that greeted the birth of an heir, a surplus son, or merely a daughter.[40] While English women were not excluded from systems of inheritance to the extent that French women (subject to Salic law) were, nevertheless the birth of a daughter as the only heir to a powerful domain would have been an occasion for sorrow and disappointment. Likewise, it would have introduced a profound degree of uncertainty into Walter and Griselda's marriage. While the Clerk reports the public hope that Griselda would bear a son next, the very nature of that optimism reveals the potential for failure. Griselda's womb offers no guarantee of its future fertility, and for all Walter knows, this daughter might well be the only child borne to him.

Moreover, it is within Griselda's womb that the limits of Walter's ability to translate and transform her are made manifest. Walter can redress Griselda as a noble woman, destroying all vestiges of her peasant identity, but even he cannot control her womb or its productions. The womb is Griselda's link with Eve, and thus with female betrayal and female illusion. Without her reproductive potential, Griselda's external semiotics would be far more worthy of trust (although rendered useless for the dynastic purposes for which Walter had married her). It is the womb that matters to Walter and his subjects, but it is also the womb that eludes their control.

It is this ambiguity, between revelation and obfuscation, which draws Walter and his people into repeated attempts to read Griselda's womb, even as they simultaneously resent its lack of reliable signification. From disappointment at the birth of a girl, they move immediately to a reconfiguration of their expectations

---

[39] *The Trotula: An English Translation of the Medieval Compendium of Women's Medicine*, ed. Monica H. Green (Philadelphia, PA: University of Pennsylvania, 2002): 95.

[40] Lianne McTavish describes the scene from Bourgeois's diary in which the long-awaited Dauphin was finally born to the French King. Bourgeois agreed to perform a secret gesture to alert one of the ladies-in-waiting of the infant's sex. She did so and the lady alerted the King, but he refused to believe her because Bourgeois's face was too serious. Once the King finally believed he had had a son, he "cried tears of delight, informed the Queen, and then allowed some two hundred people into the ante-chamber to celebrate the birth." Lianne McTavish, *Childbirth and the Display of Authority in Early Modern France* (Aldershot, UK and Burlington, VT: Ashgate Publishing, 2005): 98.

according to the new information that Griselda has provided them. They base an empirical evaluation on the evidence of her daughter. "She may unto a knave child atteyne/By lyklihed, sin she nis nat bareyne" (447–8). Although at the time of her initial marriage to Walter, Griselda is surprisingly exempt from this type of intrusive speculation as to her reproductive potential, from the moment she per- forms her procreative duty, her body becomes a set of generative signs, determin- ing her chances of producing a viable male heir. This was a form of evaluation that Chaucer's readers would have accepted as inherently unexceptional; despite the generally progressive trend, for example of Anne of France's fifteenth-century *Lessons for My Daughter*, she is careful to warn the girl that men will constantly evaluate her body for its capacity to bear male offspring. She tells the story of a daughter of the lord of Poitiers whose clothing was so tightly laced (for the sake of vanity) that a potential husband judged her body to be infertile. "It seemed that, because of this weakness, she would never be able to bear a child, and he concluded in his heart that he would never be able to marry her."[41] Women's appearances were always reduced to the womb, as men searched the signs they could see for the meaning of what they could not.

It is the process of semiotic reduction of woman to womb that condemns Griselda to an endless assay, despite her subsequent production of the desired heir. Once the possibility of uncertainty has been offered to Walter by Griselda's body, he becomes fixated upon his own lack of control over Griselda and her womb. Again, it is the moment of birth that serves as the trigger for Walter's suspicions and for his desire to know her with certainty. Griselda bears him "a knave child…ful gracious and fair for to biholde" (ClT 612–3), and Walter once again begins to doubt (albeit much more slowly than he did after the birth of his daughter).[42] There is never any uncertainty as to the child's paternity nor in Griselda's general fidelity. Indeed, as the Clerk tells us, Walter "sey/the constance of his wyf" (ClT 667–8), and is himself witness to the reliability of her virtuous signs. And yet the reintrusion of the womb, as symbol of all about Griselda that he cannot definitively prove, drives Walter to act against the evidence of his own eyes, to distrust even that which he *can* see, let alone that which he cannot.

Griselda herself strikes to the very heart of Walter's intellectual confusion when she confronts him in the moment of his public renunciation of her as his wife. After Walter publicly commands Griselda to "retourneth to your fadres hous" (ClT 809), Griselda directly critiques both his mistrust of her signification and his own semiotic duplicities. As Robert Myles notes, Griselda explicitly points to

---

[41] Anne of France, *Lessons for My Daughter*, ed. and trans. by Sharon L. Jansen (Cambridge: D. S. Brewer, 2004): 42.

[42] The daughter is only given time to suck "but a throwe," while her younger brother is not removed from Griselda's care until "it was two yeer old and fro the brest/departed of his norice." Chaucer, *The Clerk's Tale*, 450, 617.

Walter's manipulation of his external signs and her trust of their internal meaning
as the flaw within their marriage:[43]

> How gentil and how kynde
> Ye semed by youre speche and youre visage
> the day that maked was oure mariage!
>
> (ClT 852–4)

Griselda notes her own early willingness to trust in Walter's appearance of virtue,
even in the absence of true certainty. She has been willing to know through faith
when human signs might be uncertain or duplicitous, a cognitive philosophy
from which Walter himself would benefit. And yet, recognizing his profound
incapacity to live without full, comprehensive knowing, Griselda offers to strip
herself (in the most literal fashion) of the very gaps in signification upon which
other women (as we will see in Chapter 2) take full advantage.

Griselda reminds Walter that he has stripped her before, seeing her "truth"
without any interference of external signs. "Naked out of my fadres hous . . . /I
cam, and naked moot I turne agayn" (ClT 871–2), she declaims. There is no need
for Walter to have faith in her; instead he can have certainty, trusting the evidence
of his own eyes. If Walter cannot abide with the ambiguities of human signification, then Griselda will remove them for her husband. She will grant him the
power to read beyond the acquired attributes that manipulate human assignation
of meaning to signs. Her willingness to walk naked through the town (a scene
whose climactic, if titillating, role in the narrative is indicated by its artistic popularity) shows how profoundly, and how deeply, Griselda is willing to show herself
to Walter, and to his people.[44] It also, of course, bears strong religious resonances,
redirecting to Walter to an appropriate humility for the abject nakedness with
which God has placed him in the world. By identifying her own naked movement
to and from Walter's house with Walter's own humble and transitory time on the
earth, Griselda sharply reminds Walter of the limits of his own authority.
God knows Walter in a way that Walter himself can never, and should never,
know Griselda.

---

[43] Robert Myles, "Confusing Signs: The Semiotic Point of View in the *Clerk's Tale*," *Chaucer and
Language: Essays in Honour of Douglas Wurtele*, ed. Robert Myles and David Williams (Montreal and
Kingston: McGill-Queen's University Press, 2001): 107–25, at 115.
[44] I am thinking here particularly of the Sienese group of panels painted around 1490, referencing
Boccaccio's version of the Griselda story from the *Decameron*. In one of the three panels, Griselda's
stripping and subsequent nudity is dramatically depicted; her smock certainly does not cover her
womb (the viewer can clearly perceive her navel), and both breasts and pudendum appear on display
as well. The fact that the artist chooses to show Griselda twice in this unclothed state (both undressing
and later so close to nude) highlights, I believe, the particular fondness that those familiar with the
story felt for its most erotic scene. For more on these panel paintings, see Jill Dunkerten, Carol
Christensen, and Luke Syson, "The Master of the Story of Griselda and Paintings for Sienese Palaces,"
Technical Bulletin 27 (2006): 4–71.

Thus, despite the nakedness which Griselda attests herself so willing to display, this scene should be read as one of sharp rebuke from wife to husband, in criticism of the overweening nature of his desire to know. For, even as she offers her naked body to public perusal, Griselda simultaneously holds one part of her body off from such display.[45] As he prepares to reject her and cast her off, Griselda declares:

> Ye coude nat doon so dishoneste a thing
> That thilke wombe in which youre children leye
> Sholde biforn the peple, in my walking,
> Be seyn al bare...
> Wherfore in guerdon of my maydenhede,
> Which that I broghte, and noght again I bere,
> As voucheth sauf to yeve me to my mede
> But swich a smok as I was wont to were,
> That I therwith may wrye the wombe of here
> That was youre wyf."
>
> (ClT 876–9, 883–8)

Here Griselda both solicits and denies visual access to her womb. She singles the organ out as the only part of her body that she wishes to keep private. Ostensibly, it is the common people whose eyes Griselda hopes to keep from her womb. And yet because the scene is staged as a confrontation between Walter and Griselda, her claim of authority over access to her flesh seems to disrupt his spousal hegemony. She denies the public the chance to view her womb, but it is first Walter before whom she refuses to disrobe fully, first Walter whose vision she restricts.

At the same time, however, Griselda assures Walter that even if he cannot see her womb he can have faith in its submission to his authority. She identifies this aspect of her own body as "thilke wombe in which youre children leye" (ClT 877), displacing her own claim to ownership over both children and womb. In fact, Griselda offers Walter this admonition, but she herself barely figures within it. Not only does she identify their children as exclusively his, but she removes herself almost entirely from even the activity of uterine exposure. The choice of whether or not to display her womb is Walter's alone, dependent on the question of whether or not he can "doon so dishoneste a thing"(ClT 876). Moreover, it is not "my womb," but rather "thilke wombe," further alienating Griselda from her

---

[45] In Petrarch's earlier version of the *Tale*, as Emma Campbell attests, Griselda uses this moment instead to reaffirm her spiritual rather than significatory wholeness. "In claiming that she has always remained a maid in spirit (*animo semper ancilla permansi*) (17.5, 12–15), Griselda emphasizes her role as a servant and the embodiment of Christian virtue rather than as a wife, associating herself with that other (rather more famous) handmaid of the Lord, the Virgin Mary." Emma Campbell, "Sexual Poetics and the Politics of Translation in the Tale of Griselda," *Comparative Literature* 55.3 (Summer 2003): 191–216, at 206. Campbell goes on to note that Chaucer's Griselda, on the contrary, "does not mention her spiritual virginity" (Campbell, 210); her identity is firmly grounded as a sexually active wife.

own body. The only part of this moment that Griselda identifies as under her own control is the act of walking. All is under Walter's control, Griselda asserts, except the capacity to verify his dominion.

Griselda's willing surrender of any claim to mutual possession of their children is an example of the medieval division of paternal and maternal conceptive roles taken to its furthest extreme. Men indeed were considered the "actors" in the creation of children, women the passive material upon which, and through which, the actions of generation took place.[46] And yet, as the procreative matter from which life was created, women were still fundamental to reproduction. Neither Galen nor Aristotle espoused a reproductive science in which men assumed exclusive dominance of the filial product. Likewise, even in the case of the Virgin Mary's conception of Jesus, an example which might understandably place emphasis upon the central role of the Father, Mary herself was credited with substantial contributions to her child.[47] In her desire to assuage Walter's fears, Griselda has abnegated herself to an extent that both medieval science and theology would condemn. Perhaps we may identify this tendency as originating within the moral philosophy of the *Tale* itself, in which, as Emma Campbell notes, women are forced to "both acknowledge the negative representations of them-selves by male authors and reproduce those stereotypes through their own behavior."[48] Certainly Griselda argues for a female passivity that is embedded within the body, re-enacting the role of submissive wife to an extreme that ren-ders it (and the image of motherhood) grotesque. But, she also goes beyond the dictates and witticisms of male authors, presenting a vision of herself to her hus-band's court in which all personal identity has been leeched out by marriage. When they look at her, they should see Walter's power, she claims; even when they look at that which they cannot see (her womb), they should imagine only Walter, and the unsurpassed extent of his authority.

To ground her argument that Walter should have faith that he may control her womb even if he may not see it (and thus, by extension, trust in other things he cannot see), Griselda appeals to that more visible female sign: the hymen.[49]

---

[46] Cf. Joan Cadden, *The Meanings of Sex Difference in the Middle Ages: Medicine, Science, and Culture* (Cambridge: Cambridge University Press, 1995): 117–30; Danielle Jacquart and Claude Thomasset, *Sexuality and Medicine in the Middle Ages*, trans. Matthew Adamson (Oxford: Polity Press, 1988): 53–60.

[47] For more of a discussion on the problematics of Christ's incarnation within Mary's potentially menstrual womb, cf. Cadden, *Meanings of Sex Difference*, 173–7; Theresa Coletti, "Purity and Danger: The Paradox of Mary's Body and the En-Gendering of the Infancy Narrative in the English Mystery Cycles," *Feminist Approaches to the Body in Medieval Literature*, ed. Linda Lomperis and Sarah Stanbury (Philadelphia, PA: University of Pennsylvania Press, 1993): 65–95, at 68–71.

[48] Campbell, "Sexual Poetics and the Politics of Translation," 212.

[49] Sarah Stanbury remarks that lines 218–20 early in the *Tale* indicate that Griselda's heart is con-tained "within the protective membrane of her virginity." Sarah Stanbury, "Regimes of the Visual in Premodern England: Gaze, Body, and Chaucer's "Clerk's Tale," *New Literary History* 28.2 (Spring 1997): 261–89, at 280. This is a provocative reading, since it would suggest the same parallelism between hymen and heart that Griselda attempts to establish between womb and heart.

"Wherfore in guerdon of my maydenhede,
Which that I broghte, and noght again I bere…"

Griselda reminds Walter that she has already offered him tangible proof of her virtue. Virginity was understood to be a highly verifiable condition, one that husbands would investigate on the wedding night, and from which evidence might be publicly displayed.[50] Yet again, she turns his mind's eye to what he has already seen, so that he might create a logical extension between the two reproductive signs. Moreover, these lines serve to reference the verifiable changes of her external body from virgin to mother, changes that Walter himself might be able to see and accept as vestigial markings of his control. He has had the proof of her virginal blood and witnessed the alteration of her flesh as a consequence of his sexual mastery. Surely, that is enough for him to rely on in evaluating her as a woman.

Griselda asks Walter to accept her virginity and her maternal markings as synecdoche for that which he cannot see: her womb and heart. To do so would be to accept the mutuality of their sinful, human state with grace. Griselda has humbled herself to Walter as far as one human being can to one another; she has been willing to render all of her flesh to his control, and to provide reliable signs for that which he cannot verify. It is this humility that serves to emphasize the inappropriateness of Walter's refusal to accept his own human restrictions and relative inferiority. Lines like Griselda's "I ne heeld me nevere digne in no manere/ to be youre wyf, no, ne youre chamberere" (CIT 818–9) only serve to draw a sharp contrast with her husband's pride. For Walter has of course always thought he was good enough to be Griselda's husband, and far too good to be her servant. Even more importantly, he seems to think that he is good enough to be her judge, good enough to assay her for that truth which he demands. Griselda's refocusing of his attention to her womb at the very moment she denies his view of it thus may be read as a sharp rebuke of such intellectual pretensions. She clearly shows him both the extent and limits of his power.

In his earlier version of Griselda's story, Boccaccio jests that another woman would have run to a new man if thrown out of her house.[51] Chaucer has removed such types of humor from his own version since it would undercut the power of Griselda's message to Walter. She tells him that he can rely on the signs of her body that he has already perceived in order to predict her inner feelings and her future behavior. The argument by Boccaccio that married women can behave with impunity, since sexual sins will be hidden by the absence of corporeal signs post-virginity, is thus roundly dismissed by Griselda.

[50] Jane Cartwright discusses both historical and literary testings of a medieval bride's virginity in "Virginity and Chastity Tests in Medieval Welsh Prose," *Medieval Virginities*, ed. Anke Bernau, Ruth Evans, and Sarah Salih (Toronto: University of Toronto Press, 2003): 56–79.
[51] Giovanni Boccaccio, *The Decameron*, trans. by Richard Aldington (Garden City, NY: Garden City Books, 1949): 556.

Til I be deed, my lyf ther wol I lede:
A widwe clene, in body, herte, and al.
For sith I yaf to yow my maydenhede,
And am youre trewe wyf, it is no drede

(CIT 835–8)

Griselda argues that her maidenhead is not a transitory sign, meaningless once assessed, but rather a consistent marker of her virtue, one to which Walter can repeatedly return for reassurance. Her reproductive experiences have permanently altered her body, rendering her signification stable and worthy of trust. Walter should believe those external signs he sees in her to be perfectly reciprocated by their internal meanings because reproduction has exerted his dominance over her body not once or twice, but irrevocably. He can use what he has known about her in the past to know her in the future.

Walter's investigative struggle within the *Tale* is described as an attempt to force Griselda "to the uttereste preve of hir corage" (CIT 785). And yet far more of the *Tale* may be seen as a negotiation between husband and wife as to what, if anything, might qualify as the "uttereste preve." For, while Griselda might be the most patient of wives, she is far from a skilled rhetorician. The flaw in her argument that the womb might suffice as a sign in which Walter might place his faith and obtain certainty, is proved by Chaucer's other wives: the Merchant's May, the Miller's Alisoun, and Alisoun of Bath herself. *The Canterbury Tales* is replete with stories of women whose signs of virginity were certain, but whose signs of marital chastity were rightly suspect. The type of reproductive metonymy that Griselda argues for as a mode of knowledge acquisition for her husband is the precise model upon which so many other husbands have floundered. This is, in many ways, the central conflict of the narrative. For Griselda, the womb *is* the "uttereste preve" of her virtue. It is the only external marking that she possesses that she can reliably present to Walter as outside of her own control, visibly subject to his own intervention (through the transformations of parturition). But, for Walter, Griselda's womb is yet another lying, human sign, unreliably attached to its intrinsic meaning. There is no solution for the two to live in harmony as long as such a sharp division exists between them as to what degree of semiotic uncertainty is acceptable for life, what amount of cognitive humility can be borne by man.

Thus, when Walter does indeed decide to end Griselda's ordeals, it comes to the reader as a bit of a shock. The narrative has thrived on the cyclicality and inevitability of its plot; Walter tempts, Griselda overcomes, Walter appears to fall back into his obsession. Surely Griselda's attempt to offer her womb as reliable sign appears as the last hope for a man poisoned by his own doubt? Chaucer's challenge in resolution surely lies in providing the happy ending to the story as established within his source texts without offering Walter the demonstrably false reassurance that semiotic certainty is an attainable goal for human beings. The ending to the *Clerk's Tale* indeed seems rather excessively happy, reintegrating the two spouses into a peaceful and satisfying marriage, despite the years (and, one would imagine, lingering trauma) of Walter's system of inquiry and abuse. "Ful many a year in heigh prosperitee/liven thise two in concord and in reste" (ClT 1128–9). Walter's obsession and Griselda's sufferings no longer operate as twin halves of a doomed debate about reliable semiotics; they are now confined to the restricted narrative of the past.

Therefore, Walter must have received his answer, or at least an answer he can accept. But from whence did it come? It is my argument in the final pages of this chapter that Walter's change of heart (and his newfound trust in the steadfastness of Griselda's own) functions not as a matter of revelation, but rather as one of resignation. Walter and Griselda do not discover some purer, more reliable sign than that of her womb; they merely come to peace with the fact that no better sign will be forthcoming. Their unnamed daughter, whose birth precipitated Walter's intellectual crisis, also resolves it with her re-entry into the story. As a female infant, she provoked concern about Griselda's fallibilities, and by extension, about Walter's own. When she appears as his putative wife, Walter must face the only certainty delivered to him in the *Tale*: he will know this new spouse no better than he did his last.

His people, on the other hand, are quick to endow the young girl with immense possibility. They perceive her as a dramatic improvement upon Griselda, largely because of her supposed lineage and rank.

> For she is fairer, as they deemen alle,
> Than is Grisilde, and moore tendre of age,
> And fairer fruyt bitwene hem sholde falle,
> And moore plesant, for hire heigh lynage.
>
> (ClT 988–91)

Here we have a nice dramatization of Walter's earlier observation that children often do not resemble their parents. Reading the evidence of the girl's lineage, they fail to perceive its mendacity, despite their longstanding knowledge of her biological father and his appearance. This moment of misperception serves to underline the story's motif of semiotic confusion, while also dramatically increasing the stakes of such false readings. As they imagine the fair children who will be born from such a marriage, the reader must imagine the monstrous results of incestuous intercourse. Moreover, in his desire to know Griselda with certainty, Walter puts himself and his daughter at risk of most deadly sin. To quote a late medieval didactic text, "wher ys fleshly knowlege between kyn and kyn; in the most helly pein their soules xall rest."[52]

This new young wife brings potential sin, but no solution to Walter's intellectual frustrations. She is no more knowable than her mother; Walter's cognitive

---

[52] Peter Idley, *Peter Idley's Instructions to His Son*, ed. C. D'Evelyn, The Modern Language Association of America Monograph Series, Volume 6 (Boston, MA: D. C. Health and Co., 1935): 202.

powers are no more omnipotent with a different wife. Griselda recognizes the potential for Walter's new marriage to get caught by the same lust for knowledge, counseling him that "ye ne prikke with no tormenting/this tender mayden, as he han don mo" (1038–1039). Griselda understands that Walter's obsession with proving his skill as a reader of people is not confined to the particularity of her own person, but rather applies to her sex as a whole, and is thus readily transferable between women. It is the female sex whose signs he mistrusts, his own eyes whose power he doubts. Once rid of his existing wife, Griselda assumes, he would only begin the process again with a new bride. As soon as the marriage was consummated (with the destruction of the hymen, that supposedly reliable visual sign), Walter would once again begin searching for his wife's heart.

Confronted by his own cognitive impotency, Walter capitulates. He reclaims Griselda as his wife and as the mother of his children, resolving to take her steadfastness on faith, and thereby abjuring his investigative eye for a more appropriately conjugal one.

> This is ynogh, Grisilde myn…
> Be now namore agast ne yvel apayed;
> I have thy faith and thy benignitee,
> As wel as ever womman was, assayed.
> In greet estaat, and poverliche arrayed,
> Now knowe I, dere wyf, thy stedfastnesse.
>
> (CIT 1051–6)

Griselda has been tested, not to a reliable conclusion but rather in the more limited sense: "as wel as ever womman was." There is no "utterest" proof, no certain sign. Walter's investigative defeat is not a triumph of the human intellect, but rather an acceptance of its limitations and flaws. There are no signs a human body can render that may be fully relied upon, and no human brains capable of interpreting semiotic meaning beyond the shadow of a doubt. True to form, Walter asserts that "now knowe I" Griselda's "stedfastnesse," yet he does not know her any better (albeit, or any worse) than he did upon first beholding her in her poverty. Walter does not become a better reader of the feminine text over the course of the story. He only abandons his own prideful hopes to know in ways that a man cannot know, embracing the inevitability of doubt and uncertainty. Walter reclaims "Constant Griselda" as his wife, even as he confronts his human incapacity to judge the accuracy of that appellation.

Conclusion

It was within the female reproductive body that medieval fears of adultery and of human intellectual limitation coalesced, turning the image of the fecund mother into one of anxiety and doubt. The threat posed by one's wife and one's supposed sons had psychological ramifications for men far beyond the practical details of inheritance. Thus, consider the following quote from a fourteenth-century didactic text, *The Mirroure of the Worlde*. "There be som that be covert theefes, the whiche stelith heritages...[like] the wyfe the whiche knoweth welle that shee hatthe geten hir childe in aventure the whiche bereth therytage and disseheriteth the right heyris."[53] The most explicit conflict here occurs in terms associated with the preservation of patrimony; the wife is seen in conflict with her husband's heirs, breaking down the marital association in favor of one that links husband and his male relatives in opposition to the wife. And yet while the text purports to be concerned with the condemnation of theft, it cannot separate its imagining of such a reproductive scenario from a discourse on knowledge. The wife's sin is not only that she has stolen property through an illicit pregnancy. Instead, her primary fault is that she "knoweth welle" whether or not she has done so. It is the wife's certainty here that singles her out for censure, particularly in juxtaposition with the apparent lack of knowing that afflicts both husband and heirs. Men might have the authority in marriage, but women have the privilege of certainty, of knowing their children. According to one medieval author (paraphrased by James Brundage), "maternity was a matter of fact, but paternity was a matter of opinion."[54]

The womb, in all its unknowability, symbolized the state of human cognition: flawed, unverifiable, and unstable. The act of a father recognizing his children could therefore be seen as a performative modeling of correct epistemological behavior, a privileging of faith over that which could not be proved. Women's wombs tempted male eyes, urging them to try to interpret the signs before their eyes. And yet to give in to the temptation was to fall towards sin and towards obsession. Walter's lust to know Griselda is an explicitly negative example of what happens to men who proudly overvalue their own intellect. The lust to know is as virulent a disease as any other form of lust, an act of defiance against the natural order of a post-Edenic world. After humanity's fall, language and cognition were reconstructed around principles of doubt and inevitable gaps between sign and meaning, while the bodies of Eve's daughters became the universalized symbols of that degradation. Even the most virtuous of women, like Griselda, cannot force their bodies to signify with certainty, any more than the most intelligent and perceptive of men, like Walter believes himself to be, can trust what they read on their wives' flesh.

---

[53] *The Mirroure of the Worlde: A Middle English Translation of* Le Miroir Du Monde, ed. Robert R. Raymo and Elaine E Whitaker, assist. Ruth E Sternglantz (Toronto: University of Toronto Press, 2003): 162.

[54] James A. Brundage, *Law, Sex, and Christian Society in Medieval Europe* (Chicago, IL: University of Chicago Press, 1990): 430.

It seems fitting to conclude this chapter with a story from *Le Menagier de Paris*, a text contemporaneous with the *Clerk's Tale*, containing a Griselda analogue, and ostensibly written by an elderly husband to dictate the behavior of a young wife. In this story, a dying woman confesses to her husband that he is not the father of one of their children.

> She continued her admission, but her husband cried out and said, "Ho! ho! ho! say no more!" He then kissed her and pardoned her, chiding, "Never speak of this again, nor tell me or anyone else which of your children it may be, for I want to love them all equally, so that you will not be blamed either during your life or after your death."[55]

The father here, realizing the fallibility of his wife's flesh and that he had indeed dramatically misread one of the signifiers of her womb, nevertheless pleads for ignorance. While the rationale he gives to remain in ignorance appears to be a fundamentally altruistic one (so that he will not change the degree in which he loves his children), surely it is also a more practical epistemological one. Having once misread his wife's body and the flesh of a beloved, if illegitimate, child, how could he ever trust subsequent signs provided to him by the same woman, whether visual or verbal? Instead, he chooses the certainty of ignorance, embracing the limitations of his human understanding. Even as the Manciple must write out an entire reproductive plotline from his Ovidian source so as not to introduce the specter of doubt to his story, and as Walter must accept the curse of his own inability to know, so too must all men, Chaucer seems to say, choose to live with faith, rather than to chase the blind promises of doomed empiricism and "assay." As Chaucer highlights masculine failures of perception and feminine failures of reproductive signification, he turns the reader's eyes away from the futility of reliance upon the science of human signs, to that source of signification that does not, cannot fail: "his visage, that oghte be desired to be seyn of al mankynde" (ParsT 279).

---

[55] *The Good Wife's Guide (Le Menagier de Paris): A Medieval Household Book*, ed. and trans. Gina L. Greco and Christine M. Rose (Ithaca, NY: Cornell University Press, 2009): 144–5.

2

The Uneasy Institution

Lineage and the Wife of Bath

To attract her fifth husband, the Wife of Bath pretends to have had a violent dream.

> I seyde I mette of hym al nyght,
> He wolde han slayn me as I lay upright,
> And al my bed was ful of verray blood
> 'But yet I hope that ye shal do me good,
> For blood bitokeneth gold, as me was taught.'
>
> (WBT 577–81)

This is an unusual means of entrancement. The dream—Jankyn's violent intentions and the bed covered in blood seem strange stuff with which to woo a lover, for they appear rather as a warning to both man and woman alike to forebear from matrimony. The Wife of Bath's association of blood and gold at the end of the lines perhaps provides a bit more clarity, however. She woos him with the prospect of her own death, holding out in front of a twenty-year-old clerk the opportunity of becoming a rich widow's young heir. Blood does indeed "bitokeneth gold" if the privileges of marital union are first bestowed. Marry me and I promise to die, says the Wife of Bath; our bed will be enriched with my blood.[1]

This is a contractual exchange with which the Wife of Bath, widow of five husbands, is herself intimately familiar. She too has benefited from the death of her spouses, has been endowed with worldly goods via the blood of others. And in promising Jankyn a bed full of blood, the Wife of Bath toys with the unnatural means of that inheritance. For the blood through which property was meant to be transmitted in late medieval England was male blood, and the locus of its distribution was not intended to be the marriage bed. Man's blood fed and stirred his semen; his semen sired his heirs, perpetuated his blood.[2] There is thus a hidden darkness to the Wife of Bath's vision of the bloody bed, for the great effusion of blood that she imagines to have seen within those sheets has been misplaced. Her

---

[1] For a different interpretation of the Wife of Bath's dream as related to sexual violence, see H. Marshall Leicester, "'My bed was full of verray blood:' Subject, Dream, and Rape in the Wife of Bath's *Prologue* and *Tale*," *Geoffrey Chaucer: The Wife of Bath*, ed. Peter G. Beidler (Boston and New York: Bedford Books of St. Martin's Press, 1996): 235–54.

[2] Cadden, *Meanings of Sex Difference*, 23–4, 77–80.

Father Chaucer: Generating Authority in The Canterbury Tales. Samantha Katz Seal, Oxford University Press (2019).
© Samantha Seal.
DOI: 10.1093/oso/9780198832386.001.0001

bed is full of blood because it is the space where male bloodlines die, not where they are reborn into some new posterity. The blood is gold, indeed, but it is her gold alone, the wealth that she has mined from the bloodlines of her men. And Jankyn, the foolish clerk, cannot discern the trap into which he soon will fall, for he thinks of mortality as something only for the old, a snare for this woman twice his age. Yet the Wife of Bath does not die. Death is the fate of men, the fate of their unborn sons. It is but the profit of the Wife of Bath, the mortal tool with which women achieve a sovereignty more binding and more eternal than that granted by men's words alone.

In this sense, the Wife of Bath assaults not only men, but also the very institutions of male authority. The flesh of her five husbands—and that of the rapist knight within her *Tale*—becomes a representative of all male flesh, and, even more significantly, a manifestation of the means by which male flesh is perpetuated within the world. Female sovereignty meant little if it left untouched the endless authority of the patrilineal bloodline. Men rest content in their own power, for they inhabit an earth held stable through the steady patterns of lineage and male descent. In lineage, God had placed the blueprint for man's fate, crafting a bond through which human men could be linked to the antiquity of their fathers, to the distant futures of their sons. The man who retains his claim to his male ancestors and descendants cannot truly surrender mastery over himself to any woman, for he cannot alienate himself from his masculine heritage of authority any more than he can alienate his full estate from its entail upon his sons. Male modes of inheritance protected the individual man by safeguarding masculinity itself, preserving the privileges of men from one generation to the next.

The Wife of Bath therefore attacks lineage, and even the linearity of male time, within her *Prologue* and *Tale* for reasons of clear self-interest. "Wommen desiren to have sovereynetee," she claims, "As wel over hir housbond as hir love,/And for to been in maistrie hym above" (WBT 1038–40). Yet female sovereignty was undermined by the male institutions that supplemented and preserved the power of individual men. In deploying the Wife of Bath to wreck men's certainty in the foundations of their world, Chaucer also demonstrates what lies at stake in the *Tale*, for author and reader alike. The idea that women wish to rule their husbands is a lively, humorous occasion for some literary play and bawdy lines. But the knowledge that his fellow men believe themselves to have gained an eternal, unchallengeable authority from the lives of their fathers is a far weightier matter. The idea of an earthly authority incapable of alienation from its human possessor is a lovely, aching dream; it is a kind of certainty capable of arming men against their deaths. And yet by extension, it also separates men from the humility they owe their God, allowing them to believe that fathers and sons can save them from the inexorable futility of the human fate. Chaucer cannot allow the constancy of lineage to continue unchecked, for its assurances are as false as the beauty of its vision is profound. So, he will set the Wife of Bath upon the road to Canterbury, a merry widow to shake men's certainty, to cast doubt upon the institutions of masculinity that undergird men's lives.

It is for this reason that the Wife of Bath never seeks to replace patriarchal structures with some vision of their feminized counterparts. Chaucer has not written an aspiring matriarch, or a ruler for some new "reign of Femenye" (KT 866) in his Wife of Bath.[3] He uses her to destroy and challenge male systems of stability and reproduction, but not to create new lineages in turn, for annihilation is ever her only goal. In this sense, the Wife of Bath truly does not claim authority; her attribute remains always experience alone, since her creator has sent her into the world to undermine the authority of men. Authority contains an inherent promise of creation and generation, but from "experience" the Wife of Bath derives the capacity to relate only tales of death and seemingly sterile sex. Even when she usurps a place in the male chain of inheritance, pushing herself forward into male lineage by claiming to be her husbands' heir, her participation leads only to further destruction. Women are the means by which men perpetuate the species, but in Chaucer's hands they are also the tools of disruption and disorder, the sowers of (albeit necessary) doubt and despair in the minds of men.

The world is unsteady, Chaucer tells his readers, and man is not enough to hold the world for future generations. And neither is a poet. For poets derive authority from male progenitors as well, from the genealogical structures of the literary world.[4] Patrilineal models of inheritance and poetic likeness are popular among authors precisely because they are seen to stabilize, to authorize, and to legitimize literary work. And yet Chaucer refuses to allow poets, like their fellow men, to seek refuge in the history of their "bloodline." Even St Paul himself is, Chaucer notes, only as authoritative as the reader who encounters him; Scripture itself cannot keep false exegetes like the Wife of Bath from overthrowing its posterity.[5] For while the Wife of Bath promises Jankyn a bed of blood, she gives him only a burned book, the sooty ashes of ten centuries of male authority. "He yaf me al the bridel in myn hond,/To han the governance of hous and lond...and made hym brenne his book anon right tho"(WBT 813–14, 816). Labor and creation can only last so long; lineage itself will soon expire. It does not take a war to destroy

---

[3] The Amazon women of Chaucer's *Knight's Tale* are the only example of matriarchy within *The Canterbury Tales*, and their potential threat to male power has already been contained by the male army by the time that the Knight picks up the story of Theseus and his conquered queen Hippolyta.

[4] As Stephen Guy-Bray writes, the imposition of reproductive metaphor (including genealogy) upon literary production is a means of enforcing order and pattern, for the impossible "metaphor brings both the 'otherwise chaotic' writing body and the 'otherwise chaotic' desiring body (and, for that matter, the 'otherwise chaotic' reproducing body) under the rule of law." Stephen Guy-Bray, *Against Reproduction: Where Renaissance Texts Come From* (Toronto: University of Toronto Press, 2009): 8.

[5] Critics have labeled the Wife of Bath as an overly literalist exegete—an attribute that (depending on the critic) either disqualifies or empowers her reading. On the Wife of Bath's literalist reading practice, see Robertson, *Preface to Chaucer*, 317–31; Dinshaw, *Chaucer's Sexual Poetics*, 113–31; Lawrence Besserman, *Chaucer's Biblical Poetics* (Norman, OK: University of Oklahoma Press, 1998): 139–59.

men nor even a devastating plague. The posterity of men's lives can end as simply and devastatingly in the petty hands of a feuding wife. The Wife is no great antagonist to mankind, but rather a reminder to men and poets alike that institutions cannot save them. All men will end, fathers and sons and the childless alike, meeting with a finality granted by the small peace of oblivion. Lineage is not a certainty that can save them, procreation not a means of winning eternal life. There is only God and men, Chaucer says, and the insurmountable distance between the two. And then there are wives, if men might momentarily forget that they are weak.

Usurping Primogeniture: The Wife of Bath as Heir

Chaucer employs three strategies in crafting a Wife of Bath ready to threaten the stability of lineage. First, he allows her fictionalized historicity, expressed through the autobiography offered within her *prologue*, to contradict the legal patterns of late medieval inheritance, throwing into doubt whether the law itself is sufficient to guard men's patrimony. Secondly, Chaucer highlights the Wife's more existential vision of time and intergenerational transmission, noting how the Wife's imposition of a lateral mode of knowledge dissemination destroys men's hopes of linear descent and genders the very idea of the future as exclusively male. And then finally, Chaucer lets the Wife of Bath tell a romantic story that can bring elements of the previous strategies together, for in her legend of Arthurian Britain, the Wife of Bath both argues against the very idea of hereditary transfer and bluntly erases the characters' natural (in Chaucer's view) orientation towards the future and towards procreation. Each of these strategies of destabilization overlap and bleed into one another, but each also remains simultaneously distinct, capable of being isolated for analysis, as I intend to do within this chapter. And thus, by beginning with the historicized fiction of the Wife of Bath's persona as the heir of each her marriages, I would like to establish her account of her disruptions of the legal hereditary process as but one of the ways in which she attempts to disrupt men's assurance in their potential procreations.

The Wife of Bath has the distinction of being the sole exclusive heir of five husbands, of whom "thre of hem were goode men, and riche, and olde" (WBT 197). Her account of the precise goods that she had inherited from these husbands places a high importance upon the accumulation of land, but also acknowledges the importance of more liquid property. Chaucer has the Wife boast in three separate instance of her legal seizures; she claims that, "they had me yeven hir lond and hir tresoor" (WBT 204), "they hadde me yeven al hir lond" (WBT 212), and also cites "al the lond and fee/That evere was me yeven therbifoore" (WBT 630). Thus, while critics have attempted to relate the Wife of Bath to the medieval weaving industry of Bath, her primary occupation remains a form of "dower economics," driven by the financial accumulations made possible in the marriage bed.[6] And yet the Wife of Bath's list of her own inheritance problematizes the critical interpretation of her situation. For the Wife of Bath is demonstrably ill content to settle for a mere portion of her husbands' estates. On the contrary, she wishes to control it all, to be named sole heir to the property of her spouses. Moreover, she also claims that, in addition to these grants of land and money, she has been granted the ability to dispose of the property in her own right, a behavior that she eventually puts into practice with her marital gift of her lands to her fifth husband, Jankyn.

As Lee Patterson has commented, it is almost impossible to discover a means of medieval female inheritance to justify the Wife of Bath's depiction of her situation, for it "will not compute with *any* of the possible arrangements for marital property available at the time."[7] Indeed, the Wife's claim that she has received all of her husbands' property means that her inheritance has far surpassed that of the dower portion typically given to widows, a life interest only in a third of the husband's estate.[8] And while some scholars have argued that her ability to inherit all of her husbands' property means that she must have been made a joint tenant in the property, others note that her ability to dispose of that property in turn makes this option less likely, since medieval female jointure was also often only for life use. Moreover, the question of how the Wife of Bath manages her legal machinations is a difficult one, for, as Susan Crane has argued, the imposition of such historical context, including questions about land tenure, may serve only to further Chaucer's pretense that the Wife of Bath is a real person rather than a literary creation.[9] Likewise, Elaine Treharne writes that "to read the Wife as if she were anything other than a fiction masterfully created by Chaucer is to fall into the trap of 'truth' that he sets through his vivid, realistic depictions."[10]

---

[6] Accounts of the Wife of Bath's connection to the cloth industry include Mary Carruthers, "The Wife of Bath and the Painting of Lions," *PMLA* 94.2 (March 1979): 209–22; Roger A. Ladd, "Selling Alys: Reading (with) the Wife of Bath," *Studies in the Age of Chaucer* 34 (2012): 141–71.

[7] Lee Patterson, *Temporal Circumstances: Form and History in the Canterbury Tales* (New York: Palgrave MacMillan, 2006): 43.

[8] On the dower as a portion of the husband's property, see Barbara A. Hanawalt, *The Wealth of Wives: Women and Economy in Late Medieval London* (Oxford: Oxford University Press, 2007): 55, 61–5. The third of the property was a typical amount, but according to London customs the Wife of Bath could have inherited as much as half of the husbands' estates in the absence of offspring.

[9] Susan Crane, "Alison's Incapacity and Poetic Instability in the *Wife of Bath's Tale*," *PMLA* 102.1 (January 1987): 20–28, at 20. Crane cites the following article as a specific example of the trend of historicizing Alison's inheritance of land with which she disagrees. D. W. Robertson, "'And for My Land Thus Hastow Mordred Me?': Land Tenure, the Cloth Industry and the Wife of Bath," *The Chaucer Review* 14.4 (Spring 1980): 403–20.

[10] Elaine Treharne, "The Stereotype Confirmed? Chaucer's Wife of Bath," *Writing Gender and Genre in Medieval Literature: Approaches to Old and Middle English Texts*, ed. Elaine Treharne (Cambridge: D. S. Brewer, 2002): 93–115, at 97.

In Patterson's defense, however, the "impossibility" of the Wife of Bath's legal situation can be used to amplify, rather than detract from, the critic's perception of the way in which Chaucer wields the fictional Wife of Bath as a very real threat against his readers. In the vastness of her uncontrollable greed, the Wife of Bath becomes a symbolic antagonist for men and male inheritance—one who, in her very improbability, cannot be controlled or contained by the legal protections of their world. She overwhelms the text, but the specific *way* in which she overwhelms it—by claiming such a vast, impossible inheritance—is, in itself, significant. Likewise, while she can tell us little about the real circumstances of wives and widows in her world, she nevertheless can bear full witness to the anxieties inherent within masculine social systems. For if no widow was likely to seize the full estates of five separate husbands, then nevertheless widows could weaken the overall condition of the male hereditary estate, tying up a significant amount of property for the unknown duration of their lives. And, even more importantly, women inherently undermined the authority and power of spouse and son alike, by their very participation in the systems of reproduction and inheritance. The mother triangulated the linear relationship; the stepmother triangulated it even further.

The Wife of Bath capitalizes upon the threats of both mother and stepmother alike, by usurping the son's position as male heir. For the Wife, the role of heir is inseparable from that of master, for she misunderstands the very dynamics of the familial system that she thwarts. Instead, she boasts that "sith I hadde hem hoolly in myn hond,/And sith they hadde me yeven al hir lond,/What sholde I taken keep hem for to plese" (WBT 211–13). The "hoolly" nature of her control over the husbands blurs with the "al" of their property transmission, as the notion of entirety becomes the Wife of Bath's measure of her own power. In this sense it is important to the Wife of Bath to inform her audience that this transfer was not initiated according to marital affection, but rather by means of female dominance alone. The land is worth as much to her as the witness of her own mastery as it is according to its economic potential, for it is proof that she has so fully seized her husbands that they will act not only against their own interests, but also against the interests of their proper heirs and of their families as a whole.

For some scholars, the Wife's intrusion into pre-existing systems of inheritance has seemed to mark a positive attribute of the character. For example, Mary Carruthers speculates that the Wife of Bath was "far too good a business woman to marry a man whose property was encumbered with children or other undesirable heirs."[11] This assessment, however, seems unlikely. Whether or not the individual men had sired children in previous marriages, they nevertheless would have remained participants in pre-existing kin networks with claims to their

---

[11] Carruthers, "Painting of Lions," 211.

property. Medieval structures of inheritance were designed specifically to ensure that no man was left without access to heirs, undesirable or not, capable of claiming his property. Property, particularly land, would continue to move according to familial proximity, even if the reproductive potential of a single generation had broken down. The inheritance would move laterally so that it might then move linearly once again, or, in other words, it would pass to the next sibling, parent, or cousin of siblings, parents, or even grandparents if necessary, before once again beginning to be passed down through linear descent. The Wife of Bath's husbands would be disappointed with such an outcome, for it meant that their own unique "genetic" combination would be annihilated in the next generation. Yet the lineage itself would survive, undaunted by the efforts of any unnaturally dominant widows to substitute themselves for the family's heirs.

English laws of inheritance were designed to protect the interests of the lineage rather than that of the individual man. The advantage of primogeniture, a system of property distribution increasingly dominant in late medieval England, had been that it maintained the family's property intact, transmitted through the male lineage alongside any titles of nobility that were thus similarly constrained.[12] This system could disadvantage the younger siblings and female members of the family by restricting their inheritance, and also curtailed the individual's freedom to dispose of his property as freely as he desired. Yet for the familial unit as a whole, primogeniture ensured that there was a reliable, replicable system in place to determine land disputes and to designate appropriate heirs for the lineage even when normal patterns of reproduction had failed in a generation or two. By the late thirteenth century, laws of entail (fee tail) had also begun to restrict the transmission of land sharply, limiting the capacity of individuals to alienate their land or goods from their family. From the passage of the statute *De donis conditionalibus* in 1285, the fee tail was, as Robert Palmer writes, "burdened with conditions: a condition on alienation (it could not be sold for longer than the current holder's life) and a condition of inheritance (it could only descend to children of the couple or of one of the parties, not to other heirs, such as cousins."[13] Such a system of land transmission made the privileging of the male heir and of the lineage itself a primary attribute of inheritance; medieval English society's vested interest was in protecting the property rights of the patrilineal chain rather than the individual interest of man or woman.[14]

---

[12] On the history of medieval patriline inheritance and primogeniture, see Eileen Spring, *Law, Land, & Family: Aristocratic Inheritance in England, 1300–1800* (Durham, NC: University of North Carolina Press, 1993); Mary Murray, "Primogeniture, Patrilineage, and the Displacement of Women," *Women, Property, and the Letters of the Law in Early Modern England*, ed. Nancy E. Wright, Margaret W. Ferguson, and A.R. Buck (Toronto: University of Toronto Press, 2004): 121–36.

[13] Robert C. Palmer, "Contexts of Marriage in Medieval England; Evidence from the King's Court circa 1300," *Speculum* 59.1 (January 1984): 42–67, at 57.

[14] Janet Loengard thus calls dower a "theoretical anomaly" in a system that privileged male inheritance so strongly, since it allowed land to be divided for the decades of a woman's life, and to be carried

To preserve their wives' land rights in the event of their own decease, men could turn to jointure (or joint tenancy), and many brides' fathers insisted that the groom's father establish a jointure from his own property before the wedding.[15] Jointure, in contrast to fee tail, made paternal land partible, and could potentially alienate one piece of land from the main line of male descent (if the heir to the jointure differed from the heir to the primary property). And yet, as Joseph Biancalana concluded in his seminal study of fee tail, jointure was not a legal system to protect the wife herself, but rather one designed to safeguard the interests of her offspring, for "jointure provided the simplest protection of the issue of the marriage against claims by children of the groom's earlier or later marriages."[16] Without offspring for the marriage, a widow's jointure could be reduced to the term of her life alone, in a manner akin to the dower property. The main patrilineal family would thus have triumphed once again, receiving its land back from the widow at the time of her eventual decease.

In this sense, the production of heirs protected the long-term financial interests of a wife, providing her ammunition for her legal battles against her husband's family. And yet for all her boasts as to her economic success within the marriage bed, the Wife of Bath never mentions having produced any offspring from any of her marriages. Desiring to be acknowledged as the sole heir of her spouses, the Wife of Bath thus faces competition from two categories of "undesirable heirs." If her marriages had indeed failed to produce children (of either sex), then she would struggle against her husband's relations, his larger lineage of male consanguinity. On the other hand, to claim true control over her property, she would have had to have an heir born from each of her marriages, in whose name she could wield authority over her deceased husbands' land. In this sense, the Wife of Bath is both incentivized to procreate and yet *disincentivized* to bring a child from her body that would be capable of contesting her authority and rights.[17] This is the conundrum that Lee Patterson referred to in the line I quoted earlier, for there is no true way for medieval hereditary law to encompass the enormity of the claims that the Wife of Bath asserts upon her husbands' property. When she recalls that, to her fifth husband, "this joly clerk, Jankyn, that was so hende...yaf I al the lond and fee/That evere was me yeven therbifoore" (WBT 628, 30–1), the

into a second marriage (although it could not be inherited by the heirs of that marriage). Janet Senderowitz Loengard, "Rationabilis Dos: Magna Carta and the Widow's 'Faire Share' in the Earlier Thirteenth Century," *Wife and Widow in Medieval England*, ed. Sue Sheridan Walker (Ann Arbor, MI: University of Michigan Press, 1993): 59–80, at 60.

[15] Joseph Biancalana, *The Fee Tail and the Common Recovery in Medieval England: 1176–1502* (Cambridge: Cambridge University Press, 2001): 144–5.

[16] Biancalana, *Fee Tail*, 144.

[17] Karen Harris has therefore argued that the Wife of Bath actively prevents herself from becoming pregnant through the use of prophylactics, although the evidence for such self-medication is somewhat thin within Chaucer's text. Karen Harris, "Wise Wyf's Remedies of Love: Birth Control in the Wife of Bath," *Graduate Research Journal* 1 (2014): 11–18.

Wife of Bath is thus remembering a time when she performed a transaction that was both against the property laws of England and against her own perpetual desire for marital control. She reintegrates her property into a male lineage, but her choice is one of low status and with no familial connection to her spouses.

This scene with Jankyn is also remarkable because it is the only time in the Wife of Bath's *Prologue* when she represents herself as the distributor of property rather than as its eternal heir. For all her desire of mastery and control over men, the Wife of Bath places all her efforts upon the accumulation of property (and other wealth) with little interest in how the property will circulate after her eventual death. And yet, upon marrying the young Jankyn, she is willing to hand over that wealth, letting the property that she has defiantly kept outside male patterns of descent become reintegrated into the systems of patriarchal control from which she wrested it. And indeed, Jankyn himself seems to expect that he will outlive the Wife of Bath and win the opportunity to found his own lineage with her property, for even when he hands her the mastery of their marriage he is careful to specify the span of time during which he imagines this new power dynamic will apply. "And that he seyde, 'Myn owene trewe wyf,/Do as thee lust the terme of al thy lyf;/Keep thyn honour, and keep eek myn estaat'" (WBT 819–821). Jankyn's investment in outliving the Wife of Bath, and then perhaps marrying a younger, more fertile, and more biddable wife, is also the foundation of the Wife's accusation against him when she pretends that he has murdered her after she has ripped the pages from his book. "O! hastow slayne me, false theef?' I seyde,/'And for my land thus hastow mordred me?'" (WBT 800–1). It is the inheritance of the Wife of Bath's land, rather than its current possession, that her words emphasize as Jankyn's secret desire here, for Jankyn has already been granted control over the land at this point of the story. What he has not received is the power of disposition, the capacity to incorporate that land into his own posterity.

Of course, this marital conflict ends up as a moot debate, for the Wife of Bath has been widowed once again by the time she joins the pilgrim fellowship. As the reward for his efforts, Jankyn has lost both his life interest in the land (reclaimed by the Wife of Bath during their fight) and also his hope of transmitting that land to his own future progeny. For all his hopes of serving as the Wife of Bath's heir, Jankyn will eventually endow the Wife of Bath with his own instead. The Wife of Bath depicts inheritance as part of the struggle between the male and female partners of a marriage. Who outlives whom becomes, in this context, an essential component of the larger conflict between the sexes, as husband and wife assess their individual economic interest in serving as the other's heir. Such a situation flies in the face of Church doctrine that, with the marriage ceremony and sacrament, husband and wife became one flesh, one legal entity with united financial interests. And, it also conflicts with the doctrine, espoused by both religious and secular law in the Middle Ages, that the point of marriage was to generate offspring. Neither medieval marriage partner should have eyed the other as a potential source of hereditable wealth, for each should have seen their interests combined within their children, the true heirs to a Christian marriage. When medieval law recognized the separate interests of husband and wife (as it did in the legal state of jointure discussed previously), it was only in relation to preserving the interests of their mutual offspring in respect to each parent alike.

In a sense, the Wife of Bath's continued investment in her own status as perpetual heir is driven by her refusal to acknowledge even the possibility that any of her marriages may have produced offspring when reciting her story to the other pilgrims. Rather than imagine the Wife of Bath exclusively as a potentially failed mother, critics should heed her own depiction of herself as a radically successful heir; within her historical context, the Wife of Bath's success at inheriting property demands that she remain silent as to her potential skill in birthing offspring. And certainly, the Wife of Bath does not appear to perceive the absence of children in her story as problematic, despite the theory of one 1950s critic that the Wife's unnatural rebellions against men stem from the psychoanalytic trauma of unfulfilled motherhood.[18] For other scholars, asserting that the Wife of Bath has failed at producing children proves the Wife to be a hypocrite in her presentation of procreation as a primary good of marriage. D. W. Robertson, for example, makes the comment that the Wife "is clearly not interested in '*engendrure*'" as part of a larger dismissal of her exegetical capacities.[19] In contrast, feminist scholars have emphasized those products that the Wife of Bath *is* interested in breeding, particularly her economic profit.[20]

I would argue instead for a third approach, for critics to approach the Wife of Bath's silence on her childbearing as part of a larger attack against both individual men, and, even more importantly, against the institutional, familial strategies of masculine reproduction. By denying her husbands the public recognition of having fathered a male heir, the Wife of Bath cuts off their memory from the very system of generation. When these husbands died, according to the story she tells her fellow pilgrims, they were truly dead; no posterity waited to pull their fathers' memory back from the brink of oblivion. If the chains of male lineage offered men the opportunity to look both forwards and backwards through time, deriving an authority from the endless progression of their male kin, then it is those

---

[18] F.M. Salter, "The Tragic Figure of the Wife of Bath," *Transactions of the Royal Society of Canada* 48, sermon 3, sect. 2 (1954): 11–13. In contrast, Kenneth J. Oberembt emphasized the moral implications of the children's absence as a contradiction of the Wife of Bath's defense of marital sexuality; he took the argument even further by speculating as to the nature of that sterility, eventually arguing that, nevertheless, "Alice's lack of children cannot be proven to be caused by some intervention into natural processes and, as a result, [to be] mortally sinful." Kennth J. Oberembt, "Chaucer's Anti-Misogynist Wife of Bath," *The Chaucer Review* 10.4 (Spring 1976): 287–302, at 296.

[19] Robertson, *Preface to Chaucer*, 328.

[20] Sheila Delaney, "Sexual Economics, Chaucer's Wife of Bath, and the *Book of Margery Kempe*," *Minnesota Review* 5 (Fall 1975): 104–115, at 104; Laurie Finke, "'Alle is for to selle': Breeding Capital in the Wife of Bath's *Prologue* and *Tale*," *Geoffrey Chaucer: The Wife of Bath*, ed. Peter G. Beidler (Boston and New York: Bedford Books of St. Martin's Press, 1996): 171–88.

very links and chains that the Wife of Bath will sever, erasing the vision of perpetual masculinity with her unacknowledged offspring. It is notable, for example, that the Wife of Bath never allows any of her first four husbands the possession of a name, as only Jankyn is allowed some form of nomenclature, and his nickname-like designation appears far from authoritative. Without sons, their names have truly disappeared into the past.

Moreover, by claiming the right to tell the story of these husbands, to characterize and describe their deeds and actions, the Wife of Bath also claims an authority over their posthumous memory. In the company of pilgrims, it is only the Wife of Bath who can offer testimony to their lives, and she will do so however she pleases. In this sense, the Wife of Bath performs truly as an heir, stepping into the breach of death to invoke the father's memory once more. And yet the stories she tells are deliberately calculated to cast shame and scorn upon her husbands' lives. "Sire olde kaynard, is this thyn array?" (WBT 235), she mocks her husbands' memory; in a nostalgic re-enactment of how she had dominated her spouses, the Wife of Bath snaps out the various insults, all focused upon the denigration of male age: "Sire olde lecchour, lat thy japes be!" (WBT 242), "with wilde thunder-dynt and firy levene/Moote thy welked nekke be tobroke!" (WBT 276–7), "olde dotard shrewe!" (WBT 291), and "olde barel-ful of lyes!" (WBT 302). And of course, the Wife of Bath never ceases from mocking her spouses' sexual performance, as when she advises the fellowship that "for wynnyng wolde I al his lust endure,/And make me a feyned appetite;/And yet in bacon hadde I nevere delit" (WBT 416–18). These men have no heir (at least within the Wife of Bath's *Prologue*) to contest her account of their lives, no fellow man to speak up and counter this abuse with praise or deep respect. They have left nothing upon the earth, their widow claims, other than the land that she has inherited and her memory of their impotence and sexual failure. While the Wife of Bath may not be willing to share the land, she is more than happy to disseminate her accounts of her husbands' failings, to expose their posterity to the contempt of strangers.

The Wife of Bath is their heir, their only link to a world that has continued after their respective deaths. And she will not allow any to share that inheritance with her, no relics of male kinship to contest the singularity of her status. She claims the right to property and narrative alike, to a retelling of their lives that accords entirely with her own desires. If she has given any of these men a son, she has no desire to acknowledge that son here, for that child, by his very existence, would take his father out of her reach, returning him to a land of men and male authority.

At only one point in her usurpation of the status of male heir does the Wife of Bath toy with the idea of allowing her husbands a moment of lineal reintegration. When her fourth husband dies, she allows Jankyn to participate in a mockery of filial piety and recognition. While previously, the Wife of Bath has spoken of Jankyn as a confederate of hers, at the time of her husband's death, he nevertheless participates in a surprisingly sober way. The Wife of Bath tells the company,

"To chirche was myn housbonde born a-morwe/With neighebores, that for hym maden sorwe;/And Jankyn, oure clerk, was oon of tho" (WBT 593–5). Jankyn's carrying of the man's corpse to the church, and the sorrow that he makes alongside the neighbors, becomes almost a performance of male kinship, as Jankyn re-enacts the correct behavior of men bearing witness to the deaths of other men. And yet the Wife of Bath, watching this procession, disrupts its piety with her very act of sight. For, of course, this is not a scene of a son following his father's bier, but rather that of a humble clerk following the corpse of a man whose wife he will soon wed. The Wife of Bath turns this funereal moment into an occasion of lust, claiming that, "As help me God, whan that I saugh hym go/After the beere, me thought he hadde a pair/Of legges and of feet so clene and faire" (WBT 596–8). Watching Jankyn's shapely legs walk behind her husband's corpse, the Wife of Bath reflects not on the intergenerational authority of masculinity, but rather upon its sexual uses, its potential exploitations.

Jankyn does indeed become the heir to the fourth husband's property; he becomes the heir to all the property when the Wife so briefly hands it over. And this is as close to a male heir as any of her husbands can hope to have. She will not render them viable offspring of her flesh, but rather adolescent interlopers into their homes, young men who will receive both the dead man's wife and his goods. For when Jankyn becomes a kind of pseudo-heir to the four dead husbands, the Wife of Bath marks that moment of lineage and heredity with her own body. If patrilineality functioned on the principles of male likeness and male kinship, then the Wife of Bath's foray into hereditary practice substitutes her own flesh for that male structure, supplanting an institutionalized system of legal code and social expectation with the binding agent of her own sexual desire. The five husbands are united, after all, with other men, but the Wife of Bath has inverted the process, so that it occurs only through her mediation. Where patrilineal genealogies wrote women out, the Wife of Bath has made a new genealogy that ignores men except as the spousal source of lands and goods. In this way, the Wife of Bath alienates her husbands from their lineages even as she alienates their property from patrilineal control. And she will not claim to have given male heirs to any of the men; she will stand no competition to her own inheritance, no opportunity for patrilineality to reassert itself. Her husbands are dead and buried, and the Wife of Bath's inheritance is hers alone to hold.

Against Male Time

As her husbands' heir, the Wife of Bath attacks male lineage itself, ripping the traditional patterns of descent and inheritance in order to fashion a new structure around her own flesh. And yet the system of inheritance that the Wife of Bath envisions as replacing father/son heredity has fundamentally different goals than the structures that had been designed to perpetuate male interests and continuities across time. For while the male system of heredity engaged with time on both ends, allowing past, present, and future to flow together in an ecstasy of male continuity, the Wife of Bath's system of "heredity" could more truly be called a system of disruptive change, designed to facilitate only immoderate accumulation. The Wife of Bath inherits from each husband in turn, tying the past together to her present state, but she refuses to acknowledge that those goods will eventually pass from her grip into some distant future. Linear time pulls humanity's attention to their own individual decease, to the necessity of naming heirs, but the Wife of Bath refuses to countenance the existence of an heir other than herself. The Wife of Bath, according to her own account, has considered inheritance only insofar as it can serve as a means of personal enrichment, without considering her own potential need one day for an heir of her own.

Chaucer's depiction of the Wife of Bath's antagonism towards the consideration of future time is deliberate. For Chaucer has no use for a Wife of Bath capable of building her own edifices of continuity, of permanently alienating male property from a familial line only to capitalize upon such wealth in the founding of a new, matrilineal line. Such acts would be inherently constructive, and would demonstrate a true female capacity to exist and thrive outside of male structures and restraint. And Chaucer is not enough of a feminist to give us a Wife of Bath capable of naming an heir to her own life. Continuity belongs to men, for Chaucer, and he will allow women like the Wife of Bath only the power to disrupt that stability, never the authority to build their own to replace it. The Wife of Bath's task within the *Tales* operates within the sharp limitations of just how radical Chaucer is willing for her to be. When she breaks down men's worlds, she acts as an agent of the divine, reminding men of their own frailty. But if she were to rebuild those edifices anew, then she would be truly an unnatural woman, for she would have *succeeded* in her challenges to the male order. Thus, Chaucer writes a Wife of Bath who is uninterested in the very idea of posterity, who sees no future nor feels any sense of impending time. She is an heir incapable of further transmission, for she breaks the temporal structures of her own enrichment once she has partaken of their bounty.

Critics have noted the extent to which the Wife of Bath remains in a static temporality, caught in the endless repetitions of marriage and widowhood. Borrowing a term from Tzvetan Todorov, Sachi Shimomura writes that the Wife's narrative slips into a "perpetual present...she orders her narrative not through references to husbands one, two, and three, but through a succession of her own—primarily verbal—tactical moves against the collective husbands."[21] Historical continuity, like male lineage, is sacrificed to the Wife of Bath's larger

---

[21] Sachi Shimomura, *Odd Bodies and Visible Ends in Medieval Literature* (New York: Palgrave MacMillan, 2006): 93.

rhetorical strategy; her husbands all occupy a simultaneous past from which she can derive the power of her experience. Progressive time is a privilege of masculinity, for the Wife depicts the passing of time itself as an assault upon women and womanly prerogatives. She tells us that she married for the first time at twelve and for the last time at forty, and mourns the loss of the vitality and beauty associated with her youth.

> Unto this day it dooth myn herte boote
> That I have had my world as in my tyme.
> But age, allas, that al wole envenyme,
> Hath biraft my beautee and my pith.
> Lat go. Farewel! The devel go therwith!
> The flour is goon; ther is namoore to telle.
>
> (WBT 472–7)

The effects of lineal time upon women serve to silence them, at least according to the Wife of Bath, for forward-moving temporality becomes synonymous with the affronts of aging. And age impacts her and her fellow women in economic terms, leaving them with inferior products to vend upon the marketplace ("the bren, as I best kan, now moste I selle" [WBT 478]). Men may grow old and depend upon their riches to buy them young wives, as the Wife of Bath knows from her own experience, but the quality of what women have to sell deteriorates with that same process, tilting the battle between the sexes more firmly in favor of men and their dominion.

And yet the Wife of Bath moves almost immediately to reject her own conclusions. Time has moved against her, stealing her beauty, but "yet to be right myrie wol I fonde./Now wol I tellen of my fourthe housbonde" (WBT 479–80). She might have only bran to sell, but it has sold as well as her flower, and will continue to do so, she trusts, for a sixth time. In this sharp move to the discussion of her fourth husband, the Wife navigates the collision of two temporalities, one of which sees her growing old, while the other preserves her as an endlessly eligible marital prospect. Marriage serves the Wife of Bath as a means of continuous renewal, an opportunity to move away from lineal time and its degradations and back into the cyclical process through which her value is ever restored.[22] Within the space of a few lines she has moved from mourning that, with her flower gone, there is no more to tell, to remembering that, on the contrary, she has yet to tell the company of her fourth husband (or of her fifth). One temporality invokes silence with its reminders of personal mortality, while the other allows her to proceed, refreshed,

---

[22] Aranye Fradenburg likewise argues that the romance genre itself, with its inherent nostalgia, also allows the Wife of Bath to "elude the time of the clock" and dream about the hag's magical ability to switch from age to youth. Louise O. Fradenburg, "The Wife of Bath's Passing Fancy," *Studies in the Age of Chaucer* 8 (1986): 31–58, at 43.

in narrating the mortalities of her men. No wonder that her idea of "purveiance," of accommodating future contingency, operates solely around the marital state, for, as she assures the fellowship of pilgrims, "was I nevere withouten pureveiance/ Of mariage, n' of othere thynges eek" (WBT 570–1). Marriage allows her to escape the march of the future and its incursions upon her person, and providing for future marriages is not a means of combatting her age, but rather of reinscribing her life into a pattern of temporal movement that brings her ever back to where she started.

Indeed, even when the Wife of Bath directly references her age—admitting that she was twice Jankyn's age—she immediately counteracts that acknowledgement by reasserting the perpetuity of her youth.

> He was, I trowe, twenty winter oold,
> And I was fourty, if I shal seye sooth;
> Yet I hadde alwey a coltes tooth...
> As help me God, I was a lusty oon,
> And faire, and riche, and yong, and wel bigon"
>
> (WBT 600–2, 605–6)

And yet all of these things could not have been true at the same time, for the Wife has told us that her riches came from the husbands that she married in her youth, from the process of inheritance, and thus her wealth did not coincide with the time of her beauty and youth. By conflating these two, apparently sequential, periods of her life, the Wife of Bath claims youth as yet another attribute that belongs to her cyclical, female process of time. She and her colt's tooth have always managed to possess "youth," in defiance of the very meaning of the life span's division into stages. And the Wife of Bath makes it clear how she has managed to maintain youth so indefinitely, despite her earlier claims to the contrary; the almost supernatural quality of her *quoniam* ("I hadde the beste quoniam myghte be" [WBT 608]) has allowed her to enforce her own interpretation of female aging upon the world. For her *quoniam* remains superior, untouched by age, eternal in its divinely granted vigor.

As her husbands age and die in male time, the Wife remains static through the preservations of her own marital temporality and its "purveiances." And as her husbands' heir, she prevents them as well from attaining the true measure of their temporal movement, for she lets them die, but keeps them from their lineage. Her temporality is apparently endless, always renewable, and so it keep accumulating past the point at which men begin to think of mortality. The Wife of Bath has no designated heirs of her own, or at least none to whom she will admit, for she has (almost) successfully avoided the implications of her own death. Death is something that men do in the *Wife of Bath's Prologue and Tale*; women marry. And thus women also inherit and absorb property, for they remain present in a world from which their husbands persist in departing, capable of gaining experience and wealth from the past, but refusing to allow the memory of past men to move them into the path of historical, advancing time.

The Wife of Bath's only reference to a future posterity for her own life comes in the two brief mentions of a "nece, which that I loved weel" (WBT 537). This unnamed woman participates in two of the Wife of Bath's schemes, serving (along with Jankyn) as a false witness to the lies that the Wife of Bath presses upon her aged husbands (WBT 379–383), and then again as a witness to the secret information about her husbands ("hadde myn housbonde pissed on a wal,/Or doon a thyng that sholde han cost his lyf...I wolde han told his conseil every deel" [WBT 534–5, 538]) which the Wife of Bath divulges to her female circle. In this younger woman we have a hint of feminine continuity, some vestige of the intergenerational transfer so precious to medieval men. Moreover, she gives the Wife of Bath a more definite position within an unnamed kin network, grounding her in some form of linear time as living proof of a new generation. And yet the figure of the niece does not maintain her forward-looking orientation for very long; she collapses into the homogeneity of the Wife's older female circle, and becomes secondary to the Wife's "gossib," a woman also named Alisoun (WBT 530).[23] Likewise, the designation of the woman as a niece, rather than a daughter, keeps her at some distance from the Wife of Bath. The younger woman remains the unnamed recipient of the Wife of Bath's gossip, a far cry from being designated the recipient of her goods.

The Wife of Bath does imagine one definitive mode of feminine transmission, albeit one based upon the dissemination of speech rather than upon the hereditary distribution of property. The Wife of Bath tells her audience that she learned her feminine marital "wisdom" from the tutelage of her mother, for "my dame taughte me that soultiltee...I folwed ay my dames loore,/As wel of this as of othere thynges moore" (WBT 576, 583–4). The image of the mother teaching the daughter moral lessons was a common one in late medieval didactic texts, but here it has become a twisted perversion of that pattern.[24] For women, according to the Wife of Bath, transmit neither moral truths nor prized possessions between their ranks, but only the tools to persevere in an intergenerational conspiracy against men. There is thus a pettiness to the modes of feminine heredity that the Wife of Bath describes; men pass down honor, kinship, and worldly respect along their lineage, while women offer their daughters only tricks and enchantments to

---

[23] Mary Carruthers has argued that, according to fourteenth-century Middle English lexicon, "gossib" should be interpreted not as "gossip" or "confidante" (as it is typically glossed in editions of the text), but rather as "godsib," or the baptismal sponsor of one's child. Mary Carruthers, "Clerk Jankyn: At hom to bord/With my gossib," *English Language Notes* 22.3 (March 1985): 11–20. Such a reading would be significant for the question of whether or not the Wife of Bath has children, but it seems strange that Chaucer would use "godsib" so precisely (twice) in the *Parson's Tale* only to change its spelling here for no apparent reason of meter, especially when the force of these lines reinforces a gossiping relationship between the two women with no reference to religious ceremony.

[24] See, for example, "How the Good Wife Taught Her Daughter".

practice upon men. The contrast between the serious forms of male lineage and their inconsequential female imitations becomes a moment in which the Wife of Bath fully embodies her Ovidian origins, her designation as a *magistra amoris* rather than as an instructor of more serious subjects.[25] That prized inheritance from her mother, "my dames loore," is worth little more to the male listener than the old woman's speeches ("her babbling") on love to the skeptical hero in the *Roman de la Rose*.[26] For what the Wife of Bath learned from her mother was how to entrance a humble clerk with well-shaped legs, hardly a monumental inheritance for her or for her audience.

And yet that moment of petty transmission between mother and daughter is still innately superior to the modes of dissemination that the Wife of Bath herself employs, for it is at least the intimate transfer of some kind from a parent to her posterity. In contrast, the Wife of Bath's own forms of transmission bear even less likeness to the familial, authoritative intimacy of male inheritance. Some critics have argued otherwise, postulating an equivalency between the Wife's inheritance of female lore and her respective distribution of the same, without noting the clear distinctions that the Wife of Bath draws between these separate modes of transmission.[27] For example, Robert Sturges attempts to tie the Wife of Bath into a full spectrum of temporality when he writes that "the Wife learned how to gain power over men from her mother in the past; in the present, she shares that knowledge and power with a community of women. As for the future, she hopes to expand the female community by passing her lore on to her listeners and, by implication, to the reader."[28] For such critics, it is impossible to imagine a mode of inheritance outside of the bounds of continuity and the complete range of temporality. But the Wife of Bath herself is quite comfortable with asynchrony, and inherently at peace with the disruption of such systems.

The ways that the Wife of Bath participates in the dissemination of her mother's lore to a new generation is not that of the careful lineage described by Sturges, but rather a haphazard, inconsistent scattering of her knowledge into the closed circle of her present. When she offers herself up as an example to "wyves that been wyse" (WBT 229), she does not assume a maternal role, but rather that of a companion to her fellow women. These wives are already married, already conversant

---

[25] Alastair Minnis explores the extent to which the Wife of Bath can be classified as a *magistra amoris* and eventually concludes that the Wife's depiction of her sexual desires unambiguously connects her to Ovid and Jean de Meun's versions of the *magistra amoris*, even though Chaucer also allows the Wife of Bath to transcend these literary models and dispense true wisdom on higher matters. Minnis, A. J., "The Wisdom of Old Women: Alisoun of Bath as *Auctrice*," *Writings on Love in the English Middle Ages*, ed. Helen Cooney (New York: Palgrave MacMillan, 2006): 99–114, esp. 108–11.

[26] Guillaume de Lorris and Jean de Meun, *The Romance of the Rose*, 3rd edition, trans. Charles Dahlberg (Princeton, NJ: Princeton University Press, 1995): 225, ln. 12987.

[27] Robert S. Sturges, "'The Canterbury Tales' Women Narrators: Three Traditions of Female Authority," *Modern Language Studies* 13.2 (Spring 1983): 41–51; Charles R. Sleeth, "'My Dames Loore' in 'The Canterbury Tales,'" *Neuphilologische Mitteilungen* 89.2 (1988): 174–84.

[28] Sturges, "'The Canterbury Tales' Women Narrators," 44.

with the struggle between the sexes that is the heart of the Wife of Bath's discourse. And moreover, some of them are already wise, and "kan understonde" (WBT 225); her experience is not proscriptive for such women, but rather a reflection of what they already know. There is no deference here, no establishment of a transgenerational authority. Instead, all the women function as one collective generation, endlessly buoyed by the testimony of their simultaneous sisters. Thus, when the Wife of Bath calls to her fellow wives to listen to her story, she does not set herself up as a mother speaking to a daughter (or even to a niece), but rather as a peer among her peers, unmoored by temporal chains.

> Now herkneth hou I baar me proprely,
> Ye wise wyves, that kan understonde.
> Thus sholde ye speke and bere hem wrong on honde,
> For half so boldely kan ther no man
> Swere and lyen, as a womman kan.
> I sey nat this by wyves that been wyse,
> But if it be whan they hem mysavyse...
> But herkneth how I sayde.
>
> (WBT 224–30, 234)

Listen to me, "herkneth," calls the Wife of Bath to what you wives already know; practice the lies and false oaths that are already an inherent aspect of your character. Listen to my example and recognize me as one of your own.

If the Wife of Bath has little interest in serving as a parent to other wives, she is even less invested in functioning in a maternal role to the pilgrims or to the reader. While she is happy to tell them of her life, the relationship she forms with the male pilgrims is one of revelation rather than inheritance. This is not information that these men have earned as a function of their lineage, but rather secrets to which they are explicitly not privy by virtue of their gender. When the Pardoner, for example, reacts violently to her speech, protesting that "I was aboute to wedde a wyf; allas!/What sholde I bye it on my flesh so deere?/Yet hadde I levere wedde no wyf to-yeere!" (WBT 166–8), he represents himself as a man about to be made the victim of this violent female inheritance. Likewise, when he pleads with her to "telle forth youre tale, spareth for no man,/And teche us yonge men of your praktike" (WBT 186–7), he not only offers her the recognition suitable for an instructor, but also acknowledges that her "praktike" is something that does not belong naturally to young men. The Pardoner knows that he is not the rightful heir to this story, and that the Wife of Bath's openness to telling it to him and the other pilgrims is thus not an act of hereditary endowment, but rather a quirk of rare benevolence.

Jerry Root has argued that the Wife's speech to the company of pilgrims is in itself a form of maternal generation, for, instead of producing children, the Wife ties "her salvation to an economy that is reproductive only in discursive and textual terms."[29] And yet such a reading would appear to imagine a very different Wife of Bath than the one who rides with Chaucer to Becket's shrine at Canterbury. In response to the Pardoner's anxious entreaties, she offers him the rather callous dismissal, "Chese wheither thou wolt sippe/Of thilke tonne that I shal abroche" (WBT 176-7). In other words, the Pardoner can listen to her story and make up his own mind; she is not responsible for, nor interested in, his future welfare. And at other times, her audience even appears uninterested in her story, such as when the Friar and Summoner almost derail it altogether through their quarrel (WBT 829-56). She is not their mother, and these men are not her sons. And thus, significantly, she never tells truly them her "mother's loore"—a point that some critics have seemed unfortunately to elide. She keeps her recipes for enchantment to herself, her own inheritance to her own breast. The Wife of Bath teaches of love, but not in any invocation of lineage or descent. "Myn entente nys but for to pleye" (WBT 192), she tells her audience, and the fluidity of her ever-renewed temporality ensures that she—unlike the male pilgrims, unlike Chaucer himself— can speak only to amuse, without the encroaching sense of creeping death.

Sterile Futures, Sterile Pasts: The Hag Against Heredity

The present (encompassing as well a flattened version of the past) is everything to the Wife of Bath; it is the dizzy cycle in which her lust remains ever new, her flesh ever desirable despite its years of experience. And thus it might initially appear disconcerting to find her *Tale* beginning in the past, at the time of King Arthur's court in a distant England. It is one of the knights of ancient Camelot who rides out one morning and rapes a young virgin, within the story, and it is a mythical Queen Guinevere who allows the knight to save his life only if he can discover the answer to the riddle of what women truly want. Even the old woman who gives the knight the crucial response is introduced to the tale through the trappings of a pagan past, for she appears as part of a magical frolic within the deep woods ("he saugh upon a daunce go/Of ladyes foure and twenty, and yet mo" [991-2]). Yet, as the reader soon learns, this is not the past in any historical linear sense, for it is a world wholly disconnected from its future, a world in which fertility is alienated from human flesh and children dispossessed from their familial past. The Wife of Bath imagines the Arthurian world not as a past origin point for her own medieval one, but rather as a parallel function of the present, with only the absence of fairies to mark the difference between them. Carolyn Dinshaw has written that the human perception of time depends upon the observation of change, yet, as I have argued in this chapter, the medieval perception of time depended as

---

[29] Jerry Root, "'Space to Speke:' The Wife of Bath and the Discourse of Confession," *The Chaucer Review* 28.3 (1994): 252-72, at 259.

well upon the observation of lineage and of the unending, ancient linkages between individual men.[30] The Wife of Bath has erased such ties, breaking down the system of male genealogy so inseparable from the function of history itself. And so time is a funny thing within this *Tale*; men move unmoored from the familial structures and kinships that allow temporality to be observed. In short, this is a world devoid of human generation, and so men must search in other places for their authority or, perhaps, acquiesce to the surrender of that authority altogether. It is a test case for Chaucer, a vision of male terror and male submission to be dismissed with laughter and relief at the end of the Wife of Bath's narration, and then remembered, somewhat anxiously, as his *Tales* move ever closer to their end.

The Wife of Bath has taken two stories and merged them together; she has added a "loathly lady" story to a "romantic" tale of knightly rape, or perhaps vice versa. And in bringing these two forms together, she has managed to remove the elements of each that had been designed to reinforce systems of patrilineal control. She has destroyed the inherent promise of future fertility from the rape story and annihilated the structures of the past upon which all other loathly lady analogues depend. Taken each on their own, these stories are firmly grounded in the male expectation of male reproductive authority, and affirm the social structures upon which masculine kinship and inheritance were based. Yet, brought together by the Wife of Bath, these tales instead have become obsessively circled around the present, caught in that same cycle of female renewal that seems to appear, to the Wife of Bath, as the only potential temporal location for women's power. It is not enough for men to concede sovereignty to their wives if they maintain their investment in genealogical structures that inherently grant dominion and authority to men. True sovereignty, the Wife of Bath implies with her *Tale*, can only be rendered to women when men are cut off from both their futures and their pasts, when all kinships with other men are severed and husbands must rely only upon the kindness of their wives.

To begin with the male alienation from the past, it is important to note that the "loathly lady" analogues almost all introduce, and then continue to center, the hero according to his lineage. For example, in both *The Weddyng of Sir Gawen and Dame Ragnell* and the *Tale of Florent*, the knight is not only emphatically *not* a rapist, but he is moreover a significant member of a powerful family and noble ancestry.[31] *The Weddyng of Sir Gawen* divides its male protagonists between King Arthur ("that Kyng curteys and royall") and his nephew, "gentyll Gawen knyght,"

---

[30] Dinshaw, *How Soon is Now?*, 7–16.

[31] "The Weddyng of Sir Gawen and Dame Ragnell," ed. John Withrington and P. J. C. Field, *Sources and Analogues of The Canterbury Tales*, Vol. II, ed. Robert M. Correale and Mary Hamel (Cambridge: D. S. Brewer, 2005): 420–41; "The Tale of Florent," ed. Withrington and Field, *Sources and Analogues*, 410–19.

and both are characterized according to the aristocratic roots of their behavior.[32] Likewise, in his *Tale of Florent*, John Gower presents Florent as "a worthi knyght...neveou to th'emperour."[33] The depth of male sacrifice in marrying the ugly bride—as well as in offering her sovereignty over his decisions—is therefore amplified by the perception that it is not only the individual man himself whose sexual future and progeny are thus jeopardized. Rather, like Arcite mourning the destruction of the Theban lineage, each man's vulnerability to the demands of their magical bride represents the simultaneous vulnerability of his lineage, and the ancestral investment in his future.

In both texts as well, the resolution of the story provides a solution to a problem of patrilineal injustice. King Arthur is charged with his quest to learn what women most desire because he has erroneously disinherited a knight, Sir Gromer Somer, who holds his life in forfeit, and Florent must set off on his identical quest because he has robbed another family of their male heir, killing "Branchus, which to the capitain/Was sone and heir, wheof ben wrothe/The fader and the moder bothe."[34] Each man's willingness then to sacrifice his own lineage to make amends for his crimes against the larger patrilineal system further entrenches the importance of male heritage within the story. And each man finds himself well rewarded for his hazard, since he ultimately receives a wife with whom he can willingly and productively procreate. Florent's bride is of "eyhtetiene wynter age," while Gawen's bride gives him a son within the course of the story.[35] Indeed, as Sheryl Forste-Grupp notes, Gawen's wife Dame Ragnell makes an even larger investment in the preservation of Gawen's lineage, by dying well before she and her dower claim could pose a threat to their son, Gyngolen's, inheritance.[36]

In fact, the authors of these loathly lady analogues go to some trouble to establish that the assault against the patrilineal system does not lie within the women themselves, but rather exists external to them; they are the tools with which an evil, magical stepmother (in both stories) has attacked their father's lineage, and by extension, also their new husband's. Far from being lowborn female monsters, the women announce themselves to be of noble birth; one is the "kings dowter of Cizile," and the other, Dame Ragnell, is revealed to be the sister of Sir Gromer Somer himself.[37] In each case, the woman makes it clear that she is aligned with her father (and now with her husband) against the enchantments and wiles of older women. She is on the side of the patriarchy, and longs only for reintegration into the limited, reproductive role offered to women in male genealogies. The story closes with the male lineage augmented, for by his self-sacrifice the knight

[32] "Weddyng of Sir Gawen and Dame Ragnell," 420 ln. 6, 422 ln. 142.
[33] "Tale of Florent," 410 lns. 13–14.   [34] "Tale of Florent," 411 lns. 33–5.
[35] "Tale of Florent," 418 ln. 408; "The Weddynge of Sir Gawen and Dame Ragnell," 440 ln. 799.
[36] Sheryl L. Forste-Grupp, "A Woman Circumvents the Laws of Primogeniture in 'The Weddynge of Sir Gawen and Dame Ragnell,'" *Studies in Philology* 99.2 (Spring 2002): 105–22, at 121–2.
[37] "Tale of Florent," 419 ln. 446; "The Weddynge of Sir Gawen and Dame Ragnell," 432 ln. 475.

has proved his likeness to his ancient ancestors, and his ability to preserve and perpetuate their memory by siring offspring on his young, newly docile wife. The "sovereignty" that the women supposedly maintain melts away after the man's initial choice, for it was only in their loathly form that they desired such an unnatural imposition upon male authority.

The Wife of Bath has erased all of these elements from her story. Her knight is of uncertain ancestry and her loathly lady never denies the charge of low ancestry. Even King Arthur appears demoted; the several lines of praise devoted to him by Gower become merely "Kyng Arthour/Of which that Britons speken greet honour" (WBT 857–8). The Wife of Bath is uninterested in offering her own praise of the mythical king, for he is yet another representative of the male systems of power against which she (and the hag of her story) find themselves aligned. The original offense against patrilineality has been transformed into a sexual offense against womanhood. And, perhaps most significantly of all, the loathly lady's transformation into a beautiful, younger woman owes not to any stepmother's wicked curse, but rather only to her own control. Her transformation is not the revelation of her true form, but rather her assent to appear in one of the many forms that she appears able to wield. Thus, as other critics have noted, the new bride's power remains supreme, and the procreative potential of her body is placed in far more doubt than in any other version of this story. Moreover, without the context of the beloved father from whom she has been separated, the reader is given no indication that the bride herself has any investment in upholding patrilineality. Her marriage serves not as a reintegration into a new lineage, but rather a challenge to the importance of paternal ancestry, particularly since she is so willing to continue to live without naming her father.

In medieval romance, familial disruption and confusion often dictate the protagonist's development and journey, as he or she seeks to restore or replace the fractured bonds of their kin network.[38] It is the destruction of patrilineality that sets all future conflicts into motion. And yet according to the speeches of the Wife of Bath's old hag, after she has successfully demanded the rapist-knight's hand in marriage, the opposite instead is true. Aristocratic lineage itself becomes the obstacle to be attacked and dismantled through argumentation, and the successful conclusion of the romance can only be achieved once the knight has accepted the meaninglessness of his (still unnamed) male heritage. The old woman argues that lineal inheritance is fundamentally dysfunctional for it is incapable of transmitting virtue, the only property that truly matters in the world. Instead, all virtue derives from the divine desire to distribute grace, the exercise of God's free will to

---

[38] Many examples of this paradigm can be found in Joanne Charbonneau and Desiree Cromwell, "Gender and Identity in the Popular Romance," *A Companion to Medieval Popular Romance*, ed. Raluca L. Radulescu and Cory James Rushton (Cambridge: D. S. Brewer, 2009): 96–110.

offer "gentillesse" where He will.[39] As the Wife of Bath charges the rapist-knight, "Thy gentillesse cometh fro God allone./Thanne comth oure verray gentillesse of grace;/It was no thyng biquethe us with oure place" (WBT 1162–4). The knight's faith in his own intrinsic "gentillesse" is thus to some extent undermined, for it is determined by an authority outside of his control; his forefathers cannot help him gain this prize.

Chaucer offers two superficially similar attacks upon gentilesse in his other works. One appears in a minor poem entitled "Gentilesse," and the other undermining of lineage can be found in Walter's speech upon the uncertainties of heredity within the *Clerk's Tale*. However, the likeness between these three speeches is far thinner than one would initially think. For in the *Clerk's Tale*, Chaucer emphasizes the unreliability of lineage as a mechanism of transmitting virtue down the generations; sometimes (and *only* sometimes) the mechanism fails and a son is born with only a weak moral resemblance to his father. And in his short poem, Chaucer notes that the inheritance of "gentilesse" is a participatory system, one that demands for sons to imitate their father's moral qualities in an active manner. Chaucer writes:

> The firste stok, fader of gentilesse—
> What man that claymeth gentil for to be,
> Must folowe his trace, and alle his wittes
> Vertu to sewe, and vyces for to flee.[40]

Chaucer claims that men who wish to be known as "gentil" cannot rely upon lineage alone to win that title for them. Instead, they must perform their likeness to their father, following that ancestral habit of distributing virtues in their midst. As Chaucer notes, "ther may no man, as men may wel see,/Bequethe his heir his vertuous noblesse." And yet by providing his son with the image of his own moral rectitude, a father may shape and condition his son to fit within his lineage, even as his own father must have encouraged him to model himself in virtue after that "firste stok."

In other words, lineage still *works* in Chaucer's poem on "gentilesse;" heredity simply cannot substitute entirely for human will and human activity. Men are called upon to be active participants in their own ancestry, to behave themselves in a way that mirrors the moral behavior of their forefathers. From a paternal perspective, such a dictate is labeled with uncertainty, for, as Walter laments in the *Clerk's Tale*, men cannot trust to their seed alone to sow virtue in their sons. This is an undermining of the authority of heredity, an acknowledgment of how

---

[39] This section of the *Tale* has been difficult for some critics to parse, since, as Gloria Shapiro writes, the earlier elements of the story stand in contrast to "the purity of religious feeling" supposedly displayed within the hag's speech. Gloria K. Shapiro, "Dame Alice as Deceptive Narrator," *The Chaucer Review* 6.2 (Fall 1971): 130–41, at 132.

[40] Chaucer, "Gentilesse: Moral Balade of Chaucier," *Riverside Chaucer*, 654, lines 1–4.

limited paternal power truly is as a proscriptive for an heir. Still it is far from an attack upon lineage itself. On the contrary, lineage is the means of providing men with models of morality, of reminding them of how much higher their aspirations to virtue may be aimed. The memory of fathers past uplifts the filial generations, linking them with a nobility not passively placed within their hands, but rather one which calls to them to be better men, men more like their fathers, and to seize their place within that moral lineage for themselves.

The speech given by the old woman in her marital bed is thus an emphatically different speech than these other two, although most critics have tended to conflate them without question. Instead of elucidating the limitations of lineage, she lambasts the hubris of men who think that the status of their fathers matters at all within the modern world.

> "But, for ye speken of swich gentillesse
> As is descended out of old richesse,
> That therfore sholden ye be gentil men,
> Swich arrogance is nat worth an hen."
>
> (WBT 109–12)

The hag thinks of lineage only in terms of riches and wealth; male ancestry is always fully divorced from virtue within her speech. While Chaucer, speaking in his own voice rather than that of the Wife of Bath, can easily imagine a moral lineage that links father and son in a mode analogous to that represented by property transmission, the old woman begins her argument by assuming that lineages are exclusively concerned with the distribution of wealth. Those men who call themselves noble after the nobility of their fathers thus base their claims to morality entirely upon the accumulations of mammon.

This is a coarse, crude way to look at men's heredity. And the old woman uses the ugliness of the vision of paternity that she creates to draw a contrast with the purity of Christ as a progenitor, saying,

> "Crist wole we clayme of hym oure gentillesse,
> Nat of oure eldres for hire old richesse.
> For thogh they yeve us al hir heritage,
> For which we clayme to been of heigh parage,
> Yet may they nat biquethe for no thyng
> To noon of us hir vertuous lyvyng,
> That made hem gentil men ycalled be,
> And bad us folwen hem in swich degree.
>
> (WBT 117–24)

Again, "heigh parage" was not merely a matter of wealth or of accumulation. As the analogous stories of the loathly lady make clear, male heroism was still a matter of high birth, for virtuous men like Gawen and Florent could imitate (if not fully inherit) the noble qualities of their male kin. Yet for the old woman, lineage offers nothing to men other than an inflated sense of their own worth. She, a humble lady, may turn to Christ and find within him more nobility than any noble's son will find within his wealthy father.

The lack of certainty within reproduction—emblematized by the occasional failure of sons to resemble their fathers well—becomes the old woman's ultimate proof of the entire system's decay. As she argues, "if gentillesse were planted natureelly/unto a certeyn lynage doun the lyne...they myghte do no vileynye or vice" (WBT 134–5, 138). If any genetic variance is found within a man's heirs—as Chaucer and his readers will readily admit is a common fact—then no virtue may be planted within that lineage at all, she reasons. It either yields its fruits in perfect reciprocity of their original generation or that lineage must admit that no virtue was ever planted in its line, that its men have claimed nobility when all they had was their forefathers' wealth. And those men who do resemble their fathers in nobility, who fight and strive to mirror the virtues of their family's past, as Chaucer called upon them to do, cannot be held up as to defend the (limited) mechanism of lineage—for they, as she has said, derive their virtue only from God. Any resemblance to a male parent is inconsequential, for all nobility must be triangulated through the Lord.

Men may worry that there is no authority in reproduction, since there is no certainty in the resulting quality of one's procreative endeavors. But the Wife of Bath's old woman tells them that they have far more to worry about than merely that. Lineage and all the familial institutions that support male power are feeble, useless things, designed only to accommodate man's greed and doom his soul. "For of oure eldres," she teaches, "may we no thyng clayme/But temporal thyng, that man may hurte and mayme" (WBT 1131–2). She cannot deny that riches and wealth do pass, with relative reliability, through male ancestral hands, strengthening the institution of male patrimony. So instead, the old woman will denigrate wealth itself, turning—with a piety somewhat startling in a woman we first met when she was dancing with the faeries—a harsh judgment upon the riches of the world. There is nothing superior to be found in noble families, only a debilitating arrogance and a false estimation of their virtue. And even in defense of her own origins, the hag turns simply to God. "Al were it that myne auncestres were rude,/Yet may the hye God, and so hope I,/Grante me grace to lyven vertuously" (WBT 172–4). She makes no claims to a virtuous mother or a moral father, no appeals to her own family for their pious grace. The old woman will dally with no lineages at all, not even her own; the only power she will acknowledge is that of the individual and of the individual's God.

In this sense, the *Wife of Bath's Tale* denies men the authority of their own past. Ancestry and lineage are robbed of all meaning within the hands of her didactic hag. If one imagines this speech on "gentilesse" as a retort in some way to those

666

fears articulated by Walter in the *Clerk's Tale* (even as the Clerk himself responds to the Wife of Bath at the end of his narration), then the old woman would appear to answer Walter's question of how a man can procreate with authority when he cannot procreate with certainty. "You can't," she seems to say; "you men have no authority at all." The institutions of masculinity meant to insure man's continued dominion within the world have fallen with her words, and, in their absence, the rapist-knight (no advertisement after all for the genetic potential of virtue) might as well surrender his future to that same wife who has annihilated his sense of his own past.

And that male future has been well and truly surrendered, within the *Wife of Bath's Tale*. Even beyond the matter of the transference of sovereignty, the old woman's very presence within the story has transformed an inherently fertile story of a young man and woman into a much stranger story of a rapist, a rape victim, and the rapist's ugly new wife. Chaucer's *Wife of Bath's Tale* is the only version of the "loathly lady" story to insert a rape as the catalyst for its knight's need to learn what women most desire. And critics have thereby noted how powerfully that initial assault transforms the meaning of the knight's unwilling marriage to his old wife, and debated to what extent the loss of male sovereignty restores justice for a female violation.

I would argue, however, that we can also reverse the direction of our critique, and speculate upon what transformations the addition of the loathly lady wreaks upon the narrative of the rapist's tale. The most famous and controversial analogue for the rape within the *Wife of Bath's Tale* is the ballad, "The Knight and the Shepherd's Daughter;" while the analogue lacks any type of loathly lady, the mirroring of the rape and the knight's surrender to a forced marriage with a now sovereign woman bears close resemblance to that depicted within the *Tale*.[41] Needless to say, I am not arguing for the direct relation between the two, particularly since the latter is almost certainly significantly later than Chaucer's poem. Instead, I wish to use the ballad to demonstrate the type of traditional heterosexual story that the Wife of Bath has interrupted and hybridized with her addition of the loathly lady trope.

The most significant aspect of the "Shepherd's Daughter" ballad is therefore the fact that in that poem it is the rape victim herself who demands justice for her rape and forces the knight into a marriage. In contrast, after the sexual assault within the *Wife of Bath's Tale*, the girl who has been attacked disappears from the narrative, subsumed under the more powerful female figures of the queen and the loathly lady. Marriage to a rapist appears as a less than desirable result to a

---

[41] "The Knight and the Shepherd's Daughter," *The English and Scottish Popular Ballads*, Vol. 2, Part IV, ed. Francis James Child (Boston, MA: Houghton Mifflin Co., 1886): 457–77. The argument in favor of this ballad as an analogue for the *Wife of Bath's Tale* was made in G. H. Maynadier, *The Wife of Bath's Tale: Its Sources and Analogues* (London: D. Nutt, 1901): 115–20.

modern reader, but for a medieval rape victim (and particularly for the women within both stories) the ability to demand marriage of an unwilling partner granted a mode of remuneration, safeguarding their social status and personal authority.[42] Moreover, from the point of view of the storyteller and reader, the marriage of the young girl to her attacker would seem to resolve the anxieties triggered by violence, for it reintegrates both man and woman into a productive social institution, and provides for the possibility of future procreation.[43] And, it should be noted, Francis Child collected several versions of this ballad in the late nineteenth century, implying that it remained a popular romantic story (despite the violence of its opening scene) well into the modern era.[44]

The Wife of Bath appears to position her *Tale* to be a similar "romance:" she is careful to narrate that both assailant and victim are eligible for marriage, since the rapist was a "lusty bacheler" (WBT 883) of King Arthur's court, who encountered a "mayde" and "by verray force, he rafte hire maydenhed" (WBT 887–8). At this point in the story it would appear perhaps most natural for the unmarried knight to rectify his actions by offering the girl the protections of matrimony—an act which medieval theologians could classify "as penance for his crime."[45] And, of course, the knight does indeed find himself forced into matrimony within the course of the story. But wedding the "loathly lady," while traumatic to his sense of bodily integrity, does little to ameliorate the offense that he has committed against this specific woman. The maiden herself never re-enters the story; we are given no sign if she desires the man's death or rather the protections of his name.[46] Indeed, while in the "Knight and the Shepherd's Daughter," the woman herself runs to the court for justice, here it is only the passive intervention of "swich clamour/And swich pursute unto the kyng" (WBT 889–90) that wins some mode of vengeance for the woman.

[42] Barbara Hanawalt notes that "rape could be a prelude to marriage, particularly when there was initial resistance on the part of the victim or her family…cases do appear in which the woman later married the rapist." Barbara Hanawalt, *Crime and Conflict in English Communities, 1300–1348* (Cambridge, MA: Harvard University Press, 1979): 106.

[43] In another story that George Coffman has suggested should be seen as an analogue for the rape in the *Wife of Bath's Tale*, the man does not offer the woman marriage, but the rape results in the birth of St. Cuthbert. George R. Coffman, "An Analogue for the Violation of the Maiden in the 'Wife of Bath's Tale,'" *Modern Language Notes* 59.4 (April 1944): 271–4.

[44] Lynn Wollstadt also argues that, as an orally transmitted ballad, the story may well have been perpetuated by female singers; she believes women may have connected strongly to the young woman's triumph within the tale. Lynn M. Wollstadt, "Repainting the Lion: 'The Wife of Bath's Tale' and a Traditional British Ballad," *The English 'Loathly Lady' Tales: Boundaries, Traditions, Motifs,* ed. S. Elizabeth Passmore and Susan Carter (Kalamazoo, MI: Medieval Institute Publications, 2007): 199–212, at 201–3.

[45] Kathryn Gravdal, *Ravishing Maidens: Writing Rape in Medieval French Literature and Law* (Philadelphia, PA: University of Pennsylvania Press, 1991): 9.

[46] Corinne Saunders argues that the girl's silence within the tale may be an indication of the strength of female solidarity, since the other women are able to plead effectively on her behalf. Corinne Saunders, *Rape and Ravishment in the Literature of Medieval England* (Cambridge: D. S. Brewer, 2001): 302. Yet the girl's silence is so complete and her disappearance from the story so comprehensive that it is difficult to maintain this more optimistic perspective.

After the rape in the ballad, on the contrary, the young woman immediately demands that her rapist tell her his name, and the knight, apparently thinking that he will not be held responsible for his actions flippantly responds,

> 'In some places they call me Jack,
>   In other some they call me John;
> But when into the queen's court,
>   O then Lithcock it is my name!"

Lithcock, the lady soon deduces, is Latin; when she translates the name into English it turns out to be Richard, and the rapist is revealed to be Earl Richard, the brother of the queen. The ballad establishes that it is important for the girl to know the rapist's name not only so that she can demand justice for his attack upon her, but also so that she can evaluate the lineage of the man whom she will insist upon receiving in marriage. She is offered either his death or his marriage, and the revelation of his lineage leads her to decide that she will demand for him to marry her. In this sense the eventual marriage at the end of the poem rewards the deliberate calculations of the female victim; it matches her assessment of what she is owed, and what manner of male lineage she is willing to join.

Thus, even though the knight is rewarded by marriage to a beautiful woman who, of course, is revealed to be of noble birth, the power reversal of the *Wife of Bath's Tale* remains here as well. He begs her to leave him his body; she refuses, and snaps at him, "O haud your tongue, young man."[47] Moreover, when the knight, like that of the *Wife of Bath's Tale*, complains of the shame of the marriage to a woman of low lineage, the girl retorts that low social class did not give him a reason to rape her.[48]

> 'O may be I'm a shepherd's dochter,
>   And may be I am nane;
> But you might hae ridden on your ways,
>   And hae let me alane.'[49]

The woman proves to be as invested in lineage and noble heredity as the knight himself, but her vision of justice accommodates the width of the united womanhood presented by the Wife of Bath. Aristocratic privilege here is held up as naturally coexistent with morality.

A knight has no more reason to rape a peasant girl than he would the daughter of a king or earl. And if a man of high birth commits that violation, then he should be punished with matrimony to that specific, humble maiden; her potential

---

[47] "The Knight and the Shepherd's Daughter," 461, stanza 24.
[48] Elizabeth Helsinger notes that the revelation of the girl's secret parentage serves to "reinscribe her within the patriarchal hierarchy of the family." Elizabeth K. Helsinger, "Consumer Power and the Utopia of Desire: Christina Rossetti's 'Goblin Market,'" *ELH* 58.4 (Winter 1991): 903–33, at 915.
[49] "The Knight and the Shepherd's Daughter," 462, stanza 32.

suffering as a violated woman without the protection of marriage warrants a greater intervention from the king's court than the potential degradation to his lineage. And the knight's punishment fits his crime, for, since he has degraded his lineage with his violence, the "shepherd's daughter" will degrade it even further with her low blood. For this remains a fundamentally reproductive story, even though no children are born from the marriage within the poem. The knight's horror at wedding a beautiful young girl is a horror born from misplaced snobbishness, rather than repulsion at her looks. His fear is not of the sexual act itself (in which he has already engaged with her), but rather the institutional joining of his family with that of a shepherd, and the devastation that such a marriage will wreck upon his offspring. The girl therefore taunts him with imagined tales of her humble parents—telling him, for example, that her mother would "lay down her head upon a poke,/Then sleep and snore like ony sow"—so that he experiences the full horror of the lineage into which he has been forced to marry.[50] His forefathers will be forced to reside with her peasant mothers, their respective lines united in their progeny. And yet as the girl reminded him, he had no need to rape her mother's daughter.

It is impossible to know how the Wife of Bath's story of rape would have continued without the intrusive introduction of the loathly lady; indeed, it is impossible to imagine that story without its most prominent character. But it is instructive to reflect upon how the rape is set up to progress along the lines of a very different type of story than the one to which the Wife pivots. The story might not have progressed in the same path as that of the "Knight and the Shepherd's Daughter," but that poem's emphasis on the remediation of rape through enforced matrimony to the victim herself appears highly plausible. And in that poem, the knight is not only allowed to maintain the virtues of his past ancestry (however much the girl might scare him with stories of her own), but the woman herself also testifies to the importance of lineage and hereditary institutions to provide context for the litigation of violence and the matrimonial production of progeny. Both the knight and the victim of his attack are given a very specific type of heterosexual, reproductive future by their poem, and both end their story with their personal and familial authority reinforced and enhanced.

And thus while the Wife of Bath's Tale effects a feminine seizure of power within the marriage bed, it also should be seen as severely restricting the future procreations of its participants. For however beautiful the old woman turns at the very end of the tale, their marriage never appears to possess the same potential for procreation that is found in this ballad analogue, or in the loathly lady analogues, or indeed, that would have been found within the story itself if the rapist-knight had been commanded to marry his initial victim. The old woman has dictated to

---

[50] "The Knight and the Shepherd's Daughter," 467, stanza 43.

him the unimportance of his lineage, the inconsequentiality of the relationship between a man and his fathers. Thus, although she informs him that she will be "bothe fair and good" (WBT 1241), no promise of procreation or contribution to his family is thereby promised. Instead, the Wife of Bath emphasizes the finality of death, once again, by transitioning quickly between the sexual bliss found in the marriage bed to the fact of their demise. "She obeyed hym in every thyng/That myghte doon hym plesance or likyng./And thus they lyve unto hir lyves ende" (WBT 1255–7). If the knight had married the girl he raped, they might have become the progenitors of a dynasty, as in other Arthurian romances; instead, married to the loathly lady, he will receive pleasure in bed until he dies.

Likewise, the Wife of Bath demonstrates no investment in male futures more generally. As she concludes her *Tale*,

> And eek I praye Jhesu shorte hir lyves
> That noght wol be governed by hir wyves;
> And olde and angry nygardes of dispence,
> God sende hem soone verray pestilence!
>
> (WBT 1261–4)

All men die, in the Wife of Bath's philosophy. Whether they expire of sexual bliss or Jesus's wrath, a queen's anger or a divinely chosen pestilence, men are meant to die and be replaced. There is a finite limit to their lives, one which women are delighted to determine. And there is no future promised to them, no progression of offspring to soothe their passage or fathers to welcome them at the last. Men are allowed no lineage in the world of the Wife of Bath, no fertile wives, no progeny to serve them as their heirs. To obtain sovereignty she has had to circumvent the institutions designed to maintain men in the continuity of time, to keep them grounded in the authority of their blood. All pleasures now must be found in the present moment, for the Wife of Bath will allow no other mode of time to any of her men.

Literary Lineage

To bring men to the realization of their own insufficiency and impotence, Chaucer has given them a jolly widow and her cheerful account of how easily she can break the hard structures of men's lives. Men knew they were mortal, but still the family stood against the overwhelming annihilation that waited within death. Kin networks promised men that they would live within the memories of their sons, and reside in turn in the bosoms of their own fathers. Men's lives were short, but their lineages were long. Men existed after death through their bonds to sons, brothers, and grandsons, preserved within present time by the privileges of gender, class, and blood. And all that faith, that certainty that they were promised some small part of the patrilineal whole, falls at the feet of Alisoun of Bath. The law cannot save their land from her grasping hands, and their fathers cannot reach them across her arguments against heredity. Each man is alone, the old hag tells her rapist-knight, unmoored from all but the occasional benevolence of his God. And Chaucer knows that men do not want to be alone, that there is no authority to be had for the man cut off from his fellows, left solitary with the fact of his own death.

Poets seek genealogy for the same reason, to tie themselves to something larger within the world. No wonder then that Chaucer's hag not only calls men to abandon their hope in their fathers, but also calls upon Chaucer himself to remember how even Dante, a poet of two generations before, cast off father and son alike. As she recites,

> Wel kan the wise poet of Florence,
> That highte Dant, speken in this sentence.
> Lo, in swich maner rym is Dantes tale:
> 'Ful selde up riseth by his branches smale
> Prowesse of man, for God, of his goodnesse,
> Wole that of hym we clayme oure gentilesse;'
> For of oure eldres may we no thyng clayme
> But temporal thyng, that man may hurte and mayme.
>
> (WBT 1125–32)

Dante is a strange fit within this otherwise devotional speech, for the passage that Chaucer appears to be referencing from within the Florentine poet's *Convivio* has far less to do with divine authority than it does with imperial power.[51] Likewise, the reference to the Roman author, Valerius Maximus (WBT 1165), as another source for this philosophy paradoxically serves to establish a strong secular basis for the Wife of Bath's words, despite their otherwise prominent religious content.

Moreover, by using and naming these specific sources for the hag's speech against nobility and male inheritance, Chaucer invokes the ghosts of his own literary fathers, of the men whose exalted ranks Chaucer longs to join. It is not enough for Chaucer to stand aloof and destroy the hopes of other men. His faith too will be consumed, his fathers—both biological and poetic—exhumed as evidence for the distance between the generations of men. Chaucer writes Dante into the world of *The Canterbury Tales* only so that Dante may therein reject him, may disclaim the very possibility of a meaningful likeness between poetic "fathers" and "sons." Thus, it is important to note that the hag's speech wanders briefly in its terminology here, for Chaucer's Dante does not reject the reproduction of

---

[51] John Livingston Lowes, "Chaucer and Dante's 'Convivio,'" *Modern Philology* 13.1 (May 1915): 19–33, esp. 19–24. See also Donald C. Baker, "Chaucer's Clerk and the Wife of Bath on the Subject of 'Gentilesse,'" *Studies in Philology*, 59.4 (October 1962): 631–40, at 632 n.2.

"gentillesse" but rather of "prowesse" (WBT 1129). We are supposed to be speaking of the inheritance of nobility within this passage, but the introduction of Dante changes the very vocabulary of the speech. For Chaucer does not dream of inheriting aristocratic status from his literary progenitors, but rather that skill and talent which he has read indited in their books. And so it is the reproduction of talent itself which will be denied here, that dream of poetic resemblance and lineage.

In a sense, the hag's speech on "gentillesse" therefore also stands as a rebuttal to the more ambitious, hopeful Clerk of the Canterbury pilgrims. For the Clerk will recite (or perhaps has already, depending on how one aligns the tales) a story that he claims to have learned from a different Italian poet, Francis Petrarch.[52] The Clerk claims Petrarch to be the "worthy man/That taught me this tale, as I bigan" (ClT 39–40). In other words, the Clerk attempts to position himself as literary heir to Petrarch, who "is now deed and nayled in his cheste" (WBT 29); he can imitate Petrarch's talent by virtue of his own education supposedly as Petrarch's pupil. And yet from the very start, the Clerk tells us that he cannot in fact imitate the "heigh stile" (ClT 41) in which Petrarch wrote, and begins to list excuses for why his story will be different (and likely inferior) to the one which he first heard "at Padowe of a worthy clerk" (ClT 27). For all the optimism of his attempt to step into the void left by the death of his literary master, the Clerk must almost immediately accept that his inheritance from Petrarch is incomplete and imperfect; as the hag would tell him, a man's genius or authority cannot be transmitted to another man. And so he ends his *Tale* by ceding the ground to the Wife of Bath, that skeptic of man's heredity, "whos lyf and al hire secte God mayntene/In heigh maistrie" (ClT 1171–2).

Both Petrarch and Dante intrude into Chaucer's text only to demonstrate the impossibility of either man serving as a reliable, legitimizing source of authority for later poets. Dante disclaims the hereditary mechanisms of talent altogether in the hag's speech, while the Clerk demonstrates how even a man personally instructed by the poet can fail to assume his mentor's literary authority and style. Indeed, after narrating the full story of Griselda and Walter, the Clerk notes that the tale has limited efficacy in the modern world. Virtuous, patient women "were ful hard to fynde now-a-dayes...the gold of hem hath now so badde alayes/With bras" (ClT 1164, 1167–8). Time itself has intervened to shatter the likeness between contemporary women and their legendary sister; the generations of inheritance between women have been only a means of degradation and decay. The identification of both Griselda and Petrarch with some virtuous past of noble women and excellent poets foregrounds the despicable state of modernity, how

---

[52] For the intertextual relationship between Chaucer's *Clerk's Tale* and Petrarch's story of Griselda, see John Finlayson, "Petrarch, Boccaccio, and Chaucer's 'Clerk's Tale,'" *Studies in Philology* 97.3 (Summer 2000): 255–75.

far it has fallen from some antique vision of the past. The men and women of Chaucer's current day may make claims upon the lives of their ancestors, but they are incapable of portraying themselves as true likenesses of the past. There is no lineage, neither female nor poetic, sufficient to transmit the "prowesse" and authority of these dead exemplars to the modern-day men and women who wish so desperately to be their heirs.

The longing to serve as heir to the glories of the past is a means of seeking contemporary legitimization, of laying claim in the present day to a status derived from actions undertaken long before one's life. Chaucer breaks the stability of that chain, undermining man's assurance that he (or his wife) can ever access the authority and virtue that should be theirs by birth. Yet Chaucer also undermines man's confidence in his contemplation of the future, for Chaucer demonstrates how fragile are the goods that men create within their lives. Men cannot claim likeness with the past, but they also cannot feel confident in the preservations of the future. The material products of their creative lives are as easily broken as their links with their fathers ands sons. Those "temporal thyng[s], that men can hurt and mayme" may not survive the ravages of time. Books are fragile, foolish objects, expensive to create, easily destroyed. The "book of wikked wyves" (WBT 685) that Jankyn reads to the Wife of Bath is a massive intellectual undertaking, a compilation of Latinate detail pruned from Chaucer's lifetime of reading. And yet it is so simple to destroy.[53] That book represents not only Chaucer's labor, but also the labor of dozens of ancient men's lives, derivations of their (misogynistic) genius. In fact, by listing the enormous number of sources in the book ("mo legends and lyves/Than been of goode wyves in the Bible" [WBT 686–7]), Chaucer refuses to allow his reader to retreat from the sheer enormity of knowledge contained within the covers of this book. From St Jerome to Ovid, from the Christian writings of Tertullian to the gynecology of Dame Trot, the book spans a wide assortment of genres, a vast spectrum of time and space. The reader may share the Wife of Bath's antagonism to the anti-female discourse used as a selection mechanism for the compilation of the volume, but nevertheless such feelings of distaste should not obscure the degree to which Chaucer constructs Jankyn's book as a material object of wide authority, one that contains the vast gleanings of ancient genius, brought together by happenstance.

It is happenstance again that decides which texts are initially destroyed by the Wife of Bath's violent hands, and which texts will be destroyed by her command to Jankyn to "brenne his book anon right" (WBT 816). For despite the centuries of intellectual effort that the book's compilation represents, it is incredibly simple

---

[53] John Steadman has documented analogues of the book-burning scene from across Asian and European traditions, but he notes that Jankyn's book is unusually broad, erudite, and specific in naming its intellectual progenitors. John M. Steadman, "The Book-Burning Episode in the Wife of Bath's Prologue: Some Additional Analogues," *PMLA* 74.5 (December 1959): 521–5, esp. 524.

for the Wife of Bath to rip out its pages. The modes of literary generation are as fragile as those of biological reproduction, since each relies upon material forms for its perpetuation. Chaucer never tells us which authors have their work ripped apart by the Wife of Bath's anger, and that lack of specificity reinforces the reader's sense that such a fate could have befallen any of them. Perhaps it was a final page from the *Parables of Solomon* and the first few pages of Heloise's writings that were destroyed, or perhaps a bit of Ovid.[54] The uncertainty inherent within the Wife of Bath's violent selection renders all the poets vulnerable, for the Wife of Bath reports only to her audience that, "al sodeynly thre leves have I plyght/Out of his book, right as he radde" (WBT 790–1). The sudden unpredictable nature of the attack amplifies its power, as the Wife of Bath triumphs not only over her domineering husband, but also over the literary men and women who thought to leave their posterity safe in the hands of other future readers.

There was no fee tail to protect literary property, no legal court to hear the appeal if one's creations fell into the wrong hands. In life, Chaucer may still amend the violations done to his work by scribes like Adam Pinkhurst, for as Chaucer writes in *Adam Scriveyn*, "So oft adaye I mot thy werk renewe,/It is to correcte and eke to rubbe and scrape,/And al is thorugh thy negligence and rape."[55] But after the poet's death there will be no one to renew his work and scrape out the mistakes. Instead he will have to depend upon the care and kindness of unknown men to keep his literary creations safe from destruction and catastrophic happenstance. For all that is left after death is the fragile, material form upon which the memorialization of men must be founded. There is no innate authority to be found in the links with other poets, in the claims to intellectual lineage. The Wife of Bath has shaken all men's certainty in the preservation of their posterity.

The Wife of Bath presents this promise of destruction as a specifically female task, born from the conflict between the genders.

Thou liknest eek wommenes love to helle,
To bareyne lond, ther water may nat dwelle.
Thou liknest it also to wilde fyr;
The moore it brenneth, the moore it hath desir
To consume every thyng that brent wole be.
Thou seyest, right as wormes shende a tree,
Right so a wyf destroyeth hire housbounde

(WBT 371–8)

---

[54] Indeed, Alice Hamilton argued that there is a strong parallel between the burning of Jankyn's book and the destruction of Peter Abelard's works. Alice Hamilton, "Helowys and the Burning of Jankyn's Book," *Mediaeval Studies* 34 (1972): 196–207.

[55] Chaucer, "Chaucers Wordes Unto Adam, His Owne Scriveyn," *Riverside Chaucer*, 650, lines 5–7.

And yet the modes of annihilation that she describes (barren desert, wild fire, insatiable worms) are not specific to women's love, but belong more broadly to the categories of human crisis. They encompass not only the death of the individual, desiccated or consumed, but also the destruction of any hope of progeny or posterity. The infliction of sterility, the incineration of the full flesh—these are modes of decease that emphasize the comprehensive destruction of man's desire to preserve past his own mortality. There is nothing left of such men; fire will burn their flesh and worms will eat their family tree.

For all the Wife of Bath's boasting, women are not the catalyst for catastrophe. They are instead the mechanisms by which men dream of avoiding mortality, although technologies of fertility fail, and female bodies may give their husbands little fruit in which to place paternal faith. What men should fear within their wives is neither female love nor even sovereignty, but rather the female witness to the fictionality of lineage, the mockery that women like the Wife of Bath can direct at men who believe that the patrilineal bonds will be enough to save them from destruction. Men fear to be forgotten, fear that their fathers and sons are not sufficient to hold them within the larger course of the forward-moving world. And the Wife of Bath tells them that they are right to worry, that she can shake their certainty in their own heritage as easily as she can burn a simple book. The medieval world and its patterns of inheritance were made to soothe the fears of men, to calm anxieties and promise that something mortal and specific would remain after all a man's mortality had ceased. But Chaucer will let neither his readers nor himself rest in this false certainty, in this fiction of self-indulgence and release. Men should be anxious; they should stir beset with doubts in their own authority. The Wife of Bath mocks where men should mourn, and breaks the structures that they believe were meant to save them. For Chaucer will allow no man to place his faith within the human race, no man to rest content with his future or his past.

SECTION II
ON CREATION

3

Uncertain Labor

Conception and the Problem of Productivity

Labor was the curse of medieval man, the payment with which God had requited his sins. After eating the forbidden fruit of knowledge, Adam and Eve are told their respective punishments; Eve will bring forth children "in sorrow," and Adam will be condemned to win his food with "labor and toil."[1] Human reproduction and physical work are simultaneously united and made distinct. They are delineated by sex, and yet both are clearly imagined as mutual endeavors. The blurring of the respective roles of Adam and Eve in the creative processes attests not only to female participation in agriculture ("the grete alquemie"), but also to male participation in reproduction.[2] In medieval texts it is the latter which stands out as particularly prominent, as men are invested with creative primacy not only in traditional labor-related fields, but also in the labor of human generation.[3] Insemination becomes the pivotal moment of generation; conception is privileged over gestation. Scientific texts imagine the creation of the fetus as a form of agricultural production, the man "pour[ing] out his duty in the woman just as seed is sown in its designated field."[4] Similarly, the common metaphor of children as the "fruit of the womb" (ex: Luke 1:42) figures the female body as container rather than cultivator in its own right.

We must therefore think about medieval rhetorics of creation and generation as spaces within which production as mode of individual and social fulfillment

---

[1] Genesis 3:16–17.

[2] Agriculture is referred to as "the great alchemy" within *The Dicts and Sayings of the Philosophers*, ed. Curt F. Bühler (London: Oxford University Press for the Early English Text Society, 1941): 29. The full reference is as follows, a praise of those who "laboure in the grete alquemie, that is to seye the labourers of the erth, suche as sowen the seedis and planten fruytes and alle other labourers, by thewhiche is proufite unto the peple, and knighthode multiplied, and the houses full of ricchesses, and the realms susteyned, by thewhiche alle suche thingis is necessarie to be wel saved & kepte." Ibid. What is remarkable about this passage is how easily it visualizes the transformations of agricultural production within the context of alchemical transformations. Furthermore, it then resituates both forms of production within the greater context of social reproduction, arguing that these endeavors on the parts of Adam's heirs allow Eve's task to be carried out, as the aristocratic ranks "multiply."

[3] In contrast, in modern times as reproduction is typically thought of as exclusively a "woman's issue," we see its almost wholesale exclusion from intellectual engagements with issues of labor and production. The Marxist tradition, in particular, has proved remarkably resistant to incorporating female, biological forms of labor into its vocabulary and analyses. See, for example, the critique offered in Silvia Federici, *Caliban and the Witch: Women, the Body, and Primitive Accumulation* (Brooklyn, NY: Autonomedia, 2004): 7–10.

[4] *The Trotula*, ed. Green, 65.

Father Chaucer: Generating Authority in The Canterbury Tales. Samantha Katz Seal, Oxford University Press (2019).
© Samantha Seal.
DOI: 10.1093/oso/9780198832386.001.0001

was subject to exploration and critique. As Isabel Davis writes, "fashionable moral discourses... continually related men's sexual and laboring roles, making industry and the social cohesion it would necessarily produce an attractive masculine commission by liking it to sexual success and patriarchal authority."[5] The procreation of offspring allowed men to negotiate their larger relationships with their sexual labor and with its material fruit. Man possessed the active power in reproduction; it was his spirit that worked on the female uterine matter, shaping it into the new life form of the child.[6] Alan of Lille speaks of male hammers and female anvils, a vision of human reproduction as craft-like labor.[7] The Pseudo-Albertus Magnus gynecology, *De secretis mulierum*, articulates a similar metaphor for the male act of spermatic creation: "Just as a carpenter alone is the efficient cause, and the house is the effect, in that he alters and disposes the matter of the house, so the male seed alters the female menses into the shape of a human being."[8] The late medieval theories of reproduction focused on male labor, male spirit, and male virility, with women serving only as the defective material with which a man's craftsman skill was forced to work.

Moreover, the rhetoric of procreation as craft-based or agricultural labor allowed Chaucer's audience to imagine themselves performing very different types of work than they probably experienced in daily life. The affluent audience of *The Canterbury Tales* probably had an intimate awareness of the labor involved in producing food or material goods, yet they themselves would encounter such work primarily in the role of consumer.[9] Conceptualizing sex as carpentry or blacksmithing therefore allowed an aristocratic or upper bourgeois class to fantasize about their own capacities for material production. There were few creative and generative opportunities available to men and women whose economic and social functions typically removed them from the direct relationship between labor and produced object. Even Chaucer, with the advantages of his status as an author (and thus a producer of physical text) demonstrates the anxieties incumbent upon the dis-placement of the creator's link to the material form in his complaint about the inadequacies of his scribe, *Adam Scriveyn*.[10]

---

[5] Isabel Davis, *Writing Masculinity in the Later Middle Ages* (Cambridge: Cambridge University Press, 2007): 10.

[6] According to Aristotelian theory, man is the "efficient, agent cause" and woman is the "material cause." Cadden, *Meanings of Sex Difference*, 127.

[7] Alan of Lille, *The Plaint of Nature*, ed. and trans. James J. Sheridan (Toronto: Pontifical Institute of Medieval Studies, 1980): 69.

[8] Helen Rodnite Lemay (ed. and trans.), *Women's Secrets: A Translation of Pseudo-Albertus Magnus's De Secretis Mulierum With Commentaries* (Albany, NY: State University of New York Press, 1992): 64. A few lines later, the same author refers to conception as an ironsmith working metal.

[9] For the aristocracy as consumers of the products of peasant labor, see Barbara Harvey, "The Aristocratic Consumer in England in the Long Thirteenth-Century," *Thirteenth-Century England VI*, ed. M. Prestwich, R. Britnell, and R. Frame (Woodbridge, Suffolk: Boydell and Brewer, 1997): 17–37.

[10] Perhaps the best critical statement on the tension between author and scribe within Chaucer's poem comes from Glending Olson, who argues that Adam Scriveyn "construct[s] the speaker as a particular kind of *auctor* whose inventions transcend their scribal incarnations, yet at the same time

For such individuals, sex re-established the likeness between Adam, the first father, and his more affluent sons. Their wealth exempted them from the physical labor of the human struggle to produce food, and yet they too must labor and struggle in a way, to produce a human fruit no less desired, despite its metaphorical nature. Procreation makes every man a generator, an active source of new creation. It soothes the very aristocratic anxieties that the rebels of 1381 sought to ignite when they chanted "Whan Adam delved and Eve span, who was then the gentleman?"[11] Chaucer's gentle readers delve like Adam, they produce like Eve. They simply have the luxury to do so within a corporeal rather than pastoral field. And these reproductive acts of creation are as tied to physical survival as the production of food, as the widespread fifteenth-century extinction of aristocratic bloodlines (including that of Chaucer himself) would come to prove.[12] Reproduction is a labor and a mode of creation that levels social hierarchies (the spermatic power of peasant and knight are, after all, grounded in gender rather than class), even as it also offers justification for their existence and their continued regeneration.

Or, at least, it should do so in an ideal natural state. And yet Chaucer does not consider his modern age to possess the characteristics of such idealized normativity. Instead, he shows character after character in *The Canterbury Tales* who wishes to reproduce and create in inappropriate ways and with inappropriate partners. The heterosexual mutuality of the Biblical mode of procreation is overthrown, while the radical power differentials supported by medieval religious and scientific interpretations of male creativity and female materiality were amplified. This chapter will examine two modes of alternative generation from within *The Canterbury Tales*: a religious alternative and a scientific alternative. Perhaps unsurprisingly, Chaucer treats devotional reproductive alternatives with the most respect, acknowledging the historical tradition of creating with the help of God. Chaucer's God created the heterosexual conceptive patterns of humanity; he can circumvent them according to his will. In contrast, on scientific reproductive innovations, Chaucer takes a much harsher tone. These are reproductive strategies doomed to failure, indicted first and foremost for their hubristic attempts to innovate that which has been divinely created and thus should be exempt from human innovation, and secondarily condemned for their implicit endorsement of non-normative structurings of the sexes.

---

registering the dependence of authors on scribes and the limitations of authorial power in medieval manuscript culture." Glending Olson, "Author, Scribe, and Curse: The Genre of *Adam Scriveyn*," *The Chaucer Review* 42.3 (2008): 285.

[11] For an analysis of John Ball's use of this chant as a transformation of a conservative religious precept into a radically egalitarian one, see Nicola Masciandaro, *The Voice of the Hammer: The Meaning of Work in Middle English Literature* (Notre Dame, IN: University of Notre Dame Press, 2007): 59–70.

[12] For the gap in male population replacement among peasant families, see Sylvia L. Thrupp, "The Problem of Replacement-Rates in Late Medieval English Population," *The Economic History Review* 18.1 (1965): 101–19.

And yet, in typical fashion, the strictness of Chaucer's condemnation is modulated by his fascination with the technological and emotional frameworks that have facilitated such aberrant possibilities. His narrative conclusions are typically orthodox, his depictions of human labor and human creative potential always inferior to those wrought by God through the mechanisms of gendered human flesh. At the same time, however, Chaucer explores with avid detail those very reproductive strategies of which he so strongly disapproves. He appears intellectually engaged by the almost aggressive erudition that he associates with alchemists and philosophers, while simultaneously cognizant of the moral and religious failings of their experimentation. We may read this as another of Chaucer's breaks with empiricism as the means of acquiring knowledge and certainty, similar to his condemnation of Walter's testing strategies in an earlier chapter. At the same time, however, Chaucer is also fascinated by how such strategies operate, and how the creative desires and labors of human beings are made manifest in a world whose sources of data and links with ancient philosophy are exponentially expanding. Innovative forms of generation are doomed to failure, Chaucer writes, but the desire to generate and create by whatever means available is fundamentally human, both in terms of its universality and in its ultimate epistemological frailty.

Conceiving with God: the *Second Nun's Tale*

In Fragment VIII of *The Canterbury Tales*, Chaucer offers up a pair of stories about partner-based production, narrated by the Second Nun and by the Canon's Yeoman, in turn. The former relates a hagiographic account of the "Life of St. Cecilia," explicitly drawn from an authoritative Church-approved source, the *legenda* authored by Brother Jacob of Genoa.[13] In contrast, the latter offers up a bipartite account of a series of alchemical attempts, even though the practice of alchemy had been banned by Pope John XXII in the bull, "*Spondent quas non exhibent*" (1317). Scholars have traditionally seen the two *Tales* either as unlinked apart from placement, or deliberately juxtaposed in order to highlight virtue's opposition to sin.[14] Yet as Jennifer Sisk notes, that dialectic of polarity not only operates between the discrete *Tales*, but also within them. Sisk locates these encounters with binarization as part of an epistemological nostalgia, as both nun and alchemical apprentice confront, and long for, the more primitive yet more knowledgeable

---

[13] Chaucer gives the attribution to Jacob of Genoa with a Latin insertion located between SNT 84 and SNT 85.

[14] Joseph Grennen offers up an excellent summation of such contrasts between the two from the work of Marchette Chute, Raymond Preston, and Charles Muscatine respectively. Grennen summarizes the contrast as "some more or less perfunctory statement about the contrast they provide—honesty, piety, and the odor of sanctity being opposed to duplicity, avarice, and the sulphurous fumes of the alchemists' laboratories." Joseph E. Grennen, "Saint Cecilia's 'Chemical Wedding': The Unity of the 'Canterbury Tales,' Fragment VIII," *The Journal of English and German Philology* 65.3 (July 1966): 466–81, at 466.

ideals of past practitioners.[15] In this chapter I likewise identify an internal system of binarization within each *Tale*; however, where Sisk saw such oppositions pointing to the past, I argue that instead they are meant to implicate Chaucer's narrators in specific, polarized visions of man's reproductive future. Each character looks back upon the past for procreative inspiration, but that retrospective impulse never escapes the greater sense of propulsion to some future generation.

The internal contraries of the *Second Nun's Tale* have been paralleled to the alchemical process as a whole. Joseph Grennen argues that we may see St Cecilia's marriage and martyrdom as a metaphorical invocation of alchemy's "chemical wedding," albeit one that serves primarily to indict alchemy as "a perversion of orthodox religious ideals such as zeal and perseverance, and as a profane parody of the divine work of Creation and an unwittingly sacrilegious distortion of the central mystery of the Christian faith."[16] Similarly, Bruce Rosenberg cites the wide diversity of contraries within the two linked *Tales* to argue that "the philosophical polarity of Fragment G then, embodies one of the most debated intellectual problems of the Middle Ages: reason and revelation," while Alcuin Blamires summarizes the fragment as a "polarity of busy fruitfulness on the one hand, and on the other hand a heap of barren inchoate thoughts."[17] These explorations of medieval contraries provide an excellent analysis of the scientific necessity of contraries for alchemical production, but they avoid the question of human generation almost entirely. On the contrary, human generation appears to me as the essential productive process (both religious and scientific in its categorization) against which alchemy or poetic productions must be compared.[18] In short, the fragment is rife with contraries not because that is the nature of alchemy, but because that is the nature of human reproduction according to medieval thought, and therefore the binaries of "sterile science" and "fruitful faith" operate only to the extent that the technologies and ideologies of procreation allow.

The Second Nun's aspiration to fruitfulness focuses upon her literary production, even as the Canon's Yeoman's emphasizes a more financial product.[19] In the *Prologue* to her *Tale*, the Second Nun therefore can turn deliberately to reflect upon a devotional past, remembering the reproductive possibilities offered up by

---

[15] Jennifer L. Sisk, "Religion, Alchemy, and Nostalgic Idealism in Fragment VIII of the *Canterbury Tales*," *Studies in the Age of Chaucer* 32 (2010): 152, 171–7.

[16] Grennen, "St. Cecilia's Chemical Wedding," 466–7.

[17] Bruce A. Rosenberg, "The Contrary Tales of the Second Nun and the Canon's Yeoman," *The Chaucer Review* 2.4 (Spring 1968): 278–91, at 289; Blamires, *Chaucer, Ethics, and Gender*, 214.

[18] This is where I differ from Robert Longsworth's reading of both *Tales* from Fragment VIII as invested in an epistemology of transformation, because while certainly both the Canon and Cecilia wish to transform the objects and people before them into something new, they also go much further than that, to articulate their desire explicitly as one for the power of generation; the changes that they demand in the objects of their attention is so great, it is as if the objects (or people) have been not just transformed but created anew. Robert Longsworth, "Privileged Knowledge: St. Cecilia and the Alchemist in the 'Canterbury Tales,'" *The Chaucer Review* 27.1 (1992): 87–96.

[19] For a longer discussion of the Second Nun's "fruitfulness" as a product of her faith, see Blamires, *Chaucer, Ethics, and Gender*, 212–14.

the Christian tradition as she muses upon how best to go about to produce her book. More specifically, she explores the spectrum of procreative partnership, moving rapidly between allegory, dogma, and biological science, as she searches for someone or something which whom she can join in a de-eroticized yet not desexed coupling. Thus, she begins with an invocation of human productive qualities, imagining herself coming together in succession with Idleness and with "hire contrarie" (SNT 4), Busyness. To attack Idleness as a potential partner for the human desiring to create, the nun begins with an attack upon Idleness's qualifications as a conceptive mate, calling it, "the ministre and the norice unto vices," (SNT 1–2). Her metaphors invoke reproduction, while also displacing it; they imagine Idleness instructing and nurturing the vices, but as an externalized figure, a spiritual rather than biological parent. The actual vices are born within the bodies of the men and women who fall prey to the sin. In other words, Idleness is a bad partner for a parent, an evil shadow of the "good" spiritual parents (such as those created through the baptismal rite) who help to nurture virtues within a child. This point is underlined by another negation of Idleness's creative capacity. "Ydlenesse is roten slogardye,/Of which ther nevere comth no good n'encrees" (SNT 17–18). Idleness is condemned both for what it produces and what it does not.

Moreover, by alienating men from their proper productive partner, "leveful bisynesse" (SNT 5), Idleness also serves to turn men away from creation, towards destruction and an excess of consumption. Those who join with this figure live "oonly to slepe, and for to ete and drynke,/And to devouren al that othere swynke" (SNT 20–1).[20] To partner with Idleness is to turn oneself entirely over to the animalistic impulses of the human body. And yet copulation and conception, while seemingly natural and animalistic impulses, are excluded from the Second Nun's characterization of the dangers of creating with Idleness. Her vision of an exclusively corporeal, non-reasoning creature is one that is fundamentally sterile, a creature in a chain of endless consumption, producing only new variations of nothing. In an apophatic sense, therefore, the acts of eating, drinking, and sleeping become negative creative activity; they are actions that, when partnered with Idleness, conceive destruction and "greet confusioun" (SNT 23).

Instead, the Second Nun will couple with "faithful bisynesse" (SNT 24) to produce a translation of St Cecilia's "glorious lif and passioun" (SNT 26). And yet for all her renunciation of Idleness and praise of its contrary, the Second Nun does not appear to think very highly of busyness as a conceptive partner either.[21] She has

---

[20] This sentiment is repeated in other devotional works, such as in the *Book of Vices and Virtues*: "Hie [asolkenesse] me haveth imaked hevy and slaw on godes weorkes thurh idelnesse; hie me haveth ofte idon eten othermannes sare swink all un-of-earned." *Vices and Virtues: Being a Soul's Confession of its Sins with Reason's Descriptions of the Virtues, A Middle English Dialogue of about 1200 A.D.* Vol. 1, ed. F. Holthausen (London: Oxford University Press for the Early English Text Society, 1888) 2–3.

[21] Despite the Second Nun's presentation of herself as caught between a fully polarized binary of idleness and busyness, Gregory Sadlak observes that religious or academic workers such as the Nun occupied a separate category of activity in which both models were understood to overlap. These workers participated in a model of "productive idleness," or *otium negotium*, that allowed them to

given us four verses arguing against the former, but when at last she has dismissed it and turned to the allegorical good, she immediately starts looking for yet another new partner for her production. Instead of relying upon an active form of labor as her productive counterpart, the Second Nun turns to the Virgin Mary, in a classical mode of poetic invocation. Unlike the ancient muses however, the Virgin Mary's value as a conceptive partner is well established by the Christian dogma of her cult. She has already served to reproduce as the partner of God; the Second Nun hopes that the Virgin will condescend to partner her as well ("do me endite/Thy maydens deeth" [SNT 32]).

The Second Nun's plea to the Virgin Mary to join with her to conceive the story is remarkably like the earlier invocation of the Prioress, begging the Virgin Mary to do the same with her. Both women tie the conceptive requirements of creating a *Tale* directly to Mary's experience of creating the Son of God. The Prioress cries:

> Of whos [Mary's] vertu, whan he thyn herte lighte,
> Conceyved was the Fadres sapience,
> Help me to telle it in thy reverence!
>
> (PrT 471–3)

The Prioress appears to see no strangeness or arrogance in juxtaposing Mary's success at conceiving of the Father's "sapience" with her desire for Mary to help her in turn conceive of wisdom. The Virgin brought the former into the world, and so the Prioress seems to expect that the Virgin will have no qualms at doing the same with her own. Similarly, the Second Nun turns towards retelling the Annunciation/Nativity narrative as an essential component of her request for conceptive aid.

> Thow nobledest so ferforth our nature,
> That no desdeyn the Makere hadde of kynde
> His Sone in blood and flesh to clothe and wynde.
> Withinne the cloister blisful of thy sydis
> Took mannes shap the eterneel love and pees.
>
> [SNT 40–4]

Mary's skill at creation is remarkable.[22] Surely, both religious women ask, she would not be opposed to helping them to generate as well?

---

produce outside of more traditional labor patterns. Gregory M. Sadlak, "Otium, Negotium, and the Fear of Acedia in the Writings of England's Late Medieval Ricardian Poets," *Idleness, Indolence and Leisure in English Literature*, ed. Monika Fludernik and Miriam Nandi (New York: Palgrave MacMillan, 2014): 17–40, at 31–2.

---

[22] Corey Marvin indeed argues that even the *Alma redemptoris mater* becomes a maternal space within the *Tale*, reinforced by Mary's essential maternity, and "drawing [the clergeon] to the very

However, there is a problem with these nuns' aspirations. The perfection of the divine conception is predicated upon a sexed version of God, thus fulfilling the scientific and theological understandings of procreation as something that happens between a man and a woman. Indeed, the version of Mary's conception of Jesus that both women recount emphasizes its alignment with traditional medieval theories of fetal generation. It is a desexualized and (sometimes, as in the Prioress's metaphor of God "lighting Mary's heart," an almost painfully) allegorized conceptive act, but it is still a recognizably Aristotelian image of male spirit acting upon female matter to craft a child. Even as spiritual allegory, medieval understandings of procreation restricted catalytic generative activity to men alone.

Medieval religious women's use of procreation as allegory for spiritual triumph similarly emphasized the female role as one of reception and gestation. Nicole Rice reads the late medieval devotional text, *The Book of the Mother*, as arguing that, "preaching authority need not be wrested away from official authorities but may perhaps be fruitfully embodied alongside them."[23] In other words there was a way for devout women to mimic Mary to gain a spiritual authority through their reception of men's seeds of faith, and thus to perform as women and as mothers even as simultaneously they lived chastely. Such an intellectual scheme depends upon a rigid gender binary and a fluid approach to embodiment; the process of insemination must remain emphatically metaphorical, and the feminine virtue of receptivity must remain eager in its passivity. This is the type of spiritual insemination that the Prioress imagines taking place within her body, through the corporeal (but de-eroticized) image of the lighting of a woman's heart. Such a metaphor is of the flesh without being fleshly, generative without being graphic in its physiology.

The Second Nun's understanding of the divine conception is, in contrast, quite visceral. She imagines God clothing and winding his son in Mary's most intimate flesh and blood, with no disdain for kynde and apparently no disdain for the natural ways that a child was thought to take shape from the retention of the menses. This actually then becomes quite theologically interesting, since as Charles Wood has documented, Church doctors were deeply divided on the existence of Mary's menses.[24] The Second Nun does not commit to a theory of Marian menstrual emission (a somewhat radical precept due to the association of the menstrual flow with the curse of Eve), but she certainly does seem to imagine a Mary who has retained the menstrual material of blood and humoral excess upon which God

threshold of the symbolic." Within such a reading, Mary not only creates and nurtures the divine, but she also nurtures and brings forth language, meaning, and the symbolic-determined entry into selfhood. Corey J. Marvin, "'I Will Thee Not Forsake'" The Kristevan Maternal Space in Chaucer's *Prioress's Tale* and John of Garland's *Stella maris*," *Exemplaria* 8.1 (1996): 35–58, at 45.

---

[23] Nicole R. Rice, *Lay Piety and Religious Discipline in Middle English Literature* (Cambridge: Cambridge University Press, 2008): 124–6.
[24] Charles T. Wood, "The Doctors' Dilemma: Sin, Salvation, and the Menstrual Cycle in Medieval Thought," *Speculum* 56.4 (October 1981): 710–27.

will work his "spermatic" power. Her reference to Mary as a flower ("that flour of virgines" [SNT 29]) manages to be both courtly and anatomical, invoking the symbolic attribution of flowers with maternal menstrual matter while simultaneously idealizing the association through poetic euphemism.[25] Mary's fruitfulness is tied analogically to her flowering blood; as Albertus Magnus opines, "Just as flowers exist for the production of the fruit, so the menses relate to the production of the fetus."[26] The Second Nun demonstrates an awareness of the Virgin Mary as a bleeding, female body, in a moment reminiscent of Julian of Norwich's association of Christ with (to quote Liz Herbert McAvoy) "a woman's purging menstrual blood as well as the more copious blood-loss of childbirth."[27] Her admiration for the Virgin is predicated not upon a decorporealized vision of spiritual maternity, but rather upon an understanding of the virgin as a woman whose flesh will be twisted to feed her fetus, whose womb is not only "a blisful cloister" but also full of menstrual tissue (and no less blissful for that).[28]

Both the Second Nun and the Prioress value Mary for her capacity to produce fruit, although their own aspirations in that direction are far more modest. And yet since both women understand conception as facilitated through the conjoining of active and passive powers, they must reorient the power dynamic between themselves and the Virgin Mary in order to accomplish a successful generation of their textual offspring. The same-sex partnership that they hope for must be one predicated upon hierarchies of power that may symbolize the sexual act, without recreating it. The Prioress establishes this power hierarchy by infantilizing her own body so as to de-eroticize it, referring to herself as a "child of twelf month oold, or lesse" (PrT 484). The Prioress "may the weighte nat susteene" (PrT 483) and so she opts out of any claim to the productive process, requesting that the Virgin instead ventriloquize her voice. Indeed, the Prioress's *Prologue* emphasizes the mechanisms of dissemination to the full exclusion of any metaphors of

---

[25] One late medieval edition of the *Trotula* was renamed *Flos mulierum*, for example, in reflection of this nomenclature for the menses. Monica H. Green, "From 'Diseases of Women' to 'Secrets of Women:' The Transformation of Gynecological Literature in the Later Middle Ages," *Journal of Medieval and Early Modern Studies* 30.1 (2000): 5–39, at 26.

[26] Albertus Magnus, *Questions Concerning Aristotle's On Animals*, 306.

[27] Liz Herbert McAvoy, "'The Moders Service': Motherhood as Matrix in Julian of Norwich," *Mystics Quarterly* 24.4 (December 1998): 181–97, at 189.

[28] It is important to acknowledge Catherine Sanok's point that the blissfulness of the Second Nun's vision of Mary is itself quite restrictive in its spatial allowance for female authority. Sanok writes: "The Second Nun's strongest argument for women's performance of sacred speech itself recalls the restriction of that speech to the intensely private space of the womblike cloister." Catherine Sanok, "Performing Feminine Sanctity in Late Medieval England: Parish Guilds, Saints' Plays, and the *Second Nun's Tale*," *Journal of Medieval and Early Modern Studies* 32.2 (Spring 2002): 269–303, at 291. The contrast for Sanok between public/private female speech is particularly stark, since she is comparing the *Tale* to dramatic performances of female legends. For this study, on the other hand, domestic legitimations of speech and authority are indivisible from their public iterations, since Chaucer's vision of poetic authorship allows both for private creation and public dissemination. Furthermore, I would say that while the womb may be the Virgin's cloister, the global ascendance of her Son/Word proves for the Nun how powerfully public the privately produced may become.

production. "O Lord, oure Lord, thy name how merveillous/Is in this large world ysprad" (PrT 453–4) exclaims the Prioress, before she notes that "to telle a storie I wol do my labour" (PrT 463). The story that the Prioress tells will spread God's name and praise, but her labor is only to further the dissemination of other's (Mary's) conceptions. The only "original" conceptive or productive activity in the story is God's lighting of Mary's heart. The Prioress in turn begs to be allowed to partake of that conception without initiating one of her own. She pleads for Mary to "getest us the lyght, of thy preyere" (PrT 479), but not to light a new fire within the Prioress's own flesh. The Prioress wishes to remain product not producer, to borrow her words and her prayers from the divine Creation rather than have new ones created within her vessel.

In contrast, the Second Nun refuses to abdicate her role as a partner in the conception of her story. While she too turns to Mary as the natural, female object of her prayers, she does not merely want to borrow the light of Mary's conception of Christ, but rather for Mary to aid her in her own conception of holy words. To accomplish this productive act, the Second Nun explores a multitude of active/passive pairings to stand in for the two women's bodies, and thus de-eroticize the conceptive moment. The Second Nun suggests that Mary might serve as her "sonne" (SNT 52), her "leche," (SNT 56), her "advocat" (SNT 68), and her "light" (SNT 71). In each scenario, the Second Nun imagines Mary taking on a masculine conceptive role. Mary will be the one who lights the Nun's heart, who stirs the Nun's passive matter with the active energy of the Virgin's spiritual seed. Since the conceptive catalyst was definitionally male, then it is far safer and less radical for the Second Nun to imagine herself as the passive, female matter upon which the divine will, embodied by the Virgin Mary, will conceive a story. Mary's divine status allows for a flexibility in her gendering; she is a woman in comparison to God, but she can act like a man in comparison to the humble Second Nun.

The Second Nun's very title within the poem establishes her as the inferior and lesser partner in a female relationship. When establishing the humility of her flesh and of her capacities as a narrator, she likewise articulates her personal status in terms of an evaluation of woman vs. woman. While the Prioress portrayed herself as an infant child "on the brest soukynge" (PrT 458), the Second Nun articulates her identity as that of an adult human, undermined not only by individual inadequacies, but rather by the general frailties of fallen men and women. "I, unworthy sone of Eve" (SNT 62), the Nun names herself, in a moment of gender fluidity and transgression that signifies strongly for the rest of the poem. The paradox of a woman referring to herself as a son of Eve, rather than a daughter, parallels the Nun's earlier reference to the Virgin as "Mayde and Mooder, doghter of thy Sone" (SNT 36). The Nun explores the entire spectrum of familial and sexual paradox engendered by the Virgin's reproductive incarnation of her God. She speaks of "Thow humble, and heigh over every creature" (SNT 39) and "Virgine wemmelees,/Baar of thy body" (SNT 47–8), emphasizing the extent to which the Virgin Mary's existence as virgin and mother challenges the limits of signification and human interpretation. The Nun notes as well how the Virgin embodies a crisis of lineage—"Thow Cristes mooder, doghter deere of Anne" (SNT 70)—caught between the bonds of human blood and divine miracle. The Virgin Mother represents a conflict between epistemology and genealogy on one side, and faith on the other. Thus, while the Prioress turned to the Virgin when speaking her *Tale* for aid to avoid any inference of sexual fluidity, the Second Nun turns to the Virgin for assistance in imagining a form of poetic and spiritual generation both sexed and sexless.

Within her *Invocacio ad Mariam*, the Nun therefore lays out the terms of the relationship that she desires with the Virgin Mary. The Nun's soul is tied down by "the contagioun/Of my body" (SNT 72-3), and her body in turn is plagued by "the wighte/Of erthely lust and fals affeccioun" (SNT 73-4). In other words, her identity as a poet is characterized by precisely those corporeal attributes whose miraculous absence in the Virgin Mary placed her beyond nature ("Thiw nobledest so ferforth oure nature" [SNT 40]). Moreover, the Nun is able to demonstrate how fully her own flesh is already bound by the binary; she is the fusion of holy soul and damnable skin. If her soul will suffer the disease of its vessel, then surely the Virgin might condescend to work her spirit within a human form. For, as the Nun reminds the Virgin, "no desdeyn the Makere hadde of kynde" (SNT 41), and thus how could the Virgin, herself born in human flesh, disdain to couple with that inferior matter which her own Maker nevertheless judged not unworthy of impregnation? The Nun calls on Mary:

> Now help, thow meeke and blisful faire mayde
> Me, flemed wrecche, in this desert of galle;
> Thynk on the womman Cananee, that sayde
> That whelpes eten somme of the crommes
> That from hir lords table been yfalle;
> And though that I, unworthy sone of Eve,
> Be sinful, yet accepte my bileve
>
> (SNT 57-63)

The Canaanite woman, whom the Nun references (Mark 7:24-31), called on Christ on behalf of her daughter, who had been possessed by demons.[29] Christ initially refused to help, claiming that he had been sent only to help the children of Israel. But, in her humility, her faith, and her insistence, the Canaanite woman won a divine healing for her daughter too.

There is thus a series of couplings referenced within the Bible verse, all of which the Second Nun draws upon in her invocation of the Virgin. She wishes the Virgin to join with her like Christ did with the Canaanite woman—the active

---

[29] For a discussion of the larger parallels between the Canaanite woman and the Second Nun, particularly as women wielding authoritative speech, see Elizabeth A. Dobbs, "The Canaanite Woman, the Second Nun, and Saint Cecilia," *Christianity & Literature* 62.2 (2013): 203–22.

power of a divine man coming together with the weak passivity of a helpless human woman to conceive a miracle. But, she also highlights a number of coexistent, if less dominant, dualities characterized by the combination of the strong with the weak: mother and possessed daughter, Hebrews and Canaanites, lords and hungry dogs. Moreover, the Nun transforms those combinations of contraries to reinforce the reproductive resonances of their verbal union; for example, rather than speak of "dogs" like the Canaanite woman did in the Bile, the Nun speaks of "whelps," grounding her Scriptural metaphor not only in a dichotomy of the animal vs. human, but of the adult and the newborn as well. The world she invokes for the Virgin Mary is a world in which creation occurs through the condescension of the strong to the weak, the "male-like" to the "female-like," and in which even miracles cannot escape their genealogies.

Both forms of creation (Mary's with God, and the Second Nun's with Mary) are thus positioned outside the erotic copulation typically associated with the conceptive act; even as the soul joins with the body to create life, the divine may combine with the human to sexlessly produce holy words. And yet generation (even of spiritual texts or poetry) remained such a profoundly corporeal and sexed process for medieval men and women that even this faithful Nun cannot imagine a creative process that could function without reference to the power differential at the heart of medieval conceptive theory. The generative partnership is thus inherently sexed even when it is de-eroticized, although sex and power are treated as exchangeable variables. Thus it would not be enough for the Virgin Mary to join with the Second Nun as equals, or as one woman with another woman. She must instead dominate the Nun, even as the Nun also imagines her readers dominating her text ("pray yow that ye wole my werk amende" [SNT 84]). The Nun only understands production through the domination of one contrary by another; she desires the Virgin to provide the seeds for her creation, but, failing that, she is also willing to accept the seeds and revisions of those who wish retrospectively to procreate her poems.

The Nun is aided in her poetic conceptions by the matter of her story, the *Life of St. Cecilia*. Cecilia's very name offers a diversity of contrary conjoinings, which the Nun imagines as occurring through the conceptive couplings of grammar and etymology.

> Cecile, as I written fynde,
> Is joynded, by a manere conjoynynge
> Of 'hevene' and 'Lia'; and heere, in figurynge,
> The 'hevene' is set for thoght of hoolynesse,
> And 'Lia' for hire lastynge bisynesse.
>
> [SNT 94–8]

Cecilia's name is produced through the joining of the holiness of heaven with the busyness of the world, and understood through a mode of conceptive "figuring" reinforced by human intellect. But even as in the Nun's earlier invocation of Mary, she provides an excess of conjoinings to reinforce the vision of production that she is endorsing. Thus Cecile is also derived from "hevene and "leos" (SNT 103), and a diversity of characteristics (some complementary, some contradictory) is provided for her signification. The flexibility of Cecilia's etymological origins attests to the general fluidity of production and productive partnerships within the poem.

These etymological joinings are inherently sexed, if one reads the sexual binary through ethical hierarchies and active/passive dichotomies. The second nominalistic metaphor in particular, that of "hevene" and "leos" (the latter meaning "'peple' in Englisshe" [SNT 106]), emphasizes the joining of disparities—one symbolizing (heavenly) spirit and the other dull, base matter. Cecilia's name thus privileges the masculine and the heavenly—those elements that have worked on common, humble humanity to transform sinful flesh into something holy, into St Cecilia. Moreover, the active, catalytic nature of sanctity, in contrast to the human matter that it is its purpose to mold and shape, allows St Cecilia, through her sanctity, to take an active, male-designated role in her own productions. While Chaucer's Nuns prayed for God to light their hearts and stir their prayers, St Cecilia stands as her own light. In her *Prologue*, the Second Nun repetitively asserts Cecilia's status as burning flame.

> And right so as thise philosophres write
> That hevene is swift and round and eek brennynge,
> Right so was faire Cecilie the white...
> And brennynge evere in charite ful brighte.
>
> (SNT (113–5, 118)

Cecilia is the flame that works on others' hearts; she is the spermatic spirit that turns passive matter into a new life. She is not only the flame, however, she is the "burning." Cecilia is the very act of combustion. She is always at the very moment of her activity, aggressively present tense in the minds of the men who "goostly in this mayden free/Seyen of feyth the magnanymytee" (SNT 109–10).

The story of a virgin martyr might initially appear a rather unlikely place to find such an enthusiasm for production through sexed collaboration. The "Life of St Cecilia," particularly as depicted within the Second Nun's Tale, actually functions naturally around this rhetoric. There is of course the emphasis on genealogy typically found in saints' lives; Cecilia's earthly corpus is a result of the productive joinings of "Romayns and of noble kynde" (SNT121). But more significantly, the vita as a whole may be read as a story about partnerships, and about creating a desired product through communal, paired labor. Cecilia, in her progress from young girl to authoritative saint, forms an almost staggering number of labor-based partnerships, while nevertheless also remaining partnered with Jesus. Her major allies on her holy mission include her husband Valerian, his brother Tiberius, and Pope Urban, not to mention the angel who guards her body and more minor characters such as Maximus, the Roman officer who suffers martyrdom. Her partnerships with these men are procreative, in that they produce new Christian converts. However, radically it is Cecilia herself who appears to be the active force in these conceptive pairings, working with her words upon the pagan matter of these male bodies in order to produce within them a new Christian soul. As Pope Urban remarks:

> For thilke spouse that she took but now
> Ful lyk a fiers leoun, she sendeth heere,
> As meke as evere was any lomb, to yow!
>
> (SNT 197–9)

Cecilia has taken Valerian and made something new out of him.[30] Similarly, Tiberius claims to have been "chaunged...al in another kynde" (SNT 252). She works on pagan men as if they were women and she a man, conceiving with them the spiritual offspring she desires.

Yet if Cecilia occupies the male conceptive role in her relations with other human, she nevertheless plays the female conceptive role when she joins with God. In her preaching to her followers, Cecilia highlights Jesus as creator and generator of the world around them. "That Fadres Sone hath alle thyng ywroght,/ And al that wroght is with a skillful thoght" (SNT 326–7). Not only is Jesus the sole progenitor of the world's creations, but he alone is able to do so without a conceptive partner, depending upon only a non-corporeal thought to drive his generations. The Divine Creation is singularly affected, and thus singular beyond belief. This unique capacity to produce without collaboration is in turn highlighted by Cecilia's emphasis upon the limits of creative authority of the pagan ruler, Almachius. Almachius makes it clear that his powers of production are given and restricted by a larger communal grouping of princes.

> "Han noght oure myghty princes to me yiven,
> Ye bothe power and auctoritee
> To maken folk to dyen or to lyven?"
>
> (SNT 470–2)

Almachius judges the collaborative distribution of royal power to be an enhancement of his individual authority, but it only serves to highlight the contrast between his inadequate skills of production and those of Jesus, who can create alone, with

---

[30] This authority that Cecilia is able to wield within her marriage and her marriage bed is so unique from her contemporaries' experience that David Raybin argues that the Second Nun's Tale's treatment of sex is less of an exemplum for medieval women and more of a commentary on "how rare, connubially impractical, and generally unworldly real-life saintly behavior actually is." David Raybin, "Chaucer's Creation and Recreation of the 'Lyf of Seynt Cecile,'" *The Chaucer Review* 32.2 (1997): 196–212, at 201. The same can be said of Cecilia's reproductive behavior; most medieval husbands wanted far more tangible offspring.

only a thought. Cecilia emphasizes how profoundly such a collaborative mode of sovereignty renders Almachius inferior to God by responding, "thy princes han thee maked/Ministre of deeth" (SNT 484–5). Mortal rulers may be made and created by other men, and their existence is dependent upon the vagaries of human partnerings.

The creations of God are performed alone. But, weak woman that she is, Cecilia needs assistance, and a companion, for the procreative act. And thus, Jesus does not only create in isolation; he joins with Cecilia as his partner as well, to create new virtues within the world. When Pope Urban is confronted with Valerian's desire to convert to Christianity, he praises the productivity of Jesus's joining with Cecilia.

> "Almyghty Lord, O Jhesu Crist," quod he,
> "Sower of chast conseil, hierde of us alle,
> The fruyt of thilke seed of chastitee
> That thou hast sowe in Cecile, taak to thee!"
>
> (SNT 191–4)

The Pope's vision of Christ's stimulation of sanctity within his human followers moves provocatively between its metaphors of productivity, toying with a language of erotics before immediately disavowing its associations. Thus, the Lord is a "sower" but only of chaste council; he has planted seed within Cecile, but paradoxically that seed is the seed of chastity. Chaucer's Second Nun offers a sharply sexualized image of Christ's insemination of Cecilia, but quickly moves to discount the content of these inseminations. Valerian (along with the other Christians whom Cecilia has converted) is thus not only Cecilia's husband but also her child; he is the fruit that Jesus has sown within her womb. Cecilia may take the masculine role of active creator with the pagan men, but with Jesus she reverts back to the feminine, passive designation as vessel and shapeable matter.[31]

The Second Nun thus offers up a story that contains multiple models of sexed production, with a flexible designation of who must assume the male and female sexual roles. This is in many ways a fantasy of generation, with its separation of sexed production from the sexual act, and its deprioritization of sex assignment in favor of a fluid, almost meritocratic model of procreation. It is a model grounded upon the successes and perfections of generation within a distant yet omnipresent past, citing the miraculous decorporealized modes of reproduction for the Virgin Mary and St Cecilia not from the nostalgia of loss, but rather with the hope of such flexible avenues of procreation in the future. The Second Nun may have sworn a vow of chastity, but she too aspires to produce "withinne the

---

[31] Karen Arthur similarly speaks of St. Cecilia's "fus[ion] of masculine and feminine roles" in regards to her religious vocation and the authorizations of her virginity. Karen Arthur, "Equivocal Subjectivity in Chaucer's 'Second Nun's Prologue and Tale,'" *The Chaucer Review* 32.3 (1998): 217–31, at 220.

cloistre blisful of [her] sydis," to serve as the fecund matter for another's power and thus fulfill the act of creation with her newborn text.

Conceiving with Chemistry: the *Canon's Yeoman's Tale*

In many ways the *Canon's Yeoman's Tale* appears as a bastardized version of the *Second Nun's Tale*. It too is concerned with how one may generate and create, and what types of partnerships may prove necessary for the process. However, the aspiring "parents" of the *Tale* have turned to a "slidynge science" (CYT 732) rather than to the miracles of God for inspiration, and have suffered accordingly. Indeed, in their desire to create new, productive transformations through the mediation of alchemy, these men (vocalized by the Yeoman) have instead created new, degraded versions of themselves. Chaucer seems to differentiate between the two models of creation according to their motivation. The Second Nun saw her generative labor as stemming from the glorification of St Cecilia; the Canon and his Yeoman desire generation as a form of multiplying and thus a form of greed. The desire to multiply, to generate for personal gain, is thus vilified within the *Canon's Yeoman's Tale*, even as the scientific sources to which the men turn are vilified in comparison with the religious sources so readily available.[32]

Moreover, the men find themselves in the same situation as the Prioress and the Second Nun had done; namely, trying to engage in a likeness of human reproduction without an appropriately sexed productive partner. And yet while the two religious women confronted this challenge by embracing a flexible attribution of conceptive sex (without contradicting the power hierarchies therein contained), the alchemists attempt to force their materials to combine in ways that are incapable of leading to conception. Two centuries after Chaucer wrote the *Canon's Yeoman's Tale*, as Katharine Eggert has argued, early modern alchemists would come to reflect upon the potential exclusion of women from the chemical conceptive process as a *strength* of the science, denoting a new spectrum of reproductive configurations from the parthenogenetic homunculus born outside the female body to the tripartite spermatic model of Paracelsus.[33] Indeed, even medieval alchemical texts (such as those included within the *Secretum Secretorum*) mark positive models of queer production through the linkage of human and mineral reproductive

---

[32] Robert Epstein argues that "Chaucer reviles alchemy as the obscurantist antithesis of both scientific technology and economics which are logical systems that, while artificial, can only be understood rationally and empirically." Robert Epstein, "Dismal Science: Chaucer and Gower on Alchemy and Economy," *Studies in the Age of Chaucer* 36 (2014): 209–48, at 248. I find Chaucer's observations of science and economics as artificial and unnatural to be far more damning than Epstein does, and I conclude in contrast that Chaucer's condemnation of alchemy originates not from its opposition to these other systems, but rather according to its participation with them.

[33] Katherine Eggert, *Disknowledge: Literature, Alchemy, and the End of Humanism in Renaissance England* (Philadelphia, PA: University of Pennsylvania Press, 2015): 157–68, 157–68.

theory.[34] Thus, Chaucer's negative depiction of the non-normative reproductive techniques capable with scientific innovation was far from inevitable, and can be understood as an individual and reactionary response to theories of mineral generation and transformation, even those by classical scholars whose work Chaucer treats as authoritative elsewhere.[35]

Instead of highlighting the opportunities that a new proliferation of scientific texts offered for reshaping the traditional models of how reproduction works, the Yeoman offers a harsh denunciation of those who try to reproduce with the "wrong tools." The generative problem that the men face with one another is a problem of *prima materia* (to borrow a term from alchemical theory). The matter upon which the male spirit must work in order to conceive must be of a sufficient and gendered quantity to ensure the production of offspring.

There is a significant conflict between medieval Church and Science, however, in reference to this philosophy. Alan of Lille represents the dogmatic position of the Church in a manner similar to Chaucer, claiming of men who seek to reproduce with other men, "That man in whose case a simple conversion in an Art causes Nature's Laws to come to naught, is pushing logic too far. He hammers on an anvil which issues no seeds."[36] It is worth noting here that Alan of Lille conceptualizes sodomy as a process almost identical to procreative sex (still involving the union of hammer and anvil) rather than as one involving two hammers or two anvils. It is merely the anus's insufficiencies as conceptive matter that renders the sexual act non-procreative here, rather than any difficulties in fit or function. There seems therefore to be an implicit theory here that the hammer's *desire* to pound any and all anvils available is natural in and of itself, but rather that for the sake of its productivity as a tool, the hammer must seek out an anvil capable of producing seed (according to the Galenic two-seed model of reproduction). Alan's argument is in fact rather destroyed by the widespread, if rather inconsistently applied, transition of medieval intellectuals to a belief by Chaucer's time in Aristotle's one seed, one matter theory. From an Aristotelian perspective, if all productivity is contained in the hammer, then as long as the anvil is composed of passive matter (as Alan appears to assume it is), then perhaps sodomy too might prove to be procreative sex?

Church theologians refused to consider this possibility, even when, like Albertus Magnus, they thoroughly identified with an Aristotelian vision of the reproductive world. Medieval scientists, on the other hand, were far more willing to explore the potential in a deprioritization of the maternal conceptive role from mutual

---

[34] Cf. Cynthia Masson, "Queer Copulation and the Pursuit of Divine Conjunction in Two Middle English Alchemical Poems," *Intersections of Sexuality and the Divine in Medieval Culture: The Word Made Flesh*, ed. Susannah Mary Chewning (New York: Routledge, 2005): 37–48.

[35] This is particularly true of Chaucer's willingness to treat Aristotle as an authority on the human and animal body, but not the mineral form.

[36] Alan of Lille, *Plaint of Nature*, 69.

inseminator to latent matter. The authors of the *De secretum mulierum*, for example, speculate on alternative forms of conception that continue to rely upon male sperm as a catalyst but embrace a new variety of "maternal" matter. One of the commentators on the text, for example, states as biological fact that, "If a cat ejaculated on some sage, and a man ate some of this sage, then cats would be generated in his stomach and would have to be expelled by vomiting."[37] Here the man's stomach becomes the feminized "prima materia" upon which the male active power (the feline semen) can work its procreative power. This opinion is offered as part of a duality of scientific theorization on alternative conception, that also speculates whether women can provide the catalystic sperm for their own pregnancies. The text moves fluidly, if confusingly, between the one- and two-seed theories of procreation, but asserts that yes indeed, female nocturnal emission may result in the growth of a mass of flesh within the abdomen which will represent as a false pregnancy.[38] Again we see the malleability of the conceptive matter in comparison to the power of the semen; the text even warns that such procreations do not only happen in the stomach but can occur "whenever the sperm falls elsewhere," a rather terrifying prospect.[39]

These gynecological commentaries' willingness to consider alternative modes of conception, based upon alternative materials, reflect similar trends within medieval alchemical science. The Canon, his Yeoman, and his fellow alchemists indeed appear to adhere to such radical reproductive thinking. The act of bringing the two metals together within the matrix of a clay container is an attempt to recreate theories of human generation though the conjoining of "metals with a certeyn quantitee" (CYT 900). And yet Chaucer (through the Yeoman's vocalization) immediately dismisses the possibility of such unnatural combinations succeeding. The pots break quickly, destroying the elements that they contain, in what Michael Calabrese names "a fruitless, sterile orgasm."[40] The Yeoman blames this disastrous, destructive result upon the unnaturalness of the metals' non-contrary conjoining.

> Thise metals been of so greet violence
> Oure walles mowe nat make hem resistence,
> But if they weren wrought of lym and stoon;
> They percen so, and thurgh the wal they goon.
>
> (CYT 908–11)

The spirit and matter that the alchemists are attempting to bring together are inherently incompatible. Both are active, "violent" forces in the creative process, and thus nothing can be created. The gendered vision of procreation through the

---

[37] *Women's Secrets*, ed. Lemay, 66.   [38] *Women's Secrets*, ed. Lemay, 67–8.
[39] *Women's Secrets*, ed. Lemay, 67.
[40] Michael A. Calabrese, "Meretricious Mixtures: Gold, Dung, and the 'Canon's Yeoman's Prologue and Tale,'" *The Chaucer Review* 27.3 (1993): 277–92, at 285.

conjunction of contraries, one weak and one strong, is an essential obstacle to such alchemical experiments that bring together two catalysts without the matter neces- sary for catalyzation. Such a poorly calculated joining of two active, masculine spirits cannot seem to result in productive generation. Moreover, brought together in this "unnatural" way, the two male metals become the catalyst for destruction, rather than for creation. What matter there was—the pot, each metal's own material form— is destroyed, transforming latent matter into to nothingness.

The alchemists are blind, however, to the unnaturalness of the violent and unbalanced copulations that they have attempted to effect. Instead, they attempt to blame the environment surrounding this commixtion. Particularly, they blame the pot, the one passive element of feminized material referenced within the chemical experiment.

> Some seyde it was long on the fir makynge;
> Somme seyde nay, it was on the blowyng...
> It was nat tempred as it oghte be.
>
> (CYT 922–3, 926)

They turn away from the clear causality (which the Yeoman has already identified as originating in the nature of the metals that were being brought together) to focus on the critiquing the nature of the effect. The Canon then concludes that "I am right siker that the pot was crased" (CYT 934). These avid men with their false science turn to the container of conjunction, that symbol of the womb, as if that was the cause of their mistakes, rather than looking inside it to consider the sexed properties of what it contains. Similarly, they visualize the alchemical process as if it consisted of the active power of the fire acting upon the passive material of the pot, not grasping the way both fire and pot represent merely external forces out- side the main scheme of chemical procreation.

The Canon's Yeoman grounds his exposition on the dangerous generative lures of alchemy by presenting his own body as one that has been degenerated by such false processes.

> Of his science am I never the neer.
> Al that I hadde I have lost thereby...
> Wher my colour was bothe fressh and reed,
> Now it is wan and of a leden hewe-
> And of my swynk yet blered is myn ye.
> Lo, which avantage is to multiplie!
>
> (CYT 721–2, 726–31)

The Yeoman's corporeal state has been materially damaged and comprehensively transformed by his attempts to partner the Canon in the transformation of metals.

He speaks of multiplying and of generation to remind his listeners that not all generation is healthy generation, not all creation (through alteration) to be praised.

From an Aristotelian perspective, alteration is identified with the generative state. In *De generatione and corruptione*, Aristotle notes the intellectual debate over whether "the nature of alteration and generation is the same or different."[41] In his separation between the Monists and Pluralists (concerning the status of original matter), Aristotle presents a polarized discourse between "those who construct everything out of one thing [and] necessarily identify generation and corruption with alteration" and those who "allow a plurality of kinds [and] have to distinguish alteration from generation, since for them generation and corruption occur when things come together and separate."[42] In breaking with the Pluralists, who, Aristotle claims, disavow birth itself, Aristotle offers a vision of generation that depends upon change and transformation, whether those changes represent a coming into being or a passing away. Generation and corruption are intrinsically linked, as the contraries of one another. Nature has decreed the process to be continuous and never to fail; while God "has filled up the whole in the only way that remained by making generation perpetual."[43] As Thomas Aquinas notes in his commentary on Aristotle's *Physics*, the complexities of Aristotle's arguments about generation allow for two types of generation to be conceptualized: simple generation (in which subjects move from not-being to being) and accidental generation (in which an object transforms the specificities of its beings).[44]

The Canon's Yeoman's body has therefore undergone a process of accidental generation, cousin to the simple generation of human reproduction, yet differentiated by his pre-existent state of being. Alchemists think only of multiplication, he charges, of the endless division of matter into ever more and more matter. And yet generation is also about transforming matter from one state into another, whether that matter is coal changing into silver, or a human body changing from health to weakness. Moreover, they forget that multiplication is as likely to end in its contrary, corruption, as it is likely to see generation. The inseparability of generation and corruption as concomitant aspects of creation privileges both the primacy of initial matter and the singularity of eventual loss.

> Konne he lettrure or konne he noon
> he shal fynde it al oon.
> For bothe two, by my savacioun,
> Concluden in multiplicacioun

---

[41] Aristotle, *De Generatione et Corruptione*, trans. and ed. C. J. F. Williams (Oxford: Clarendon Press, 1982):1.

[42] Aristotle, *Generatione et Corruptione*, 2.

[43] Aristotle, *Generatione et Corruptione*, 55.

[44] Thomas Aquinas, *Commentary on Aristotle's Physics*, trans. Richard J. Blackwell, Richard J. Spath, and W. Edmund Thirkel (Notre Dame, IN: Dumb Ox Books, 1999): 319–21.

> Ylike wel, whan they han al ydo,
> This is to seyn, they faillen bothe two.
>
> (CYT 846–51)

No matter how one brings together contraries, the corruption of matter is the inevitable result of any form of reproduction or generation. The Yeoman's description of his body's degeneration has many parallels in medieval devotional descriptions of the decay of man with age. As the contemporaneous text, *The Prick of Conscience,* warns, "als tyte als a man waxes alde/than waxes his kynde wayke and calde."[45] Death is the inevitable result of all generation, all attempts to multiply.[46] How foolish to accelerate that process with one's prideful, acquisitive desires!

The attempts to reproduce outside of the "natural" generative order combine that process's corruptive mortality with the absence of normative offspring. When alchemists generate together, their offspring is as queer as their hope of same-sex reproduction. In Chaucer's biting critique, these scientists are first indicted by their procreative status as men who wish to create with other men.

> "This instrument," quod he [the alchemist], "which that thou seest,
> Taake in thyn hand, and put thyself therinne
> Of this quyksilver an ounce, and heer bigynne,
> In name of Crist, to wexe a philosofre."
>
> (CYT 1119–22)

Chaucer's "instruments" are frequently, if not exclusively, references to human genitalia. The Wife of Bath, for example, famously declares, "In wyfhod wyl I use my instrument/As frely as my Makere hath it sent" (WBT 159–60). Karma Lochrie has noted the phallic resonances in the Wife of Bath's understanding of her own instrument; and yet here the instrument (belonging to a man) is a gynocentric device, a crucible.[47] The confusion of gender and even of genitalia here is Chaucer's point. These are alchemists and priests who neither know how to recognize an instrument nor how to employ it.

Moreover, the scene which Chaucer has imagined between the two men is itself a mockery of reproduction, a literal insemination of this pot with a spermatic power. Take it in your hand, the priest is told, and put the quicksilver therein and, due to the ambiguities of the syntax, perhaps put yourself therein as well. Here we see one of the essential paradoxes of alchemy's technologies of reproduction.

---

[45] Richard Morris, *Prick of Conscience*, ed. Ralph Hanna and Sarah Wood (Oxford: Published for the Early English Text Society by the Oxford University Press, 2013): 24.

[46] On medieval understandings of aging as the visible imprint of death's inevitability, see Rosenthal, *Old Age in Late Medieval England*, 178–84.

[47] Karma Lochrie, *Heterosyncrasies: Female Sexuality When Normal Wasn't* (Minneapolis: University of Minnesota Press, 2005): 71–102.

The scientists envision this alternative mode of creation as one that occurs outside of themselves, displaced entirely from the human body into the confines of the clay crucible. And yet the alchemist is never truly separate from the act of creation, and thus Chaucer shows a persistent elision of the active spirits of the minerals with the active, male power of the alchemist himself. Moreover, he implies that science itself is not the de-eroticized act of creation that its practitioners might present. This scene between the priest and alchemist is rife with erotic allusion, as these two men decide to generate together in privacy.

> And shette the dore, whils we been aboute
> Oure pryvetee, that no man us espie,
> Wils that we werke in this philosophie.
>
> (CYT 1137–9)

Similarly, Chaucer's descriptions of the creation process focus on the male labor of the scientists rather than on the male labor of the minerals and metals that they are combining. The alchemical process of generation appears thus less grounded on the specifics of the conceptive science, even displaced into a laboratory, than on the male desire to labor with his own body. For example, the priest "faste blew the fir/For to come to the effect of his desir" (CYT 1260–1), while later he offers the Canon his own body (CYT 1289) in exchange for the success of their procreation.[48]

Even the ancient philosophers relied on male/male pairings as the essential combination of generative science. "Ther may no man mercurie mortifie/But it be with his brother knowlechyng" (CYT 1431–2), the Yeoman offers as a point of ancient lore, even as "the dragon [Mercury]...ne dyeth nat but if that he be slayn/With his brother" (CYT 1435–7). The successful discovery of the Philosopher's Stone, the *Secretum sectretorum*, relies upon the coming together of like with like, man with the image of man, in a relationship that is as incestuous as it is queer, and above all unnatural in its rejection of the principle of conceptive contraries in favor of sexual likeness. The Yeoman references the heterosexual (yet as Bonnie Wheeler notes, incestuous) pairing of Sol and Luna (CYT 1440), sun and moon, often pointed to by alchemists as proof of the normativity of their generations, but only to allow it to serve as an origin point for the "abnormal" sexual proclivities of the chemicals being combined.[49] For within medieval alchemical texts the union of Sol and Luna resulted in a bicephalous hermaphrodite. As Lawrence Principe observes, such a "birth" makes sense when discussing the conjoining of minerals, for "unlike with animals whose procreation produces offspring while

---

[48]   Isabel Davis also speculates as to the sexual relationship between Canon and Yeoman, since they have labored so together. Davis, *Writing Masculinity*, 121.

[49]   Bonnie Wheeler, '"The Prowess of Hands': The Psychology of Alchemy in Malory's 'Tale of Sir Gareth,'" *Culture and the King: The Social Implications of Arthurian Legend*, ed. Martin B. Shichtman and James P. Carley (Albany, NY: State University of New York Press, 1994): 180–95, at 184.

elaving the parents intact, the combination of two material substances causes
them to unite in a new, third substance with a new identity, losing their own inde-
pendent identities in the process."[50] Thus the dragon and his brother Mercury,
while born themselves from a heterosexual union, nevertheless come together
in a union (made manifest through the orgasmic language of eroticized death)
that is not only fundamentally queer, but which also retrospectively queers that
of their parents, who lose their sexual distinctions through the transformations of
their offspring.

These conceptions without women are inherently false in Chaucer's hands, and
their potential for offspring is equally false. The creative union of male alchemists
might "wexe a philosofre" (CYT 837, 1122), but it is unlikely to grow anything
else unless one considers the Yeoman's claim "we wexen wood" (CYT 869) as a
productive conception. The only result of such generation is corruption: the loss
of man's health, his wealth, and his judgment. To reproduce with other men, with
science rather than the divine ordination of the sexes as the primary facilitator of
creation, is an attempt doomed to failure, and to the degradation of self (through
the loss of financial and corporeal stability) that is worse than failure. As the
Yeoman remarks wryly, "A man may lerne, if he have aught/To multiplie and bring
his goods to naught!" (CYT 1400–1). The offspring of these alternative reproductions, when practiced by mortal man, are only multiple layers of destruction.

Moreover, those who set themselves up to produce in such a manner, mimicking
the queer productive philosophy of the alchemists' chemicals, set themselves up
against the divine will. The philosophers have sworn not to reveal the secret of
the Philosopher's Stone, "for unto Crist it is so lief and deere" (CYT 1467). The
Canon's Yeoman's Tale attacks reproductive alternatives, but, like the Second Nun's
Tale, it holds out the hope that one can reproduce with God, through faith and
the disavowal of empirical knowledge. God is not bound by the system of conceptive
contraries; indeed, one should emphatically avoid becoming God's opponent if one
wishes to produce or generate.

> Whoso maketh God his adversarie
> As for to wyrken anything in contrarie
> Of his wil, certes, never shal he thryve.
> Thogh that he multiplie terme of his lyve.
>
> (CYT 1476–9)

Contraries may produce, but not the contrasting pair of man and God. God
chooses to produce as he wishes, with whom he wishes. This is a particularly
nominalist moment in The Canterbury Tales, as Chaucer rejects any form of

---

[50] Lawrence M. Principe, The Secrets of Alchemy (Chicago, IL: University of Chicago Press, 2013): 78.

limitations on the divine power, even those observed by natural law. He throws away all the limits and logics that he has allowed from the precepts of how reproduction works; when God is involved, it simply does not matter. If God chooses to "sende every trewe man boote of his bale!" (CYT 1481), then He does not need to adhere to his own precepts restricting procreation. This is the alternative reproduction that always works, must always work, even if it directly disregards all the knowledge man has of his own creation. The alchemical vision of reproduction is therefore not only a perversion of the "normal" human generative order, but also an attempt to replicate the most singular form of reproduction.[51]

Alternative Conceptions

Engendrure is the metaphor that Chaucer turns to again and again to describe the process of coming to be within the world, and thus all sorts of non-human things become engendered in the *Tales*. "Cold engendreth hayl" (WBT 46) as the Wife of Bath testifies and "ire engendreth homycide" (SumT 2009) as the Summoner adds. Not to be outdone, the Parson proceeds to list all the different things, starting with hate, that ire can also engender (ParsT 562), while Dame Prudence teaches Melibee to consider the genealogy of the advice that he hears: "Thanne shaltow considere of what roote is engendred the matiere of thy conseil/And what fruyt it may conceyve and engendre" (Mel 1209–1209A). And, of course, the most famous engendering of all within *The Canterbury Tales* comes at the very beginning of the *General Prologue* when, in a mimicry of the sexual act, April's sweet showers "the droghte of March hath perced to the roote,/And bathed every veyne in swich licour,/Of which vertu engendred is the flour" (GP 1–4). There are plenty of ways to describe the coming of new spring flowers without asking one's audience to imagine a copulation between the respective weather patterns of March and April, and the fact that Chaucer begins his *Tales* with exactly such a copulation and subsequent engendering is remarkable both for the erotic imagination it bespeaks on the part of the poet and for the utter primacy which it grants to the reproductive mechanism as *the* central mode of being and becoming in the world.

And yet all the creative copulating and birthing that happens in the margins of Chaucer's more poetic flourishes only serves to highlight the truly restrictive nature of the generative options available to his pilgrims. Metaphors do not need procreative partners, but humans, for all their scientific and technological

---

[51] The relationship between alchemical production and the Immaculate Conception provoked medieval intellectuals whether they approved or disapproved of alchemy. Lawrence Principe notes that while some medieval authors saw alchemical claims as a parody of the divine, others, like Petrus Bonus of Ferrrara, argued that alchemical knowledge provided proof of the Immaculate Conception and thus could be utilized to convert pagans to Christianity. Principe, *The Secrets of Alchemy*, 62–9, esp. 68.

innovations, still do, Chaucer claims. In his *Sentences*, Peter Lombard had differentiated between making and creating as follows:

> A creator is one who makes some things from nothing, and, properly speaking, to create is to make something from nothing; but to make is to produce something not only from nothing, but also from matter. And so, a man or an angel is said to make things, but not to create them; and he is called a maker or an artificer, but not a creator.[52]

Lombard is concerned here with establishing the singularity of God's creative capacity, and restricting the human ambition to imitate such divine generations. However, his words also lay out a vision of human production that returns to the union of maker and matter as the central generative act. Men shape and make, women are shaped, and children are made.

To make something out of nothing is God's purview alone. And yet such a procreative heresy is precisely what Chaucer's "alternative generators" attempt to effect, rejecting the "natural" reproductive technologies available to humanity in favor of creative techniques that thereby trespass onto the divine prerogatives. The Second Nun is aided by the miraculous power of God; her prayers grant her the power to sidestep the restrictions associated with her status as a chaste woman and nevertheless become the fecund matter upon which another (whether Mary or God) will work their spermatic will. Alchemists, on the other hand, are not so easily assimilated into the traditional narrative of miraculous conceptions. They have turned not to God but to Science in their desire to forge a new mode of generation. Moreover, they are unwilling to assume the passive, feminine role in this reproductive relationship. The Second Nun is content to be mere matter; the alchemists wish to be the ones who shape and mold, who imbue a material with the active powers that will transform it, who create something out of nothing. They throw off even a pretense of adherence to a traditional, heterosexual model of procreation. They experiment with hitherto unprecedented quantities of matter and of catalytic spirit, in unnatural combinations, and subject to perverse treatments with heat. There is nothing that the alchemists wish to take from the divinely instituted mode of creation except its limitless power, and that God will not allow. To attempt creation outside of a traditional reproductive pattern is to create only degradation and the loss, rather then multiplication, of the self.

This would seem to be Chaucer's final and rather unforgiving statement on the matter. And yet if he condemns the enactment of such hubristic ambitions, then he nevertheless appears to sympathize with the intellectual spirit from which this dream might be born. For he too notices the miraculous engendrures in the world, the copulations of rains and the births of flowers, the anger that breeds

---

[52] Lombard, *The Sentences: Book 2, On Creation*, 3–4.

ever-new emotions, the somethings that are created everyday out of a readily observable nothingness. He, a medieval Christian just like the Second Nun, has learned the dogma of an Immaculate Conception that broke all rules of reproduction, while birthing the world from the darkness of sin. He is familiar not only with the list of alchemical ingredients, but, more significantly, with the records of ancient philosophers who claimed that such recipes had worked, and who bore empirical witness to that which a medieval philosopher must deny as impossible. In short, Chaucer appears as fascinated by the opportunities of "unnatural" creation as he is opposed to their implementation. Thus, in the *Physician's Tale*, Chaucer has Nature boast of the birth of the beautiful young Virginia:

> "Lo, I, Nature
> Thus kan I forme and peynte a creature,
> Whan that me list; who kan me countrefete?"
>
> (PhyT 11–3)

This is a strident rejection of the aspiration of any man to imitate Nature or the perfection of her creative ability. And yet Nature immediately continues with a list of those who have dared the attempt.

> "Pigmalion noght, thogh he ay forge and bete,
> Or grave, or peynt; for I dar el sayn
> Apelles, Zanzes, sholde werche in vain
> Outher to grave, or peynte, or forge, or bete
> If they presumed me to countrefete."
>
> (PhyT 14–8)

It may be impossible to create in this "unnatural" matter; such an attempt may be a mere counterfeiting and theft (a presumptuous one at that). But, Chaucer tells us, those who try and inevitably fail earn fame with Nature and poet alike, and thus create their own posterity.

4

Adultery's Heirs

Multiplying Excess

Creation is important because men die. Each man lives in flesh formed by his parents, flesh that he in turn must shape into new matter in the brief moment before his death. Joining together in a repetition of their own creation, men employed the female body as the essential technology of self-perpetuation. And then, having shaped their own matter into a new form, it was the human task to surrender their own flesh to death, and so to dematerialize their individual incarnation of their lineage. In this idealized image of the human lifecycle, procreation provides the compensation for the dignity men lose in death. Man's authority must be reinforced even as it is lost, and women are the mechanisms by which that sustaining mode of masculine self-respect may be achieved. And therein lies the rub. For men may no more fully control their female productive tools than they may trust with certainty in the filial objects of their production. Thus we find medieval wills like that of John Chelmswyk of Shropshire (*d.*1418), who, without "heires of my body lawfully begete," declared his wife Jonet to be his heir *provided* that she remained without any male company for a year after his decease.[1] Erotic jealousy blends here with patriarchal uncertainty; by demanding that his wife perform her chastity publicly after his death, John demands that she remain his mechanism of procreation, pregnant with the possibility of a posthumous heir, long after he has left the world. Women who accepted such testamentary terms, or even augmented them by vowing lifelong chastity, Mary Erler has argued, offered to their husbands' memory a "promise[e] of stasis, the absence of unsettling change—a kind of personal, rather than legal mortmain, in which the husband's 'dead hand' continued to exert his grip."[2] Male wealth could, in this sense, seek to transcend mortality's limitations on human flesh, coercing man's female reproductive tools long after his own decease.

---

[1] John Chelmsywk, Esq. Shropshire, "Will," *The Earliest English Wills in the Court of Probate, A.D. 1387–1439; with a Priest's of* 1454, ed. Frederick J. Furnivall (London: Published for the Early English Text Society by Trubner and Co., 1882): 33–4.

[2] Mary C. Erler, "Three Fifteenth-Century Vowesses," *Medieval London Widows, 1300–1500*, ed. Caroline M. Barron and Anne F. Sutton (London and Rio Grande: Hambledon Press, 1994): 165–83, at 180.

Father Chaucer: Generating Authority in The Canterbury Tales. Samantha Katz Seal, Oxford University Press (2019).
© Samantha Seal.
DOI: 10.1093/oso/9780198832386.001.0001

Man's desire for a lasting authority in the production of his children was condemned as avarice by fourteenth-century authors. As John Gower acerbically comments in the *Confessio Amantis*:

> Men mai wel make a liklihiede
> Between him which is averous
> Of gold and him that is jelous
> Of love, for in on degre
> Thei stoned bothe, as semeth me.[3]

Man's tight cling upon his wife's "love," and thus upon her procreative capacities, is to Gower only one more example of a destructive, immoral worldliness. To guard against loss, whether of the gold itself or of the female mechanism capable of producing a new owner for that gold, was to rebel against the natural order of life and death. For, as the *Prick of Conscience* warns,

> As he com naked and ful porely
> The fyrste day from his modur body,
> Nought he brought with hym that day
> Ny no thyng schalle he bere away
> Bot a wyndynge cloth oonly.[4]

Men are born with the knowledge of their deaths already writ upon them. There is no authority in that nor, as Chaucer reproduces the devotional argument, should men demand certainty and full fidelity from wives when their true heir will be not a son but a tomb.

And yet for all that, his pilgrims are fixated upon the threat of cuckoldry. They are men of the world and they will search for ways to preserve their flesh within that world. His merchants and reeves, millers and shipmen, turn to their wives to protect their own authority, through the pleasurable reproductions of their flesh. And yet by offering coin in exchange for that reassurance, investing their money in their wives' wombs in hope of an heir to inherit their gold, these husbands transform a productive partnership into a financial transaction. Their avarice creates the circumstances through which the avarice of other men may find a willing object in their wives. These husbands have nurtured their wives' faithlessness by encouraging a domestic atmosphere of frenetic increase and accumulation, one that eventually drives women to redirect their mechanisms of productivity towards the multiplication of lovers and possessions rather than to the measured production of offspring. We can see here a break with older Aristotelian traditions

---

[3] Gower, "Confessio Amantis," 418. For Gower's belief that "the wealth of money brings no profit even to those who accumulate it," see Epstein, "Dismal Science," 224.
[4] Morris, *Prick of Conscience*.

that taught, to quote Howard Bloch, that "money is dead, unproductive, sterile, an unfruitful good incapable of breeding, that is, of yielding profit."[5] Here money is not dead but rather too intensely alive, too full of its own spermatic possibilities to allow for a stable, sufficiently productive marriage. As Robert Epstein concludes, "Chaucer clearly had a sense of productive capital."[6] This perspective on the exponential fecundities of money as a metaphor for marriage is anti-scholastic in its understanding of economics, but in sympathy with the Renaissance poets who named cuckoldry "the horn of abundance;" a cuckolded husband possessed such a cornucopia of ever-multiplying, sexual largesse in the body of his wife, so that some overflow to other men was to be expected.[7] The exponential qualities of money, long expressed in Christian diatribes against usury for (to quote D. Vance Smith) "producing fruit from money," served as a useful metaphor for the reproductive possibilities of wealthy men's young, fertile wives.[8]

The medieval rhetoric of cuckoldry thus combined the terror of deprivation with that of unnatural excess. An excess of possessions predicted loss, as the avarice represented by the accumulation of economic or sexual goods demanded a moral requiting. The question thereby raised in cuckoldry narratives was whether it was more authoritative to produce a plentitude, in anticipation of some loss, or rather to produce little (or nothing), but to be certain of that production? Chaucer's Miller advises the husbands in the party to enjoy the sexual excesses of their wives, without greed or the presentiment of loss: "So he may fynde Goddes foyson there/Of the remenant nedeth nat enquere" (MilT 3164–5). And yet Chaucer's Shipman reminds the company of the dangers of such unbounded indulgence. For a medieval wife was not a treasury, but rather a technology; she is the mechanism by which man brings himself anew to life and thus to allow other men to generate with one's wife was to risk the proliferation of other men's products in one's domestic space. Countering the Parson's attempt to speak, the Shipman warns of the dangers of unlimited multiplication: "He wolde sowen som difficulte,/Or springen cokkel in our clene corn" (MLT 1182–3). The Parson's words (his seeds) do not fall harmlessly in some boundless, fecund field. Even as a hatching cuckoo bird pushes the native birds out of the nest, so too do errant

---

[5] R. Howard Bloch, *Etymologies and Genealogies: A Literary Anthropology of the French Middle Ages* (Chicago, IL: University of Chicago Press, 1986): 173.

[6] Epstein, "Dismal Science," 224.

[7] See for example, *Henry IV, Part II* when Falstaff mocks another man with "for he hath the horn of abundance, and the lightness of his wife shines through it." (*Henry IV, Pt. II*, Act I, Scene 2). While Douglas Bruster identifies several merchants in Early Modern drama who profit from the selling of their wives' abundant sexuality, in medieval texts that cuckoldry is always figured as a form of loss. Douglas Bruster, "The Horn of Plenty: Cuckoldry and Capital in the Drama of the Age of Shakespeare," *Studies in English Literature, 1500–1900* 30.2 (Spring 1990): 195–215, at 205–7.

[8] D. Vance Smith masterfully argues that "in usury, especially, a number of medieval writers saw a tendency that ultimately robbed the body of meaning because it avoided the obligations of labor." D. Vance Smith, "Body Doubles: Producing the Masculine Corpus," *Becoming Male in the Middle Ages*, ed. Jeffrey Jerome Cohen and Bonnie Wheeler (New York and London: Garland Publishing, 1997): 3–20, at 11.

adulteries rob men of their full largesse.[9] To lose a little is to lose all, according to the Shipman; an individual's authority depends upon their ability to maintain an exclusive hegemony over female tool and filial product.

Chaucer plays with both arguments, granting no more authority to the Shipman than he does to the Miller. Indeed, he later takes his chances with "cokkel corn," letting the Parson (that "Lollere in the wynd" [MLT 1173]) end the *Tales* with a sermon. Moreover, Chaucer acknowledges the universality of the human desire to possess and to produce, even as he explores the resultant multiplicity of misproductions and monstrosities. Men wish for heirs, for wealth, for loyal and fertile wives, and Chaucer does not fault them for that wishing. Yet as this chapter will argue, he also does not reassure them in their hope. He is no more certain than any of his pilgrims that man can find a lasting authority in the product of his own flesh. Instead, he provides his audience with one *Tale* after another of how that dream falls apart in female hands, indicting women for the humbling of their male partners. Tales of adultery are tales of failed collaboration, dark accounts of technology's rebellion against its scientists. That failure and that rebellion may stem from man's avarice, the hubris of his very desire to create despite the fact of his own death. And yet the blame for the disaster will be attributed to his wife. Chaucer's adulterous *Tales* thus leave us with a paradox. Women are the means by which man's dream of a human authority are brought to life, but they are also, always, the mechanism of his destruction.

Against Sufficiency: The Productivity of Excess and Absence in the *Summoner's Tale*

Chaucer approaches human productivity (whether biological or economic) as a process caught between overabundance and insufficiency. Lacking the capacity to be satiated with sufficiency, men transgress against others in the pursuit of their own gain, driven not by need, but rather by the desire to accumulate excess or, even worse, to deprive others of their goods.[10] That mode of excessive productions is in turn self-replicating; from an allegorical perspective, for example, sin breeds upon itself, multiplying from its own excess. Such unholy multiplications

---

[9] Legislation against adultery often emphasized the illicit birth of offspring as a precondition for judicial involvement, and would demand the adulterous male offender to offer financial restitution to the man whose adulterous wife had borne the offender's child. Vern L. Bullough, "Medieval Concepts of Adultery," *Arthuriana* 7.4 (Winter 1997): 5–15, at 9.

[10] My argument is therefore the exact inverse of Alcuin Blamires's theory of the "ethics of sufficiency" within *The Canterbury Tales*, reaffirming the virtue of those who trust in God for their sustenance. While Blamires is correct in identifying Custance of the Man of Law's Tale as a figure of holy resignation, the theme of multiplying insufficiencies is far more pervasive and threatening throughout Chaucer's full text than he allows. He sees the *Shipman's Tale* as a moral-reinforcing parody; I see it as one of several *Tales* in which unbalanced multiplications threaten to spin out of control and are only reined in at the very last minute. Blamires, *Chaucer, Ethics, and Gender*, 117–29.

break with the Aristotelian definition of commerce as elucidated by Lianna Farber, who writes, "commerce therefore rests firmly on necessity and is an inevitable outcome of the uneven distribution of goods... [it] is the name given here to exchange when it is used to procure sufficiency."[11] But enough is never enough for Chaucer's fathers; whether it is one heir, one coin, or one coital act, these are men driven to accumulate in fear of death. And their exponential accumulations dictate the rate of their unstable reproductions, driving them to sire unnatural, monstrous outputs that are as sinful as they are insufficient.

This imbalance of production, predicated upon a polarized spectrum of complete possession or exhaustive loss, swings its adherents wildly between joy and despair. Its antithesis is therefore not only sufficiency but also the balancing of needs that sufficiency implies, the collaborative efforts of production. Chaucer provides a model of this holier, more stable state with his holy brothers, the Parson and the Plowman. The Plowman produces in moderation ("a trewe swynkere and a good was he... his tithes payde he ful faire and wel" [GP 531, 539]), and the Parson consumes in moderation ("he koude in litel thyng have suffisaunce" [GP 490]). Both men understand their duty within the world to be the balancing, rather than the augmentation, of the extremes of economic inequality. The Parson gives freely "unto his povre parisshens aboute/Of his offryng and eek of his substaunce" (GP 489), turning the scarcities of the poor into sufficiencies for them, and refusing to augment his own personal wealth from sufficiency to surplus. Likewise, the Plowman's labor is directed at producing material sustenance for others rather than for himself, and he perceives an equivalency embedded within that productivity of exchange, for he loves "his neighebor right as hymselve" (GP 535). It is difficult to imagine either Parson or Plowman engaging in the marital jealousy, let alone the sexual machinations, of Chaucer's more immoderate husbands; these holy men balance communal needs with love and a free exchange of goods, and thus are able to produce without the fear of loss.

In contrast to his own behavior, the Parson therefore criticizes not only those who are discontented with moderation, but also those who tie production too tightly to the extremes of abundance or poverty. He thus, for example, bases his criticism of sinful human dress for its reliance upon either extreme: "namely in to muche superfluite, or elles in to desordinat scantnesse" (ParsT 415A). Moreover, he argues that these sartorial sins do not merely perform immorality, but again *produce* it. The excesses of costly clothing "maketh it so deere, to harm of the peple" (ParsT 416). The superfluity indeed produces scarcity for the gowns, "trailynge in the dong and in the mire, on horse and eek on foote... is verraily as in effect wasted, consumed, thredbare, and roten with donge, rather than that it is yeven to the povre, to greet damage of the foreseyde povre folke. And that in

---

[11] Lianna Farber, *An Anatomy of Trade in Medieval Writing: Value, Consent, and Community* (Ithaca, NY: Cornell University Press, 2006): 20.

sondry wise; this is to seyn that the moore that clooth is wasted, the moore moot it coste to the peple for the scarsnesse" (ParsT 419–20A). The Parson's detailed complaint about these excesses of clothing emphasizes how an overindulgence upon the part of the wealthy inevitably results in the increased deprivation of the poor. For if the rich ladies had contented themselves with dresses of sufficient length, then those dresses would have been in sufficient condition for the poor ladies who would be their clothing's heirs. Sufficiency gives birth to sufficiency; excess and deprivation give birth only to one another.

This theme of the unfortunate productions of human extremes appears in a more explicitly reproductive context within the *Prologue* to the *Summoner's Tale*. Within the Summoner's opening remarks, designed to requite the anti-summoner ramblings of the Friar, a friar is spiritually transported to Hell, and marvels at the scarcity of friars there to be found. " 'Now, sire,' quod he, 'han freres swich a grace/ That noon of hem shal come to this place?' " (SumT 1683–4). The friar claims the absence of friars as a product and a proof of virtue, only for his accompanying angel to counter absence with overabundance. For "many a millioun" (SumT 1685) friars are revealed to inhabit Hell. Moreover, they are born into the absent space with an astounding superfluity.

> And er that half a furlong wey of space,
> Right so as bees out swarmen rom an hyve,
> Out of the develes ers ther gonne dryve
> Twenty thousand freres on a route,
> And thurghout helle swarmed al aboute,
> And comen again as faste as they may gon,
> And in his ers they crepten everychon.
>
> (SumT 1692–8)

According to the Summoner, Hell is a realm with an alternating excess and absence of friars. By nesting within the Devil's anus, the friars only come forth into the world as a too-large teeming group, twenty thousand friars flying like a swarm of bees. Once born out from their anal womb, the friars overwhelm Hell with their numbers, the very space marked previously by their comprehensive absence.[12] Moreover, the transformation in their numbers happens with celerity. Their hasty exit from the Devil's anus, and their re-entrance thereto, both occur as unsteady vacillations between shortage and surplus. All too quickly, this fast-flying swarm may overwhelm their new habitation, before retreating under the Devil's tail by "comen again as faste as they may gon."

---

[12] As Tiffany Beechy notes, sodomy and greed were understood as overlapping behaviors in the Middle Ages "because they violated the always tenuous principle that desire must serve procreation." Here they serve a reversed, unproductive procreation. Tiffany Beechy, "Devil Take the Hindmost: Chaucer, John Gay, and the Pecuniary Ass," *The Chaucer Review* 41.1 (2006): 71–85, at 73.

From the Devil's anus, no sufficiency will come to Chaucer' world. Evil instead embraces its excesses and its inequalities, urging men to aspire to produce glut and surplus as their partner. Even that single, dreaming friar who, upon watching the swarm of his fellows fly in and out of the Devil's asshole, decided that he "looked hadde his fille" (SumT 1700), must almost immediately reject his new-found restraint. Instead, "the develes ers [remains] ay in his mynde,/That is his heritage of verray kynde" (SumT 1705–6). The friar is haunted by his vision of the demonic birthing of his brethren not because such persistent memories might help him turn away from sin, but rather because of the inevitability of his future residence beside them. The Summoner turns at the end of his prologue to this language of inheritance and natural law to remind his listeners of precisely how profound the friars' perversion truly is. They twist the traditional laws of labor and production, since they gather sustenance and wealth by feeding parasitically off of other's productivity, and therefore rob men's heirs of the full amount that they should inherit from their fathers. And yet such unbalanced excess and avarice will have its own reward, as each friar inherits as patrimony his personal habitation within the teeming, overabundant, glut of the Devil's anus.

The friars sin by stirring men to long for an abundance that they lack but do not need; the pursuit of these unnecessary goods only serves to rob men of the sufficiencies that they already have. It is thus significant that the *Summoner's Tale* as a whole appears to function on the paired doubles of a father who has lost a child and a child who gains a "father."[13] The Summoner's evil friar breaks down the bonds of inheritance and family with his incessant urging for alms and his extravagant promises of excessive reward; likewise, the young squire, Jankyn, with his inventive solution for the problem of the indivisible fart, reduces the excess of friars into a single joined body capable of sharing the stench, and simul-taneously establishes himself within his lord and lady's favor, closing the circle of a new domestic unit. The story thus becomes a moral tale of the need for families to fight off both the terror of loss and the lure of surplus, to prioritize the struc-tures of traditional reproduction and heredity (and the sufficient authorities incumbent within) over the false promises of the devil's clerics.

The peasant couple targeted by the friar within the *Summoner's Tale* suffers from three significant reproductive challenges. First, they appear to have no liv-ing children; the man and wife are the only acknowledged occupants of their

---

[13] Robert Emmett Finnegan reads the doubling of the two children quite differently, arguing that each might potentially be the son of Friar John, and thus serve less as mirrors of one another than as dual signposts of the friar's virility. I do not find this argument fully convincing, particularly since squire Jankyn is so antagonistic to the "friar;" Chaucer's father/son pairs are many things, but not hostile to one another. I also object to the assumption that the peasant child was a boy, since if that child was symbolic of a specific masculinity rather than a more generalized productivity, it would have been easy enough to have the wife say "son." Robert Emmett Finnegan, "The Wife's Dead Child and Friar John: Parallels and Oppositions in the 'Summoner's Tale,'" *Neuphilologische Mitteilungen* 92.4 (1991): 457–62.

habitation. Secondly, they appear unlikely to produce any future heirs, due to the bad health of Thomas, the peasant husband. His wife complains to the friar that her husband is "as angry as a pissemyre,/Though that he have al that kan desire" (SumT 1825–6), and notes as well that "oother desport noon of hym have I" (SumT 1830). The friar seems willing to help remedy this default; he "kiste hire sweete" and vows to be "youre servant every deel" (SumT 1804, 1806). And yet for all the ardor of the friar's greeting, the *Summoner's Tale* is far from the expected story of a neglected wife and a lascivious cleric. For, while the friar continually claims the wife to be in possession of surplus sexual bounty, the wife herself rebuts him by invoking her list of losses and reproductive struggles. For example, when the friar claims "saugh I nat this day so fair a wyf/In al the chirche" (SumT 1808–9), the wife responds with the dampening, "Ye, God amende defautes, sire" (SumT 1810). He praises "youre grete goodnesse" (SumT 1813); she replies in turn with an account of the unproductivity of that goodness within her marital bed. "Though I hym wrye a-nyght and make hym warm,/And over hym leye my leg outher myn arm,/He groneth lyk oure boor, lith in oure sty" (SumT 1827–9). To describe a lack is not necessarily to demand compensation for the deficiency, particularly when one is confiding in one's confessor. And indeed, the friar's sexual strategy has not been focused upon offering to compensate inadequacies of her marital life, but rather on aggrandizing the "excessive" nature of her sexuality so that some of the surfeit might fall by accident to him. The peasant's wife denies his sexual advances by denying the very existence of an erotic surplus.

Unlike the lascivious cleric within the *Shipman's Tale* to be discussed later in this chapter, the Summoner's friar becomes less (rather than more) sexually avaricious when informed of such a dearth within another's erotic life. All kissing of lips occur when he judges her to be full of abundance, and he loses interest quickly in her once she claims a sexual lack. A variation of this attitude to the wife as a source of "sexual surplus" can perhaps be found in certain scholarly interpretations of the character. For example, as Robert Finnegan speculates upon the wife's sexual attractiveness, "the [peasant] wife must be conceived as much younger than her husband in order to have Friar John's attention so concentrated on her."[14] I disagree with this conclusion both in terms of its implicit assumptions around female desirability and aging, and to the extent that it absorbs the peasant's wife of the *Tale* into a category of Chaucerian adulterous wives, full of unsatiated desires, rather than allow her to be judged by her own account of providing exhausting spousal labor to soothe her husband at night.[15] This is a wife complaining that she is unable to please, rather than that she has not received pleasure in turn.

---

[14] Finnegan, "The Wife's Dead Child," at 458.

[15] John Finlayson, in contrast, focuses on the friar as aggressor, noting the Summoner's comparison of the friar to a sparrow, "a common image of indiscriminate sexual union even today." Within this reading, the guilt is placed upon the friar for his own sexual advances, rather than indirectly upon the wife as coy precipitator. John Finlayson, "Chaucer's 'Summoner's Tale:' Flatulence, Blasphemy, and the Emperor's Clothes," *Studies in Philology* 104.4 (Falls 2007): 455–70, at 461.

For all her evening labor, the peasant wife is unable to produce with her husband and, more tragically, she has recently witnessed the destruction of their past production. She tells the friar of the couple's most profound loss: the recent death of their child. " 'Now, sire,' quod she, 'but o word er I go./ My child is deed withinne thise wykes two' " (SumT 1851–2). The friar responds by attempting to demonstrate the excessive abundance that was produced by that child's death: the holy "avision" of the child's salvation granted not only to the friar himself, but also to the sexton and the infirmarian, the entire convent rising together to pray for the child's entry into heaven, plus the "many a teere trillying on my cheke" (SumT 1864). What the peasant husband and wife have experienced as loss, the friar and his brethren have experienced as an outpouring of communal sanctity; the child's death becomes a moment of useful production for the mendicants.

Scholars have tended to identify the mother's reference to the child's death as a moment of strange coldness within the *Tale*. Derek Brewer notes that Chaucer's "apparent callousness" when referencing the deaths of children can "give an effect of bathos to the modern reader, who may well think that Chaucer is trying to be funny."[16] Brewer is somewhat charitable, in that he ascribes the coldness and callousness here to Chaucer rather than to the peasant wife. Far more common is the type of harsh indictment of the woman to be found within one of David Allen's footnotes: "Earle Birney's suggestion that it is 'highly unlikely' for Thomas' wife to be comforted by the Friar's vision attributes a greater grief to the woman than she seems to display. Disgusted with her husband's unmanly malaise, she seems eager enough to forget the dead child and go on about making another one."[17] Allen's comment here is remarkable for its gendered bias, for if the wife is judged for the brevity of her remark upon her child's death, surely Thomas himself should be judged for failing to provide any comment upon his loss. Moreover, Allen's explanation for the apparent "indifference" of Thomas and his wife depends upon a generalized acceptance of the premodern parent as devoid of affective bonds to their children; for example, he writes, "children were, there-fore, widely perceived as greedy little monsters who sucked the vitality out of their parents."[18] Instead, we may see the wife's limited discourse upon her child's

---

[16] Derek Brewer, *Tradition and Innovation in Chaucer* (London: MacMillan Press, 1982): 49.

[17] David G. Allen, "Death and Staleness in the 'Son-Less' World of the *Summoner's Tale*," *Studies in Short Fiction* (Winter 1987): 1–8, at pg. 1, n.2. The work by Earle Birney that he is referencing is Birney, "Structural Irony within the *Summoner's Tale*, *Anglia* 78 (1960): Numbers, at 210–11.

[18] Allen, "Son-less World," 3. Allen's reading here is heavily indebted to the work of Philippe Aries and Lawrence Stone, who both attempted to explain the parental "coldness" they perceived within the archive as a defensive response to the high rates of infant/child mortality in a society that nevertheless needed to maintain a high birthrate to meet its labor demands. Philippe Aries, *Centuries of Childhood: A Social History of Family Life*, Trans. Robert Baldick (New York: Vintage Books, 1962); Lawrence Stone, *The Family, Sex and Marriage in England 1500–1800* (New York: Harper and Row, 1977). Aries and Stone's conclusions as to medieval parental affect have been countered over the past thirty years by countless examples of parental emotion from the time period. Nicholas Orme, for example, sum-marizes decades of successive scholarship on the medieval parent/child unit, and concludes: "None of the scholars mentioned above has found material to support the assertions of Aries; all, in different

death as stemming from her desire to rebuke the friar for his callousness to her loss, since, despite the friar's willingness to take the couple's money, he had failed to be in town to minister to their family when they needed him most. The child is not an easily dismissed detail in the way of her sexual life (as Allen in particular seems to imply), but rather evidence of the friar's pastoral inadequacies. The delay in the wife's mention of her child indicts the friar's callousness, rather than her own; after spending so long a period in their home, he has rudely not yet thought to comment upon their child's absence. To view the wife as desiring to "go about making another [child]" with the friar is both to misperceive the directionality of the expressed lust within the *Tale* (from friar to wife rather than vice versa) and to interpret an articulation of failed productivity (lost child, impotent husband) as a demand to initiate a new cycle of generation. It is the friar himself who wishes to turn every loss into profit; the wife merely wishes to mourn and, perhaps, complain.

The friar sees productivity in both excess and insufficiency. He not only expects the death of a poor child to produce a (albeit fictional) mystic experience for his entire monastery, he expects a poor couple's empty larder to produce a capon's liver, "softe breed," and a "rosted pigges heed" (SumT 1830–41) for his meal. Indeed, he is so desperate to find bounty within other men's empty purses, that he so famously puts his hand "aboute his [Thomas's] tuwel" (SumT 2148) searching for some hidden good. However, he also seeks production from those who have too much, not only running to the lord for recompense, but praising those historical figures capable of producing from their excesses. For example, while he condemns ire (the very sin that he himself later embodies), he nevertheless semi-lauds the sin as at least a means of generation. "Ire engendreth homycide…I koude of ire seye so muche sorwe,/My tale sholde laste til to-morwe" (SumT 2009, 2011–12). Murder is an evil thing, even to the friar, but it is an evil thing that never seems to rebound upon its sire. Thus, in the tale from Seneca, the angry potentate produces a triple murder of innocent knights, but the ruler himself never suffers from that production. Likewise, the story of Cambyses that the friar retells becomes within his telling a tale of an angry, murderous, excessively alcoholic man who is only rewarded for his excesses, even as he murders the child of his abstentious knight. Not only is this latter tale a remarkably insensitive narrative to offer two grieving parents of a recently deceased child, but it is also a story in which punishment only falls upon the man who urges a regime of productive sufficiency. The knight begins by urging the king to "drynk moore attemprely!" (SumT 2053), the king then murders the knight's child, and the knight is fully silenced. "What sholde I telle th'answere of the knyght?/His sone was slayn; ther is namoore to seye" (SumT 2072–3). Within the Summoner's friar's stories, excess

ways, have rebutted them. They have gathered copious evidence to show that adults regarded childhood as a distinct phase or phases of life, that parents treated children like children as well as like adults, that they did so with care and sympathy, and that children had cultural activities and possession of their own." Nicolas Orme, *Medieval Children* (New Haven, CT: Yale University Press, 2001): 5.

may breed evil, but that evil will fall only upon the temperate men, whose sufficiencies will thereby be turned to loss.

This is an economic philosophy of human production repeated again and again by sinful, avaricious men (particularly clerics) throughout *The Canterbury Tales*. For the Pardoner, for example, the Summoner's friar's greedy engenderings are merely another iteration of his system of duplicitous multiplications. But before discussing the multiple manifestations of this strategy of production, I first wish to note the extent to which the *Summoner's Tale*, with its crude splitting of the fart, also offers a vision of recuperative resistance to the destabilizing avarice of men and their more sinful productions. It becomes a *Tale* of measuring and containment, of enforcing order upon uncontainable excess.[19] In this sense, the alternative domestic unit represented by the lord and lady who apparently own the "cherl" living in what the friar calls alternately "youre village" (SumT 2177) and "youre toun" (SumT 2180) serves not only as a foil for Thomas the peasant and his wife, but as the provenance of an alternative theory of production to rival and defeat that of the friar. For this couple (and their squire, Jankyn) are faced with two baffling intellectual challenges: firstly, how can a single fart be redistributed to twelve men, and secondly, how and from whence does such a brilliant idea manage to be produced within the rough lewdness of a peasant's mind?

The answer to the first question is in a sense the easier one to derive. Jankyn, the lord's squire, not only provides the answer, but by doing so, produces for himself a named, stable role within the *Tale*.[20] At line 2243 he enters the story as "the lords squire at the bord,/That karf his mete" (SumT 2243–4), and it is not until after he has provided his solution that he is finally offered a name of his own (line 2288). The name is then repeated twice within five lines, as if the Summoner wishes to emphasize the boy's integration into the story and into his lord's court. As I noted earlier, there is a sense of implicit parallelism here with the peasant family; the peasants have lost a child and thereby been reduced to a supposedly barren male/female partnership, but the unexpected intellectual production of the fart in turn produces a "child" for their male and female lords, one whose presence within the court is at the least revalued according to the public recognition of his wit. Thomas's production of the fart has revealed the mendacity behind the friar's false acclamation of familial bonds ("ye sey me thus, how that I am youre brother?" [SumT 2126] as Thomas asks immediately before he farts), but it

---

[19] Glending Olson has documented the way in which Chaucer's discourse of measurement partakes of theological and scientific rhetoric about the purposes and applications of geometry, particularly noting John Wyclif's contemporaneous investment in the indivisibility of linear forms past a certain degree of constituent. Glending Olson, "Measuring the Immeasurable: Farting, Geometry, and Theology in the *Summoner's Tale*," *The Chaucer Review* 43.4 (2009): 414–27, at 416–19.

[20] David Raybin reads Jankyn as not only unnamed, but also occupying an explicitly liminal social space, arguing that Jankyn's "intermediary social role as a dependent member of the lord's household places him in a position where he might bridge the gap between peasant and noble." David Raybin, "'Goddes Instrumentz': Devils and Free Will in the *Friar's* and *Summoner's* Tales," *The Chaucer Review* 46.1–2 (2011): 93–110, at 104.

also offers up the younger boy an opportunity to strengthen far more productive ties of affect with his lord.

However, even more significantly, Thomas's production of the fart is a true product of scarcity, and is recognized as such when reviewed by the lord's court. Faced with his own poverty and his physical impotence, Thomas nevertheless manages to come up with an original product to bestow upon the friar, and a startlingly complex piece of brilliance to proffer to his lord.

> The lord sat stille as he were in a traunce,
> And in his herte he rolled up and doun,
> "How hadde this cherl ymanginacioun
> To shewe swich a problem to the frere?
> Nevere erst er now herde I of swich mateere.
> I trowe the devel putte it in his mynde."
>
> (SumT 2216–21)

The lord is struck to silence first and foremost by the idea's origination in his peasant's brain, rather than by the idea itself, although he moves within a few lines to praising its brilliance as well. The lord has identified a chain of production that he claims to be even more remarkable than "ars-metrike" (SumT 2222)—the siring of the idea within the peasant's brain, and the subsequent reproduction of that idea into the verbal/material combination of fart and proffered challenge.[21]

The lord recognizes the peasant's supposed insufficiencies, his absences and losses, and identifies them as comprehensive obstacles to productivity. Instead of immediately recognizing his peasant's achivement, a few lines later he repeats the accusation of demonic intervention once again, "I holde hym certeyn a demonyak!" (SumT 2240).[22] According to the lord's intellectual system of how productivity works within his world, the devil may logically produce copious and remarkable offspring from his excessive store of evil, while a peasant, with his incumbent scarcities, may not. Indeed, as Anne McIlhany has perceived, "the characters to whom the devil comes in the *Canterbury Tales* are *already* lacking in wit and reason and discretion."[23] It is then this point that must be most fully refuted at the end of the *Tale*. "Touchyng the cherl, they seyde, subtiltee/And heigh wit made hym speken as he spak; He nys no fool, ne no demonyak"

---

[21] This is, as Robert Epstein has argued, one of the most remarkable aspects of money: its ability to function as paradoxically material abstraction. Robert Epstein, "Sacred Commerce: Chaucer, Friars, and the Spirit of Money," *Sacred and Profane in Chaucer and Late Medieval Literature: Essays in Honor of John V. Fleming*, ed. Robert Epstein and William Robins (Toronto: University of Toronto Press, 2010): 129–45, at 136–8.

[22] Ann Haskell identifies references to the devil throughout the poem, beginning with the oaths on St. Simon, whom she reads as the demonic figure Simon Magus, perhaps a double for the friar himself. Ann S. Haskell, "St. Simon in the 'Summoner's Tale,'" *The Chaucer Review* 5.3 (Winter 1971): 218–24.

[23] Anne E. McIlhaney, "Sentence and Judgment: The Role of the Fiend in Chaucer's 'Canterbury Tales,'" *The Chaucer Review* 31.2 (1996): 173–83, at 175.

(SumT 2290–2). This acclaim for the peasant's wit at the end of the *Tale* is not, however, a praise of the inherent productivities of absence and insufficiency, such as was offered earlier by the friar in his avaricious greed. Instead, it is a recognition of the sufficiencies hidden underneath even the most comprehensive presentation of lack and poverty. The "cherl's" subtlety and high wit are just enough for him and for his wife; they are the tools by which the man has produced precisely what he needed (the vanquishing of the greedy friar) and not a crumb more or less.

Multiplying Problems in the *Pardoner's Tale*

Production should be born from sufficiency, as the *Summoner's Tale* attests. And such modes of moral production should be matched with moral terms; Chaucer uses grammatical variants of the term "engendering" when he wishes to demonstrate either a moral means of production *or* an immoral, but not unregulated, means of production.[24] In contrast, Chaucer labels reproductions as "multiplications" when they result from the excess/absence paradigm, and particularly when both present and future reproductions appear to exist outside of, or counter to, natural mechanisms of restraint.[25] This is, for example, why within the *Canon Yeoman's Tale*, productive acts are repeatedly termed multiplications rather than engenderings; the use of the terminology of "unnatural" generation reflects both the alchemists' hopes for unlimited production, and the general judgment upon them for such immoderate avarice.[26] Even the Biblical use of "multiply" within Genesis 1:28, such as articulated by the Wife of Bath, "God bad us for to wexe and multiplye" (WBT 28), was not exclusively positive, since the command to human fertility was not necessarily capable of being disentangled from the concupiscence of the sexual act.[27] As Jeremy Cohen has argued, the Christian exegetical tradition

---

[24] There are thirty uses of grammatical variants of the term "engendering" within *The Canterbury Tales*. The moral spectrum of these uses moves, in my opinion, from the noble and courtly allegory of the *General Prologue* 4 ("Of which vertu engendred is the flour"), to the relatively moral terms of sexual procreation (ex: "On which he myghte engendren hym an heir" [MerT 1272]), to the explicitly negative ("Of hym flesshly descended be we alle, and engendered of vile and corrupt mateere" [ParsT 333A]). "Engendering" can be good or it can be bad, but it is always to some extent controlled and dictated by the limitations of its progenitor. Cf. "Chaucer Concordance," http://www.columbia. edu/~hfl2110/cconcord.html.

[25] There are eighteen uses of the grammatical variants of the term "multiplication", and they are almost universally negative with the sole exception of the Parson's invocation of the marriage sacrament as "God made mariage in paradys, in the estaat of innocence, to multiplye mankynde to the service of God" (ParsT 883A). Cf. "Chaucer Concordance," http://www.columbia.edu/~hfl2110/ cconcord.html.

[26] Edgar Duncan also shows that "*multiplicatio*" indicated a specific part of the alchemical process, in which the prepared elixir "tremendously increased in strength and efficacy." Edgar H. Duncan, "The Literature of Alchemy and Chaucer's *Canon Yeoman's Tale*: Frameworks, Theme, and Characters," *Speculum* 43.4 (October 1968): 633–56, at 635.

[27] The Wife of Bath's use of the line is a controversial point in scholarly debates over how one should interpret her preaching. Alastair Minnis, for example, reads the line as indicative of the Wife of

of the Biblical command was a history of contentious negotiation with implications for how literally the Old Testament should be interpreted, how sharply the Fall had divided human history, and how widely God had intended his words to be applied.[28] In particular, medieval theologians asked how a divine command towards sexual multiplication might be reconciled with a dogma that emphasized the spiritual superiority of sexual abstinence. Thus, in *De Civitate Dei*, St Augustine used Genesis 1:28 as evidence for the postlapsarian impact upon the relationship between Reason and Flesh, arguing that in Eden, man and woman might have procreated through the reasoned impositions of the will rather than rowdy demands of concupiscent flesh. "Why should we not believe that the sexual organs could have been the obedient servants of mankind, at the bidding of the will...if there had been no lust, which came in as the retribution for the sin of disobedience?"[29] From this perspective, the morality of human "multiplication" is again assessed through its capacity for (internal and external) regulation. Faced with no external social or demographic pressures to regulate the production of offspring (the entire world after all awaited population), Adam's own human reason provided the counterweight to his productive capacities. Controlling insemination not with his member but with his mind, Adam participated in a mode of multiplication not ad infinitum, but within reason.

After the Fall, however, insemination might no longer be achieved without some degree of pleasure and concupiscence. As Alastair Minnis notes, the virtuous nature of procreation within Eden undermined by contrast its postlapsarian manifestation; medieval theologians such as Bonaventure and Thomas Aquinas put human multiplication into "its historical context—a context which denies it universal value."[30] After the Fall, man's reason and authority were defunct, his capacity to control and moderate his own flesh overthrown. Procreation remained one of the goods of marriage, although in its absence a marriage still might be proved licit.[31] Yet marital procreation was a sacramental good precisely because it was a regulated one, with boundaries reinforced both by canon and

Bath's insufficiencies as an exegetical reader. A. J. Minnis, "The Wisdom of Old Women: Alisoun of Bath as Auctrice," *Writings on Love in the English Middle Ages*, ed. Helen Cooney (New York: Palgrave Macmillan, 2006): 99–114, at 109; while on the other hand, Warren S. Smith argues that it represents Alison's correction of Jerome, bringing him more closely in line with the opinions of St. Augustine on the value of marriage. Smith, "The Wife of Bath Debates Jerome," *Satiric Advice on Women and Marriage*, ed. Warren S. Smith (Ann Arbor, MI: University of Michigan Press, 2005): 247–8.

    [28] Jeremy Cohen, *'Be Fertile and Increase, Fill the Earth and Master It:' The Ancient and Medieval Career of a Biblical Text* (Ithaca, NY: Cornell University Press, 1989): 221–70.
    [29] St. Augustine, *The City of God*, ed. Henry Bettenson (London: Penguin, 2003): 139.
    [30] Alastair Minnis, *From Eden to Eternity: Creations of Paradise in the Later Middle Ages* (Philadelphia, PA: University of Pennsylvania, 2016): 235.
    [31] There was nevertheless a debate about whether such non-procreative sex was inherently sinful, particularly insofar as it was pleasurable. See Brundage, *Law, Sex, and Christian Society*, 138–40, 197–9; Pierre J. Payer, *Sex and the New Medieval Literature of Confession*, 1100–1300 (Toronto: Pontifical Institute of Mediaeval Studies, 2009): 147–50.

civil law. Multiplication, on the other hand, entailed a much larger category of procreations—ones potentially unbounded by matrimony, unregulated by legality, and unblessed by Holy Church. Such multiplications represented a productivity opposed to sufficiency, born instead from pleasure and excess.

Thus, while the Nun's Priest's invocation of the divine command to multiply has been cited (for example, by Jeremy Cohen) as a positive example of Christian exegesis of the scriptural verse, I read the reference as a far more critical one. Before the Nun's Priest chides his avian protagonist, Chauntecleer, for engaging in intercourse with his wives "moore for delit than world to multiplye" (NPT 3345), he first establishes a model of control, regulation, and sufficiency within the figures of the old woman and her daughters. Chauntecleer's owner, a "povre wydwe," "in pacience ladde a ful symple lyf" (NPT 2821, 2826). Before we are ever introduced to Chauntecleer and his seven fowel wives, we first are given evidence of the widow's simple life: the perfect adequacy of her number of sows, cows, and sheep, and the careful limitations of her diet and medical care.[32] "Attempree diete was al hir phisik,/And exercise, and hertes suffisaunce" (NPT 2838–9). The widow's lifestyle is praised for its moderation, but the widow herself is praised even more for her capacity to take delight and comfort within its regulations. She has produced (there are those two daughters), but in a limited and moderate way. The Nun's Priest does not tell us of any unmet desires for the unmaterialized heir, nor does he inform us of any concern on the part of the widow with the posthumous distribution of her goods. She appears content with what she has produced; she has neither need nor lust to multiply.

Thus, while the Nun's Priest appears to critique Chauntecleer for his engagement in coitus for the purpose of fleshly pleasure rather than procreation, the measure of his criticism would seem unsatiated even if Chauntecleer performed sexually with his motivations in reverse. A Chauntecleer copulating with his wives in order to create a rampantly multiplying population of his offspring would hardly be more virtuous than his current state.[33] Indeed, for Chauntecleer to attempt to render his copulations more reproductively successful might in turn undermine the widow's system of sufficiency. The widow appears to be maintaining the chickens for their eggs, rather than for their meat; she eats "somtyme an ey or tweye" (NPT 2845), but her only meat appears to be "seynd bacoun" (NPT 2845). Thus, the widow, finding herself with an excess of young chicks rather than unfertilized eggs, might consider that excess to be a source of destabilizing disproportion on her farm and within her diet. Chauntecleer's pleasure

---

[32] John Finlayson reads this passage as an anticlerical critique meant to reflect retrospectively upon the Monk and his gluttonous excesses. John Finlayson, "The 'Povre Widwe' in the 'Nun's Priest's Tale' and Boccaccio's 'Decameron,'" *Neuphilologische Mitteilungen* 99.3 (1998): 269–73, at 269–70.

[33] I thus agree with Lawrence Warner's critique of Chauntecleer's antimoralist sexual practice, but would take the argument even further to condemn Chauntecleer's couplings even if they were for procreation. Lawrence Warner, "'Woman is Man's Babylon': Chaucer's 'Nembrot' and the Tyranny of Enclosure in the 'Nun's Priest's Tale,'" *The Chaucer Review* 32.1 (1997): 82–107, at 88–9.

thus maintains her sufficiency as his multiplying would never do. Moreover, Chauntecleer's life is already reinforced by excesses of multiplication. He has "sevene hennes for to doon al his plesaunce,/Which were his sustres and his paramours,/And wonder lyk to hym, as of colours" (NPT 2866–8). This is an excessive number of hens for any cock, particularly one not being called upon to father chicks. For, even if Chauntecleer copulated solely from a desire to multiply his seed, those copulations would be neither free from sin nor from the inherent pleasures of the flesh.

What Chauntecleer wishes to multiply *is* specifically his delight, his pleasure in coitus. And, strangely enough, this strategy seems to be to some extent a successful one. His seven hens are "wonder lyk to hym;" he has multiplied his own image by some wondrous power, and now will couple with it. The application of marital terms to the various fowls serves to amplify the humor of the allegory, but it also amplifies the impropriety of the sexual relations. For, Chauntecleer's hens are both "his sustres and his paramours" (NPT 2867); they are both his female family members and his concubines, in a parody both of the divine ban against human incest and the divine commandment in favor of monogamous marriage, even as he is also identified with some form of "miraculous" masturbatory fantasy made manifest through his likeness to his sexual partners. That Chauntecleer is a rooster does not elide the sexual parallels to human practice. Instead, the animal association highlights the more sexually illicit elements of the *Tale*, allowing the reader to imagine a safe and licit coupling with seven women magically like to himself, in an ancient time when "beestes and brides koude speke and synge" and perhaps judged erotic pluralism less harshly than in his own. It is a vision of all the "right" kinds of multiplications from a medieval male perspective: the multiplication of female partners, the multiplication of the individual male image, and the multiplication of carnal pleasure.[34]

Sinful, fleshly things multiply within Chaucer's world. When the Canterbury pilgrims and their characters invoke the word, they do so exclusively about worldly objects. Thus, for example, when Dame Prudence assures Melibee that if he acquires "richesse" honestly, they will "wexeth alwey and multiplieth" (Mel 1580), while the Canon's Yeoman almost exclusively speaks of chemical or financial increase in variants of "multiply." In both cases, the moral ambiguity of the word appears on full display; it is associated exclusively with worldly possessions and gain, yet multiplication is not something that can be achieved through alchemists' tricks or from "thefte and…alle othere yveles" (Mel 1577A). For as Dame Prudence reminds Melibee before holding up the lure of his

---

[34] Sexual strategies such as that of Chauntecleer might have their advantage as a model of what Ruth Karras terms "resource polygyny;" multiple long-term relationships with multiple women produced large numbers of children who could support their legitimate siblings and "enhance" their father's public performance of manhood. Ruth Mazo Karras, *Unmarriages: Women, Men, and Sexual Unions in the Middle Ages* (Philadelphia, PA: University of Pennsylvania Press, 2012): 69.

multiplied riches, "Nature deffendeth and forbedeth by right that/No man make hymself riche unto the harme of another persone" (Mel 1584–1584A). Multiplying is worldly, but it is not evil, a vanity but not a malice. Even the Parson grounds the verb in worldliness rather than outright iniquity, preaching that sins "multiplie in a man so greetly that thilke worldly thynges...he loveth" (ParsT 365A).

Multiplication is a problem of the world and its concerns, a generative process grounded in biology and acquisition rather than in sanctity and abstention. The Second Nun, wishing to generate with her spirit rather than her flesh, has no traffic with multiplication; the Canon's Yeoman, dreaming of personal gain, is, on the other hand, obsessed with it. In Chaucer's hands, faith is exempt from the need to multiply, while avarice is incapable. And yet he sees the most prominent multiplication problem offered by the human desire to generate as grounded neither in chaste nor in scientific reproduction, but rather, in extramarital intercourse. Adultery is the mirror image of alchemy, although each are equally flawed in terms of their capacity to produce. The latter wishes to create multiple offspring with too few conceptive partners; the former wishes to create a single offspring (or none at all) from too many progenitors. There are too many sexual partners in Chaucer's adulterous *Tales* and too few children. In the *Miller's Tale*, for example, Alisoun has three sexual partners from which to choose and yet no offspring; in the *Shipman's Tale*, likewise, money and seed pass unproductively between three partners in a sterile mockery of sexual and financial intercourse.[35] The remainder of this chapter therefore examines the way in which lust (in marriage or in liaison) undermines the heterosexual mechanism of creation, displacing man, woman, and child alike from their natural roles in the multiplication of the species.

Chaucer provides an explicit mediation between multiple forms of multiplication in the Pardoner's speech on the generative powers of his relics. The miracles the Pardoner promises his congregation are, of course, spurious. But, they are also contradictory; the Pardoner's miraculous claims cannot coexist with one another. He pits one form of multiplication (the multiplication of partners) against another (the multiplication of offspring), and genders the former, adulterous desire as female and the latter, reproductive desire as male. And yet neither of the generative models that the Pardoner offers to his audience adhere to cycles of "natural" reproduction, and thus neither can nor will result in viable offspring. They seem more akin to the vision of market production that David DeVries claims for Chaucer, with "money, valuables, symbolic capital all disappear[ing] into a

---

[35] In this reading of the *Shipman's Tale* I thus disagree with the common critical conclusion that, for example in Helen Fulton's words, "each makes a profit on the deal." Helen Fulton, "Mercantile Ideology in Chaucer's *Shipman's Tale*," *The Chaucer Review* 36.4 (2002): 311–28, at 318. Sexual intercourse might be a commodity that will bring pleasure to the characters of the Tale, but it is not a profitable or a productive commodity, as evidenced by the narrator's early words: "Swiche salutaciouns and contenances/Passen as dooth a shadwe upon the wal; But wo is hym that payen moot for al!" (ShipT 8–10). The pleasures of unproductive, unprocreative female company are as transient as they are expensive, according to the Shipman.

'pryvetee' that hides wives swiving to circulate more and more in a rushing swirl that has at its center nothing."³⁶ The forms of multiplication offered up by the Pardoner consume and consume, and hide the emptiness of their productions with the swirling speed of their consumptions. Such multiplications are negative reproductions; they take up intellectual, generative space with the spread of their imagined powers, but they remove from, rather than augment, the human presence within the world.

The Pardoner begins his recitation of these miraculous procreative opportunities by offering two relics—one appropriately phallic and one vaginal—for his audience to behold, a "sholder-boon/which that was of an hooly Jewes sheep" (PardT 350–1) and a "miteyn" (PardT 372). Both relics may only fulfill their creative capacities if utilized in a manner that roughly approximates a heterosexual joining. The bone is meant to be inserted into a well (PardT 353), while the mitten is meant to be penetrated by the hand of a man (PardT 373). Again, as in the earlier sections of this chapter, we may see that when procreation takes place through the intervention of non-human materials, Chaucer's narrators still theorize conception as initiated by the union of objects rendered "male" and "female" by their respective degrees of activity and passivity. The holy bone and the human hand become the catalytic forces of insemination within the Pardoner's scenario, while the well and mitten become the female matter upon which the active power will work.

The man who drinks of the well into which the holy bone has been inserted every week will witness that "his beestes and his stoor shal multiplie" (PardT 365). Similarly:

> He that his hand wol putte in this mitayn
> He shal have multipliyng of his grayn
> Whan he hath sowen, be it whete or otes,
> So that he offer pens, or elles grotes.
>
> (PardT 373–6)

This is a prototypical use of the word "multiplying" as a stand-in for generation. In both cases, whether turning to the powers of the bone or the mitten, the men who heed the Pardoner's claims wish to augment their personal wealth, to benefit from sacred intervention into the means of procreation so as to amplify their share of production. Moreover, they wish to produce and generate without reference to female partners, to allow a holy relic to facilitate the miracle of a male-only production similar in many ways to that desired by the alchemical scientists of the *Canon Yeoman's Tale*. It is wheat and oats that they themselves have sown, beasts and steers that they themselves own (seemingly in independence from a

---

³⁶ David N. DeVries, "Chaucer and the Idols of the Market," *The Chaucer Review* 32.4 (1998): 391–8, at 398.

family unit), for which they dream of a rapid acceleration of growth and production. This is not the model of mutual production and conception endorsed by the medieval Church and medieval theories of Nature; it is again a case of men aspiring to conceive with one another or on their own, and, as with Chaucer's alchemists, who are willing to pay for the pleasure.

The Pardoner offers women a similarly procreative miracle, but in their case it is their sexual partners that he promises to multiply, rather than their goods or possessions. If these women drink his holy water (women are not offered access to the holy mitten since the Pardoner appears unable to imagine what could be created by the insertion of a female hand into a "female" hole), they will be rendered capable of taking lovers without losing their husbands.

> For though a man be falle in jalous rage,
> Lat maken with this water his potage
> And nevere shal he moore his wyf mystriste,
> Though he the soothe of hir defaute wiste,
> Al had she taken prestes two or thre.
>
> (PardT 367–71).

A wife who offers her husband some of the Pardoner's miraculous soup will find herself able to copulate with as many men as she desires, as epitomized by the image of the two or three priests. However, it is not the consent of multiple men to engage in sexual intercourse that the Pardoner imagines the wives in his audience would want; rampant desire is taken for granted in this scenario. Rather, women wish for the desire to multiply their lovers without spousal interference or abandonment, to multiply the sources of seed while maintaining the social protection of the spouse who can claim paternity with trust in his wife, even when he knows such trust to be misplaced. Wives wish, according to the Pardoner, for an intervention into their husbands' processes of knowledge and perception. They do not mind if their husband acquires awareness of their misdeeds, as long as he does not make the immediate cognitive leap to suspecting them of such misdeeds or to drawing conclusions about their virtue. If there seem to be some logical holes on the parts of the wives in this scenario—for example, how do the husbands simultaneously know and not know about their wives' infidelity?— perhaps that can be ascribed to a certain general tendency within *The Canterbury Tales* to ascribe remarkably faulty intellectual processes to its female characters.

Even more significantly, however, the Pardoner's imagined audience of husbands and wives are in possession of desires that fundamentally conflict with one another. The husbands wish to multiply their goods without reference to their wives as conceptive partners, allowing a paternal certainty in their own creation; the wives wish to engage in the act of conception with as many men as possible, thus undermining their husbands' ability to be certain of their conceptive role in creating their own children, a material "good" even more significant than their

farm animals or produce. Moreover, both of these forms of "unnatural reproduction," while facilitated by supposedly holy relics, result only in alienating their
male and female practitioners from the Church. For, after holding out this vision
of sexually diverse reproductions, the Pardoner then moves to condemn those
who take advantage of such lures. To the wives to whom he has promised a conse-
quence-free mode of multiplication, he now preaches that "any womman, be she
yong or old/that hath ymaked hir housbonde cokewolde" (PardT 381–2) cannot
offer to his relics because of her sin. Similarly, if one assumes the continued existence of the parallelism from earlier in this passage, then the Pardoner's ban on
men offering to his relics who have "doon synne horrible, that he/dar not, for
shame, of it yshryven be" (PardT 379–80) may be a reference to those husbands
who likewise have wished to procreate without their wives, and have thus engaged
in sexual sins by themselves or with other men.

   It is the breaking of the heterosexual pact that the Pardoner seems to condemn,
the sexual union between men and women designed by God and Nature alike so
as to allow for the mutual production of offspring. The Pardoner's own sexual and
procreative ambiguity, derived from his famous classification as either "a gelding
or a mare" (GP 691), enhances his critique, since his body thereby rejects the
forms of balance that Chaucer (and medieval texts more generally) identified
with productivity.[37] The Pardoner's flesh is excessive in its scarcities, provoking
comment from Chaucer-the-narrator. The pervasive sense of absence that sur-
rounds the Pardoner in the *General Prologue* encompasses far more than just his
sexuality. Chaucer spends forty-five lines introducing the Pardoner within the
larger company, and the full first half of this discourse emphasizes the Pardoner's
insufficiencies and absences. The Pardoner lacks not only clear signs of masculinity, he also possesses extremely thin hair (675–9) and a voice "as small as hath a
goot" (GP 688); for the sake of style, he has refused to wear his hood (GP 680–3),
and his facial hair is noted according to its absence, "no berd hadde he, ne nevere
sholde" (GP 689). Chaucer's comment on the Pardoner as gelding or mare comes
only after this recitation. It is the climactic summation of the array of disappointing, unfulfilling traits that have come before.

   However, the line about the Pardoner as gelding or as mare also marks a transition from Chaucer's emphasis on the scarcity associated with the Pardoner to his
employment of an inverse rhetoric fixated upon the Pardoner as a figure of
inappropriate abundance. The Pardoner's insufficient masculinity serves as the
apex of this semiotic switch, but it is reinforced by Chaucer's immediately

[37] For discussion of the Pardoner's ambiguous performance of sex and gender, see:
Monica E. McAlpine, "The Pardoner's Homosexuality and How It Matters," *PMLA* 95.1 (Jan., 1980):
8–22; Dinshaw, *Chaucer's Sexual Poetics*, 156–86; Glenn Burger, "Kissing the Pardoner," *PMLA* 107.5
(October 1992): 1143–56; Steven F. Kruger, "Claiming the Pardoner: Toward a Gay Reading of
Chaucer's *Pardoner's Tale*," *Exemplaria* 6 (1994): 115–39; Carolyn Dinshaw, "Chaucer's Queer
Touches/A Queer Touches Chaucer," *Exemplaria* 7.1 (Spring 1995): 75–92.

successive comment upon the general availability of such Pardoners within the world. Chaucer-the-narrator declares, "But of his craft, fro Berwyk into Ware/Ne was ther swich another pardoner./For in his male he hadde a pilwe-beer..." (GP 692–4). The paradox of the Pardoner is thereby contained; namely, that he overflows with his own insufficiencies. He is so lacking as to be thereby abundant in this emptiness, so excessive as to be lacking any peer. The Pardoner's "male" (GP 694) is stuffed full of pardons and spurious relics; the last half of Chaucer's description of this pilgrim focuses on outlining the objects that fill the purse to its brim. And yet in its resonance of the verb "male," used by Chaucer elsewhere in the *Tales* to indicate the male sex, the Pardoner's male purse reflects the character's radical vacillations between the abundant and the scarce. He lacks the male genitals necessary to reproduce, and yet his "male" is overflowing with the false reproductions of holy relics. The Pardoner is a stranger to the sufficiency necessary for normative procreations, and thus the only creation of which he is capable is that of making "the person and the peple his apes" (GP 706).

The Pardoner is not, therefore, only a preacher against avarice; he is a preacher against avarice's favorite mode of generation: multiplication. From the example of his own body, he demonstrates the perilous losses that await those who seek out unmediated excess as their good. As the Pardoner preaches, "Radix malorum est Cupiditas" (PardT 426), an excerpt from a much longer condemnation of avarice within 1 Timothy, chapter 6. He continues, "I preche nothyng but for coveitise./ Of this mateere it oghte ynogh suffise" (PardT 433–4). The clever rhyme between "coveitise" and "suffise" reinforces the Pardoner's endorsement of moderation for his brethren even as he offers them the dream of multiplication. It is this same logic that leads the Pardoner to condemn gluttony as a mode of anti-reproduction within his *Tale*.[38]

> O wombe! O bely! O stynkyng cod,
> Fulfilled of dong and of corrupcioun!
> At either ende of thee foul is the soun.
> How greet labour and cost is thee to fynde!
> Thise cookes, how they stampe, and streyne,
> And turnen substaunce into accident
> To fulfille al thy likerous talent!
>
> (PardT 534–40)

Eating, according to the Pardoner, is but a mockery of insemination. Men, in their avarice, desire to fill the wrong womb, performing a solitary act of generation

---

[38] The Pardoner also speaks of gluttony as one of the primary sins of Adam and Eve, and as the cause behind their exile from the Garden of Eden. As Susan Hill records, this rhetoric came from a longstanding tradition among Church fathers. Susan E. Hill, "'The Ooze of Gluttony': Attitudes towards Food, Eating, and Excess in the Middle Ages," *The Seven Deadly Sins*, ed. Richard Newhauser (Leiden: Brill, 2014): 57–72, at 59–60.

within their own flesh, and thereby becoming the fathers of dung and other materials of corruption. Whereas male seed should work upon female matter within the womb, shaping and transforming it into human life, such men rely instead upon cooks to satisfy (or further stimulate) their productions. And yet for all the efforts of the cooks, such parodies will prove destructive. They destroy substance and annihilate the very matter that might, in the right womb and with the right progenitor, be brought forth as new, sufficient life.

Multiplying was reproduction done in the wrong places and for the wrong reasons, seed put into mittens or into men's stomachs rather than into the divinely ordained receptacle of female flesh. Driven by the love of excess, multiplying was a form of clinging tightly to human goods, an amalgamation of gluttony, avarice, and lechery alike. John Gower condemns such behaviors within his short poem, *Dicunt Scripture*, calling on men to "give while you have time, let your heir be your own hand;/No one will take away what you yourself give to God" ("Da, dum tempus habes, tibi propria sit manus heres;/Auferet hoc nemo, quod dabis ipse Deo").[39] And yet men did not need to embrace abnegation so fully as Gower advised in order to avoid the sins of avarice through multiplication. Gower found such sin in human practice to be a reason to disavow the entire system of personal reproductions, manifesting one's desire for perpetuation in the soul rather than within the body. On the contrary, with his comparison between wombs, Chaucer's Pardoner allows for the existence of a successful mode of human generation, albeit one driven not by "coveityse" but by sufficiency.

Within the human body, more was simply too much. Adulterous wives were receptacles of too much seed to be productive, let alone of too much seed to be certain of their offspring's paternity. Medieval reproductive theory imagined the womb as a "purse," capable of containing only the amount of "coin" for which it had been designed to hold.[40] One of the commenters in *De secretum mulierum*, for example, offers as medical fact that if new semen is provided to a womb already filled with male seed, that womb might choose to eject the previously implanted seed.[41] A similar act of physiological rebellion was imagined within the medieval romance, *Lay le Freine*, where characters debate whether a pregnancy with twins reveals female adultery; upon learning that her neighbor's wife has born two twin sons, the heroine's mother declares, "wel may ich man wite

---

[39] John Gower, "Dicunt Scripture," *The Minor Latin Works with In Praise of Peace*, ed. and trans. R. F. Yeager (Kalamazoo, MI: Medieval Institute Publications, 2005): 52.

[40] One of the commentators in the *Secretum mulierum* goes even further with this metaphor, imagining the womb as a purse as an analogy for female social behavior. "When in the text the author mentions the womb closing up like a purse, this is similar to someone having a friend giving her as a gift something that she likes very much. If the friend were afraid to lose the gift, she would close her hand tightly, and in the same way the womb desires to retain the semen and for this reason closes up tight." *Women's Secrets*, ed. Lemay, 70. The original comment (quoting Avicenna) is on p. 66.

[41] *Women's Secrets*, ed. Lemay, 102.

therfore/that tuay men hir han hadde in bour."[42] Such a medical theory proposes that female adultery will rob a man's seed of the maternal resources that should be its exclusive right.

Through adultery, women reject men's "natural" claims on their bodies and upon their reproductive capacities. Chaucer's Parson indeed dwells at some length on why women are not allowed to multiply their husbands; it is according to the rule of nature, and logic of productivity. "For if a womman hadde mo men than oon, thanne sholde she have moo hevedes than oon, and that were an horrible thyng biforn God... and forther over, no man ne sholde knowe his owene engendredure, ne who sholde have his heritage" (ParsT 922–23). A woman who multiplies her sexual partners destroys the aspirations of husband and lover alike to multiply themselves in turn through the reliable conception of offspring. Thomas Aquinas offers a similar variation on this theme within the *Supplement* to the *Summa Theologica*, although he adds as well that such a singularity of male partnership is predicated upon a practice of paternal care; a man must know his own offspring not for personal gain, but rather so that he might provide them with his protection and labor.[43] As men break this covenant with their offspring and with the purposes of procreation, so too will women break their covenants with men. When men seek to multiply their goods, women will seek to multiply their lovers.

The Monstrous Heirs of Greed: Chaucer's Cuckolds and their Cuckoos

Even Chaucer's humble Parson appreciates the importance of human reproduction as a reliable means of transferring wealth between productive parties, warning against adultery that "of which brekynge [of the marital bond] comen false heires ofte tyme, that wrongfully ocupien folkes heritages" (ParsT 884). It should

---

[42] "Lay le Freine," *The Middle English Breton Lays*, ed. Anne Laskaya and Eve Salisbury (Kalamazoo, MI: Medieval Institute Publications, 1995): lines 70–1.

[43] Thomas Aquinas, *Aquinas Ethicus: Or, the Moral Teaching of St. Thomas Aquinas: A Translation of the Principal Portions of the Second Part of the 'Summa Theologica,'* Vol. 2, ed. Joseph Rickaby, S.J. (London: Burns and Oates, 1896): 329. Don Browning and John Witte use this line to argue for Aquinas's argument as fundamental to the Christian rationale for paternal investment within the family unit. They write: "Once a rational man is certain of his paternity, he will come to see that the child is literally an extension and continuation of himself, a part and product of his own body and being (his genes, we would say). He will then care for the infant as though it is his own body." Don S. Browning and John Witte, Jr, "Christianity's Mixed Contributions to Children's Rights: Traditional Teachings, Modern Doubts," *Children, Adults, and Shared Responsibilities: Jewish, Christian, and Muslim Perspectives*, ed. Marcia J. Bunge (Cambridge: Cambridge University Press, 2012): 276–91, at 285. I find this summation of Aquinas's argument does a fine job of emphasizing the inherent human selfishness assumed by medieval theologians to be at the heart of human reproduction; a man lacking certainty in the paternity of his offspring is thereby justified according to "Nature" in an abandonment of the domestic unit, and it is only by appealing to the individual desire for self-preservation that men can be enticed to participate in paternal care.

therefore be unsurprising that Chaucer's pilgrims associate female adultery almost exclusively with the wrongful disposition of wealth. John the Carpenter (of the *Miller's Tale*) is a "riche gnof" (MilT 3188), the Shipman's merchant "riche was, for which men helde hym wys" (ShipT 2), the Merchant's January a "worthy knight…in greet prosperitee" (MerT 1246–7), and miller Symkyn is likewise marked by his pride (RT 3865, 3926, 4313) within the *Reeve's Tale*. As the Reeve comments,

> Symkyn wolde no wyf, as he sayde,
> But she were wel ynorrished and a mayde,
> To saven his estaat of yomanrye.
>
> (RT 3947–9)

This is at once both a cruel joke for Chaucer's aristocratic audience about yeomen who so prize their "lofty" station and estates, and a sharp assessment of the type of social and economic fragility experienced by men of every class when reflecting upon generative dreams. A virginal wife, educated by nuns, was an investment in a man's future as a father, in his certainty that he himself had sired his sons, and that his property would be preserved for the next generation.

In this final section of the chapter I wish to observe the parallels between two Chaucerian rhetorics of miscreation, in which fathers jealous of the distribution of their patrimony serve to create their own false heirs, thereby themselves perverting the purity of their bloodline and the very mode of reproduction itself. In their excessive avarice, the men of the *Reeve's Tale* and *Merchant's Tale* end up thwarting their own desires for reliable heirs; they make their own monstrous cuckoos from their fear of other men and the intensity of their pecuniary lust. Both become caught in the cyclical nature of greed's reproductions, as, in their longing to add and add to their storehouses of treasure and the excesses of their goods, they lose sight of the natural progressions of time. Fixated upon the preservation and augmentation of present abundance, such men forget the very reason that they need an heir: not so that they might clasp more tightly to the petty pleasures of the world, but so that they might loosen the grips upon their lives, moving towards the fatal inevitability resting at the end of linear time. True heirs are made when their fathers die, as they assume their father's place in the world around them, and thus men who refuse to relinquish that place and move towards their deaths and the repudiation of their goods, find only cuckoos waiting in their nest.

Oswald the Reeve indeed preaches on precisely this theme to the assorted company, before Harry Bailly cuts off his "sermonyng" (RT 3899) and calls for lighter fare. The Reeve presents himself as an old man caught in a generative quandary: what kind of *Tale* should old men tell and leave within the world?

> Ful wel koude I thee quite
> With bleryng of a proud milleres ye,

> If that me liste speke of ribaudye.
> But ik am oold; me list not pley for age.

(RT 3864–7)

The Miller's tale of a cuckolded carpenter has left its own "offspring" in the world; most of the company is given joy, but Oswald the Reeve receives "a litel ire…in his herte ylaft" (RT 3862). He must therefore decide how to respond, and first he reasons like a young, foolish man, wishing to proffer to the Miller that same gift which he himself has received, a vengeful fabliau.

But before requiting the Miller with a ribald poem, the Reeve first invokes a different mode of generation, ostensibly more appropriate for a man soon to leave the earth behind. He is more than capable of producing a "ribaudye" to match the Miller's own, but he recognizes that such creations are rendered inappropriate (and perhaps inaccessible) by his advanced age. The verb "pley," used by the Reeve to denote the act of literary production, is applied later in the *Tales* by the Shipman's wife to indicate the dissatisfying congress of her marriage bed; she tells Don John that in all France there is "no wyf/That lasse lust hath to that sory pley" (ShipT 116–7). Thus, the Reeve's employment of the verb resonates with motifs of failed sexuality, the aging husband incapable of satisfying his wife's avid lusts, and, even more significantly, incapable of producing some offspring from their couplings. As Placebo advises the aged Justinus in the *Merchant's Tale*, "I warne yow wel, it is no childes pley/To take a wyf withouten avysement" (MerT 1530–1). And indeed, when old men marry in *The Canterbury Tales* there are very few children (playful or otherwise) born from those marriages. Men play at speech even as they play in bed: with inverse skill as they increase in age. The jocularity of their "pley," however, is not enough to release them or their wives from the disappointments of its sterility.

Such couplings bear little fruit. The Reeve imagines his aged body as flesh so rotten, so degraded, as to become the very offal of his own generations.

> But if I fare as dooth an open-ers –
> That ilke fruyt is ever lenger the wers,
> Til it be roten in mullok or in stree.
> We olde men, I drede, so fare we:
> Til we be roten, kan we nat be rype

(RT 3871–5)

The bearing of fruit is one of Chaucer's favorite metaphors for generation, and was a common symbol in other contemporary English poems, such as William Langland's *Piers Plowman*. Moreover, for Chaucer, like the verb "pley," it resonates with a dual signification; in *The Canterbury Tales*, fructification is often the shorthand for literary, rather than corporeal, procreation. The Man of Law, for example, refers twice to "fruyt" as the product of tale-telling, the offspring that legitimates the system of poetic generation, and, as Warren Ginsburg notes, Oswald the

Reeve attacks the Miller with a reference to the Gospel of Luke that immediately precedes the evangelist's commentary on the likeness between trees and their fruit: "There is no good tree that bringeth forth evil fruit, etc."[44] Twining metaphors of fructification into the narrative of literary creation shapes a linear, causal structure for those acts of linguistic siring, so that they can be presented as a form of alternative reproduction at a remove from the human flesh but never quite divorced from it. Chaucer eroticizes his fruitful play, while always leaving the objects of his verse open to deanimation, reducible at any moment from sex to vegetation.

The Reeve's self-identification as an "open-ers" is thus blatantly sexual, and critics have recognized the homoeroticism tied up within its metaphor; however, that moment of intrusive crudity expands beyond the specifics of homosexual or heterosexual intercourse to comment and assess sexuality within procreative terms.[45] The medlar fruit, with its cleft resembling a human buttocks, was, as Carol Everest notes, associated not only with the coarse lewdity of man's body, but also with the complexional specifications (coldness and dryness) associated with aging, and with the spermatic insufficiencies of the elderly.[46] The Reeve ties the insufficiencies of his speech to the impotency of his body. He is so old that any kind of linguistic or erotic "pley" will prove only unproductive. Even worse, it will prove counterproductive, corrupting his existent body rather than reproducing it in a mimetic form. Breaking with the Chaucerian metaphor of poetic fruitfulness, the Reeve imagines a mode of production indivisible from consumption. This is the same mechanism of decay identified by Theseus in the *Knight's Tale*, discussed in the Introduction to this book, as the part, divided from the wholeness of its progenitor, becomes exponentially smaller over the "successions" of man's heredity. And yet here those generations of succession are compressed into the body of one man; the process of aging so accelerated that we move from wholeness to rotten part in the course of one generation alone. Within his own flesh, the Reeve provides an allegory of man's decay and of reproduction's counterproductive impact upon the human desire to generate its own longevity.

The Reeve himself is the only fruit that his body will ever bear, and he is rotten and anus-shaped. That "open-ers" slang for the medlar fruit can be understood to

[44] Warren Ginsberg, *Tellers, Tales, and Translation in Chaucer's Canterbury Tales* (Oxford: Oxford University Press, 2015): 12.

[45] The most extensive work done on the gendering of the Reeve through his self-identification as an "open-ers" is Anna Waymack's master's thesis. Anna Fore Waymack, "Speaking through the 'Open-Ers:' How Age Feminizes Chaucer's Reeve" (master's thesis, University of Texas at Austin, 2013). Womack argues that this rhetoric serves to feminize the Reeve, allowing him to cast off "the standard marginalized voice of old age" to "create a decaying chaotic mess...he openly utilizes that decay to create a new hole and voice with which to express desire." Waymack, "Speaking Through the "Open-Ers," 15.

[46] Carol A. Everest, "Sex and Old Age in Chaucer's 'Reeve's Tale,' *The Chaucer Review* 31.2 (1996): 99–114, at 106–8.

invoke a queer porosity, a vulnerability to phallic intrusion, but it can also be visualized as its inverse, as a form of obscene birth. Where women's wombs open to bear fruit, the aged and moldy Reeve will open his arse to find only more rotten waste. And, what is worse, he will bring forth that waste into the world, fathering only an excess of feces, even as in the *Summoner's Tale*, the devil's anus opened to reveal a teeming swarm of friars.[47] The Reeve offers a vision of profound corruption, predicated upon the desire to speak, but also recognizing the horrendous excesses that will teem from his double mouths as soon he allows them to open. There is a monstrosity inherent in the Reeve, whether it originates from his age (one is reminded of how Chaucer's old January makes love to his wife as "the slakke skyn about his nekke shaketh [MerT 1849]), his occupation, or even, as Joseph Taylor has argued, his identity as a Northerner.[48] The products of his creation are thereby rendered monstrous in turn, consumed, along with his own flesh, by his foolish efforts at generation. The Reeve makes a similar, if less scatological, point when he laments that his heart is as "mowled as myne heris." The phonological closeness of the two words, "heris" and "heires," allows for a moment of blurred play here. We know the Reeve is complaining about his moldy hair, but he leads us to reflect as well upon the quality of his heirs, of how decayed would be the offspring of a man capable of producing only moldy hair upon his head. Indeed, it makes as little sense for hair to be moldy as it would for children, and the metaphorical leap required for the reader in adjudging the former, makes the latter that much simpler of an intellectual recognition.

The Reeve embodies both the rotten potential procreations of his flesh and the monstrous process of parturition by which such heirs would come to be. And yet while the Reeve warns us of his perversions, he is nevertheless as unwilling as anyone else within *The Canterbury Tales* to let that prevent him from generating speech. He is too old to speak, he tells the company, but just wait a while, and soon he will be ready. "We olde men, I drede, so fare we:/Til we be roten, kan we nat be rype" (RT 3874–5). V. A. Kolve refers to this speech as a testimony to "the perverse longevity of sexual desire," but it is also an articulation of the perverse development of that desire.[49] The Reeve's lust is not persevering in stasis, but rather multiplying. He understands his body only in terms of positive or negative development, ripening or decay; he wishes not to maintain a status quo but to take advantage of the rapidity of corporeal change. What he first called rot he now calls ripe, transforming his rhetoric to match the swelling of his desires.

---

[47] The demonic allusions within the *Reeve's Tale* have been well catalogued by Deborah Ellis, but she does not make the connection between the two "open-arses." Deborah S. Ellis, "Chaucer's Devilish Reeve," *The Chaucer Review* 27.2 (1992): 150–61.

[48] Joseph Taylor, "Chaucer's Uncanny Regionalism: Rereading the North in the *Reeve's Tale*," *Journal of English and Germanic Philology* 109.4 (Octobrt 2010): 468–89, at 474.

[49] V. A. Kolve, *Chaucer and the Imagery of Narrative: The First Five Canterbury Tales* (Stanford, CA: Stanford University Press, 1984): 253.

> For sikerly, whan I was bore, anon
> Deeth drough the tappe of lyf and leet it gon,
> And ever sithe hath the tappe yronee
> Til that almoost al empty is the tonne.
> The streem of lyf now droppeth on the chymbe.

(RT 3891–6)

The Reeve's "tappe of lyf," coming immediately after his description of his "coltes tooth" (RT 3888), becomes intrusively, uncomfortably seminal.[50] He recasts his body from one in which all flesh has become corrupt, all possible productions rendered perverse, into one that still holds the seminal fluid of maintaining life and procreating life. The fluids given to him by God are low, but they are not gone yet! They droppeth on the "chymbe," and thus he has enough left still to create; "the sely tonge may wel rynge and chymbe" (RT 3896). His speech has been legitimated by this late turn of his rhetoric, and now he is ready to speak, however rotten his offspring may prove.

The *Tale* that the Reeve tells mirrors his verbal processes of miscreation. It is the story of men who miscreate, who exploit their financial opportunities to wreak immorality, to sire monstrous, unnatural heirs from their own rotten flesh.[51] More specifically, it offers a dual drama of paternity, centered between two men (Symkyn the miller, and the town parson, his father-in-law) whose identities as fathers merge almost seamlessly together into a single image of corrupt paternity.[52] Symkyn has inherited his patrilineal aspirations from the older male figure and, since the latter's death is not marked within the narrative, appears to represent both their simultaneous interests in reproducing on the flesh of Malyne, their daughter/wife. As John Plummer notes, "It is as father and grandfather, as progenitor rather than actor, that [the parson's] presence is felt, both causally and symbolically… [Symkyn] is the agent in situ of the parson."[53] The parson has quite literally invested in the union of Symkyn and his daughter

---

[50] For discussions of the various metaphorical possibilities incumbent within the Reeve's leaking tap, see A. H. MacLaine, "Chaucer's Wine Cask Image: Word Play in 'The Reeve's Prologue," *Medium Aevum* 31.2 (1962): 129–31; Carol Falvo Heffernan, "A Reconsideration of the Cask Figure in the 'Reeve's Prologue," *The Chaucer Review* 151 (Summer 1980): 37–43.

[51] As Elizabeth Sears writes, old age could be associated with an increase in avarice; Thomas of Cantimpre argued that "in the decrepit age, a period of weakening, avarice increases since the individual despairs of being able to provide for himself in the future." Elizabeth Sears, *The Ages of Man: Medieval Interpretations of the Life Cycle* (Princeton, NJ: Princeton University Press, 1986): 126. This interpretation of aging sets up an inverse relationship between human greed and human productivity, explaining why old men have a heightened investment in reproductive attempts.

[52] The existence of a cleric's illegitimate child was not in itself particularly uncommon in the Middle Ages. As Ruth Karras notes, the thousands of extant dispensations offered to the illegitimate sons of priests wishing in turn to enter religious orders testifies to the relative frequency with which clerical celibacy was transgressed. Ruth Karras, *Sexuality in Medieval Europe: Doing Unto Others* (London and New York: Routledge, 2005): 56.

[53] John F. Plummer, "Hooly Chirches Blood: Simony and Patrimony in Chaucer's 'Reeve's Tale,'" *The Chaucer Review* 18.1 (Summer 1983): 49–60, at 55.

through her dowry, that customary transmission of wealth between men. "With hire ye yaf ful many a panne of bras,/For that Symkyn sholde in his blood allye" (RT 2944–5). It is important to note that Symkyn the miller has been carefully selected by the parson for an alliance with his family and heritage, and that the parson has contributed a significant amount of his material wealth to bring this marriage to fruition. Moreover, the parson's financial stewardship of his daughter's family continues to the next generation, with his active strategies for, and financial investment in, the womb and body of his granddaughter/heir. It is customary to think of the *Reeve's Tale* as a story of a confrontation between a miller and two students, fought upon the eroticized bodies of the miller's women. And yet it is just as much the story of conflict between an irreligious parson and two students, albeit one displaced into the next generation of his family.[54] Symkyn the miller stands in for the parson in this larger dynastic game, representing the interests of a male lineage defined by its religious illegitimacy.

The parson's desire to found a noble bloodline is made particularly manifest through his aspirations for his granddaughter.

> This person of the toun, for she was feir,
> In purpos was to maken hire his heir,
> Bothe of his catel and his mesuage.
>
> (RT 3977–9)

Malyne, like her mother, intrudes into the story according to her sexual desirability and her capacity to transmit material goods between men. The parson's plans for the girl, "to maken hire his heir," do not endow her with his goods so much as they transform her person *into* one of his goods, "his heir" even as it is "his catel and his mesuage." The essential possessiveness at the heart of the parson's paternal strategy means that it is fundamentally suited to be achieved through female, rather than male, bodies. After all, Symkyn and his wife have another child, a young boy who is, according to patriarchal traditions of inheritance, more entitled to the status of his grandfather's heir than is his sister. And yet that child could not exclusively belong to the parson; by right of sex, he is his father's heir.[55] By that same sex, the young boy enforces a division between the male forces of the parson and the miller, breaking their unity as paternal construct through the presumption of his closer bond to his father. In contrast, the miller's daughter is

---

[54] Nicole Sidhu remarks upon how rare such a pattern is among the fabliau, "whose primary focus is on erotic relationships rather than intergenerational ones," and concludes that the plot of the *Reeve's Tale* is far closer to many classical plots, such as that of Theseus and Ariadne, than it is to its Anglo-French peers. Nicole Nolan Sidhu, *Indecent Exposure: Gender, Politics, and Obscene Comedy in Middle English Literature* (Philadelphia, PA: University of Pennsylvania Press, 2016): 77, 79–80.

[55] William Woods therefore sees the baby as the crux of Symkyn's eventual downfall, writing, "when the baby is used to ridicule Symkyn, collapse his bullying, and thus constrain his predation, he has in effect been wounded from within, bled by his own blood." William F. Woods, "The Logic of Deprivation in the *Reeve's Tale*," *The Chaucer Review* 30.2 (1995): 150–63, at 155.

up for grabs. She can be possessed fully by either man or both together, absorbed into whatever fictional construct of lineage they desire to dream. She is female so she is flexible, with no position on the linear tree of male time except that which her father(s) deign to grant to her.

The girl's potential as an heir is inseparable from her potential to be sexually possessed. She is useful to her grandfather and father insofar as her erotic capacities will forge bonds for them with other men. The Reeve describes the nature of her beauty, noting her "kamus nose and eyen greye as glas,/With buttokes brode and brestes ronde and hye" (RT 3974–5). Her hair may be fair (RT 3976), but the crudity of his description makes it clear that it is not an admiration for ethereal beauty but rather a purely erotic lust that the young woman inspires in male hearts. Indeed, it is because of this lust-creating attribute of her appearance that the parson has aspirations for her marriage, hoping to wed her "into som worthy blood" (RT 3982). He plans to take advantage of her sexual desirability to trap another man into an alliance with himself, even as he utilized his own daughter's virginity to woo Symkyn into marriage. If millers long for virgins, then, the parson appears to believe, lords must long for broad buttocks and high breasts. William Woods identifies the lure of Malyne's marriage as allowing both men, miller and parson alike, to participate in a logic of deprivation; once Malyne is married to an aristocrat, the miller will have "drained the resources of all three of the traditional estates (commons, clerics, nobles) into his own capacious pocket."[56] In each case, the parson manipulates the facts of his female descendant's body to negotiate his relationships with the men around him, and what they offer to the continuation of his bloodline; Woods therefore terms both wife and daughter "vessels of infinite increase."[57]

And yet, as the Reeve makes clear, the parson believes himself to have merged his paternal duties with his pastoral ones; it is both as a religious and as a patriarchal authority that the parson considers his bloodline to warrant perpetuation. In a radical misunderstanding of Church doctrine, the parson conceptualizes his desire to reproduce his bloodline as a religious rather than biological imperative.

> For hooly chirches good moot been despended
> On hooly chirches blood, that is descended.
> Therfore he wolde his hooly blood honoure,
> Though that he hooly chirche sholde devoure.
>
> (RT 3932–6)

The parson elides his own physical identity with that of the Church that he has served so poorly and unchastely. The social authority that it has granted him within his community has effected, from his perspective, a holistic transformation

[56] Woods, "Logic of Deprivation," 151.   [57] Woods, "Logic of Deprivation," 156.

of his flesh into something sacred. Chaucer's reference to the parson's "hooly blood," while first and foremost a mockery of the moral distance between his pretensions and his reality, is also a sharp reminder of how fluidly the paternal and patriarchal models of authority blur together, and of how easily a man may clothe his worldly lusts within a pious attire.

The parson's position within the Church has excluded him from the classic modes of reproduction and creation, but he refuses to accept that exclusion or to embrace the new productive capacities that are available to a religious man. The contrast between this parson and that "good man" (GP 477), the parson of the *General Prologue*, is most readily apparent in terms of each man's relationship with pecuniary accumulation. The parson who is traveling with Chaucer on pilgrimage is "povre…but riche he was of hooly thoght and werk" (GP 478–9); the Reeve's parson is concerned only with the acquisition of wealth. And yet this contrast is also fundamentally grounded upon precepts of creation and production. For the holy parson of the *Prologue* is a man at peace with his own productivity. Like his brother, the plowman, the parson understands what the fruits of his labor will be, and finds them utterly opposed to the possession of material goods. The plowman is a "trewe swynkere" (GP 531) and would "thresshe, and therto dyke and delve,/For Cristes sake, for every povre wight" (GP 536–7). His experience of work is removed from his expectation for remuneration. His labor results in a product for others, even as the goal of the parson's labor is "to drawen folk to hevene" (GP 519) rather than to win his own salvation. Such holy men experience their productivity as a mechanism divorced from the "natural" selfishness of its causality. They labor so that other men can eat; they pray so that other men will be saved. The poor and the laity are thus heir to what the parson and plowman create *as soon as* it is created; the subjects of the labor (the two holy brothers) never assume personal possession of the material and immaterial products that they have brought into being.

This is a form of sacral creation and inheritance of which the parson of the *Reeve's Tale* wants no part. He claims "hooly chirches good" as his own, espousing the very model of personal possession that the other parson and the plowman have both denounced. On one hand, as John Plummer has observed, the parson engages in a classic example of simony, a sin typically depicted in "images of illegitimate birth, patrimony, and fornication."[58] The material goods with which he has been invested, courtesy of his religious position, become part of his own material form, and vice versa, with his assessment of his own body as "hooly chirches blood" (RT 3934). The internal rhyme within the verses (between good and blood) highlights the unnaturalness of this elision, and the worldly contexts into which the parson has thrust such spiritual matters. Holy Church has goods far more precious than the brass pans that the parson stole for his daughter's dowry;

---

[58] Plummer, "Hooly Chirches Blood," 50.

it has blood far more worthy of honor than what may be found within the parson's veins. The parson simply does not understand the spiritual potential of his role. He treats the clergy as if it were a form of earthly power, one which endows an individual with the products of his labor, and allows that individual to transmit these products in turn upon his death. That upheaval of causality experienced by the plowman and the other parson, as they turn over what they have created to others, and take upon themselves only the labor of creation, rather than its fruits, is utterly foreign to this parson. He is a worldly man wearing the mantle of unworldliness, and thus he invests his capacities of production in biological reproduction rather than the salvation of other's souls.[59]

The two scholars at the heart of this fabliaux therefore approach these two women (mother and daughter alike) as the dual embodiment of the male desire to create, and to preserve economic resources through that creation. They are the fleshly shapes at the convergence of two men's biological ambitions. If Symkyn's wife is rather haughty about "hire kynrede and hir nortelrie" (RT 3967), it is as a byproduct of paternal and husbandly ambition. Moreover, her haughtiness (unlike that of her father or of Symkyn) is not a desire for replication, but rather an affective response to her position as the object of her father's own reproduction. Here it is important to note how displaced Symkyn's wife's pride is from her relationship to Symkyn himself. She is proud of her kindred and of her convent tutelage, both of which she received from her father. Although we can identity in Symkyn a desire to replicate himself and transmit his goods through the creation of offspring, his wife appears to identify herself solely as an object of reproduction rather than its subject. Symkyn views his wife's body as a symbol of potentiality, a promise of continued and future fecundity, but she herself reads her body only as the inscribed text of an already complete history of paternal production.

Thus, by the time that our two students, Aleyn and John, enter the story we have already established two competing visions of how the reproductive contract between men and women should function. One vision, that of Symkyn, highlights the sexual relationship between partners, for the production of an offspring who is both vital to the father's economic and social aspirations, and yet displaced from the central duality of the sexual couple. Thus, Symkyn's young son is his heir, but he is also relegated at night to a cradle at the foot of his parents' bed. The parson's vision of reproduction is, on the contrary, far less traditional; it is a vision of distended reproduction that reduces both daughter and son-in-law into the mere mechanisms by which the father himself may be regenerated. Moreover, the parson's vision of reproduction disruptively inserts the parson's own body into

---

[59] As Ruth Karras writes, there were many metaphorical ways in which medieval priests and parsons could assume modes of spiritual paternity, through the nurturing of souls. Ruth Karras, "Reproducing Medieval Christianity," *The Oxford Handbook of Theology, Sexuality, and Gender*, ed. Adrian Thatcher (Oxford: Oxford University Press, 2014): 271–86, at 282–3.

sexual acts from which it should be removed. He becomes a silent participant in the siring of his granddaughter, and aspires to repeat that process in his grand-daughter's own future procreations. His image has, in this sense, unfairly can-nibalized a process intended to allow a mutuality of reproduction, and has supplanted the paternal prerogatives of those who copulate with his female descendants.

We witness a similar dynamic within the reproductive interactions of January and May, the aged husband and young wife, within the *Merchant's Tale*.[60] While the genealogies of the *Reeve's Tale* were stretched out to encompass multiple generations, allowing the parson's paternity to stretch grotesquely out across time, here we witness instead the perverse compression of generational experience and familial investment. May's unmentioned family, unlike Malyn's, appears to have had no explicit aspirations for her marriage; she moves seamlessly into January's house, denuded of any ancestral ties other than the mention of her "small degree" (MerT 1625). However, even more significantly, January attempts to reshape the very purpose of marriage itself, at times subjugating its appropriate patrilineal benefits under an excessive cloud of emotional abstractions. January and the nar-rating Merchant alike measure marriage according to its emotional outputs, cre-ating an alternative model of assessment that dislocates the production of offspring from the marital bond for most of the *Tale*, until Chaucer slyly catapults the subject back to the center of the story with May's sudden claim of pregnancy.

The quick sliding between economics and overabundant emotion is jarring, particularly when January begins with an invocation of the economic benefits of marriage only to "prove" them with some affective evidence.[61] For example, he first claims "a wedded man in his estaat/Liveth a lyf blisful and ordinaat" (MerT 1283–4), before offering "wel may his herte in joye and blisse habounde" (MerT 1286). The former lines highlight marriage's potential to organize and regularize a man's condition, to put his affairs in a stable social order. This does not necessarily imply anything about the state of his heart, as the latter lines claim; there is no reason, so to speak, why a life that is "ordinaat" should be for that reason "blisful" as well. By rhetorically linking the economic and social costs/benefits of marriage with the emotional ones, January attempts to undermine genuinely persuasive economic arguments about the importance of creating an heir. And his

---

[60] The extreme age difference between the two has been, as A. S. G. Edwards writes, a source of considerable attention and concern by critics of the *Tale*, with some compressing the age gap to min-imize the immorality, and others expanding it to amplify the effect. A. S. G. Edwards, "The *Merchant's Tale* and Moral Chaucer," *Modern Language Quarterly* 51.3 (September 1990): 409–26, at 410–11.

[61] January's mercantile approach to marriage has long been held up by critics as a central compo-nent of his downfall. Barbara Gates noted that he is "as avaricious as he is lecherous," and Paul Olson wrote that "January's love of May is like the love of possession; it is the love of possession not as one among many goods but as the highest good." Barbara T. Gates, "'A Temple of False Goddis': Cupidity and Mercantile Values in Chaucer's Fruit-tree Episode," *Neuphilologische Mitteilungen* 77.3 (1976): 369–75, at 371; Paul A. Olson, "Chaucer's Merchant and January's 'Hevene in Erthe Heere,'" *ELH* 28.3 (September 1961): 203–14, at 208.

punishment for this series of deliberate misjudgments will fit the crime, for, at the conclusion of the *Tale*, his marriage has given him some joy but has created a monstrous heir of his own making, and a spurious one who is likely not. His excesses of emotion have produced neither son nor financial largesse, but only the sight of his "pregnant" wife being swyved in a pear tree; as the narrator mockingly concludes, "This Januarie, who is glad but he?" (MerT 2412).

Confronted with a strong statement of the essential value of marital structures for a system embedded in the hereditary transmission of property, Chaucer will have his characters or narrator immediately pivot towards a rebuke of the affective experience of living with a wife. Another example comes a few lines later with "She kepeth his good and wasteth nevere a deel./Al that hir housbonde lust hir lyketh weel" (MerT 1343–44). The sarcastic amplification of what wives do implies that all three descriptors are false. But whether or not a wife wastes some of her husband's property, in her function as his conceptive partner, she does indeed keep his goods. Moreover, in terms of the social value of marriage, surely whether or not a wife "likes" the same things as her husband matters less than how well she preserves his property. As Ruth Karras writes, "If we consider someone's work to be what she spends her life doing, and what people take to be the main contribution she makes, the main work of aristocratic women—and women among many urban elites as well—was reproduction."[62] May, as sexually available young wife, is fully embarked (however unenthusiastically) upon this procreative mission, and it is January who undermines the "naturalness" of their marital productions with his unreasonable demands for emotional, rather than filial, offspring.

The confusion between the two categories of uxorial performance (one productive, one affective) marks January's expectations of marriage. He embarks upon seeking a spouse for precisely the type of generative reasons that characterize medieval justifications of marriage.

> Whan a man is old and hoor;
> Thanne is a wyf the fruyt of his tresor.
> Thanne sholde he take a yong wyf and a feir,
> On which he mighte engendren him an heir,
> And lede his lyf in joye and in solas.
>
> (MerT 1269–73)

This speech harkens back to Oswald, the Reeve's description of his own aged capabilities to reproduce.[63] Like the Reeve, January identifies his own body in terms of its decay, but where the Reeve thereby imagined himself as the rotten

---

[62] Ruth Mazo Karras, "Women's Labors: Reproduction and Sex Work in Medieval Europe," *Journal of Women's History* 15.4 (Winter 2004): 153–8, at 155.

[63] For a detailed analysis of the visual clues that Chaucer provides to help the reader imagine January's body as undone by age, see Emerson Brown, Jr in "'The Merchant's Tale:' January's 'Unlikely Elde,'" *Neuphilologische Mitteilungen* (Helsinki, Finland: Neuphilologische Verein, 1973): 92–106.

fruit to be produced from such "pley," January conceptualizes his young wife as that fruit which his body will bring into being.[64] January thus conflates the procreative purposes of marriage, imagining that his young wife's body will serve the dual purpose of first providing the passive material for his creation, and secondly being recreated by him in turn. She will be his productive technology and his finished product, his fruit and his fruit-bearing tree.

January thus displaces the respective roles of son and wife, eliding the two distinct ancillary relationships until his dream of a young wife merges with his dream of a young son into a single vision of "childes pley." A wife is not the fruit that marriage should create; likewise, it is not a wife who grants stability and longevity, but rather the male heir who will perpetuate his father's bloodline.

> A wyf is Goddes yifte, verraily.
> Alle other maner yiftes, hardily,
> As londes, rentes, pasture , or commune,
> Or moebles, alle ben yiftes of Fortune,
> That passen as a shadwe upon a wal.
> But dredelees, if pleynly speke I shal,
> A wyf wol laste and in thyn hous endure,
> Wel lenger than thee list, paraventure.
>
> (MerT 1311–18)

This is one of Chaucer's better jokes from the *Tale*—the wife who embodies such permanence and stability that her husband will begin to pray for a little more of life's transience. However, it is also a twisted vision of social order and heredity. The material things of life, the gifts of Fortune, may indeed pass quickly and insubstantially from human lives. Yet it is not one's wife who promises the continuation of the male individual beyond the grave, even if she is destined to outlive her spouse and perhaps, like Jonet Chelmswyk at the beginning of this chapter, inherit some of his goods.[65] The man who will recreate the deceased man is his son, that child created to carry the burdens of Fortune's gifts and absolve his father from the full sting of his mortality.

January's procreative innovations inspire him to imagine creating his wife in the same manner that her womb would create their child. "A yong thing may men

---

[64] This verbal play with fructification foreshadows the pear-tree setting for the poem's eventual climax. Moreover, as Bruce Rosenberg has observed, the pear-tree setting itself evokes another fruit-based scene, that of the Virgin Mary's longing for cherries during her pregnancy. Bruce A. Rosenberg, The "Cherry Tree Carol" and the "Merchant's Tale," *The Chaucer Review* 5.4 (Spring 1971): 264–76.

[65] As Margaret Hallissy argues, there might be some strong financial advantages to recompense May for becoming January's heir, ones that would allow her an independence comparable to that of the Wife of Bath. Certainly, from a medieval female perspective, that would seem to be true. And yet I do not find Chaucer sympathizing with May's desire to be a rich widow, but instead condemning that event as a distortion of proper matrimony and reproduction. Margaret Hallissy, "Widow-To-Be: May in Chaucer's 'The Merchant's Tale,'" *Studies in Short Fiction* (Summer 1989): 295–304.

gye,/Right as men may warm wexe with hands plye" (MerT 1429–30). She is female matter, that passive malleability of form, ready to be shaped by his hands, even as her uterine matter is ready to be shaped by his seed. And yet despite his occasional mention of procreating an heir, January seems far more invested in this former mode of generation, in turning his wife into a type of incestuously intimate child. Such an idea is a crude perversion of procreation—one that bears a sharp likeness to the father/daughter incest narratives discussed in Chapter 5. In those stories, as we will see, there is a triangulated procreative cycle between father, mother, daughter, with the emptiness in the maternal space allowing the daughter to move fluidly (and unwillingly) between the erotic and the filial for her father. Here in the *Merchant's Tale*, the triangulation exists between January, his future wife, and a space marked for their offspring that he nevertheless keeps trying to fill with his wife instead.

Thus, when January complains that he cannot marry an old wife because "ne children sholde I none upon hir geten" (MerT 1437), he is highlighting the error of his erotic and reproductive reasoning, particularly since, a few lines before, he had defined an old wife as one thirty years in age (MerT 1421). Chaucer's readers would have been fully aware that men could and did "get" children on thirty-year-old women. Chaucer's own wife, Philippa, gave birth to their son Lewis in 1380, when she was probably around 34.[66] What prevents sixty-year-old January from marrying a woman half his age, instead of one a third of his age, is not the practicalities of generation, but rather the idiosyncrasies of the generative practices that he imagines. He could engage in a normative procreative relationship and focus on creating an heir; instead, he wishes to marry "tendre veel" (MerT 1420) and spend his time creating her in the monstrous, unnatural image he desires.

From this perspective it is hard to feel too much sympathy for January when May in turn decides to take over the creative process, generating her own pregnancy (the paternity of which remains uncertain) and, by the end of the poem, generating a new version of truth that January will have to live with.[67] Indeed, Chaucer offers May the opportunity to rework the reproductive wax metaphor in her own right. Once January has lost his vision (perhaps, as Carol Everest has suggested, from too much lust), May steals the key to his secret garden, and "in warme wex hath emprented the cliket/that January bar of the smale wiket" (MerT 2117–8).[68] He has not succeeded in generating her; on the contrary, May herself can shape as well, to create the key she needs to satiate her lust, and (perhaps) generate her

---

[66] For Lewis Chaucer's age, see Howard, *Chaucer*, 93.

[67] For a discussion of how the uncertainties of paternity for May's pregnancy overlap with her corporeal and reproductive desires, see Samantha Katz Seal, "Pregnant Desire: Eyes and Appetites in the *Merchant's Tale*," *The Chaucer Review* 48.3 (2014): 284–306, esp. 299–306.

[68] Carol Everest, "Sight and Sexual Performance in the *Merchant's Tale*," *Masculinities in Chaucer: Approaches to Maleness in the Canterbury Tales and Troilus and Criseyde*, ed. Peter G. Beidler (Cambridge: Cambridge University Press, 1998): 91–104.

child. In fact, the dual operations of May and Damian about wax and cliket alike is the closest the *Tale* comes to providing us with an example of successful, mutual production. May imprints the pattern of the cliket into the wax and then Damian, "the cliket countrefeted prively" (MerT 2121). Not only is there a cooperative functionality of production here, plus a reliance on images that lend themselves to phallic and menstrual symbolism, but also an assurance from Chaucer that what has been created from these material alchemies will have great significance for the rest of the *Tale* (MerT 2123). May and Damian have done that which, for all their effort, eluded the Canon, his Yeoman, and all the alchemists; they have transformed a metal into something new. If they have not created gold, they have at least still created, have shaped an object into being. And, they have done so through the partnered pairing of a man and a woman, that normative model of generation so rare within this chapter and so highly esteemed by Chaucer and his medieval fellows.

We therefore enter January's garden, in the last fifth of the *Tale*, with a multiplicity of partners for May's potential procreation. There, in the garden, a tree is already blooming, "charged...with fruit" (MerT 2211), an image of fecundity. Damian scampers up the tree, according to May's signal, and thus divides the enclosed space between two potential "cultivators." January pleads his case with May by continuing his confusion between her role as his wife and as his imagined heir. In exchange for her promise of fidelity, he offers May "al myn heritage, toun and tour...This shal be doon tomorwe er sonne reste" (MerT 2172, 2174). January will make May his legal heir, denying any hope for future progeny from their marriage, and putting into contractual terms that eroticized desire to create her as he desires. Even after his own death he wishes to dictate her behavior, to shape her life. "Neither after his deeth nor in his lyf/Ne wolde he that she were love ne wyf" (MerT 2077–8). January even expresses a desire that, instead of going blind, he and May might be killed together by a stranger (MerT 2076); in other words, although May is now his heir he still would prefer a sterile destruction rather than allow her to reproduce. For all his claims early in the *Tale* to value the transmission of his wealth along the generations, for all that that "me levere houndes had me eten/Than that myn heritage sholde falle/In straunge hand" (MerT1438–40), January seems entirely uninvested in traditional reproductive strategies or goals.[69] Instead, his love for his wife has consumed his capacity to create; she is the object of all his desires, including his generative ones. He cannot make a son in the image of himself because "ye been so depe enprented in my thought" (MerT 2178).

---

[69] It is January's disinterest in procreative love that George Economou identifies as a tie between Chaucer's *Merchant's Tale* and Jean de Meun's *Roman de la Rose*, arguing that both poems posit non-procreative sexuality as an offense against Nature, one that highlights human selfishness and greed. George D. Economou, "Januarie's Sin Against Nature: the *Merchant's Tale* and the *Roman de la Rose*," *Comparative Literature* 17.3 (Summer 1965): 251–7, at 255–6.

May is imprinted on January; Damian is imprinted on May (she "hath take swich impression that day/For pitee of this syke Damian" [MerT 1978–9]); May, if not explicitly imprinted upon Damian, has at least "so ravisshed him" that he becomes quite ill (MerT 1774).[70] That image of that passive, feminine wax being shaped by an active male hand becomes a disturbingly consistent metaphor within the poem, as each character takes a turn at the role of feminine material, conceived upon by another. Thus, when May announces that something else has been imprinted upon her, a pregnant "plyt" that stimulates "so greet an appetyt/ That she may dyen but she of it have" (MerT 2334–6), it is almost impossible to imagine who has successfully impregnated her. January, despite the comprehensive feminization of his character? Damian, despite the lack of coitus? One has the opportunity, the other has the means; neither seems a particularly likely candidate. Has May simply "conceived" of her pregnancy on her own, through the spermatic, if none corporeal, intervention of Damian stimulating her heart? Alcuin Blamires argues of May, in this scene:

> Taking what opportunity there is with both hands, she stakes a vigorous claim in her pompous husband's family tree…Moreover, she speaks down to him from "his" tree which she has now made hers, dictating in what terms he should understand the situation in it. Is there, then, a hint of a transitional moment here, a glimpse of a transition from a patrilineal to a matrilineal focus?[71]

Certainly May appears to have conquered January's tree and, perhaps as Blamires asserts, we can see that conquering as a form of matrilineal triumph. Yet the extent to which that triumph should be identified as January's tragedy should not be overlooked. It is not "natural" for May to grab that genealogical tree, nor would it have been acceptable to a medieval reader of Chaucer for a woman to sire her own offspring in the way that May appears to desire. Her generation of a child within the pear tree is an act of explicitly unnatural generation, akin in its threatening abnormality to those chemical conceptions attempted by the canon yeoman's alchemists.

January's expectation that with marriage, "thanne his lyf is set in sikernesse" (MerT 1355), has become instead May's triumphant declaration that "he that misconceyveth, he misdemeth" (MerT 2410). January has fundamentally misconceived. He sought to reproduce himself and his desires in the body of his wife, and now he strokes a womb (MerT 2414) that contains only doubt.[72] He told May

---

[70] For a reading of Chaucer's use of "imprinting" here as a reference to a medieval theory of vision and memory, see Suzanne Conklin Akbari, *Seeing Through the Veil: Optical Theory and Medieval Allegory* (Toronto: University of Toronto Press, 2004): 229.

[71] Alcuin Blamires, "May in January's Tree: Genealogical Configuration in the *Merchant's Tale*," *The Chaucer Review* 45.1 (2010): 106–17, at 116.

[72] On the possibilities associated with May's suspiciously timed pregnancy, see Milton Miller, "The Heir in the *Merchant's Tale*," *Philological Quarterly* 29 (1950): 437–40; Carol A. Everest, "Paradys or Helle:' Pleasure and Procreation in Chaucer's *Merchant's Tale*," *Sovereign Lady: Essays on Women in Middle English Literature*, ed. Muriel Witaker (New York and London: Garland Publishing, Inc., 1995): 63–81.

that he would give her "myn herte blood" (MerT 2347), and so he has. There will be no constancy of lineage, no replication of the self, no filial likeness to be relied on in the face of his own mortality. January wanted to create his wife as his child, and so he is left with only that wife, no longer juvenile in any way. As Tory Vandeventer Pearman observes, by asserting herself with Damian and January, May "knowingly terminates January's male line."[73] She, or that double-fathered child, will inherit January's fortune. No wonder that, at sight of May copulating with Damian in the fruitful pear tree, January "yaf a roring and a cry/As doth the moder whan the child shal dye" (MerT 2365). He has lost the child-wife he thought he had created, as well as his paternal certainty in the child-heir that has newly appeared in his wife's womb.

Avarice and its Inheritances

In conclusion, Chaucer's adulterous *Tales* become a space in which men can explore the limits of their authority within the very mechanisms designed by God to facilitate their reproductions. If in the previous chapter, nuns and alchemists sought some spiritual or scientific means of reproducing outside the typical technologies of Nature, then here we have looked instead at Chaucer's accounts of "normal" generations, of procreative sex between a man and a woman that should, with luck, result in the birth of an heir. And yet, overshadowed by the specter of men and women's excess, the superfluities of their desires, and the grasping nature of their perpetuations, we find instead one adulterous misalliance after another. Looking for heteronormativity in Chaucer's reproductions, one encounters a swarm of friars birthed from the Devil's anus and extramarital copulation in a pear tree, a magically multiplying mitten and a man who self-identifies as rotten fruit, but is ready nevertheless to wring every last seminal drop from his "tappe of life." These are repugnant characters, and the humor of their *Tales* does not detract in any way from our perception of that repugnance. We are meant to be appalled, even as we are certainly also meant to be amused.

And in that paradox, I think we can identify the perilous connection between men, their money, and their heirs for Geoffrey Chaucer. However natural, however expected it might be for a worldly man to wish to leave his worldly place and goods to his fleshly son, it is nevertheless a repugnant filthy thing, a thing that reeks of the body and of human greed. The urge to hold onto money after death is not a noble aspiration; it lacks even the aristocratic crafting of Walter's reaching after certainty. The authority of production and perpetuation desired by the Summoner and the Reeve, the Pardoner and the Merchant (as well as by all their

---

[73] Tory Vandeventer Pearman, "'Oh Sweete Venym Queynte!': Pregnancy and the Disabled Female Body in the *Merchant's Tale*," *Disability in the Middle Ages: Reconsiderations and Reverberations*, ed. Joshua R. Eyler (London and New York: Routledge, 2016): 25–38, at 36.

characters), stems neither from the intellect nor the soul. It comes from the desire to hold onto filthy lucre, to keep one's money in one's grasp to others' detriment and to add to one's own unnecessary surplus. However much emotion January pretends to derive from his marriage, these are not men who father in love, who hold to wife or son in some natural affection.

These, in short, are cuckolds, the men who grasp at the world so tightly that they only find its fecal matter, its money, its cheats. The women are not, in the end, the villains of these *Tales*, however many men they entertain behind their husbands' back. These are stories about what it means to be human, and about how dirty and cheap a thing that sometimes may be; these are therefore stories about men, metaphor for the species. Chaucer's women copulate and cheat, but they do so because they can, because of male culpabilities and failings. Wives like May or the anonymous wife of the *Summoner's Tale* abuse their marital bond when their husbands abuse the productive contract, when men attempt to produce from the excesses of human greed rather than the sufficiencies of human Nature.[74] Adulterous wives, for Chaucer, are creative technologies run amok, liberated from "proper" subjugation by their husbands' failings. And so they will follow Nature's commands and continue to produce, although their husbands will not recognize the offspring thereby produced. As May taunts January, perched in her pear tree:

> "Ye maze, maze, goode sire," quode she;
> "This thank have I for I have maad yow see.
> Allas," quod she, "that evere I was so kynde!"
>
> (MerT 2387–9)

May has reproduced January's sight by forcing him to witness her sin. It is up to him whether the sight will also produce repentance. In the traditional model of reproduction, woman allows man to look from a distance at his own self, recreated in a tiny image of his flesh. And so adultery provides a parodic repetition of this moment; look at me, says May, and see the perverse offspring you have sired on my flesh.

Avarice, not women, is that unnatural horror that haunts men's lives. May is "kynde," as she protests; her behaviors are reasonable within the logic of her world. It is January and all his fellow cuckolds who are the monsters. As Prudence preaches to Melibee:

---

[74] I thus disagree with readings of these "adulterous *Tales*" that emphasize the reader's sympathies for the cuckolded husbands. For example, Joseph D. Parry argues that midway through the poem one is moved to empathize with January when he begs for May's fidelity after losing his sight. Parry writes: "while this Januarie remains the materialistic, possessive, misogynist of the first part of the tale, what is different here is that he demonstrates self-awareness." 155. Joseph D. Parry, "Interpreting Female Agency and Responsibility in the *Miller's Tale* and the *Merchant's Tale*," *Philological Quarterly* 80.2 (Spring 2001): 133–67, at 155. I would argue that self-awareness is an insufficient salve for the former characteristics when it accompanies their unceasing perpetuation.

> For what cause...joyneth he hym or knytteth he hym so faste
>   unto his goodes
> that alle hise wittes mowen nat disseveren hym or departen hym
>   form his goodes,
> and knoweth wel, or oghte knowe, that whan he is deed
> He shal no thyn bere with hym out of this world?
> and therfore seith Seint Austyn that 'the avaricious man is likned
>   unto helle,
> that the moore it swelweth the moore desir it hath to swelwe and
>   devoure' "

(MelT 1614–8)

Men who treat the processes of reproduction solely as a means of knitting them-selves to their goods, of tightening their hold upon the money in their hands, will find themselves the monsters of their own creation. They are the swelling gro-tesques of the earthly world, the demon fodder to be consumed in Hell. God did not give men the mechanism for siring heirs as a means of perpetuating money, and those men who fail to see that folly, who grab after the shit of wealth and call it some new authority, will not see their line endure.

SECTION III
ON LIKENESS

5

Almost Heirs

Daughters and Disappointments

"Now was this child as lyk unto Custance
As possible is a creature to be."[1]

Four men sit down to four feasts in the *Man of Law's Tale*, and each man arises to
a future dramatically altered by the course of that consumption. Two men leave
their meals with their patrimony assured, their heir at their side. Two others see
their futures consumed in front of them, their hopes for posterity annihilated
in the same violence that claims their lives. We may identify these parallel feasts
as the Man of Law's statement on the cruelty of Fortune, who rewards and condemns
as she pleases. More significantly, however, these feasts serve as an indictment
of the entire feminine category, the mothers, wives, and daughters who create
the domestic spaces within which male bloodlines will either thrive or die. These
sumptuous meals represent the female intrusion into the course of men's lives,
and the insecurity that is innate within man's dependency on female flesh, on
her necessary mediation of his hope to live again within an external reproduction
of his life. Whether sultan or servant, king or emperor, medieval men were all
too aware that their futures would be determined within domestic confines that
might at any moment reveal themselves as hostile.

In Chapter 4 we examined the implications of female adultery as a disruptive
source of uncertainty within a reproductive collaboration whose signification
was determined by male trust. In the *Merchant's Tale* or the *Miller's Tale*, wives
revealed to the reader their willing complicity in their lovers' theft of their husbands' goods (both human and material) through sexual intercourse. Adultery
became an expression of female hostility, or at the very least one of an uncaring
indifference, towards man's reproductive ambitions. This chapter, in contrast,
examines the category of *accidental*, rather than deliberate, female obstruction to
the system of patrilineal reproduction.[2] Chaucer's *Man of Law's Tale* provides a
rather exhaustive meditation on a wide spectrum of women's interventions into

---

[1] MLT 1030–1.
[2] On the increased importance placed upon a direct patrilineal inheritance within the later Middle
Ages, cf. Eileen Spring, *Law, Land, and Family: Aristocratic Inheritance in England, 1300–1800* (Chapel
Hill, NC: University of North Carolina Press, 1997): esp. 91–122; Kathryn Reyerson and Thomas
Kuehn, "Women and Law in France and Italy," *Women in Medieval Western European Culture*, ed.
Linda Mitchell (Taylor and Francis, 1999): 136–8.

Father Chaucer: Generating Authority in The Canterbury Tales. Samantha Katz Seal, Oxford University Press (2019).
© Samantha Seal.
DOI: 10.1093/oso/9780198832386.001.0001

male posterity, documenting how even the blandest of female characters can serve to wreak havoc on the reproductive mechanisms of the world around her. The Man of Law is an ideal narrator for the story; as Carolyn Dinshaw has argued, the Man of Law "incarnates patriarchal ideology and its expressed system of law."[3] However, I disagree with Dinshaw's conclusion that therefore "the Man of Law has a profound stake in suppressing threats to the patriarchal order—in defining these threats as unnatural and outside the realm of humanity."[4] As a medieval practitioner of the law, the Man of Law is not so much invested in erasing or marginalizing female threats to the patriarchy as he is in identifying the need to respond to them through litigation and the hiring of his expansive knowledge of English law. Far from silencing women's disruptions of the patriarchal order, the Man of Law has a financial motivation to exaggerate the extent of the problem; by aggrandizing the threat of female reproductive obstruction, he justifies his own services of legal amelioration.[5]

The most problematic form of inadvertent female reproductive obstruction was the production of daughters. In a family with many sons, daughters' dowries presented a financial burden. In a family without sons, the daughter's potential assumption of the role of heir could initiate chronic, sometimes decades-long, struggles over the inheritance of the father's property. The thirteenth-century reform of inheritance law in order to allow a testator more control over the disposition of their properties outside the direct descent of blood ("fee entail" rather than "fee simple") only served to delegitimize the inheritance process by increasing its reliance upon legal strategy and conflict. For, as Eleanor Johnson notes, these new reforms proved how "land ownership could be manipulated and controlled by documentation."[6] Human sexual diversity was necessary according to medieval theologians—some babies had to be born female—but the birth or survival of a female child in the absence of a male heir offered its own destructive logistics. Fathers were lucky to have surviving offspring upon the earth, but a female heir would perhaps be more lucky for the medieval lawyers than for her own natal kin.

Such female heirs were great marital prizes, for they could bring their father's wealth to newer men. Chaucer's own heir, Thomas, owed much of his political

---

[3] Dinshaw, *Chaucer's Sexual Poetics*, 89.   [4] Dinshaw, *Chaucer's Sexual Poetics*, 90.

[5] For scholarly assessments of the Man of Law's skills as a lawyer, see Richard Firth Green, "Chaucer's Man of Law and Collusive Recovery," *Notes and Queries* 40.3 (1993): 303–5; Maura Nolan, "'Acquiteth yow now': Textual Contradiction and Legal Discourse in the Man of Law's Introduction," *The Letter of the Law: Legal Practice and Literary Production in Medieval England*, ed. Emily Steiner and Candace Barrington (Ithaca, NY: Cornell University Press, 2002): 136–53; Eleanor Johnson, "English Law and the Man of Law's 'Prose' Tale," *Journal of English and Germanic Philology* 114.4 (October 2015): 504–25.

[6] Johnson argues that the Man of Law deliberately depicts himself as a "proudly old-fashioned law-man," and "affiliate[s] himself not with the recent legal history of England but with an imaginary and idealized deep history that he would create for it." Johnson, "The Man of Law's 'Prose' Tale," 507. This reading is convincing and works well with my argument for the Man of Law's investment in supporting blood descent even to daughters.

career to his highly advantageous marriage to Matilda Burghersh, one of the two female co-heirs to the wealthy John Burghersh of Oxfordshire.[7] Nevertheless, despite the success of the marriage, Thomas Chaucer spent much of his life in litigation with his brother-in-law, each seeking to establish the boundaries of his own wife's hereditary rights.[8] England's acceptance of female inheritance in the absence of a male heir could thus turn the daughter into a semiotic of simultaneous marital opportunity and familial undesirability. A daughter's inheritance could threaten the patrilineal chain, transferring property, and even a title (if it was free from entail), to her husband, while two surviving daughters could serve as rival claimants, each offering up the overall integrity of her natal heritage to the benefit of an enriched affinal kin.[9] Contentious litigation, the disappearance of male bloodlines, and the overturning of sisterly affection in favor of co-heir competition were all too often the undesired results.[10]

The stigmatization of daughters as detrimental to patrilineal mechanisms of heredity overflowed the borders of filiation. The distinct categories of daughter, wife, mother, became fluid, flowing together into an amorphous corpus of female reproductive hostility, bound by their likeness to one another and their unlikeness to their father/husband/son. If the wife was the one whose womb most directly fails a man by denying him the production of his own likeness in the body of an heir, then the daughter was the one whose "unlikeness" reminds him of that failure, and the mother was the one who forced him to question his own likeness to his father. Analogy was an essential component of medieval epistemology. As Michael Randall writes in his monograph on the centrality of analogical systems for medieval and early modern texts, "It [analogy] allowed the human mind to understand, though imperfect comparison, the perfection of the divine. It provided a median way between equivocity, or total difference, and univocity, or complete resemblance."[11] Physical likeness was the mediation between parent and child, the corporealization of the analogy that would allow them to know one another and to be known within one another. No human being could aspire to

---

[7] Roskell, *House of Commons*, 525, 531. For a biography of Sir John Burghersh, see Roskell, *House of Commons*, 426–8.

[8] Ruud, *Thomas Chaucer*.

[9] Scott L. Waugh, "Women's Inheritance and the Growth of Bureaucratic Monarchy in Twelfth- and Thirteenth-Century England," *Nottingham Medieval Studies* 34 (1990): 71–92.

[10] Chaucer himself witnessed just such a contentious division of a noble family between its female heirs with the division of Humphrey de Bohun's property between his two daughters in 1373. Richard II interfered to prevent the earldom of Hereford and its goods from reverting to de Bohun's nephew, instead ensuring its transmission to de Bohun's daughters, Eleanor and Mary, as coheiresses. A legend has survived that when in 1376 Eleanor de Bohun married the Duke of Gloucester, the couple attempted to force Mary de Bohun to enter a nunnery so that they might have the entire inheritance. Holmes, *Estates of the Higher Nobility*, 24–5. Henry of Derby, Lancaster's heir, instead married Mary de Bohun in 1381, and certainly by 1385 Derby and Gloucester were quarreling over the division of the property between the two sisters. Chris Given-Wilson, *Henry IV* (New Haven, CT: Yale University Press, 2016): 82–3.

[11] Michael Randall, *Building Resemblance: Analogical Imagery in the Early French Renaissance* (Baltimore and London: Johns Hopkins University Press, 1996): 9.

that perfection of reciprocity represented by the Father and Son within Trinitarian theology. As Bernard of Clairvaux wrote, "It is not possible that one of these could be known without the other. That is why Christ said: 'To have seen me is to have seen the Father.'"[12] But still, men could aspire to be known in their children in a manner analogous to that of the divine, reinforced by a far more human (but still essential) mode of resemblance and reciprocity.

A daughter was therefore not only an imperfect representation of the father, but was also an imperfect *analogy* for him. Her likeness mediated unevenly between the extremes of equivocity and univocity, failing to chart out the desired middle path of invoking her father without being indivisible from him. The daughter thus makes manifest the "problem of proximity" prominent within theories of medieval queerness and racialization.[13] She is so close to, and yet so different from, her father that she undermines the stability of his masculine identity. Susan Schibanoff therefore reads the *Man of Law's Tale* as carrying out "the patriarchal solution to the threat of [woman's] proximity [which] was to reestablish woman's distance from man, to reinscribe her as inferior and subordinate to him."[14] I agree with Schibanoff's characterization of this proximity and its investment in the creation of an Other (whether religious, racial, or gendered) as integral themes of the text. And yet while Schibanoff sees the Man of Law as invoking similitude only to deny its threat through the subsequent entrenchment of binaries, I argue that the *Tale* and its speaker must ultimately move away from such binaries in recognition of their permeability; instead they reaffirm the threat of proximate likeness as man's inevitable, if undesirable, shadow. The daughter's embodiment of her father renders her a monstrously effeminate embodiment of male flesh, a perversion rather than a memorialization of his life. She is neither his like nor his antithesis, and thus breaks every binary that attempts to block her from him. In a Freudian sense, the daughter therefore becomes a manifestation of the *unheimlich*,

---

[12] Bernard of Clairvaux, *On the Song of Songs*, Sermon 8:3, 47. As Russell Peck notes, the possibility of learning "something of the creator from the study of his work appealed strongly to fourteenth-century men of letters," including William of Ockham, Thomas Usk, and probably Chaucer himself. Russell A. Peck, "Chaucer and the Nominalist Questions," *Speculum* 53.4 (October 1978): 745–60, at 750.

[13] Jonathan Dollimore's work is pivotal in the application of the term to medieval texts, but in doing so he also draws from Luce Irigaray's theorization of woman's identity as destabilized through her intimate interactions with man. Jonathan Dollimore, *Sexual Dissidence: Augustine to Wilde, Freud to Foucault* (Oxford: Oxford University Press, 1991): 230. Dollimore is particularly interested in proximity as an erotic category, but Susan Schibanoff speaks of the "simultaneous fear and exploitation of similitude" as symbolic of the Man of Law's intertwining of race and gender as categories undergoing similar processes of binary construction. Susan Schibanoff, "Worlds Apart: Orientalism, Antifeminism and Heresy in Chaucer's *Man of Law's Tale*," *Exemplaria* 8.1 (1996): 59–96, at 64. For other uses of Dollimore's "transgressive proximity" as applied to medieval texts, see Glenn Burger, "Kissing the Pardoner," *PMLA* 107.5 (October 1992): 1143–56.

[14] Schibanoff, "Worlds Apart," at 62. Elizabeth Robertson offers a corrective to Schibanoff's conclusion, however, that Custance's alterity, rather than enforcing her inferiority, marks her as superior to the non-Christians around her. Elizabeth Robertson, "The 'Elvyssh' Power of Constance: Christian Feminism in Geoffrey Chaucer's *The Man of Law's Tale*," *Studies in the Age of Chaucer* 23 (2001): 143–80, at 156.

the terrifying blend of the familiar and the foreign that "effac[es] the distinction between imagination and reality."[15] The daughter forces the father to look inwards, at the terrifying woman whose origin lies in his loins, and whose face lurks beneath his own.

The *Man of Law's Tale* thus at once treats the daughter as an image of banal legal obstruction and as a terror who violates the integrity of her father's body, while simultaneously advocating for reconciliation between the father and the monstrous child.[16] Imagination presses hard against reality within the poem, eliding the judicial and the demonic as an angry mother-in-law is revealed to be "a serpent under femynynytee/Lik to the serpent depe in helle ybound" (MLT 360), and a judicial trial is resolved when a divine hand smites a man "upon the nekke-bone... [so that] bothe his eyen broste out of his face" (MLT 669, 671). Custance, the daughter who occupies the central place of the poem and whose identity remains tied up within her filial designation throughout her journeys, signifies for her father even when she is alienated from him. As she wanders unmoored throughout the world, Custance's identity as the monstrous simulacrum of the paternal image cannot be fully eliminated until eventually she can be reintegrated into her kin network after she has produced a more acceptable heir for her father. Before that reintegration, the daughter is a terrifying and destabilizing reflection of the father. And yet, the Man of Law argues, even the most shadowed mirror of the father may aid in the future generation of the paternal line.

Women were the world's flawed heirs, the monstrous doubles of its posterity. Still, all too often, these fleshly wrinkles in the line of hereditary descent were all that a man had, the only human markers of his time upon life's journey. The Man of Law does not use his tale to hide the significance of the threat posed by female reproductive obstructions to male ambitions of transgenerational authority nor to elide the undesirability of a female heir. Instead, he counsels the pilgrims on the need to make the best of what God has delivered, to seek succor from even the smallest, most unfamiliar modes of generation. Blood is all to him, even when it is in a female form; as the narrator signals to the reader in the General Prologue's depiction of the Man of Law, "al was fee symple to hym in effect" (GP 319). Better a daughter of one's body than a conditional heir of someone else's flesh. For how

---

[15] Sigmund Freud, "The Uncanny," trans. by Alix Strachey (1919): 1–21, at 15.

[16] Elizabeth Fowler and Kathryn Lynch have each read the *Tale* as exploring the intersections of conflicting forms of law when one moves outside the English nation state, with Lynch explicitly contrasting the types of customary family law which the Man of Law probably practices with the "merchant law" that he probably does not. Elizabeth Fowler, "The Emperor and the Waif: Consent and Conflict of Laws in the *Man of Law's Tale*," *Medieval Literature and Historical Inquiry: Essays in Honour of Derek Pearsall*, ed. David Aers (Cambridge: D. S. Brewer, 2000): 55–68; Kathryn L. Lynch, "'Diversitee bitwene hir bothe lawes': Chaucer's Unlikely Alliance Between a Lawyer and a Merchant," *The Chaucer Review* 46.1–2 (2011): 74–92. Family law, or patriarchy's law, is nevertheless the one I identify as dominant within the poem, with the Man of Law touching upon "foreign" modes of legal practice only to reinforce the non-bounded geography of the law of male genealogical descent.

can even the filial embodiment of unlikeness, a daughter, compare to the harsh, annihilating severance of inevitable death? What man, Chaucer's lawyer asks, would choose nothingness over even the most fragile hope of immortality? Better instead to recognize the barest hints of likeness, however frail their form. Men must accept the heirs they have rather than mourn the heirs that they have lost.

And, as the final section of this chapter argues, so too must poets. The passing of the generations result in an ever-encroaching degradation of quality and of substance, but still no diminishment of humanity's heights will ever prove a suffi-cient excuse for silence. As the Man of Law justifies his *Tale*, "Though I come after hym [Chaucer] with hawebake. I speke in prose, and lat him rymes make" (MLT 95–6). The Man of Law is no true poet, no son nor heir of Chaucer. He has inherited a responsibility of literary creation from Chaucer and earlier poets that he recognizes himself to be insufficient to satisfy. Still, if he cannot be a perfect son, he will at least aspire to the imperfections of a daughter. An apple that has fallen far too far from the tree, the Man of Law will nevertheless speak, a humble likeness of the fathers that have come before him upon the earth, and who will soon be gone.

Imperfect Animals

The problem with much of the medieval belief in a male dominant mode of sexual reproduction was that it was so demonstrably antithetical to the conclusions that could be drawn from simple observation. If the sperm truly was capable of dictat-ing the distribution of the maternal matter, then why were some children born with a resemblance to their mothers rather than to their fathers? Indeed, why were female children born at all from a sexual union dominated by male repro-ductive power? Aristotle and his scientific peers had bequeathed a variety of sup-posed explanations to their medieval descendants, an indication that the classical philosophers themselves had perceived the danger posed by the observable real-ity of sex diversity for their argumentation.[17] The most common explanation according to classical texts was that the birth of a daughter indicated a perversion of parental coitus, in which the mother's unnaturally strong reproductive matter had triumphed over the unnaturally effeminate sperm of the girl's father.[18] The birth of a son who resembled his mother rather than his father would likewise indicate a sexual problem between his parents, albeit a less extreme occasion of

[17] Joan Cadden provides an overview of many of these philosophical arguments in *Meanings of Sex Difference*, 195–201.
[18] Vern L. Bullough, "On Being a Male in the Middle Ages," *Medieval Masculinities: Regarding Men in the Middle Ages*, ed. Clare A. Lees, Thelma S. Fenster, and Jo Ann McNamara (Minneapolis and London: University of Minnesota Press, 1994): 31–46, at 40.

misgendered intercourse.[19] An act of conception that resulted in the siring of a female child was such an assault upon the father and his prerogatives that the *Distaff Gospels'* author writes that a man typically suffers pain after creating a daughter. "When a man fathers a son, he is not much affected because he fathers his own kind. But if he fathers a daughter, who has a different constitution from his, he feels unwell for at least two or three days afterwards."[20] Symptoms of illness in the father are a diagnostic for the conception of the unlike child, thus pathologizing the daughter from her very conception.

Such a perspective corresponded well with the contemporaneous scientific identification of women as necessary "monsters;" they were necessary for the perpetuation of the species, but nevertheless represented a degradation of the male form.[21] Women were the world's "failed men," the corporeal testimonies of their fathers' weakness. Their wombs were the mechanisms by which men might recreate their image, but they were also places of pollution, error, and degeneration. So much of prenatal medical literature (both from the Middle Ages and today) therefore seeks to contain and regulate the woman's interaction with her own womb, to supervise and negate her potential impositions upon the growing child settled in the vessel of her flesh. Once inseminated, at least in theory, the mother's gestational body was only a conquered field upon which another bloodline would grow its harvest. One might therefore blame one's wife if one's child was not in one's likeness; it was her intervention that had disrupted the perfection of the system. The semiotics of the daughter in medieval literature are thus constructed both by male anxieties about sexual performance and masculinity, and by an indelible tie to the maternal figure. In this sense, the daughter inherits the erotic conflict of her parents. She becomes a liminal object, torn between two competing centers of identification, with likeness as the mediating language of the war.

Adam, before his fall, had been able to sire a son at will, in a manner reminiscent of his original creation by God.[22] Indeed, the capacity to reproduce in one's own likeness was understood by medieval authors to be a defining characteristic

---

[19] Katharine Park, *Secrets of Women: Gender, Generation, and the Origins of Human Dissection* (New York: Zone Books, 2006): 142–3.

[20] *The Distaff Gospels: A First Modern English Translation of Les Evangiles des Quenouilles*, ed. Madeleine Jeay and Kathleen Garay (Peterborough, Ontario: Broadview Press, 2006): 147.

[21] For a survey of the scientific belief in woman as a defective man in the Middle Ages and Renaissance, see: Nancy Tuana, "The Weaker Seed: The Sexist Bias of Reproductive Theory," *Feminism and Science*, ed. Nancy Tuana (Bloomington, IN: Indiana University Press, 1989): 147–71; Laqueur, *Making Sex*, 35–4; Cadden, *Meanings of Sex Difference*, 178–201; Michael T. Walton, Robert M. Fineman, and Phyllis J. Walton, "Why Can't a Woman Be More Like a Man?: A Renaissance Perspective on the Biological Basis for Female Inferiority," *Women and Health* 24.4 (1997): 87–95.

[22] Adam's creation by God was predicated upon his likeness to the divine, while Eve's resemblance to God was mediated by the intervening presence of Adam, in whose specific likeness she had been created. Bloch, *Medieval Misogyny*, 13–36. In particular, "Woman is by definition a derivative of man who, as the direct creation of God, remains both chronologically antecedent and ontologically prior," 24.

of species-level perfection. Albertus Magnus's summary of Aristotle's scientific opinion on the failures of reproductive likeness is as follows.

> The operation of a perfect animal is to produce one like itself. But, according to Aristotle, every thing has been perfect when it can produce one like itself. But many animals are imperfect, and thus it is not surprising that they cannot produce ones like themselves.[23]

Here Aristotle reflects on the reproductive perpetuation of likeness not only in terms of sex, but also concerning more general anatomical and physiological characteristics. Sexual diversity in man's offspring is not in itself enough to disqualify him from species perfection, according to Albertus Magnus's commentary, but it is nevertheless a problematic, certainly undermining, indication of how far he has fallen from the state of his first progenitor.

It is only reproductive necessity (with its corollary of human, and thereby species, mortality) that preserves sexual diversity in spite of the threat that such diversity offers to procreative systems of likeness. Magnus writes: "The generative power is bestowed upon every animal so that the species, which cannot be preserved in the animal itself, may be preserved in one like itself."[24] Woman may thus be considered a "flawed man," whose purpose it is to mitigate the mortality of the species, lending the generative potential of her body to aid (following the Fall from Eden) in man's confrontation with death and his own non-divinity.[25] Her difference to man is sexually grounded, but more significantly it marginalizes her within the biological plan. She is necessary because man was not created to be self-sufficient, because man cannot recreate an image of himself from his own body alone in the manner of God.

Man's sexual contribution and motive is nevertheless straightforward; each man engages in sexual intercourse with the biological motive of creating a male child in his likeness. It is only within the capacious depths of the womb that man's seed may go astray, that his desires may be thwarted. The mechanisms of that obstruction varied. First, a woman might engage (deliberately or inadvertently) in a reproductive obstruction through prophylactic or abortive measures.[26] Secondly, the womb itself might misdirect male seed, allowing it to take up root

---

[23] Albertus Magnus, *Questions Concerning Aristotle's* On Animals, 187.

[24] Ibid., 185–6. These lines are from the argument given in supposed opposition to the Aristotelian point, but the disagreement is not about the existence of the generative power within each organ and its desire to reproduce its like, but rather concerning whether such a microcosmic generative desire would be capable of triggering singular, rather than mutual, generation.

[25] Ibid., 144.

[26] For medieval contraceptive and abortive processes, see John M. Riddle, *Eve's Herbs: A History of Contraception and Abortion in the West* (Cambridge, MA and London: Harvard University Press, 1997); Zubin Mistry, "Alienated From the Womb: Abortion in the Early Medieval West, *c.*500–900," PhD dissertation, University College London, 2011.

within the wrong uterine space.[27] Sexual diversity was dictated according to the semen's placement within the gendered division of the seven-chambered womb; if the seed gestated within the three vessels on the left side of the womb, the child would be a girl, and vice versa.[28] Finally, and most problematically, a woman might allow the seed to lodge within the center uterine cavity, where it would birth a hermaphrodite, the corporealization of sexual diversity into a single flesh.[29] This last possibility imagined the womb as a site of sex fluidity and excess, with *The Knowing of Women's Kind in Childing*, for example, warning of a "superfluite of hete, colde, drynesse and moystour" within the center cavity, in what is both a medical diagnosis of excess and a sexual one (as the various humors were associated with the respective sexes).[30]

Men who were successful in their desire to sire sons had managed not only to overcome their wives' initial attempt at dominance within the act of sexual union, but had also in effect colonized a small segment of the female womb for the duration of their heir's gestation. The three chambers on the right side of the womb could be seen as an isolated humoral site of masculinity within that most female of organs itself. Moreover, male occupancy within a woman's womb would impact the female body in a fully comprehensive manner, with multiple medieval texts attesting to signs across the entirety of a pregnant woman's body in witness to the male fetal presence within.[31] To impregnate the female body with one's filial like-ness was to transform the female body into something temporarily superior to its innate state. At the same time, however, the transformation of male seed into a female offspring could be understood as a degradation of a finer matter into a poorer one, a perversion and corruption of seminal potentiality into only the pale double of what it might have been. A daughter was the evidence of one's own imperfection; she was the sign of a common failure, but a failure nonetheless.

---

[27] On the division of the womb into seven sections, cf. Fridolf Kudlien, "The Seven Cells of the Uterus: The Doctrine and its Roots," *Bulletin of the History of Medicine* 39 (1965): 415–23; Laqueur, *Making Sex*, 65; Park, *Secrets of Women*, 105. On the seven-chambered womb within medieval Jewish medicine and thought, see Edward Reichman, "Anatomy and the Doctrine of the Seven-Chamber Uterus in Rabbinic Literature," *Hakirah: The Flatbush Journal of Jewish Law and Thought* 9 (Winter 2010): 245–65.

[28] This placement of course corresponded to the respective association of right (*rectus*) and left (*sinister*) with good and evil.

[29] For a discussion of the hermaphrodite in medieval and early modern Europe, see Lorraine Daston and Katharine Park, "The Hermaphrodite and the Orders of Nature: Sexual Ambiguity in Early Modern France," *GLQ: A Journal of Lesbian and Gay Studies* 1.4 (1995): 419–38; Cary J. Nederman and Jacqui True, "The Third Sex: The Idea of the Hermaphrodite in Twelfth-Century England," *Journal of the History of Sexuality* 6.4 (1996): 497–517; Valeria Finucci, *The Manly Masquerade: Masculinity, Paternity, and Castration in the Italian Renaissance* (Durham, NC: Duke University Press, 2003): 189–224; Leah DeVun, "The Jesus Hermaphrodite: Science and Sex Difference in Premodern Europe," *Journal of the History of Ideas* 69.2 (2008): 193–218.

[30] Barratt, ed. *The Knowing of Woman's Kind in Childing*, 45.

[31] The uterus was understood to be an unnaturally (for a woman's body) moist place, a humoral factor that allowed male children to grow much more quickly within the womb than their female counterparts. Cf. Albertus Magnus, *Questions Concerning Aristotle's On Animals*, 305–6.

The reproductive failure evidenced by female offspring was capable of destabilizing the entire family network. In the absence of a male heir, daughters were the shadows of the patrilineal longevity that their brothers would have ensured. Twists in the genealogical chart, they promised a limited, insufficient mode of continued generation, albeit in the name of another man. However, the exclusive production of daughters within a marriage might also potentially undermine the sexual relationship of her parents. The strong primary likeness that a daughter bore to her mother not only provided testimony of her father's insufficiently dominant masculinity, but also allowed for a sexual elision between mother and daughter. Within the imaginations of medieval authors (often following classical sources), the perpetuation of affinal, rather than paternal, flesh into the next generation could trigger unnatural sexual behaviors within the thus-disordered family unit. The literary subgenre of incest narratives within medieval romance articulated incest as a state of immoral sexual sin typically stimulated within the father in response to an excess of likeness between mother and daughter. In such stories, the poet slides the daughter seamlessly into a maternal absence often precipitated by the mother's early death. For example, in the romance *Emare* (an analogue of the *Man of Law's Tale*) the mother's death is articulated both in terms of spousal abandonment ("fro her lord gan she dye") and in an assessment of how prepared her daughter is to assume her mother's place ("or hyt kowthe speke or goo").[32] Once the difference between Emare and her deceased mother is ameliorated by time (i.e. once Emare knows how to speak and move), her father desires her to complete the mimesis by becoming his wife. The likeness between mother and daughter, their mutual "fairness," precipitates the father's unnatural lust, and therefore is the direct cause of Emare's traveling and travails within the poem. Likewise, in *La Manekine*, another analogue for the *Man of Law's Tale*, the dying queen of Hungary begs her husband either to make Joy, their daughter, his heir or to marry a woman who looks exactly like herself. The king's barons conclude that since "You will have no wife except one whose appearance /Is that of the wife you had first," the king should marry his own daughter, the likeness of his wife.[33]

It is only by cutting off her left hand, thus destroying her resemblance to both parents, that Joy manages to circumvent her father's lust. More commonly within such romances, the daughter is capable of reuniting with her father only when her status *as* his daughter has been reshaped by her sexual relationship with another

---

[32] "Emare," *Six Middle English Romances*, ed. Maldwyn Mills (London: Dent, 1973): 46–74, at 47.

[33] *Feme n'[av]rés fors d'un sanlant/A cele [qu'eü]stes premiere.* Philippe de Remi Beaumanoir, *Le Roman de la Manekine*, ed. and trans. Roger Middleton (Amsterdam: Rodopi Press, 1999): 150. Cf. M. Shephard, *Tradition and Re-Creation in Thirteenth Century Romance: "La Manekine" and "Jehan Et Blonde" by Philippe de Remi* (Amsterdam: Rodopi Press, 1990): 30–4; Kathryn Gravdal, "Confessing Incests: Legal Erasures and Literary Celebrations in Medieval France," *Comparative Literature Studies* 32.2 (1995): 286, 289; Nancy B. Black, *Medieval Narratives of Accused Queens* (Gainesville, FL: University Press of Florida, 2003): 37–65.

man. As Maria Bullon-Fernandez writes, fathers participate in social patriarchy by transmitting their daughters to other men, and thus, "father–daughter incest is the negation of the social and public act of marriage, even the negation of society itself. It is therefore the worst sin against the foundations of patriarchal society and its systems of exchange."[34] It is only once the daughter has repaired her incestuous father's breaking of the patriarchal chain, through his attempt to monopolize her sexuality, that father and daughter can resume their familial relationship. When the daughter has become the sexual object of another man's conjugal bond, her resemblance with her mother (the sexual object of her father's conjugal bond) is loosened to a sufficiently significant degree to ameliorate her father's unnatural claims upon her. By becoming a mother herself, the heroine has actually managed to lessen rather than to augment her resemblance to her own mother; the counterintuitiveness of this mechanism is clear evidence of how essentially sexual the maternal role was imagined to be within a medieval context. Moreover, the reappearance of Emare in her father's life, accompanied by her husband and her young son, allows her father to move to a less threatening locus in his own genealogy. Rather than a man without an heir, he becomes the oldest link in an already existent male chain. He is given the visible evidence of a successful future for his patrimony, one that will skip with ease over the feminine intrusion of his daughter in order to celebrate his likeness within her son.

Incest within such poems can be understood as a genealogical response to the generation of a daughter, a reproductive rather than sexual reaction to Fortune's provision of only an unsatisfying female likeness for one's heir.[35] When fathers attempt to marry their female heirs within medieval romance, they do so in a desperate attempt to provide themselves with another opportunity to sire in their own likeness. Incest appears to offer the chance for a man to rectify his previous failures by integrating the image of that failure (his daughter) into a sexual system that subjugates the imperfect likeness between them in preference to the possible perfection of their male offspring.[36] Moreover, it is the daughter's existence *as a daughter*, made manifest in her likeness to her mother, which has supposedly prevented her father from assuming his natural role as paternal progenitor. Such a logic manages to blame the female victim of incest twice over, first for the "unnatural" gap in likeness with her father, and secondly for the "excessive" likeness to her mother. In turn, the natural reproductive system itself comes under critique for its culpability in perpetuating the sex diversity in the species that allows

---

[34] Maria Bullon-Fernandez, *Fathers and Daughters in Gower's Confessio Amantis: Authority, Family, State, and Writing* (Cambridge: D. S. Brewer, 2000): 18.

[35] Black, *Medieval Narratives of Accused Queens*, 38.

[36] Such an argument connects directly to Judith Butler's vision of incest and incest taboos as social means of enforcing of enforcing "certain gendered subjectivities through the mechanism of compulsory identification." Judith Butler, *Gender Trouble: Feminism and the Subversion of Identity* (New York: Routledge, 1990): 76.

for such sexual perversions, while simultaneously denying men the perfection of their Edenic progenitor's ability to sire sons in his likeness, whenever he so desired.

Incest and the Erotics of Unlikeness

Custance's first appearance within the *Man of Law's Tale* contextualizes the character according to her relationship to her father, the Emperor of Rome. This introduction would seem to establish a solid filial identity for Custance, by grounding the character both within the established hereditary network of Roman imperial royalty and within a specific paternal bloodline. And yet while Chaucer's source material personalizes and individualizes that component of Custance's characterization, Chaucer's own text erases the majority of its meaning, allowing Custance's filiation to become a structuring fiction on the margins of the story rather than an essential determinant of her character. Chaucer reduces the Emperor to his imperial rank, whereas Trevet had explicitly named him as Tiberius. More significantly, Chaucer elides the likeness between Custance and her father, undermining one of the poem's sole sources of semiotic stability for Custance. Chaucer's Custance sheds that identification with her father to manifest a blank representational space precisely where one would expect to find a reflection of the paternal image. It is, as I will argue, this aggravated lack-of-likeness that amplifies Custance's image as daughter; she is an uber-daughter, so to speak, since she is far more alienated from her male progenitor than sex diversity itself would account for. Moreover, it is this embodiment of unlikeness to a paternal source that seems to occupy the heart of Custance's sexual desirability, both for the men she encounters and for her own father.

Custance's identification as the daughter of the Emperor of Rome occurs almost seamlessly with a public recognition of her singularity and lack of likeness. The common people of Rome tell the Syrian merchants (and thus, the reader), "Oure Emperour of Rome—God hym see!—/A doghter hath that, syn the world bigan,...Nas nevere swich another as is shee" (MLT 156–7, 9). It is Custance's very incomparability that marks her out as worthy of the Syrian sultan's esteem, her lack of likeness to those who have come before her that makes her so exceptional among women. Similarly, rather than reflect the images or characteristics of her parents, Custance bears a likeness only to virtue itself: "She is mirour of alle curteisye/Hir herte is verray chamber of hoolynesse" (MLT 165–6). Her position within the royal family codifies her character by providing her with the noble birth and lineage necessary for marriage to a series of sovereigns, but it does not manifest in a more specific mode of likeness. In contrast, Nicholas Trevet explores at length the issue of parental/filial resemblance between Emperor Tiberius and his daughter. Trevet's Emperor imagines his daughter as his heir, and serves to reinforce that lineal acknowledgment by crafting his daughter even more explicitly in his own likeness. "And because he had no other child, therefore with great diligence, he caused her to be taught the Christian faith and instructed by learned masters in the seven sciences, which are logic, physics, morals, astronomy, geometry, music, perspective, which are called secular sciences; and he had her instructed in various tongues."[37] Custance masters these masculine arts so that she may be a more effective heir, and thus a more effective image of her father; the implication is that if the Emperor had had a son to serve as his heir instead, it would have been unnecessary for him to fashion Custance in such a way. Custance's education makes her less female, if by female we understand an inherited alterity predicated upon sex.

Chaucer's Custance never intends to replace her father on the Roman throne. Indeed, until the reader is told at the end of the poem that Custance's son, Maurice, becomes her father's heir, it is unclear whether or not Custance is an only child. Trevet's Custance is defined by her singularity as a woman whose father has amplified their shared likeness through an educational regimen, but Chaucer's Custance is distinguished by a sharp alienation from her family as a whole. Her singularity is so holistic that it disqualifies her from inclusion within the model of inheritance, at least until her affective reintegration into the family at the end of the poem. Scholars have remarked upon Custance as a space of absence within the *Tale*, with Carolyn Dinshaw, for example, arguing that '"Woman" in the ideology of the *Man of Law's Tale* is an essential blankness that will be inscribed by men and thus turned into a tale; she is a blank onto which men's desire will be projected; she is a no-thing in herself."[38] Such readings account well for Custance's erotic desirability to the men who long to possess and inscribe that blankness. However, it treats patriarchal desire as a monolithic entity within the poem, with no distinction between the sexual desire of a husband and the genea-logical desire of a father.

On the contrary, from the Emperor's perspective, Custance's blankness repre-sents an unnatural *failure* of his paternity to mark his progeny, and (as I will argue in this chapter) his perspective is the most relevant within the poem due to how profoundly the Man of Law privileges Roman patrimonies over Syrian or English. The relationship between father and son-in-law is one of patriarchal collaboration, but it is also one of "genetic" competition. The very possibility of female inherit-ance from a father makes clear how much of a fiction the supposed erasure of female natal identity upon incorporation into an affinal kin group was for medieval families. Custance's odd blankness, her absence of paternal marking, does not

---

[37] "Et pur ceo que nul autre enfaunt avoit, pur ceo a grant diligence la fist enseignier la foi christien, & endoctriner par mestres sachaunz en lez sept sciences, que sount logicience, Naturel, Morale, astronomie, geometrie, Musique, perspective, que sount philosophies seculeres apeletz; & la fist endoctriner en diverses langages." *Origins and Analogues of Some of Chaucer's Canterbury Tales* (London: Published for The Chaucer Society by N. Trubner & Co., 1872): 2–5.

[38] Dinshaw, *Chaucer's Sexual Poetics*, 110.

benefit patriarchy, but rather undermines its structures of paternal authority. "Daughter" should not, as Gail Ashton observes within the *Tale*, be a term that "begins and ends as 'absence;' " it is rather a term that should begin and end with the image of the father.[39]

The enhancement of Custance's sexual desirability according to her singular "blankness" represents an erotic desire to efface the wife's father and bloodline. In contrast to most medieval women, Custance appears to embody the promise of a complete feminine malleability on a genealogical level. The relationship between Custance and the men who desire her throughout the poem is thus the opposite of the genealogical crisis that Angela Florschuetz identifies in the *Clerk's Tale*, arguing that "Walter's tests of Griselda follow a genealogical logic whereby he represents Griselda as a lower-class and lineal intruder, one who transmits her own class heterogeneity to 'her' children...Tellingly, in his fantasy, Walter does not identify Griselda herself as the genealogical contaminant, but rather her father, Janicula."[40] If, in the *Clerk's Tale*, Griselda's desirability was mediated by the extent to which she could be severed from her father's line, then in the *Man of Law's Tale*, Custance's desirability is significantly augmented by her refusal to name her father ("what she was she wolde no man seye" [MLT 524]). No affinal pollution will haunt her offspring. To procreate with Custance would be almost partheno-genesis, or solitary reproduction. Custance's father may "han a doghter," but as long as Custance herself has so little of her father within her, once her physical body is in her husband's power, he might consider himself to "have" her in a mode beyond that which was possible for most men. Thus, the Sultan articulates his desire for Custance as a desire to possess her likeness, to monopolize her image and maintain exclusive control over his wife in a way that is beyond that typically available to husbands. "This Sowdan hath caught so greet plesence,/ To han hir figure in his remembrance" (MLT 1876–7). While in the *Merchant's Tale* January similarly experienced love as assimilation of a female image into his mind ("many fair shap and many a fair visage/Ther passeth thurgh his herte nyght by nyght" [MERT1580–1]), there the assimilation of that image was characterized by its ephemerality. Instead, the Sowdan does not wish for Custance's figure to pass through his remembrance, but rather to be enclosed within it, confined according to his exclusive will.

The Sultan's desire to possess Custance's image is eroticized within the *Man of Law's Tale*, and placed outside the system of a traditional medieval marital alliance. Since medieval marriage was a process of kin network unification reinforced by a belief in the individual's likeness to the blood-linked collective, Custance's

[39] Gail Ashton, "Her Father's Daughter: The Realignment of Father–Daughter Kinship in Three Romance Tales," *The Chaucer Review* 34.4 (2000): 416–27, at 418.
[40] Angela Florschuetz, "'A Mooder He Hath, but Fader Hath He Noon:' Constructions of Genealogy in the *Clerk's Tale* and the *Man of Law's Tale*," *The Chaucer Review* 44.1 (2009): 25–58, at 40–1.

alienation from her paternal line serves to stimulate sexual lust within the Sultan, long before it stirs him to consider the potential of a strategic alliance with Rome. Indeed, the Sultan's preferred method of sexually possessing Custance is explicitly *not* marriage but rather "magyk and abusioun" (MLT 214)—two mechanisms that would allow him a level of sexual domination beyond that of a marital contract. The decision to offer Custance a marital bond only comes when his councilors advise that the Sultan can accomplish his erotic wishes "noon oother wey, save mariage" (MLT 217).

In contrast, Trevet's Sultan expresses his wish to marry Custance with full awareness of how such a marriage would be shaped by her relationship with her father and the larger Christian community. In fact, his desire for Custance is initially provoked by the deliberately evangelistic preaching of the messengers, whom Custance has personally converted to send back to the Sultan. Celia Lewis notes that this aspect of the story coincides with a fourteenth-century theory of strategically using marriage to Christian women as a lure to convert Muslim leaders.[41] The Sultan's lust is an expression of affective subjectivity contextualized within a much larger international encounter between nations and bloodlines. Custance and her father appear united in their hope to convert the Sultan and his people to their shared Christianity, and at no point is Custance presented as the unmoored sexual image that she appears in Chaucer's *Tale*. Indeed, the Sultan explicitly acknowledges how deeply Custance is embedded within her natal culture and kin group by exclusively approaching the problem of wooing her as one of international strategy rather than individual sexual conquest. Thus, Trevet's Sultan turns not to magic and treachery as his romantic tools, but rather to the accepted traditions of diplomacy, negotiating with the Pope a "peace and alliance between the countries of the Christians and the Saracens" so that he might wed Custance.[42] Here the Sultan acknowledges how profoundly both he and Custance function as likenesses of their culture and family. Their union can only be facilitated by the deliberate articulation of a larger family unification. Custance's sharing of her father's Christian faith enhances the likeness between the two family members, filling in the "natural" gap of resemblance between father and daughter with an alternative mode of familial integration and investment, which the Sultan recognizes and endorses.

The Christian likeness between Chaucer's Custance and her father is far less developed, although it still remains explicitly present within the story, as we will see in a moment. The Sultan, however, is presented as entirely unaware of how these modes of embodied likeness might threaten his ability to possess Custance;

---

[41] Celia M. Lewis, "History, Mission, and Crusade in *The Canterbury Tales*," *The Chaucer Review* 42.4 (2008): 353–82, at 365.

[42] Nicholas Trevet, "The Life of Constance," *Originals and Analogues of Some of Chaucer's Canterbury Tales*, ed. F. J. Furnivall, Edmund Brock, and W. A. Clouston (London: N. Trubner Press, 1872): 6.

instead he imagines himself yet again as the embodiment of an isolated subjectivity, buffeted by excesses of individual affect, but divorced from any network of collective investment. Thus the Sultan earnestly affirms to his council "But he myghte have/To han Custance withinne a litel space,/He nas but deed" (MLT 207–9). To threaten to die over the potential consummation (or not) of sexual lust is not just a romantic trope in the Sultan's mouth because the specificities of his position disqualify the Sultan from occupying a purely romantic or sexual position. He is also a political actor in whom his country has invested their security, and a patrilineal actor representing the immense chain of his male ancestry. To contemplate the death of his dynasty over sexual pleasure would be an act of erotic transgression akin to that which Rachel Moss has observed in the incestuous medieval romances when fathers endanger their bloodlines for unnatural gratification.[43]

The Sultan's council must remind the Sultan that both he and Custance bear indelible likenesses to their respective progenitors, and that Custance is far from an unfixed object to which he might lay claim. Rather, she is the child of a "Cristen Prince" (MLT 222), even as the Sultan himself derives from those people "taught by Mahoun, oure prophet" (MLT 224). Not only does Custance's status as "his child" (MLT 223) negate the Sultan's ambitions to possess her in a definitive and exclusive manner, but it also serves as a fundamental impediment to their sexual union, since "ther was swich diversitee/Bitwene hir bothe lawes" (MLT 220–1). Custance's likeness to her father is in indirect proportion to her likeness to the Sultan, and stands in as well for her likeness to her community and Christian faith. The extreme unlikeness characterized by the religious diversity of Custance and the Sultan, on the other hand, precludes a successful sexual union between the two. A medieval romance between Muslim and Christian is predicated upon an assumption of violence and infertility. To quote Jeffrey Cohen, "When pagan and Christian subjectivities seem close enough almost to touch, violence erupts to redraw the faltering self/other boundary, this time in blood."[44] Even in the absence of outright violence, such as in the contemporaneous poem (and Constance analogue), *The King of Tars*, interracial union is associated with the inevitability of "miscegenation." In this story, a Muslim Sultan begets upon his Christian wife a child "withouten blod and bon," who thus bears neither a likeness to his respective parents nor one to the broader human species.[45] As a Christian, Custance will always bear a primary likeness to other Christians, superseding the specificities of particular resemblance or sex diversity.

[43] Rachel E. Moss, *Fatherhood and its Representations in Middle English Texts* (Cambridge: D. S. Brewer, 2013): 141.

[44] Jeffrey Jerome Cohen, "On Saracen Enjoyment: Some Fantasies of Race in Late Medieval France and England," *The Journal of Medieval and Early Modern Studies* 31.1 (Winter, 2001): 123.

[45] *The King of Tars*, ed. John H. Chandler (Kalamazoo, MI: Medieval Institute Publications for TEAMS, 2015): 37.

It is only by a comparison with the "extreme" of racial alterity, however, that Custance's representational blankness can be intuitively reintegrated into her kin network. Custance's likeness to her father is thus a varied, mostly invisible, object within the *Man of Law's Tale*. Most disturbingly, it typically only intrudes when others evaluate her potential to form conjugal relationships. For the Sultan is not the only one to identify Custance's singularity of representation as an enhancement of her sexual appeal. Despite all their praise of Custance, for example, the Roman people refuse to recognize her as his likeness and heir. Instead, they emphasize her conjugal capacities, crying that they "wolde she were of al Europe the queene" (MLT 161). The Romans do not wish to be under Custance's direct rule, but rather to pay tribute to the remarkableness of her affinal charms. The praise they give to her imagines her as the wife of a Roman Emperor, indeed as the wife of a man very like her own father. The difference between father and daughter from this perspective is almost as insurmountable as that between Custance and the Sultan. As a woman, Custance's character is conditioned towards a state of submission and passivity that is well suited for a consort but poorly arranged for a sovereign. Her "heigh beautee" and "yowthe, without grenehede or folye" (MLT 162-3) are attributes that highlight her femininity, a sexual distinction with as profound consequences for her capacity to rule as that "humblesse hath slayn in hire al tirannye" (MLT 165). Custance's singular perfection is conceptualized explicitly through her renunciation of power and authority; as Custance herself claims, her acquiescence to this marriage should be understood through the taxonomy of gender, for "wommen are born to thralldom and penance,/And to been under mannes governance" (MLT 287). According to her speech here, Custance regards herself not as her father's daughter (united with him in familial likeness, and thus in possession of authority and power), but rather as a metonymic member of the universal feminine (characterized by the lack of authority and by an insurmountable distance from the father).

Custance's address to her father has typically been treated as an ardent denunciation of the patriarchal control of woman within medieval society.[46] Thus, Elizabeth Archibald notes that Custance's complaint of "thraldom" and the story's participation in a "Flight from the Incestuous Father" plot can be read today as a "searing indictment of patriarchy, which has such unlimited power over women...and which abuses and harasses them in so many ways."[47] Likewise, as Yvette Kisor sees "the emperor's disposing of Constance in marriage [as becoming]

---

[46] See, for example, David Salter, "'Born to Thraldom and Penance:' Wives and Mothers in Middle English Romance," *Writing Gender and Genre in Medieval Literature: Approaches to Old and Middle English Texts*, ed. Elaine Treharne (Cambridge: D. S. Brewer, 2002): 41–60. Salter's readings of the performance of femininity in multiple readings is fantastic, but he often elides the conjugal and maternal classifications of his objects of study into a single example of female experience.

[47] Archibald, *Incest and the Medieval Imagination*, 161. It is worth noting, however, that later in the same chapter (179), Archibald moves away from this reading as distinct from their medieval popularity.

a less noisome and more socially accepted version of what is at the heart of father–daughter incest: a father asserting control over his daughter's body."[48] And yet, as Catherine Cox has noted, Custance herself is a "polysemous text, resisting closure and troubling any attempt to fix her within orthodox parameters."[49]

We should be suspicious of Custance's attempt to confine herself within such a narrow box, particularly a gendered one from which her privileges of class and noble blood should somewhat liberate her. Custance could easily offer her submission to her father's will as that of a child to its parent; indeed, that language would make far more sense within the scenario.[50] By choosing instead to speak of the lack of reciprocity between the two, Custance eroticizes the relationship in full disregard of its consanguinity. While certainly medieval daughters had little power in the negotiation of their marriage contracts, the complete renunciation of authority and consent that Custance articulates is radical in its intensity. In The King of Tars, in contrast, the Christian princess's agreement to wed the Sultan is coerced not by her father, but rather by the Sultan's violent defeat of the Christians in battle.[51]

Instead, Custance's denunciation of herself, an imperial Roman princess, as every man's slave may serve as a critique of the excessive binarizations of domestic law. A world that refuses to allow a woman to be her father's heir makes her instead only his slave. It denies her the protection due to her according to her blood, and, even more problematically, forces both father and child to relate to one another as sexual beings. For if a man cannot recognize to his female child as an indirect mirror of his image, then he will relate to her as a man to a woman. If one privileges gender over blood, then one risks all the potential sexual consequences of this recharacterization of familial ties. Custance elides the fact that it is her father's paternity, rather than his masculinity alone, that gives him such control over the deployment of her sexuality. She imagines him as a participant within the sexual trafficking of the medieval marriage market not in order to critique his limited advocacy for his own flesh and blood, but rather to merge the paternal and the soon-to-be-conjugal into a single category of conjugality. Her father becomes indistinct from her future husband(s) within such a reorganization of domestic relationships; it is Custance, womanhood's martyr, against all men, father and husband alike. If Alison of Bath utilized a vision of the "war between the sexes" to turn the gaze away from the diminishing returns of the next generation, then Custance of Rome will use it as a powerful means of alienation from the family to which she has been born. If she is not like enough to her father

---

[48] Yvette Kisor, "Moments of Silence, Acts of Speech: Uncovering the Incest Motif in the 'Man of Law's Tale,'" The Chaucer Review 40.2 (2005): 141–62, at 142.

[49] Cox, Gender and Language, 73.

[50] Jill Mann identifies Custance's words here as part of a larger, gendered spiritual allegory within the poem. She writes: "Woman's subjection to 'mannes governance' becomes in this tale a paradigm of the human condition. Woman's 'thraldom' to man is replicated in man's 'thraldom' to God." Mann, Feminizing Chaucer, 105.

[51] The King of Tars, ed. Chandler, 26–9.

to be his heir, then that space of difference will be vast enough to render him undistinguished from her male oppressors.

This is beyond patriarchy. The Man of Law has Custance take medieval systems of female hereditary exclusion (such as the Salic Law) to their logical extremes, demonstrating the monstrous perversion of kinship ties represented by such a severing of natural relationships between father and (even a female) child.[52] Custance's relationship with her father is marked by her elevation of the wrong kind of likeness (sex) over the more powerful, and more socially stable, mode of likeness (blood). Thus, when Custance separates herself from her father, the narrator claims instead for her a likeness with classical female models.

> I trowe at Troye, whan Pirrus brak the wal
> Or Ilion brende, at Thebes the citee,
> N'at Rome, for the harm thurgh Hanybal...
> Nas herd swich tendre wepyng for pitee
> As in the chamber was for hire departynge
> But forth she moot, wher-so she wepe or synge.
>
> (MLT 288–94)

The theme that unites these women with one another, and with Custance, is their sorrow as they wait for sexual violation.[53] Custance's characterization of femininity is not only focused upon female behavior (submission, passivity, etc.) but a more fleshly and embodied experience of female suffering. She is a woman because she too can suffer such violations and, by extension, her father is a man because he can enact them. Thus, the comparisons with these classical scenes of sorrow only allow men to become visible in the role of aggressor, like Pirrus or Hannibal. Within the imagination of the *Tale*, men are only allowed to be the perpetrators of violence and women the victims. Thus when women commit violence in the story (such as when Custance's mothers-in-law commit murder) they are labeled as demonic or "mannysh" (MLT 782). To see the sexes as entirely polarized, with no modes of blood-based resemblance to mediate between them, is to imagine a form of patriarchy far more horrific than that even of the medieval experience. It is an undermining of the kinship networks that bound the world, and a repudiation of the sufficiency of any heir (even a female one) to carry on a

---

[52] There is some debate over whether or not the Salic law was widely applied to the Valois/Plantagenet inheritance crisis of the fourteenth century, or if that application was an innovation of the early fifteenth century. Regardless, it was certainly known as a means of dictating patterns of ordinary inheritance, if not yet of royal or international inheritance. Daisy Delogu, *Theorizing the Ideal Sovereign: The Rise of the French Vernacular Royal* (Toronto: University of Toronto Press, 2008): 86.

[53] The communal aspect of the sexual violence of classical stories seems to have been a consistent theme in medieval retellings, with an additional focus on the sharing of female sorrow in these circumstances. See, for example, Corinne Saunders's analysis of the lamenting of the Trojan women from the *Gest Historiale*. Saunders, *Rape and Ravishment*, 181–3.

man's substance to the next generation. It allies fathers with rapists and daughters with the victims of such rapes, severing the more natural alliance between members of a single family, of a single bloodline.

Recognizing the Daughter, Part I: Islam as Irreconcilable Difference

To deny likeness in the face of difference is to risk the alienation of blood and the transgression of sexual taboos. And yet the denial of likeness can also be understood as a failure of human cognition, a deliberate rejection of the world's limited, yet still significant, signs. The Man of Law makes it clear from his frequent moralizing asides within the *Tale* that man's stubborn refusal to interpret the signs before his eyes, however flawed, is a demonstration not of intellectual prowess or prudence, but rather of foolish pride. The decision to marry Custance to the Sultan, for example, is thus met with the Man of Law's harsh comment, "Imprudent Emperour of Rome, allas!/Was ther no philosophre in al thy toun?" (MLT 309–10). He continues:

> Is no tyme bet than oother in swich cas?
> Of viage is ther noon eleccioun,
> Namely to folk of heigh condicioun?
> Noght whan a roote is of a burthe yknowe?
> Allas, we been to lewed or to slowe!
>
> (MLT 311–5)

There are many layers to this complaint. First, the Man of Law mourns the Emperor's failure to consult those learned in semiotic interpretation, those philosophers and astronomers whose wits are uniquely shaped according to the duties of such reading. This is the chiding of a professional to an amateur who has wrongly assumed a professional's authority.

However, it is also a criticism of the way in which the Emperor has not only overlooked the professionals whom he might employ to give him advice, but also the very signs themselves. As the Man of Law notes, not only are there individuals employed and trained in such prognostications, but there are also hermeneutic systems in place that even the inexperienced and uneducated should be able to consult. Man's nature is typified by cognitive flaws, but his "lewed" and "slowe" nature should be in relation to his attempts to perceive the future from the markers of the present, rather than in his condemnable failure to consult any signs at all. For the import of the Man of Law's rhetorical questions is to assert that indeed all such systems of discernment do exist. Man's capacities to interpret them completely may be limited, but that is no excuse for pretending that no such resources are available to him.[54] From this perspective, the Man of Law's multi-line critique of the Emperor becomes a performance of condemnation, justifying the epithet "imprudent" that he assigned the Emperor at the beginning of the verse.

This critique of man's cognitive engagement with semiotics is noticeably distinct from that offered in the *Clerk's Tale* and discussed in the Chapter 1 of this book. There, Chaucer condemned men who refused to accept the fallibility of material and linguistic signs, those who demanded certainty from an interpretative system designed with doubt in mind. In the *Man of Law's Tale*, in contrast, Chaucer remarks upon the folly of those men who refuse to seek any mode of guidance from temporal signs. A likeness need not be perfect for it to be of use to those who wish to read its signification. A "roote of a burthe," for example, is not evidence capable of endowing certainty, but it is at least evidence capable of being read and used for meaning. In this sense, Custance's interminable wanderings around her world can be interpreted as a journey in search of semiotic recognition, a cognitive peripatetic to locate a more prudent reader capable of deriving meaning from likeness rather than from perfection.

Indeed, we can recognize how dominant this concern with man's failure to read likeness is within the *Man of Law's Tale* by noting how many characters the Man of Law specifically condemns for the same behavior. The Sultan is also criticized by the Man of Law for refusing to process the legible signs around him, available to the human eye "in thilke large book/which that men clepe hevene" (MLT 190–1). While more extensive, the Man of Law's critique of the Sultan is almost identical to that which he offers about the Emperor; again he focuses on the inefficiencies of human interpretation because "mennes wittes ben so dulle" (MLT 202). However, while the criticism of the Emperor's imprudence focused upon his general inability to seek knowledge in correct locations and from skilled practitioners, the Sultan is even more specifically condemned for failing to perceive his *own* likeness to other figures in history.

> In sterres, many a winter therbiforn,
> Was written the deeth of Ector, Achilles,
> Of Pompei, Julius, er they were born;

---

[54] My reading of the *Tale's* explicitly epistemological passages relies upon my understanding of the story having a coherent and consistent strategy for human cognition based upon the perception and interpretation of analogical likeness, one within whose boundaries all the characters, including Custance, function according to their respective capacities. I therefore break with readings of the *Tale* that argue for the existence of competing epistemological systems that are stratified according to religious dogma. For example, I disagree with the strict nominalist approach of Roger Moore, who reads the lines on astrology and cognition to represent the invoking of a form of knowledge inferior to Custance's Ockham-like resignation to the unknowability of God and of his powers. Roger E. Moore, "Nominalistic Perspectives on Chaucer's *The Man of Law's Tale*," *Comitatus: A Journal of Medieval and Renaissance Studies* 23.1 (1992): 80–100, at 86–9.

The strif of Thebes; and of Ercules,
Of Sampson, Turnus, and of Socrates
The deeth.

(MLT 197–202)

The examples chosen to admonish the Sultan for his limited vision are a mixed grouping. All are male, even as all the classical analogies claimed for Custance's sorrow were female; since the issue within the poem is the resolution of cross-sex likeness, the Man of Law tends to ground his supposedly accessible analogies in the more easily recognizable same-sex resemblance.

And yet it is hard otherwise to find too much likeness within this grouping. The references to Troy and Thebes is identical to those offered concerning Custance, although while Custance wished to be judged according to her likeness to universal feminine vulnerability, here the Sultan is contextualized with the men who failed to keep those women safe. There is thus a theme of impotency and human flaw within the names the Man of Law cites, foreshadowing the Sultan's own ignominious death at the hands of his mother. Those whose deaths were written in the stars before their births are those men whose deaths transmit a resonance of shame into the memorialization of their lives. Indeed, one of the primary themes within these analogous stories appears to be the experience of betrayal by an intimate inferior, either a female lover or political disciple. Thus the Man of Law's claim to connect an individual character with a gendered universality again falls flat. "The deeth of every man" (MLT 196) may indeed be written in the stars, but it is only those men who bear a likeness to the Sultan, whose lives resemble the Sultan's in their specificities, whose histories are pointed out within the heavens.

Moreover, the likeness between the Sultan and these heroes of classical and biblical antiquity is not only one of shame and ultimate inadequacy, but also a far more immediate resemblance in terms of religious practice. The Man of Law's list of men is composed entirely of non-Christians. In fact, they are all pagans except Samson, the ancient Hebrew judge known for his famously disastrous marriage with a woman of a different faith. It is the Sultan's religious alterity that allows him to serve as such an ideal model of poor human interpretation; medieval Christians imagined their Muslim contemporaries to be explicitly poor readers of a shared devotional semiotic, explaining the overlaps between Christian scriptures and the Koran as the relationship between truth and its false likeness.[55] Peter the

---

[55] The Christian awareness of such textual overlaps was sharply amplified by what Norman Daniel calls the "almost universal reluctance to realize that the Qur'an did not accept any Scriptural text used by Christian writers as valid for polemic purposes." Norman Daniel, *Islam and the West: The Making of an Image* (Edinburgh: Edinburgh University Press, 1962): 23. Christian authors were perturbed by such moments of interfaith confluence, but also required the shared textual language that such provided for their evangelist strategies.

Venerable, for example, based his denunciation of Islam upon its "heretical" mixing of Christian doctrine with human deception, claiming that "the utterly monstrous one joined 'to a human head a horse's neck, and the feathers' of birds...thus, mixing good things with evil, confusing true things with false, he sowed the seeds of error."[56] Muslims shared an essential likeness with their Christian neighbors, but they required Christians to teach them to discern the truth hidden within their texts. From this perspective it was also relatively easy for medieval Christians to elide contemporary Muslims with the pagans of the classical past, since in each case the failure to accept Christian truth was mitigated by the respective inaccessibilities (whether of historical period or distorted text) of that devotional knowledge to the individual.[57]

The Sultan's failure to read the image of his situation within the stars is thus not only attributable to the general human inadequacy that likewise cursed the Emperor, but also a marker of the supposed "Muslim hybridity" of his mind. As John Tolan writes, to medieval western Christians such as Guibert de Nogent (d.1124), "Orientals are clever flighty intellectuals whose brilliant circumlocutions carry them off into heresy, contrasted implicitly to the stodgy, earthbound, authority-respecting Latins."[58] The instability of Islam, according to Guibert, was one of its primary attributes—"searching for novelty, always exceeding the bounds of true belief"—but such abundant, if poorly applied, rationality was also a potential strength, if correctly disciplined by Christian imposition of the correct boundaries of understanding.[59] Indeed, the Sultan's casting off of "magyck and abusioun" as wooing techniques in favor of the bonds of Christian matrimony may be seen in and of itself as a conversionary moment. Rather than experience an epiphany of Christian truth, the Sultan instead accepts Christianity by adhering to its limitations and rigidity.

---

[56] Peter the Venerable, *Writings Against the Saracens*, ed. and trans. Irven M. Resnick (Washington, DC: Catholic University of America Press, 2016): 45. Daniel notes that this became a common image with which to describe Islam's relationship to Christianity, but spread more from the Cluniac annotations of the Koran where Peter the Venerable accessed it, rather than from his repetition in his own polemical work. Daniel, *Islam and the West*, 163–4.

[57] Suzanne Conklin Akbari, *Idols in the East: European Representations of Islam and the Orient, 1100–1450* (Ithaca, NY: Cornell University Press, 2009): 200–47. In contrast, Jewish ignorance was often tied to the inheritance of blood-guilt by contemporary Jews from their ancestors. For the "deliberate" nature of Jewish misreading in *The Canterbury Tales*, see Samantha Katz Seal, "Reading Like a Jew: The *Physician's Tale* and the Letter of the Law," *The Chaucer Review* 52.3 (2017): 298–317.

[58] John V. Tolan, *Saracens: Islam in the Medieval European Imagination* (New York: Columbia University Press 2002): 145.

[59] Guibert de Nogent, *The Deeds of God Through the Franks: A Translation of Guibert de Nogent's Gesta Dei Per Francos*, ed. Robert Levine (Woodbridge, Suffolk: Boydell and Brewer Press, 1997): 30. Tolan treats this excerpt as a form of Crusader self-justification; the Muslims of the East require Christian military intervention due to the instability of their reasoning abilities that leads them to idolatry. Tolan, *Saracens*, 144–7. Also writing on Guibert, Steven Kruger similarly observes the characterization of Muslims as an "uncontained, perhaps uncontainable enemy," although he emphasizes Guibert's vision of the uncontrollable and excessive Muslim *body* rather than the uncontrollable and excessive Muslim mind. Steven F. Kruger, "Medieval Christian (Dis)identification: Muslims and Jews in Guibert of Nogent," *New Literary History* 28.2 (Spring, 1997): 185–201, at 194.

His conclusion, "Rather than I lese/Custance, I wol be cristned" (MLT 225–6), marks his reasoned acquiescence to the consequences of a Christian world that saw itself as intolerant of excess and instability. Thus the Sultan's willingness to convert for the sake of sexual love similarly denotes his incapacity to bring together disparate meaning correctly. For the Man of Law, conversion to Christianity is a positive good and so indeed is Custance, yet the Sultan's causal unification of the two undermines the value of each. While King Alla, as I will discuss later in this chapter, converts to Christianity (from paganism) due to a moment of spiritual epiphany after witnessing a miracle, the Sultan knows no more about Christ after his decision to become a Christian than he did before. Instead, he saves his soul to satisfy his lust.[60] While his conversion nevertheless represents a moral good, it therefore fails to transform the Sultan fully into the likeness of the Christian community. Whereas in *The King of Tars*, the Sultan's skin turns from black to white when he accepts Christ, the Sultan's own conversion remains enough in doubt that, later describing the post-conversion slaughter at the wedding feast, the Man of Law still distinguishes between "the Sowdan and the Cristen everichon" (MLT 429).[61] The "diversitee" between the Sultan and Custance remains rigid even after their union under a single divine law. As Alan Ambrisco has argued (about the roughly contemporaneous romance *Sir Gowther*), the text "constructs for the convert a space of radical indeterminacy in which his identity is never fully fixed."[62] Thus, the Man of Law would see no inherent contradiction in his careful distinction between the massacred Christians and those "Surryen ... that was converted" (MLT 435), a subtle (if unconscious) evocation of boundaries variably indelible and erased.

A more deliberate distinction, however, is written between the Sultan and his mother, the Sowdanesse. The latter shares her son's designation as a failed interpreter of the temporal signs that surround her, but in her that incapacity is identified as evil rather than morally neutral. For, if the Man of Law criticizes Sultan and Emperor alike for their inadequate and foolish avoidance of analogical reasoning, he far more harshly condemns the Sowdanesse for her unnatural hybridization of entirely unalike ideologies (one good, one evil) in the pursuit of her own personal authority. She creates the very model of racial and religious binarization for which she is simultaneously condemned, not only by drawing her human body (the image of God) close to the Devil, but by also by desecrating Christian truth with her falsehoods. The polemic of the Man of Law against the Sowdanesse therefore bears far more likeness to Christian slanders of Mohammed as a *heresiach*, as a mixer of good and evil, than it does to the more supposedly

---

[60] For more on how medieval Christians associated Muslims with lust and excessive corporeality, see Daniel, *Islam and the West*, 135–61; Kruger, "Medieval Christian (Dis)Identification," 194–9; Tolan, *Saracens*, 93–5, 166; Akbari, *Idols in the East*, 155–99.

[61] *The King of Tars*, ed. Chandler, 44–5.

[62] Alan S. Ambrisco, "'Now y lowve God': The Process of Conversion in *Sir Gowther*," *Studies in the Age of Chaucer* 37 (2015): 195–225, at 197.

persuasive evangelizing texts directed by theologians to the common people. The Sowdanesse does not merely consume falsely hybridized religious belief; she produces it.

The Man of Law draws attention to the Sowdanesse's devilish mixing of truth and error by allowing her to articulate her own opposition to Christianity through a sermon on Muslim doctrine (as Chaucer imagines it).

> "What sholde us tyden of this newe lawe
> But thralldom to oure bodies and penance,
> And afterward in helle to be drawe,
> For we reneyed Mahoun oure creance?"
>
> (MLT 337–40)

The Sowdanesse offers a vision of the conversion to Christianity that is the precise inverse of the "true" salvation promised. As Chaucer's audience believed, it was not Christianity, but rather Islam, that called for slavery to the body on earth and eternal torture in the fires of Hell. The Sowdanesse mixes the truth with deception, twisting the precepts of the new Law so as to pervert its promise. Perhaps on one hand this "Muslim sermon" from the Sowdanesse speaks to the ethnocentricity of a Christian author who can only conceive of religious doctrine within Christian terms of sinful materiality and eternal punishment. It also, as Christine Rose has observed, may represent a conflation of Islam and Judaism as similar, hegemonic threats to the Christian order.[63]

However, the familiarity to a Christian audience of the Sowdanesse's devotional vision also explicitly serves to enhance its monstrosity. As Sarah Salih notes of the hybridized monsters in *Mandeville's Travels*,

> Hybrid representations are subject to rational explanations; hybrid creatures are themselves reasonable. The pagans and the cynocephali confirm the ultimate primacy of monotheism and warrior masculinity not by being worthy objects of conquest, conversion, or elimination, but by being revealed as having been all along cognitive representations of the familiar.[64]

Islam has been with Christianity since the beginning, to believe the Sowdanesse's encapsulation of its theology; whether idolatry or heresy, it is fundamentally "retrogressive," to borrow Suzanne Akbari's term for this phenomenon.[65] Islam

---

[63] Christine M. Rose, "The Jewish Mother-In-Law: Synagoga and the *Man of Law's Tale*," *Hildegard of Bingen: A Book of Essays*, ed. Maud Burnett McInernay (New York and London: Taylor and Francis, 1998): 191–226 esp. at 214–15.

[64] Sarah Salih, "Idols and Simulacra: Paganity, Hybridity, and Representation in *Mandeville's Travels*," *The Monstrous Middle Ages*, ed. Bettina Bildhauer and Robert Mills (Cardiff: University of Wales Press, 2003): 113–33, at 128.

[65] Akbari, *Idols in the East*, 227–8.

appears here first and foremost as a cognitive mistake, the familiar precepts applied to the wrong law. Such depictions rendered the religion at once both more accessible for Chaucer's audience and more horrifying.

Moreover, Islam, as the Sowdanesse preaches it, is an evolving faith, codified almost exclusively by its opposition to Christianity through the substitution of "Makometes lawe" (MLT 336) for Christ's own. The juxtaposition of like and unlike is essential to Chaucer's understanding of Islam, and he makes sure to emphasize the shared belief in a monotheistic God. The Sowdanesse swears by "grete God" (MLT 334), and to all appearances she means the same God that the Christians do. It is instead the specificity in divine messenger that twists the recognizable precepts of Christianity into "the hooly lawes of our Alkaron" (MLT 332). Even as medieval Christians condemned the Talmud for its ambivalently unalike relationship to Christian scripture, so too did they identify the Koran as a distortion of Christian truth.[66] These texts embodied the persistence of religious difference and untruth; to eradicate them and their messengers was to heal the sharp differences of the world, peeling off the lies that obscured the likeness of the truth. And indeed, the Sowdanesse is precisely just such a false messenger, not only believing in the twisted malformations of her unchristian faith, but also disseminating and augmenting those lies to others. She calls upon her lords to "maken assurance,/ As I shal seyn, assentynge to my loore,/And I shal make us sauf for everemoore" (MLT 341–3). The Sowdanesse's "loore," her teaching, is in this sense an exegetical invocation of the texts that she cites. She shows no hesitancy, despite her sex, in offering up her interpretation of the political situation or the religious text. Her call to her lords to obey and accept her teaching is not enforced with violent threat of worldly harm, but rather through the persuasive resonances of her preaching, and her earnest promise to ensure their shared salvation.

It is therefore within this context that the Man of Law's extended denunciation of the Sowdanesse must be read. He attacks her as the embodiment of a conjoined disparity, good and evil, a false union of two unlike halves. More importantly, she helps establish the reconcilability of Custance's daughterly unlikeness to her kin network by providing a harsh exemplum of what truly monstrous difference would look like. The Sowdanesse's monstrosity is not characterized by a degraded but still apparent likeness, but rather by the hybridized conjunction of the truly incompatible. Indeed, Sue Niebrzydowski comments that the "Sowdanesse's monstrous (m)othering is emphasized through her comparison with creatures that are *monstrous in their combination of the human and the bestial*, in their reproductive potential and in their care of their young" (my emphasis).[67] In this

---

[66] Daniel, *Islam and the West*, 47–78.

[67] Sue Niebrzydowski, "Monstrous (M)othering: The Representation of the Sowdanesse in Chaucer's *Man of Law's Tale*," *Consuming Narratives: Gender and Monstrous Appetite in the Middle Ages and the Renaissance*, ed. Liz Herbert McAvoy and Teresa Walters (Cardiff: University of Wales Press, 2002): 196–208, at 202.

sense, the Sowdanesse's attempt to bring forth a violent plot is comparable to the radically dysfunctional procreative models of the Canon Yeoman's alchemical experiments; where the alchemists foolishly combined two identical materials, she maliciously combines two opposing ones. Thus the Man of Law addresses her as "O feyned womman, al that may confounde/Vertu and innocence, thurgh thy malice,/Is bred in thee, as nest of every vice!" (MLT 363–4). Whereas the alchemists' union of materials proved sterile, the Sowdanesse's union of virtue and innocence with their opposing quality, malice, allows for the birth of all the vices. Moreover, she is a "feyned womman," the unnatural coupling of God's own image (woman) with his adversary (Satan), a "serpent under femynynytee,/Lik to the serpent depe in helle ybounde!" (MLT 360–1).

Women represent an ambivalent category here, and thus many scholars have read the Man of Law's connection between the Sowdanesse, Eve, and Satan, as explicit misogyny.[68] Certainly the claim that Satan "wel knowestow to women the olde way" (MLT 367) is anti-woman in its bias. And yet women, for all their flaws, are still aligned with the divine likeness and the divine creation. They are not in themselves in the likeness of Satan, but rather invested within "oure heritage" (MLT 366), and thus Satan's natural antagonists, although also all too often his "instrument" (MLT 370) through their folly. Woman and Satan are antithetical creatures, only united when someone like the Sowdanesse (or her ancestress, Eve) is willing to fall prey to Satan's wiles, and to join with him in the generation of evil. The slaughter that results from her evil plans is the product of this perverse copulation of unlike with unlike. By bringing together her human soul with that of the devil, she destroys the natural (if limited) likeness between herself and her divine father in favor of a new horrific likeness with Satan. This is an act of extreme destruction, resulting in the violent deaths of all the Christians (excepting Constance), and ending her bloodline with the death of her son. But it is also, to some extent, an act of creation, the origination of a violent sin.

Recognizing the Daughter, Part II: Likeness and its Litigations at King Alla's Court

Critics typically group the Sowdanesse together with Custance's other monstrous mother-in-law, Donegild. However, as Margaret Schlauch notes, the story of Donegild's monstrous accusations against Custance are part of a far more common plot within medieval romance, and thus appear within the majority of Constance

---

[68] Indeed, Angela Weisl has argued that the connection between the Sowdanesse and Eve is what legitimates the subsequent violence against the Sowdanesse and her subjects. Angela Jane Weisl, "'Quiting' Eve: Violence Against Women in the *Canterbury Tales*," *Violence Against Women in Medieval Texts*, ed. Anna Roberts (Gainesville, FL: University of Florida Press, 1998): 115–36, at 124–5.

analogues.[69] In contrast, the Sowdanesse/Sowdan plot line is relatively rare, appearing in Nicholas Trevet's text, and then subsequently in Gower and Chaucer's derivations of that work.[70] *The King of Tars*, for example, can be considered a Constance analogue due to its similar plot of the Christian/Muslim marriage, but the rest of the story is quite different, particularly in contrast with the much stronger similarity between the Constance story and the "accused queen" motif.[71] I thus place additional emphasis on the Sowdanesse and her son for the Man of Law's overall strategy of narration, since their inclusion within the romance is in a sense an unnecessary addition to an otherwise functional plot. Moreover, the Sowdanesse and Sultan occupy such a primary role in establishing the rhetoric of the poem that the later characters are filtered through their image, shadows of the earlier characters' likeness. Thus the charge against Donegild that she is "mannysh" or a "feendlych spirit" (MLT 782–3), draws part of its impact upon the reader from the earlier castigation of the Sowdanesse as a "feyned wommen." The denunciation of Donegild is significantly shorter than that of the Sowdanesse, and lacks the vituperate specificity of those earlier accusations. Where the Sowdanesse was coupled with the Devil, Donegild is simply like a man or like an evil spirit. These are potent accusations, but they rely for their power upon the reader's memory of the far more explicit, yet similar, condemnations of the Sowdanesse.

Donegild's plot to pretend that her grandchild is an elf is in many ways a less radical and interesting plot than the Sowdanesse's plan to reject conversion to Christianity, and carve up all of the Christian dinner guests (including her son) into pieces while they eat. The variation between Trevet, Chaucer, and Gower's explanations of Donegild's motivation for her libel against Custance can be understood as an adaptation to a certain inherent inexplicability on that point. Whether Donegild's actions are ascribed to a sexually motivated jealousy (in Trevet and Gower) or to a suspicion of Custance's ancestry (in Chaucer), Donegild's plot against Custance and her son seems needlessly cruel. In contrast, the Sowdanesse's violent reaction to her son's desire to convert the entire country away from their shared faith would have been somewhat comprehensible for a medieval reader. Indeed, the language offered up by the Sowdanesse in the face of the command to leave her faith ("the lyf shal rather out of my body sterte" [MLT 335]) mirrors what would have been the appropriate Christian response to a similar circumstance of mandated apostasy. The Sowdanesse unites falsity with Christian truth to create evil, but to do so she first embraces a mimicry of Christianity. Donegild, in contrast, seems only to mimic the Sowdanesse; her evil is only a refracted one, although its impact upon Custance is nevertheless immediate and severe.

---

[69] Margaret Schlauch, *Chaucer's Constance and Accused Queens* (New York: New York University Press, 1927): 12–22.

[70] Schlauch, *Constance and Accused Queens*, 74–6.

[71] The theme of the intermarriage would seem to put *The King of Tars* into a closer dialogue with a romance like *Sir Gowther* than it would with Custance's story.

Likewise, when the Man of Law offers up critiques of male characters throughout the rest of the text, he does so in a manner that reflects the models of masculinity and masculine cognition established earlier in the characters of the Emperor and the Sultan. The messenger whom Donegild manipulates with her false messages, for example, is criticized not only for his overconsumption of alcohol, but more specifically for the way in which that consumption of alcohol serves to destroy his powers of discernment: "Thy mynde is lorn, thou janglest as a jay" (MLT 774). The messenger's incapacity to perceive Donegild's manipulations of the letters that he carries is a severe enough ramification of indulgence, but the Man of Law also augments his speech against excessive drunkenness by criticizing the way that alcohol impairs the ability to discern the implications of one's own speech. "Ther dronkenesse regneth in any route,/Ther is no conseil hyd, withouten doute" (MLT 776–7). Drunkenness is a voluntary limitation of one's ability to interpret one's own behavior correctly, as well as the behavior of others. Indeed, the Man of Law struck a similar theme when retelling the feasting in honor of Custance and the Sowdan's wedding, pairing his description of the "deyntees" (MLT 419) with the tragic price paid for them ("al to deere they boghte it er they ryse" [MLT 420]). Such meals as the Sultan's and messengers facilitate an excess of insatiable consumption, in which men abdicate their responsibilities of perception and discretion. And when the authority of proper men is undermined, evil man-like creatures may seize that authority for their own twisted purposes.

The cognitive recognition and acceptance of likeness (and thereby truth) is of such import precisely because Custance's world is so thoroughly steeped in monstrosity, peopled by those who either fail to perceive Christian truth or deliberately wed it to evil incarnations. Thus the attempted rapist who boards Custance's ship is not only a violent thief, but also "hadde reneyed oure creance" (MLT 915). His attack on her is also therefore an attack upon the faith from which he has apostatized; appropriately, it is the Virgin Mary, in recognition of Custance's own virginal likeness, who intervenes in her defense. And yet the thief's violence against Custance is also articulated as deriving from a cognitive impairment. Even as the Messenger was condemned for his self-blinding indulgence in alcohol, the would-be rapist is condemned for ceding his authority over his body to lust. "O foule lust of luxurie, lo, thyn ende!/Nat oonly that thou feyntest mannes mynde,/But verraily thou wolt his body shende" (MLT 925–7). The vices that the Man of Law highlights in his diatribes against these incompetent men are the vices that destroy man's capacity to understand the world around him, undermining the human mental process that controls the integration of semiotic information. Custance is the likeness of a holy virgin, and the thief's inability to perceive that resemblance, instead reading her as a "lemman" (MLT 917), is a symptom of how his mind has been clouded by "lustes blynde" (MLT 928).

Within the *Tale* there are many additional invocations of the narrative of human cognitive impairment, the most significant of which is that of the blind man healed by Dame Hermyngyld, when "with thilke eyen of his mynde" (MLT 552) he recognizes her Christian virtue. As Edward Wheatley notes, Chaucer diminishes the importance of physical sight for this character in comparison with Trevet and Gower, placing the rhetorical emphasis instead upon the spiritual sight that has allowed the man nevertheless to perceive the truth of Dame Hermyngyld.[72] Indeed, the blind man's feat of vision is contrasted with the blindness of Dame Hermyngyld's husband, who not only has failed to perceive his wife's conversion to Christianity, but who also appears aggressively blind to Christian truth, since he "wolde hire for Jhesu Cristes love han slayn" (MLT 565). Dame Hermyngyld's husband yet again displays his poor powers of perception when, finding his wife slain in bed next to Custance, he judges Custance herself to be the murderer (MLT 603–9). Like Donegild's messenger, this Constable is more than capable of being manipulated by a more cunning brain, particularly when that human mind is joined together with "Sathanas temptacyiouns" (MLT 598).

In contrast, the Man of Law designates King Alla as a sufficient reader of signs and their representations. Indeed, at times in the poem, such as when he first meets Custance and recognizes her inherent nobility, he is quite a skilled one. Unlike the Emperor or the Sultan, both of whom he mirrors to some extent within the narrative, Alla is never reprimanded by the Man of Law for a failure to turn to likeness and analogy as the foundations of understanding. Instead, he is singled out for his perspicacity. When the Constable, Hermyngyd's husband, brings Constance before King Alla to accuse her of murdering his wife, King Alla immediately perceives the lack of semiotic reciprocity between Custance and the deeds of which she has been accused.[73]

> The kynges herte of pitee gan agryse,
> Whan he saugh so benigne a creature
> Falle in disese and in mysaventure
>
> (MLT 614–6)

Alla, "the very *lex animata* in England" to quote Kathy Lavezzo, is capable of recognizing the incompatibility between Custance and her situation.[74] Moreover, he identifies the radical unlikeness between evil and good, and then seeks to rectify the extent to which they have been joined together by the false accusation against Custance.

---

[72] Edward Wheatley, *Stumbling Blocks Before the Blind: Medieval Constructions of a Disability* (Ann Arbor, MI: University of Michigan Press, 2010): 181.
[73] As Kathryn Lynch observes, King Alla is not even in this scene in Trevet or Gower's versions, "where the scales of justice tilt so quickly in the heroine's direction that judgment never truly stands in abeyance." Lynch, " 'Diversitee bitwene hir bothe lawes,' " 89.
[74] Lavezzo, "Beyond Rome," 168.

> This gentil kyng hath caught a greet motyf
> Of this witnesse, and thoghte he wolde enquire
> Depper in this, a trouthe for to lere

(MLT 628–30)

While the Sowdanesse and Alla's mother, Donegild, deliberately thrill in uniting virtue and vice in the pursuit of malice, King Alla comprehends the need to remedy such a forceful conjunction of disparity. The witness to which he responds is that of the common people who "kan nat gesse/That she had doon so greet a wikkednesse" (MLT 622–3), who similarly trust the evidence of Custance's image and behavior rather than the evidence of murder with which she has been found. The claim that "they han seyn hire evere so vertuous" (MLT 624) is in this sense the inverse of those concerns expressed by Walter in the *Clerk's Tale* and discussed in Chapter 1. Walter's observation of Griselda's appearance of virtue drove him to a sadistic program of inquiry, since he was unable otherwise to accept the probability that her internal state was represented with certainty by her external state. In contrast, Alla and his populace do not hesitate to accept the likeness of virtue as virtue itself, treating the probability of semiotic reciprocity as if it were in itself a cognitive good, and they are thus unfettered by doubt.

Certainty is not the desired intellectual mechanism for these characters; analogy has instead supplanted it. They discern truth by judging its closest likeness among the human matter subject to interrogation, and are willing to accept inference even from an imperfect object. Thus, when Custance is brought before Alla ("as the lomb toward his deeth is broght,/So stant this innocent bifore the kyng" [MLT617–8]), he and his common people appreciate the anagogical relationship between Custance and the imagined lamb as a means of augmenting their discernment of her moral state. She is innocent to them because she is *like* the lamb, whereas Griselda's Walter would have been unable to accept such an acceptance of likeness as truth, or indeed anything less than a literalist equivalency of girl and sheep. In other words, King Alla has learned to appreciate metaphor as an epistemological tool, in a way that Walter never could.

That is not to say, however, that the principle of intellectual certainty does not also intrude within the *Tale*. The Man of Law's persistent and moralizing narration legitimates to some extent his reliance upon analogy and likeness as diagnostics. The people see that Custance is like a lamb and therefore likely innocent, but that judgment is confirmed for the reader by the Man of Law himself. Moreover, the more immediate divine intervention in Custance's defense serves to justify the public interpretation of her likeness almost as soon as it has been delivered. When her accuser swears to her guilt upon a holy text, a divine hand strikes him down so that "bothe his eyen broste out of his face/In sighte of every body in that place" (MLT 671–2). As Margaret Schlauch has noted, medieval narratives of accused queens typically delay their resolution, sometimes for years, as the queen suffers the torments of popular condemnation and misjudgment.[75] Yet the story Chaucer has chosen for his Man of Law to retell is a story that, for all the wanderings of its heroine and its plot, delivers public and unquestioned justifications of its heroine's virtue. In the court of law that Alla has assembled to discern Custance's guilt, judgment proceeds through the customary mechanisms of litigation, witness testimony and personal evaluations of the accused. In other words, it proceeds through the assemblage of a series of likenesses that will allow the court to establish the comprehensive likeness of the accused to an ultimate good or evil. As the Man of Law tells it, characters tend to be motivated and aligned either with God or with the Devil; their fellows must discover which through careful inquiry and observation.

The metaphor of the false, devil-allied accuser whose eyes burst forth from their eye sockets in front of the eyes of the entire crowd who has already witnessed against him, places all the emphasis and responsibility upon the characters charged with perception, rather than those invested with the act of representation. Thus it is the capacity of the crowd to perceive and interpret the evidence of their eyes that is placed at the center of the litigation, rather than Custance's capacity to signify and represent innocence in a satisfactory manner. But at the same time, Custance's virtuous likeness is never far from the public assessment of her character. As the Man of Law informs the reader, she bore a distinct likeness to men on their way to the gallows.

> Have ye nat seyn somtyme a pale face,
> Among a prees, of hym that hath be lad
> Toward his deeth, wher as hym gat no grace,
> And swich a colour in his face hath had
> Men myghte knowe his face that was bistad
> Amonges alle the faces in that route?
> So stant Custance, and looks around her.
>
> (MLT 645–51)

This analogy depends upon the comparison of Custance's pale and stricken face with that of a condemned man, whose innocence or guilt is not established by the Man of Law; the emphasis of the likeness is on the suffering (virtuous in its own sake) of the individuals rather than upon the ultimate judgment of their sins. Such an analogy indeed undermines the power of the legal system within the poem, as the Man of Law reminds us of the fallibility of the human powers of cognition, especially as applied to the assessment of one another. He has no wish to present us with a means of deriving certainty, but rather only a means of assessing

---

[75] See for example her account of the variants of *Octavian*, in which the couple's children grow to adulthood before the redemption of the mother, and reconciliation between the parents is effected. Schlauch, *Chaucer's Constance and Accused Queens*, 86–8.

ALMOST HEIRS: DAUGHTERS AND DISAPPOINTMENTS   197

the probable meaning of the surrounding world and, most importantly, living with the accompanying layer of inevitable doubt.

Men may know that a man has been condemned by the color of his face; so too may they know Custance's suffering according to her countenance. But that visual evidence is in itself insufficient to bear the weight of meaning. So, Custance provides the company with a more comprehensive list of analogies for herself.

> "Immortal God, that savedest Susanne
> Fro false blame, and thou, merciful mayde,
> Marie I meene, doghter to Seint Anne,
> Bifore whos child angeles synge Osanne,
> If I be giltlees of this felonye,
> My socour be, for ellis shal I dye!"

(MLT 638–44)

Custance places the emphasis here upon her virginity, for it is that corporeal attribute that allows her to claim likeness with the two holy virgins whom God has already saved from public misunderstanding and condemnation. Chaucer makes a subtle play with this mention of the Virgin Mary, for while Custance crafts her appeal as if it is directed equally in turn to God and to the Virgin, the clause that contains the Virgin's name could as easily represent an additional object of divine intervention rather than a new active power of the same. God's salvation of Mary from the false blame associated with her pregnancy makes Mary the likeness of Susanna, even while her pregnancy with God makes her more like Him than like a human woman. Mary is the replication of mortal femininity, the "doghter to Seinte Anne," but she is also at once an embodiment of genealogical alterity through her relationship with her son, a child at once both fatherless and indivisible from its Father. With "bifore whos child angeles synge Osanne," Custance emphasizes the unbridgeable distinction that exists between the divine Child and his blessed, but inferior, mother. Custance's prayer thus highlights the fluidity of the female representational form—perfect in its likeness when called upon to be a source of individual authority, but effortlessly transcended by its male offspring when that space of incommensurable difference will codify male power.

In thinking of Custance as embodied analogy, scholars have typically focused on these models of sacral female likeness, both in regards to Custance's personal resemblance to female saints and to those female saints' resemblance to one another.[76] And indeed, Custance's position as the prayerful object of repeated acts of divine intervention solidifies the comparison to a *vita* of a female saint. But, at

[76] Hagiographic readings of the *Man of Law's Tale* are varied and numerous, but for example see Michael R. Paull, "The Influence of the Saint's Legend Genre in the 'Man of Law's Tale,'" *The Chaucer Review* 5.3 (Winter 1971): 179–94.

the same time, that perfection of likeness always functions as the inverse of the more immediate *unlikeness* that Custance also embodies in relation to her father, husbands, and son. Her performance as a spiritual analogy for the holy is directly linked to, and perhaps even precipitated by, her failures of kin-based signification within the temporal realm. The Man of Law's narration of Custance's wedding night, for example, emphasizes the mutability of feminine sanctity by noting "thogh that wyves be ful hooly thynges/They moste take in pacience at nyght... And leye a lite hir hoolynesse aside" (709–10, 713). Custance's body is an image of holiness except when it must be a vehicle for masculine reproduction; she is part of the sisterhood of "ful hooly thynges" who must nevertheless signify first and foremost according to their husbands' earthly desires.[77]

Moreover, even as Custance demonstrates her willingness to make her feminine holiness subject to her husband's reproductive needs, so too does she articulate a voluntary rejection of her likeness with the feminine divine, Mary, if so doing will be the only way to preserve Alla's bloodline. As she sails forth in her little ship with infant Maurice, Custance prays to the Virgin Mary again to help her. And yet, where before she constructed her prayer as part of an articulation of likeness with other threatened virgins, here Custance prays to be saved from experiencing a true mimesis. She reminds the Virgin that:

> Thanne is ther no comparison bitwene
> Thy wo and any wo man may sustene.
> Thow saw thy child yslayn bifore thyne yen,
> And yet now lyveth my litel child, parfay!
>
> (MLT 846–9)

There is no comparison between the sorrow of the Virgin Mary and that of any woman, nor, Custance argues, should there be. She has no desire to experience that maternal torment, to achieve an authentic mimicry where before she had claimed likeness. In defense of her son, Custance pleads with the Virgin to preserve that difference between them, so that Custance might never have to witness the death of her (still living) child.

This is a moving plea, grounded within an affective understanding of the maternal/filial bond. And yet it is also simultaneously a genealogical one, as Custance makes it clear that her hesitation to see the child killed is inseparable from his legal and fleshly connections to his father. She tells the Constable, in a plea for salvation that blends almost seamlessly into the immediately preceding one that she had offered to the Virgin, "If thou darst nat saven hym, for blame,/ So kys hym ones in his fadres name!" (MLT 860–1). Alla's paternal claim upon

---

[77] For the conflict between Custance's marital sexuality and her sanctity, cf. Melissa M. Furrow, "The Man of Law's St. Constance: Sex and the Saeculum," *The Chaucer Review* 24.3 (Winter 1990): 223–35.

Maurice not only dictates the question of the latter's survival ("why wil thyn harde fader han the spilt?" [MLT 857]), but also endows both the child's birth and potential death with their supposed meaning. It is the paternal right to acknowledge the child or not, and Custance recognizes that essential component of paternity when she asks the Constable to stand in for Alla and acknowledge the child as the legitimate heir by means of a kiss. It is unclear from the text whether the Constable indeed accedes to her plea to kiss the child in his father's name; but regardless, Custance's articulation of masculine intervention as fundamental for her son's survival, and for the demarcation of his claims to a kin-based identity, treats the chain of masculinity in which both father and son participate as superior to her own maternal affect. Her pleas to first the Virgin and then the Constable reveal the extent to which Custance perceives herself and her son to be caught within the middle of a dynastic and patrilineal struggle, as indeed Donegild, with her forged letters, has determined Custance and Maurice's exile to be. If Alla has supposedly refused to recognize his son as his own likeness and heir, then Custance will call upon his servant to do so by proxy, and remind the Virgin that Alla's resemblance to, and claim upon, his son take precedence over even the most holy likeness between women. Even if the men around Custance repeatedly fail in their powers of perception and capacity to navigate the space between inconsistent forms of likeness and representative meaning, Custance herself has a full understanding of how mutable her patterns of likeness and unlikeness must be for her to survive in a world that cannot recognize her as her father's daughter nor as a person of her own.

Recognizing the Daughter, Part III: Custance's Likeness, Maurice's Lineage

Daughters like Custance represent a monstrous threat to their fathers, but also, ideally, a temporary one. For, once they have provided a male child in turn, they themselves may be erased and elided from their fathers' and sons' stories. As Rachel Moss notes, within medieval romance, narratives of daughter-heirs reflect anxieties of patriarchal inheritance, but also reinforce male bonds of kinship when the daughter reproduces her father's likeness through the production of a male grandchild.[78] And yet while that generation of a new male heir solves the problem of the legal distribution of the father's property and titles, it still does not manage entirely to mitigate the ongoing problem of the daughter's difference from her father. The daughter remains an embodiment of unlikeness and a threat to the integrity of the paternal identity. Moreover, while property may thus

---

[78] Moss, *Fatherhood and its Representations*, esp. 144–5.

leap-frog the female generation of hereditary descent, bloodlines will nevertheless need to travel through that female link of the kinship chain, risking dilution and pollution from the mingling of the father's hereditary material with that of the daughter's husband. And indeed, the *Man of Law's Tale* (as well as its analogues) attests to perseverance of the female image within the successive generation. Both King Alla and the Emperor of Rome remark upon the significant likeness between the child, Maurice, and their wife/daughter, Custance. As the Man of Law himself attests, "Now was this child as lyk unto Custance/As possible is a creature to be" (MLT 1030–31). Previous readings of reproductive patterns within the *Man of Law's Tale* have therefore focused upon the likeness between Custance and Maurice as key to the interpretation of the poem. Angela Florschuetz, for example, reads this story as one which "validate[s] maternal transmission" of traits to children, concluding that therefore "Chaucer roundly critiques and dismantles the reflex that…makes maternal transmission an object of horror."[79] From the microperspective of the Custance/Maurice generational descent, I agree with that reading; the likeness to his mother does not in any way pass on monstrosity to young Maurice. But to focus on only those two generations is to artificially constrict the lens of analysis. It is not two generations that the story has been concerned with from its inception, but rather three, and it is upon the perspective of that first generation, the progenitor of the other two, that the evaluation of both reproductive and political consequences within the narrative should be based. From the perspective of Emperor or father, maternal transmission is a necessary mechanism; it is only through the body of the daughter that the father's own specific likeness may be reproduced. But the degree to which a daughter can transmit her father's likeness is of course limited by the extent to which she has possessed it to begin with. In this sense, the reproduction of this third generation offers both father and daughter the opportunity to reassess their likeness to one another, and to integrate and elide the persistent modes of unlikeness tied to their respective sexes into a new (male) form that signifies and represents them both. If the daughter's unlikeness to her father renders her a kind of monstrous shadow of his truth, then how can even the most perfect of male children redeem such a fragmentation of the paternal self?

It is notable that almost as soon as Custance has produced a male heir, both her husband and her father's analytic capacities precipitously improve. Upon receiving the forged letter from his mother that Custance has given birth to "so horrible a feendly creature" (MLT 751), Alla demonstrates a profound degree of wisdom by surrendering his human will to the discernment of Christ.[80] "Welcome

[79] Florschuetz, "Constructions of Genealogy," 27.
[80] Peggy McCracken notes that Chaucer has changed the accusation slightly from the version contained within Nicholas Trevet's *Chronicle*. While in both versions (as well as Gower's) the monstrous birth functions both as a rupture of the expected paternal/filial likeness and as a supposed revelation of Custance's own internal perversion, Trevet's story has Constance accused of being an evil spirit,

the sonde of Crist for everemoore/To me that am now lerned in his loore!"
(MLT 760–1). Alla's conversion to Christianity is depicted here as a pedagogical
experience, one which has opened his eyes both to the teachings of Christ and
to the necessity of subjugating his human cognition to the divine wisdom capable
of more fully addressing his situation. Thus it becomes somewhat unclear from
the successive lines if Alla's solution to the letter is his own or rather that of a
divine suggestion; in either case, the reader can be assured of the strength of his
decision. And, indeed, Alla decides to maintain his conjugal relationship and to
integrate his monstrous child into the family unit.

> Kepeth this child, al be it foul or feir,
> And eek my wyf, unto myn hoom-comynge.
> Crist, whan hym list, may sende me an heir
> Moore agreable than this to my lykynge."
>
> (MLT 764–7)

Alla's prudent reply to his mother's allegations against Custance demonstrates a
sharp break within the narrative of the *Man of Law's Tale*. No longer does the
manifestation of unlikeness or diversity result in violence, exile, or incest. Alla,
guided by Christ, does not erase the extent to which this supposed child has created a distance between itself and its father. He makes it quite clear that he will
not consider this monstrous child to be his heir, that its fleshly deviation disqualifies it from serving as his posthumous likeness in the kingdom. And yet that
acknowledgement of difference, and even of the possibility of filial monstrosity,
does not necessitate eradication. The temperate view offered here by Alla is one of
submission to the divine will, and acquiescence to the natural limitations placed
upon man by his God. He is not promised a more agreeable heir in the future;
he recognizes that this child may be the only product of his flesh and blood. But
he prays for another, and in the devotion of his prayer he is willing to tolerate the
threat to his person posed by the horror of a monstrous wife and son.

Guided by Christ, Alla recognizes that the appropriate response for a father
confronted by a terrifying lack of resemblance to his child is submission to the
divine will and preservation of the family network. Alla's "hoom-comynge" will
reunite the domestic unit, allowing the child, however horrible to look upon, to
be fully integrated within the patrilineal line. The imagined child, Maurice's
monstrous shadow, will not be allowed to reproduce or inherit within that line,
but his inclusion, however liminal, will persist within kin boundaries of alliance

---

since her child "que ne recemble pas a fourme de home," rather than a fairy as in both Chaucer's and
Gower's stories. McCracken, *Curse of Eve*, 73–5. Trevet's words work to make explicit that which is
only implied in Chaucer; Custance is accused of breaking not only the secondary level of resemblance
between son and father (since presumably Alla himself is not too horrible for anyone to look upon),
but also the primary resemblance of humanity itself. It is the form *of* man rather than the form of *a*
man (namely the child's father) that Custance is believed to have subverted.

and affect. With this decision from king and God alike, the Man of Law presents the indivisible family as an ideal blessed by both secular and supernatural authority. A true family must be elastic enough to accommodate all its disparate members despite even the most visible forms of disparity. Moreover, the Man of Law's endorsement of this type of domestic category as *the* model of paternal/filial indivisibility advances a model of the kin network that privileges legal modes for the authentication of paternity (such as Donegild's letter) over "natural" means of assessment grounded upon the visual affirmation of likeness and resemblance. This approach, on one hand, undermines the epistemological functions of paternity, since it breaks the assurance of signification grounded in the visually verifiable relationship between father and son. But, on the other hand, since the Man of Law has consistently presented such perfection of semiotic reciprocity as entirely beyond the human reach, this rhetorical move allows him to urge man instead to value the flawed, but far more accessible, means of self-perpetuation within his grasp. A monstrous child will never revivify his deceased father in the world's memory, but he will nonetheless carry the father's blood to a new man, in a new generation, more worthy of acclaim.

Alla's remarkable realization of the importance of including even monstrous children within the family network is only one specific example, however, of a larger trend at the end of the *Man of Law's Tale*. Even as the beginning of the story witnessed a wide spectrum of shattered likenesses, broken families, and violent joinings of good and evil, so too does the end of the poem emphasize processes of healing and reunification. In fact, Part III of the *Man of Law's Tale* marks a clear break with the earlier sections of the poem, ushering in a series of moments of perceptive recognition; these moments of understanding then, in turn, precipitate a variety of retributive acts that provide both judicial and familial closure to the poem's conflicts. Whereas before, blindness and misapprehension prevailed over all encounters, now the Man of Law depends on motifs of recognition and rediscovery to draw his story to a close.

As Custance and Maurice float for their five years upon the sea, suspended from the progress of the narrative until the world's cognition is capable of valuing their reappearance, Alla's capacities of discernment grow. His discovery of his mother's betrayal—"By wit and sotil enquerynge,/Ymagined was by whom this harm gan sprynge" (888–9)—marks one of the cognitive achievements of the *Tale*, and thus foreshadows the recognition scenes to follow later at the Roman feasts. The Man of Law narrates, "the hand was knowe that the letter wroot/And al the venym of this cursed dede" (MLT 890–1). Alla is now capable of reading analogies. The likeness of his mother's writing (her hand) allows him to visualize her material body (her hand) so as to intuit her guilt and malice. The Man of Lawe seeks to cast some uncertainty upon the deductive process, with "but in what wise, certeinly, I not" (MLT 890, 892), although this narrational move does not undermine Alla's conclusions as to his mother's guilt, but rather seeks to prevent the human Alla from taking credit for the full weight of his inspiration. His process of recognition may, the Man of Law implies, stem from his Christian teachings, in the same way that his advocacy of tolerance for filial monstrosity did.

In shaping this new turn towards the victorious human intellect over the evil and deceptive, the Man of Law intentionally fails to distinguish between the divine and the human sources of cognitive success. One of the only epistemological points in the *Tale* that this narrator leaves vague, this prevarication over the question of how much credit for cognition is owed to a single human mind in comparison to what is owed to an all-powerful Creator, allows the Man of Law to maintain a sense of inherent mystery around the human powers of perception. Have men's wits simply become less dull by this time in the story, than they were at the poem's beginning for the Sultan or the Emperor? Or does God simply intervene for the religious Christian mind in a way that He does not for the Muslim one? The occurrence of horrible violence and the threat of monstrous unlikeness within the family unit have both remained stable throughout the course of the *Tale*. In the absence of such mutability of circumstance, it must be the male capacity of interpretation that has undergone so fundamental a shift.

Alla's recognition of his mother's iniquity is also a recognition of how powerfully her behavior has threatened his patrilineal chain. "Alla, out of drede,/His mooder slow—that may men pleynly rede—/For that she traitour was to her ligeance" (MLT 893–5). The female role in man's reproduction of the male self is to help not hinder; moreover, that demand for beneficial female support does not extend only to the issue of the immediate generation. Instead, like the *Man of Law's Tale* as a whole, the story of conflict between Alla and his mother, Donegild, emphasizes the connectivity between three, interwoven, generations. Donegild's "ligeance" should be to her "lineage," or rather it should be given to the lineage of the son whom she has produced in the image of an absent father. Her crime is thus neither murder nor sexual jealousy; it is treachery, a rebellion against the political and familial authority of her son, and of his son, the future King, in turn. We can perhaps therefore extend to Donegild what, in reference to the Sowdanesse, Alcuin Blamires refers to as the "destruct[ion] of elementary bonds of fellowship."[81] Once again within this story, we have a mother-in-law draw together two fundamentally disparate categories, unalike and unalike, to claim that some meaning has been born from their union. Whereas the Sowdanesse drew together Christian truth with the devil's lies, here too Donegild had attempted to force a semiotic union between Custance and Maurice's Christian virtue and the devilish character of a magical, demonic world. Donegild's treachery is thus not only a matter of violence, but also one of hermeneutics. She has created a false mirror of Custance and, far more importantly, of

---

[81] Alcuin Blamires, *Chaucer, Ethics, and Gender* (Oxford: Oxford University Press, 2006): 35.

Maurice, to undermine their claims to kinship; it is for this that she is a traitor to Alla's male bloodline.

Alla's execution of his mother is thus a judicial sentence passed by an authoritative royal figure upon one of his subjects. While the bond from mother to son is referenced throughout the story as an extremely affective and sentimental one on the part of the mother, no son, not even Maurice, is depicted as possessing in return an equally powerful emotional tie to his mother. Alla's deed of matricide will eventually require penance from him, but not mourning; it is a sin of bloodshed, but not of emotional betrayal. For the Man of Law assesses Alla's own debt of loyalty as belonging first and foremost to the masculine collective of his blood, rather than to the individual associations or relationships of a subjective self. The mother exists upon the margins of that collective; a good mother will nurture its continuance through her care of her husband's male offspring. But, failing to perform such appropriate maternal behavior, the mother herself may be excised from the family line without negative consequence for anyone except herself. When the Man of Law concludes "thus endeth olde Donegild, with mischance!" (MLT 896), he is able to celebrate the visitation of justice upon Donegild as an individual without concern for her death's impact upon the family. A mother can be "endeth" at will without any jeopardy for the patrilineal chain.

Thus Alla's recognition of his mother's distinctive handwriting upon the evil missive, and his immediate, somewhat mystical, comprehension of her larger evil plot is inseparable from his simultaneous recognition of her lack of value to his dynastic project. His actions in killing her and eliminating the maternal threat occupying the margins of his male line therefore represent as much of a profound insight as his deductive reasoning. He has understood something vitally important both for his specific circumstances and for the collective: if mothers obstruct male heritage, they must be removed. Their proximity to the process of male descent should not allow them to seize an unnatural power over its successive progress. Donegild's complaint that Alla had chosen "so strange a creature unto his make" (MLT 700) is thus a cruel and rebellious imposition of female will where it does not belong; the perpetuation of Alla's line is not of her concern, and her status as his mother does not allow her to so question his authority.

The Man of Law tends to use the duality of his husband/mother-in-law plotline to reinforce his major points with doubled repetition. Thus, once Alla has had his essential epiphany as to his mother's evil treachery of thought and deed, so too does the Emperor stir finally to vengeance.

> The Romayn Emperour,
> That out of Surrye hath by lettres kowe
> The slaughter of christen folk, and dishonor
> Doon to his doghter by a fals traytour."
>
> (MLT 954–7)

Time becomes oddly distorted at this point in the poem. Those letters from Syria surely should have made the passage to Rome long before this point in Custance's story. Instead, it is as if the Man of Law has withheld the culmination of the Syrian plotline until the Northumbrian one is first fully ended. Until Alla has had his essential realization of his mother's obstruction of his desire for an heir, the Emperor and the Sowdanesse will remain in narratively reinforced limbo, awaiting Alla's moment of insight so that they may re-enact both its realization and its consequences.

The Emperor of Part III, in contrast to that of Part I, has fully opened eyes. Whereas before he was unable to read the signs of the world, now he has full recognition of the "cursed wikked Sowdanesse" (MLT 958). He accordingly sends an army to Syria, where "they brennen sleen, and brynge hem to meschance/Ful many a day; but shortly—this is the ende—/Homward to Rome they shapen hem to wende" (MLT 964-6). The fate of the Syrians (who as a collective group elide seamlessly in the Man of Law's mind with the singular Sowdanesse) is thus identical to that of Donegild. Both are brought to "mischance/meschance;" both are "ended" or excised from the story. This final section of the poem emphasizes (with a rapidity at odds with poor Custance floating perpetually at sea) how comprehensively these female threats to male perpetuation may be destroyed. Once men are awakened to the dangers within their domestic spaces, and may correctly interpret the likenesses and symbolisms of the world, they have no difficulty in reading these women for whom they truly are. The Sowdanesse and Donegild are finally recognized not as daughters (whose unlikeness to the father offers hope for reconciliation), but as the vestigial remains of reproductions long ago achieved, who, useless now for the perpetuation of human heritage, bear likeness only to the Devil. They can be safely ended now, as justice for their crimes, and in recognition of how much of their individual value ended much earlier, after they had born their sons.

By the final section of the poem, Custance too has born a son, but it is not yet time for her to be "ended." In contrast to Donegild or the Sowdanesse, she still has a vital role to play in the achievement of male genealogical success; before Custance can be excised from the plot, she must first reconcile with her father and husband so that her son may be reintegrated into their kin networks. Custance will solve Maurice's alienation from his paternal bloodlines, and Maurice will, in turn, cure Custance of the problematic "unlikeness" that has severed her from her own father. It is within this context that I read both of the "recognition scenes" at the end of this *Tale*. When first Maurice is urged by his mother to attend the visiting King Alla at a feast and stare directly into the king's face, he precipitates a scene of recognition and paternal reintegration that redeems for him his patrimony.

> Now was this child as lyk unto Custance
> As possible is for a creature to be.

> This Alla hath the face of in remembrance
> Of dame Custance, and ther on mused he.
>
> (MLT 1030–1034)

As I noted earlier, Maurice's extreme resemblance to Custance has been seen at times by critics as signifying some dysfunction within the mother/son relationship, characterized by an overdeveloped degree of maternal marking.[82] And in turn, as I noted before, other critics have attempted to redeem the relationship by seeing Chaucer here as legitimating the maternal transmission of traits, and in effect endorsing a female obstruction of the traditional models of visually dominant paternity. I break with both these readings in turn; I see this passage of Alla's recognition of his son, Maurice, due to the child's likeness to Custance as a purely secondary moment of paternal recognition in comparison to the Emperor's recognition of the same. Alla's role here is to foreshadow the reintegration of the Emperor's paternal line, not his own. Like his source in Trevet, Chaucer is constructing an origin story for Maurice as Holy Roman Emperor, one that is given added value by the ties to English royalty, but is first and foremost grounded in a male genealogy of imperial blood. Custance's likeness to her son is a means of preserving the essential relationship between Maurice and his grandfather; if, in order to ensure the reciprocity of likeness between Emperor and imperial heir, Alla's paternal prerogatives must be somewhat overshadowed, then that is a sacrifice the Man of Law is more than willing to make.

Paternity, as the perpetuation of the male bloodline across time and in defiance of death, is thus neither a universal virtue nor a universal human right. It is restricted not only by gender but by class, with the more prestigious man winning the right to dominate the likeness of a mutual heir. As I noted in the Introduction, Chaucer's own emblem is absent from his son's tomb; what Alice Chaucer decided to celebrate in memory of her father's mortal life was his blood relationships with royalty (however much more distant such were than the blood he shared with his own father). Therefore there is no contradiction or reproductive crisis in the strong resemblance between Maurice and Custance, as long as it reinforces the bond between Maurice and the Emperor. Once the plot has moved out of Northumberland (where Alla was the sole paternal figure) and back into the Emperor's Rome, the bond between Alla and his son is subjugated almost entirely to that between the Emperor and his heir.[83] Moreover, Maurice's likeness to

---

[82] Florschuetz, "Constructions of Genealogy," 48–60.

[83] My reading of the Emperor's bloodline as more dominant and central for Maurice than that of King Alla deemphasizes the theme of Maurice's "Englishness" which has become a crucial component of scholarship on the *Man of Law's Tale* as resonant of medieval English anxieties about how they fit with the rest of the world. Kathy Lavezzo summarizes the latter argument as follows: "That delirious topographic 'splitting' of Custance between England Rome points to the instability upon which the Man of Law's national fantasy is founded. At once attracted and repulsed by her maternity, alternately repudiating and embracing Roman authority, both proud of and anxious about his isolated homeland,

Custance despite their diversity of sex is precisely what gives him value as her proxy to her father. She sends her son "so lyk her face" to her father to prove the victory of blood over sex. Maurice is her human witness that resemblance and the recognition of likeness can span the diversity of sex. For if the Emperor is capable of thinking on his daughter when he looks upon this boy, then surely he must grant that his daughter may remind others of himself.

Thus the reproductive crisis on display in this final part of the poem is not Custance's displacement of Alla's likeness within their son, but rather the challenge of reintegrating Custance into a familial structure when the preceding trajectory of the narrative has so consistently emphasized her alienation. Custance indeed assumes the active role in forcing this her way back into the family, plotting a feast at which she will compel her father to recognize her as his daughter, if still not as his heir. By sending Maurice to invite the Emperor, Custance utilizes her son's male likeness to offer up a new, more pleasing version of her own to her father. Looking upon Maurice, the Emperor "on his doghter thoght" (MLT 1096); Custance reasserts herself into her father's cognition. Indeed she demands both space in his mind and a full recognition of her status as his daughter in her subsequent public confrontation with the Emperor. " 'Fader', quod she, 'youre yonge child Custance/Is now ful clene out of youre remembrance'" (MLT 1105–6). The accusation that the Emperor has entirely forgotten his daughter is in fact never challenged nor refuted. On the contrary, the Man of Law's comment that, looking on Maurice, the Emperor thought of his daughter, seems to imply that thinking upon Custance is something that the Emperor needs a visual stimulus to effect.

It makes sense, therefore, that it is Custance who recognizes and claims her father rather than the other way round—"whan she saugh hir fader in the street/ She lighte doun, and falleth hym to feet" (MLT 1103–4). Moreover, Custance explicitly claims her status as his daughter, forcing the Emperor to recognize her finally without equivocation as his child. " 'I am youre doghter Custance', quod she" (MLT 1107) immediately after she has accused him of having forgotten her entirely. Whereas in her youth Custance had been willing to identify with a universal femininity ("wommen ben born," etc.) that created an impassable space between herself and her father, now she refuses to be denied her rights of kinship. She uses "fader" as a weapon against the possibility of his indifference. "It am I, fader, that in the salte see/Was put alone and dampned for to dye./Now, goode

---

Chaucer's lawyer exhibits a version of the ideological vacillation and uncertainty that Homi Bhabha and other contemporary theorists associate with nationalism." Lavezzo, "Beyond Rome," 178. And yet I would argue that the important difference lies in a distinction of race vs. lineage. Maurice, through his father's seminal contribution, has an innate English racialization that he will carry with him within his body; from his grandfather's less immediate but more powerful seminal contribution, he has a history of patrilineal descent from the imperial throne and, moreover, the promise of carrying on that male tradition himself. Thus, I see Maurice as bearing an internal *likeness* to Chaucer's Englishmen, a corporeal trait of similitude, without seeing him as fully incorporated into even an unstable nationalist theory of imagined power.

fader, mercy I yow crye!" (MLT 1109–11). The Emperor may have overlooked his paternal obligations previously, but Custance will not let him escape from her again. Her invocation of "fader" ties the Emperor's paternity directly to Custance's suffering, and allows her to articulate the depth of his responsibility towards her. With her immediately successive lines, "sende me namooure unto noon hethe-nesse" (MLT 1112), Custance confronts her father with the extent to which he, as much as the Sowdanesse or Donegild, has kept Custance (and now her child) floating endlessly upon the sea. It is not the likeness between them, therefore, upon which Custance justifies her demand of her father. Rather, she refers to him as her father in a way that elides that paternity with the disastrous distance he has ceaselessly sought to maintain between them.

It is this distance, this space of non-recognition between father and daughter, which is eradicated through Custance's publically articulated claim upon the Emperor. "Who kan the pitous joye tellen al/Bitwexe hem thre, syn they been thus ymette?" (MLT 1114–5), the Man of Law comments after Custance's plea. Interestingly, the Emperor offers no response to Custance's aggressive acclamation of him as her father. She publicly recognizes him, but his assent to the new codifi-cation of this otherwise dormant relationship appears far more passive. We are told that we cannot guess at the joy between them, and that they immediately attend the feast "in joye and blisse at mete" (MLT 1119). But after the high dra-matics framing this scene, it would be natural to expect something more of this parent/child reunion. Instead, all the emotion and the recognition come from Custance. Her reintegration into her bloodline occurs through her father's recog-nition of her son and then through her own recognition of her father; both of these events are driven exclusively by Custance's passion and commitment to reclaim a filial role and force the paternal one upon her father. The Emperor is silent on his feelings about being reunited with his daughter. That "pitous joye," in fact, only exists between a kin network trio (the Emperor, Custance, and Maurice). No such similar joy is expressed between the father/daughter pair alone, nor does Alla appear to qualify to join their bond.

It is this patrilineal trio, with Custance the unlike space holding the others together, that provides the happy conclusion to the poem. Maurice becomes the Emperor's heir, and Emperor in his turn. No mention is made again of him serv-ing as his father's heir in Britain; Alla has been fully supplanted by the Emperor. Alla thus dies (somewhat conveniently) after a year, and Custance, returning to Rome, once more "she hir fader hath yfound" (MLT 1152). The Man of Law's heroine will simply keep on finding her father however he might evade her, until finally she has fully erased the difference between them. "In vertu and in hooly almus-dede/They lyven alle, and nevere asunder were/Til deeth departeth hem" (MLT 1156–8). The embrace of this holy lifestyle allows Custance finally to efface the gap of representation inflicted by her sex, for there is neither male nor female in Christ (Galatians 3:28). Dying in each other's arms, Custance and her father can finally revel in the reciprocity of their resemblance.

Coming After Chaucer: The Man of Law as Chaucer's Heir

The *Man of Law's Tale*, like almost all the Canterbury narratives that deal with reproduction, is a story of coming to terms with the compromises man faces in his fallen world. Before closing this chapter, therefore, I wish to note how closely the Man of Law ties the moral of his story (the overlooking of difference and disappointment in the face of encroaching death) to his own limited capacities as a narrator. From the very beginning, his *Tale*'s telling is justified not by its quality but by the company's increasing loss of time. As Harry Bailly reminds the pilgrims at the beginning of the *Tale*:

> "Lordynges," quod he, "I warne yow, al this route,
> The fourthe party of this day is gon.
> Now for the love of God and of Seint John,
> Leseth no tyme, as ferforth as ye may"
>
> (MLT 17–9)

The Man of Law gives his *Tale* in response to the company's realization of how much time they have already lost, to fulfill his "biheste" (MLT 42) in response to common plea. He does so with an acknowledgement that urgency will prevent him from perfection, that his lack of time will keep him from being worthy of Chaucer, his poetic progenitor, for "I kan right now no thrifty tale seyn/That Chaucer…Hath seyd hem" (MLT 46–7, 9). If the Man of Law has inherited Chaucer's stories, nevertheless the passing of time—both heightening the urgency and distancing him from his poetic progenitor—will prevent him from telling the stories as Chaucer would have.

Alfred David saw these lines as proof of the inherent reciprocity between the Man of Law and Chaucer, arguing the Man of Law's "doubts about his own ability to tell a 'thrifty' tale…reflect Chaucer's own uncertainty on the same score."[84] And certainly, we should not forget that Chaucer is ventriloquizing the Man of Law's praise of Chaucer's poetry. Yet what seems to me to be significant here is not how easily the Man of Law and Chaucer may be collapsed into a single poetic anxiety, but rather how sharply Chaucer maintains their respective distance as poetic father and son. Chaucer's attitude to his poetic forbearers, if that is indeed what we should read the Man of Law as modeling, is thus one of determination

---

[84] Alfred David, "The Man of Law vs. Chaucer: A Case in Poetics," *PMLA* 82.2 (May 1967): 217–25, at 217.

rather than of the defensive uncertainty of his works' merit. He acknowledges that he is an imperfect man and an imperfect poet; still he will recognize the very fathers that he cannot hope to resemble.[85] Poets, like daughters, may be inadequate in comparison with their ancestors, but that inadequacy does not excuse them from picking up the burden of their blood, any more than does the rapid passing of the time.

The Man of Law's story of imperfect but functional likeness also responds directly to the Host. Harry Bailly had utilized models of analogical perfection for his assessment of the time.

> [He] saugh wel that the shadwe of every tree
> Was in lengthe the same quantitee
> That was the body erect that caused it.
> And therefore by the shadwe he took his wit"
>
> (MLT 7–10)

At "ten of the clokke" (MLT 14) all is perfectly referential, representing perfectly that object which has brought them into being. It is from this perfection of reciprocity that the Host depicts himself as deriving meaning. He trusts his deductions based upon analogical objects because he has already assessed how minutely they reproduce their sires.

But the point that Harry Bailly misses and the Man of Law appreciates is that after this moment in the day's progress when all aligns without flaw, the sun will continue its movement across the sky, distorting the shadows that are born from the trees. The very brevity of this analogical ideal reinforces its rarity. The Host calls for the Man of Law to hurry and waste no time, but it is already too late. Nothing will allow the Man of Law nor any other storyteller to signify perfectly with the poets who have come before them. Human heredity is "the streem that turneth nevere agayn/Descendynge from the montaigne into playn" (MLT 23–4). As a poet, the Man of Law may be superior to the flat mediocrity of the plain, but he has already fallen far from the mountain.

"Looth to be likned, douteless,/To Muses that men clepe Pierides" (MLT 91–2), still the Man of Law has no excuse for silence.[86] As he concludes, "though I come after hym with hawebake./I speke in prose, and lat him [Chaucer] rymes make"

---

[85] Robert Hanning has argued that Chaucer incorporates his inability to mimic his predecessors perfectly into his literary persona. Hanning identifies this inability as stemming from Chaucer's irreverent attitude to his society's cultural authorities, but I would counter that it instead derives from the innate human incapacity to maintain paternal likeness and authority throughout the generations. Robert W. Hanning, *Serious Play: Desire and Authority in the Poetry of Ovid, Chaucer, and Ariosto* (New York: Columbia University Press, 2010): 105, 111.

[86] Here the Man of Law further demonstrates his undesirability as an heir for Chaucer, since, as Maura Nolan notes, he has muddled the reference to the *Pierides* from between two distinct Ovidian works. If Chaucer can grant his voice to a man who mixes up his Ovid, then surely other men can also accept their heirs. Nolan, "The Man of Law's Introduction," 150.

(MLT 96). He may be humble in his claims to likeness to the great poet, but he will not be silent. And indeed, the Man of Law appears to find more resemblance to his father than he first supposed, for, after all, he does not tell his story in prose but in poetry, like Chaucer. However poorly the Man of Law assesses his worth as a poet, Chaucer—his father and creator—redeems this literary lawyer and allows him to join the ranks of those "fadres of tidynges/And tales" (MLT 129–30) who, imperfect heirs every one, reproduce the likenesses of those who gave them life.

6

Father Chaucer's Heirs

In his extraordinarily influential biography *Geoffrey Chaucer* (reissued a full ten times between 1934 and 1970), John Livingston Lowes condemned the very association of Chaucer with paternity, writing:

> Nothing more unlucky, I sometimes think, could have befallen Chaucer than that he should have been christened "the father of English poetry." For father in such a context conveys to most of us, I fear, a faint suggestion of vicarious glory—the derivative celebrity of parents, otherwise obscure, who shine, moon-like, in the reflected lustre of their sons…And so to call Chaucer the father of English poetry is often tantamount to dismissing him, not unkindly, as the estimable but archaic ancestor of a brilliant line. But Chaucer—if I may risk the paradox—is himself the very thing that he begat. He is English poetry incarnate, and only two, perhaps, of all his sons outshine his fame.[1]

Lowes imagines the creative power to rest not with the father at all, but rather with the father's sons. Paternal authority in this model is still reinforced by an imitative resemblance between parent and child, but that resemblance finds its purest form in the face of the filial object rather than that of its progenitor. Heredity degrades backwards through time, minimizing the ancestor in order to elevate the contemporary son. And so Lowes must save Chaucer from the diminishment of being termed the father of other poets, for, rather than granting authority to England's great medieval poet, such a designation would (Lowes believes) steal it away, covering Chaucer's glory under the intrusive assaults of his literary sons.

In Lowes's words, we can identify the stark divide between medieval perspectives on the authority of paternity and those of the twentieth century. For "fatherhood" is far from a stable category, and that vision of poetic progeneration that Lowes describes as a source of instability for the father would be, in Chaucer's own estimation, the purest form of human power. What more could a medieval man wish, than to know that he has fathered so successfully, and that his literary authority has been borne into the future by his blood?

---

[1] John Livingston Lowes, *Geoffrey Chaucer* (Bloomington, IN: Indiana University Press, 1958): 1.

Father Chaucer: Generating Authority in The Canterbury Tales. Samantha Katz Seal, Oxford University Press (2019).
© Samantha Seal.
DOI: 10.1093/oso/9780198832386.001.0001

Moreover, Lowes's highest praise, that Chaucer is "the very thing that he begat," would appear alien to Chaucer's own depiction of paternal authority. That high degree of likeness, that perfection of reciprocity—these are not qualities that Chaucer desires to seize for humanity. As Chapter 5 asserted, such semiotic perfection across the procreative generations was reserved for God (Son and Father) alone. And, even at the most optimistic moments of his ambition, Chaucer does not wish to seize divinity for his fellow men. He wishes only to make more space beneath its maxims for humanity, to allow men to sire in sufficiency if not in perfection. That linkage across the generations, that preservation of some level of likeness from one man's body into another's, is of far more value to Chaucer than the lonely glory expounded upon by Lowes.

This difference helps to clarify, I believe, the space that Chaucer presupposed to exist between progenitor and progeny. Man did not need to be "English poetry incarnate" to father a tradition (note the singular) of vernacular poetry. Nor must a poet be peerless in order to sire with authority. The false competitions with John Gower or Thomas Usk imagined by centuries of critics and readers imagine fatherhood as a singular occupation; only one man can be the "father of English poetry" and only one lineage can survive and be held to be authentic. And yet, again, that approach appears un-Chaucerian. In *The Canterbury Tales*, only foolish men like the Miller and Reeve, the Friar and the Summoner, compete against one another, and they are hardly shown to augment their own authority by so doing. Most men compete against their own potential, against the limits set upon their generations by both God and their own self. Whether they fail in that competition, like January of the *Merchant's Tale,* or somehow stumble upon some measure of procreative triumph, like the Man of Law's Emperor of Rome, they are judged only insofar as they succeed in siring the future, in (to return to Chaucer's allegory from the *House of Fame*) generating a son to read their names upon that icy rock of arbitrary fame.

Within this chapter we will look at some examples of concurrent sirings within the *Tales*, of men's contemporaneous, but not competitive, ventures to leave some part of themselves behind. And finally, we will discuss Chaucer's acquiescence to the impossibility of ever siring with surety in one's own authority, as night begins to fall upon the road, with Canterbury still far off in the distance. Nothing, not even heirs, are enough to leave behind within the world. No man knows if his specific siring will last, if his line will continue or perhaps end. All he can do is sire in faith, trusting in his own virility and taking his chances with Fortune. The Parson is prepared to teach men of their sins, bidding them to cast off the vanities of the world. And even poets like Geoffrey Chaucer must choose between their children, claiming their literary offspring according to their embodiment of virtue and disowning those whom, like *The Canterbury Tales*, appear too sinful to be saved. Man's ambition now is ended, his authority ceded to his God.

Fallen Fathers and the Dream of the Tredefowel

Within this conclusion, therefore, I wish to consider the last two poems of Fragment VII of *The Canterbury Tales* (according to their most common order)— the *Monk's Tale* and the *Nun's Priest's Tale*—before finally moving to the *Parson's Tale* and the *Retractions*. If the *Parson's Tale* offers up a hope of Heaven, as recompense for man's humility, then the *Monk's Tale* is the story of man before he turns his eyes up to God. It is a recounting of each man's second Fall, that moment when he realizes that at best he has fathered only another humanlike himself. His heir will be merely a new man, and men are not enough to leave upon the earth. In the *Prologue* to the *Monk's Tale*, the Host allows the Monk's own body to become the primary metaphor for Chaucer's disavowal of patrilineal production and inheritance as reliable mechanisms of posterity. The Monk's dynastic associations, according to the Host's publically offered assessment, embody both man's potential generative glory and the frustration of his worldly ambitions.

> Thou woldest han been a tredefowel aright.
> Haddestow as greet a leeve as thou hast myght
> To parfourne al thy lust in engendrure,
> Thou haddest bigeten ful many a creature.
>
> (MkT 1945–8)

The Monk appears an especially virile specimen according to the Host's calculations.[2] He is flesh full and overflowing with the waste of its potential, characterized both by its inherent capacity to produce and by the external frustrations of its efforts. The Monk is exceptional in his procreative potentiality, and yet he also manages to symbolize a far more universal potential for his fellow men. For surely most medieval men could have begotten more children if they had had "as greet a leeve as thou hast myght," or at least supposed they might have done. The Host's denunciation of the social strictures that have foiled the Monk's natural capacity to reproduce, to make his own heirs upon the earth, is thus at once both highly specific in its critique of clerical celibacy (at least for this cleric) and almost overreaching in its nostalgic invocation of what might have been for any man, if only his world (and perhaps his wife) had bound him less tightly.

The Host's vision here is one of unlimited production, of an animalistic "tredefowel" process of replication. If the Monk had been born a rooster, Harry Bailly claims, then his lusts could have been put to some purpose, and rendered

---

[2] Michael Sharp argues that the discourse of procreation allows "the potentially homoerotic implications of the Host's initial remarks are deflected onto the safely heterosexual discourse of reproduction." Michael D. Sharp, "Reading Chaucer's 'Manly man': The Trouble with Masculinity in the *Monk's Prologue* and *Tale*," *Masculinities in Chaucer*: 173–85, at 176–7. I disagree with this conclusion, since, as I have argued throughout this book, procreation was not so safely heterosexual as Sharp assumes, nor would it as a discourse exclude the modes of homoeroticism of which he speaks.

almost virtuous through their natural productivity. This is perhaps the other side of what Chaucer the narrator had argued about the Monk at the very beginning of *The Canterbury Tales* when, in the *General Prologue*, Chaucer had characterized the Monk according to his unnatural investment in lay consumption and simultaneous abhorrence for modes of religious production. There Chaucer describes him with "of prikyng and of huntyng for the hare/Was al his lust" (GP 191–2), and notes the Monk's refusal to "swynken with his hands, and laboure,/As Austyn bit" (GP186–7). In the *General Prologue*, moreover, the Monk's refusal to work and labor in the manner prescribed for men in religious orders is tied explicitly to his perception of its unproductivity. As Chaucer asks, for all the Monk's labor in his cloister, "how shal the world be served?" (GP 187). There is a sharp mockery in Chaucer's query when we imagine it proffered from the Monk's own self-serving mouth; yet in Chaucer's own voice, the mockery becomes more bitter and universal. For how indeed would the world be served by the barren efforts of such a spiritually sterile man?

In a sense, it is this same question that the Host answers when, much later in the *Tales*, he assesses the Monk's untapped powers of progeniture. The Host looks at the Monk and perceives within him a latent fecundity, whose actualization has only lacked a commensurate investment of labor. By naming the Monk's superlative capacities for creation, Harry Bailly thus also grants the religious man a source of authority more appropriate to his nature than that granted to him his brethren by St. Augustine. The Monk may be an indifferent cleric, always escaping his cloister to consume the world's bounty, but within the Monk's selfish flesh, Chaucer has his Host give us a glimpse of the Monk's supposedly boundless ability to *replenish* that same multitude which he has slain. There is indeed something that the Monk can give to the world, a manner in which he too may offer his contribution to the common good. Seen through the Host's eyes, the Monk's very body is reinterpreted according to its capacity for productive labor; the Host newly appreciates as "muscle" that which Chaucer had mocked as "a lord ful fat" (GP 200). The Host characterizes the Monk as filled with a fire capable of boiling over a pot, with his "eyen stepe, and rollynge in his heed,/ That stemed as a forneys of a leed" (GP 201–2). It is, however, a fire still contained; the Monk has devoted himself not to stoking cooking fires, but rather to eating the products cooked thereon by others. As narrator Chaucer notes, "a fat swan loved he best of any roost" (GP 206).

Thus, the Host's assessment of the Monk's procreative capacities is restricted to the speculative. It is a wistful retrospection of what might have been, rather than what the future might still hold. The Monk is no more likely to become a "tredefowel" with a lively brood of children than he is to follow the Parson's advice that "whan the pot boyleth strongly, the beste remedie is to withdrawe the fyr" (ParsT 951A). To continue the metaphor, he is neither the fecund fowl nor the cooked food; he is only and ever a man with the potential of what more he might have been, divorced from that "fader kyn" from which he has fallen away.

The Monk bears a likeness to men who were of greater worth, to fathers who set forth their seed in hope of some offspring capable of carrying forth their image to their world. But an image of those fathers is all that the Monk bears within the world; he is all the shadows of authority, without their substance. The Host therefore invokes the Monk's likeness to a productive, paternal past as only a particularly jocular moment in a much longer recitation of a catalogue of loss, predicated upon all that the Monk could have been and is not.

> Thou art nat lyk a penant or a goost:
> Upon my feith, thou art som officer,
> Som worthy sexteyn, or som celerer,
> For by my fader soule, as to my doom,
> Thou art a maister whan thou art at hoom;
> No povre cloysterer, ne no novys,
> But a governour, wily and wys.
>
> (MkT 1934–40)

The Host sees the likeness of great authority written upon the body of the Monk, upon the body of the Monk's paternal past. And yet the Monk is not an officer, sexton, or cellarer. He is neither man's master nor his governor, whether at home or on the road. He may be the son of such men, but he will father none; for all his likenesses, the Monk is merely a man who likes to hunt and eat. He has ceded his authority to his flesh, and been mastered by it in his indifference.

It would be simple to dismiss the Monk's lack of authority as indicative of a specific inadequacy of the character, to ascribe the Monk's air of unrealized potential to a flaw within his subjective self. And yet, if in the *General Prologue* Chaucer acted to differentiate and individualize, here he reaches towards the universal. The Monk has too many names, none of which he claims as his own. As the Host inquires of him, "by my trouthe, I knowe nat youre name./Wher shal I calle yow my lord daun John,/Or daun Thomas, or elles daun Albon?" (MkT 1928–30). The Monk never answers the Host's question. He is all those men and none of them. Without the hope of passing on a name to his offspring in turn, what does it matter what a man is called? It is only after the Monk's own story (or, rather, his collection of stories) has been interrupted and the Monk has been displaced as a narrator in favor of the Nun's Priest, that the Host can finally put a name upon him. In disparaging the Monk's story ("youre tale anoyeth al this compaignye" [NPT 2789]), the Host calls him "sire Monk, daun Piers by youre name" (NPT 2792). Now instead, the Nun's Priest receives the praise (and the name) that once was proffered to the Monk, "this sweete preest, this goodly man sir John" (NPT 2820). The *Chaucer Name Dictionary* claims that the Host "discovers that [the Monk's name] is Piers by the time the monk has finished his story," but the eventual naming of the Monk by the Host seems to be a moment of pejoration rather than epiphany.[3] Before the Monk spoke he was all potential and all names; after his disappointing *Tale* he becomes only one man, with a name to be spoken once and then forgot.

For all his multitudes of virile likeness, the Monk is unmarked by the claims and structures of a specific patrilineal lineage. The names offered up by the Host (John, Thomas, Albon) would offer a strong spiritual heritage for the Monk. To claim the name Daun Albon, in particular, would emphasize the transhistorical link between the first English martyr (St. Alban) and his distant sons, a likeness capable of persisting across the centuries to be recognized even by the lowliest of Hosts.[4] Instead, by claiming no name, the Monk claims no father; he reaps no rewards from past masculine achievement, even as he invests no hope in the future reproductions of his line. This anonymity of past and future frustrates the Host, who demands for the monk to identify his father: "Of what hous be ye, by youre fader kyn?" (MkT 1931). The Host's evaluation of the Monk as a producer of stories or young fowl must be predicated upon the productions of the past. He struggles to situate the evidence of his eyes, his evaluation of the Monk's present person, within a mode of authority unmarked by time. The Host attempts to combat the Monk's disavowal of paternal likeness with an invocation of his own, legitimating his capacities of evaluation (if not their object) as a form of filial mimetics. "For by my fader soule, as to my doom..." (MkT 1937), the Host protests, grounding his temporal judgment within the authority of his father's soul. To ask for a man's name and be refused, to invoke one's own father's authority and be rebuffed, force the Host to confront the possibility that human authority and human lineage are as fictional and arbitrary as the *Tales* he has been told.

The struggle to name the Monk becomes a symbolic manifestation of man's desire to impose his own authority over the things of the world. Even as the Host locates the power of his own judgment within his paternal origins, he also gestures to the minuteness of such strategies within a larger cosmological context. He grounds his judgment upon his father, but his father's soul is a weak supplicant to Divine Judgment; the Host's father has no power to intercede on earth, no interpretative authority to bequeath to his son. The Host's reliance upon paternity as a means of authentication is thus undermined even in the moment that it is offered; the Host may judge the Monk by his potential, but God will judge all men, fathers and sons, by their acts. The Host's confrontation with the Monk over naming and paternal heritage therefore gets at the very heart of Chaucer's search for some mode of human authority, even while it also conceals its seriousness under an air of frivolity and an eroticization of poultry. Even as Custance's refusal to claim her father or her name when cast upon the shores of pagan England threatened the royal reproductive structures of Alla's family and of analogy itself as epistemological

---

[3] Weever, *Chaucer Name Dictionary*, 290.
[4] Weever, *Chaucer Name Dictionary*, 12.

strategy, so too does the Monk's abjuration of paternal (even spiritually paternal) markings stand as a rejection of a primary source of human authority. For Custance, the rejection of her father's name facilitated his full recognition of the likeness between them and her reintegration into the familial heritage. For the Monk, however, the process of defiliation is both less temporary and more significant. It is a marker of the larger unlinking of fathers and sons within the world, the destabilizing enforcement of difference between man and his heir.

The Host identifies the flaws in the system of patrilineal descent as an apocalyptic sign.

> For al the world is lorn!
> Religioun hath take up al the corn
> Of tredyng, and we borel men been shrympes.
> Of fieble trees ther comen wrecched ympes.
> This maketh that oure heires been so sklendre
> And feble that they may nat wel engendre.
> This maketh that oure wyves wole assaye
> Religious folk, for ye mowe bettre paye
> Of Venus paiementz than mowe we;
> God woot, no lussheburghes payen ye!"
>
> (MkT 1953–62)

Here the Host articulates a vision of human failing surprisingly close to that put forth by Theseus in the *Knight's Tale*, as I cited at the beginning of this book.[5] The Host, like Theseus with his ever-degraded "successiouns," describes a reproductive system tortured by its own temporality as it reinforces, with each successive generation, the insufficiencies and inadequacies of its forebears.[6] This is a radical mode of multiplication; as man multiplies, he contributes to the exponential disappearance of his line. Indeed, he contributes to a quite literal disappearance, for the Host makes it clear that what he imagines is not merely the moral degradation articulated by Walter, for example, in the *Clerk's Tale* ("God it woot, that children ofte been/Unlyk hir worthy eldres hem bifore" [ClT 155–6]), but rather a physical, fleshly degradation as each man's heir becomes smaller and more slender than the man himself. Man still reproduces within this system, but less and less of him

---

[5] As A. C. Spearing notes, Chaucer also uses the same biblical reference to bad fruit coming from bad trees (Matthew 7:17) at the beginning of the story of Phyllis in the *Legend of Good Women*. A. C. Spearing, *Medieval to Renaissance in English Poetry* (Cambridge: Cambridge University Press, 1985): 99.

[6] I therefore disagree with Jeffrey Jerome Cohen's more optimistic argument that "masculinity in Fragment VII is best described as an economy of flows: male sexuality diminishes and expands throughout as if it were a liquid." Jeffrey Jerome Cohen, "Diminishing Masculinity in Chaucer's *Tale of Sir Thopas*," *Masculinities in Chaucer: Approaches to Maleness in the* Canterbury Tales *and* Troilus and Criseyde, ed. Peter G. Beidler (Cambridge: D. S. Brewer, 1998): 143–56, at 144. I see masculinity as moving always towards diminishment in *The Canterbury Tales*, always descending towards the inadequacies of its reproductions.

is passed via each transmission. Eventually, given time enough, this system of perpetuation will instead make all traces of its men disappear.

Compared to such a threat, the problem of a female heir appears miniscule; likewise, no doubt over a child's paternity or a wife's fidelity could pose such profound danger. The fears of fathers in *The Canterbury Tales*, the petty doubts over the possibilities for certainty, creation, and likeness within the world, fade away. Instead the Host warns the pilgrims of reproduction itself. It is man's pride, his lust to create an image of himself, which ultimately undermines all his attempts, all his likenesses. The Host blames this situation on religion, presenting the orders of monastic chastity as a harsh scythe across the genetic pool. The Church reaches out to grab those whom it desires, robbing mankind of all its "corn," its collective hopes for the future. The Church, according to the Host, therefore acts to decrease human authority within the world, in a program of reverse eugenics meant to leave "feble" man with no other hope than heaven. Faced with the "ympes" to which their paternal line has devolved, even "shrympes" like the Host will turn to God, as indeed the Host does by requesting the Monk to speak to the company at large. As the Host charges the still nameless Monk, "no lussheburges payen ye!" (MkT). The Monk has true coin to offer, true seeds to sow with his virility; if men's wives hasten to experience these monks' idealized bodies, then surely men should hasten to listen to their words.

The Monk's story does not cheer the Host. His *Tale* is one story after another of loss, reproductive degradation, and the failure of human authority. From Croesus's daughter, who prophetically observes "thou shalt anhanged be, fader, certeyn" (MkT 2755) to Balthazar, son of Nebuchadnezzar, who "by his fader koude noght be war" (MkT 2185), the Monk tells a "tragedy" of one failed father after another, followed by a hapless son or, even worse, by no son at all. Sons destroy their parents, as Nero kills his mother "hire wombe slitte to biholde/ Where he conceyved was" (MkT 2484–5). Bloodlines are ended by the battle failures of a father, such as when, after Nebuchadnezzar's victory over the ancient Israelites, "the faireste children of the blood roial/Of Israel he leet do gelde anoon" (MkT 2151–2). The gelding of the sons of Israel is not a typical aspect of the story of the Babylonian conquest, and yet for the Monk (and Chaucer) this enforced sterilization is an essential component of any such historical degradation.[7] Perhaps the purest metaphor of this incessant imagery of human loss re-enacted through the ending of man's offspring comes with the more contemporary story of Ugolino of Pisa.[8] Starving with their father in his prison, his three young sons

---

[7] In fact, with the line "amonges othere Daniel was oon" (MkT 2154), the Monk appears to be claiming that Daniel had been rendered a eunuch as well, in addition to being rendered a "thral" (MkT 2153). This is an extremely idiosyncratic retelling of the story of Daniel's dream interpretation.

[8] For the larger historical contexts of this story, and a comparison with Dante's version, see Piero Boitani, *The Tragic and the Sublime in Medieval Literature* (Cambridge: Cambridge University Press, 1989): 20–55.

offer their father their own flesh to sustain him. Telling him not to cry, they plead "rather ete the flesh upon us two./Oure flesh thou yaf us, take oure flesh us fro" (MkT 2450–1). The cannibalistic father (although Chaucer leaves it mercifully vague as to the question of whether Ugolino partook of his children's offer) becomes the epitome of paternal reproduction's failure to suffice as a source of human authority. Instead, man will eat his own likeness, consuming the petty creations of his flesh.

The pilgrims hate the Monk's story, perhaps with some justification. The Knight, that father riding to Canterbury with his son, interrupts the Monk and begs him "good sire, namore of this!/That ye han seyd is right ynough, ywis" (NPT 2767–8).[9] The Host likewise accuses the Monk of telling the wrong kind of tale and thereby alienating his audience. "Swich talking is nat worth a boterflye,/For therinne is ther no desport ne game" (NPT 2790–1). The Host's initial judgment of the Monk's procreative capacities has proved to be inaccurate; the Monk has not given birth to a worthy tale, but rather one worth in exchange not even the most ephemeral of creatures. Or at least, so the Host claims. But, as the Host himself acknowledges, the disattention and disapprobation of one's audience do not necessarily decrease the "truth" of a tale. "Whereas a man may have noon audience,/Noght helpeth it to tellen his sentence" (NPT 2801–2). The Monk has told his sentence, and while the Host claims his evaluative powers more than equal to the task ("wel I woot the substance is in me,/If any thyng shal wel reported be" [NPT 2803–4]), the deficiencies appear to be within his audience rather than in the sentence of his *Tale*.[10]

For although the *Monk's Tale* made the Knight sad and the Host likely to "han fallen doun for sleep" (NPT 2797), it nevertheless offers the company an important message of morality. It is, in many ways, the likeness of the sermon preached by the Parson at the end of the *Tales*, and the Monk can therefore be understood to offer his denunciation of earthly power in order to prepare the pilgrims for that closing sermon. Both men offer accounts of human weakness and inadequacy, stories that advocate for men to turn their eyes away from their humble flesh, up to the glory of God. And yet while the Parson is presented as holy from his entry into the company of pilgrims, the Monk's own inherent earthiness endows his story with the weight of experience, if not authority. When he speaks of Adam ("With Goddes owene finger wroght was he,/And nat bigeten of mannes sperme unclene" [MkT 2008–9]), Chaucer's readers understand that the Monk

[9] For a discussion of the Knight's possible motivations for interrupting the Monk, see R. E. Kaske, "The Knight's Interruption of the *Monk's Tale*," *ELH* 24.4 (December 1957): 249–68.

[10] Indeed, Renate Haas has argued that the *Monk's Tale* is progressive in its genre and extensive in its learning, a progressive development towards later humanist forms of Tragedy. The failure of the company, especially the courtly Knight, to appreciate it thus becomes an ironic indictment of literary innovation and unappreciative audiences. Renate Haas, "Chaucer's 'Monk's Tale': Ingenious Criticism of Early Humanist Conception of Tragedy," *Humanistica Lovaniensia* 36 (1987): 44–70, at 57–9.

too was begotten of that unclean sperm; indeed, from the Host's prolonged dwelling on the Monk's virility, the reader has already been moved to reflect upon the Monk's own individual possession of unclean sperm. The Parson's otherworldliness brings men to God. But first, men must be disentangled from their own bodies and their own hubris. It is for that task that the Monk, with his denunciations of fathers and paternal systems of authority, offers up his words.

The pilgrims, of course, do not listen. Upon being told that the Monk has "no lust to pleye" (NPT 2806), they call upon the Nun's Priest, Sir John, to offer up a better, more playful tale. The Priest agrees, noting "but I be myrie, ywis I wol be blamed" (NPT 2817). And yet while he offers a far more appealing *Tale* in terms of its humor and philosophy, the Nun's Priest gives a meditation on paternity that is notably similar to that offered first by the Monk. For it is still that mistaken desire to draw individual legitimacy from the figure of the father that sends Chauntecleer into danger. Dame Pertelotte recognizes this tendency when she uses the imagery of patrilineal descent to urge Chauntecleer away from reflection upon his mortality and his dream; she chides him, "be myrie, housbonde, for youre fader kyn!" (NPT 2968). This is the same enforced merriness, grounded upon a stabilizing legitimacy of the father, that led the Knight and Host to interrupt the Monk, precipitating the telling of this story.

Likewise, it is through reassuring references to Chauntecleer's father that the fox tricks him into almost becoming his prey. The fox urges that Chauntecleer imitate his parents, who had in the past apparently visited the fox's den.

> My lord youre fader—God his soule blesse!—
> And eek youre mooder, of hire gentillesse,
> Han in myn house ybeen to my greet ese;
> And certes, sire, ful fayn wolde I yow plese."
>
> (NPT 3295–8)

The inheritance offered to Chauntecleer from his parents is not a pleasant one, at least not from the perspective of a rooster or a chicken. Even as man is born from unclean, sinful sperm, chickens are born to be eaten by foxes or by poor peasant ladies and their daughters.[11] Chauntecleer might take a lesson from his parents' fate, and flee the fox. But instead he wishes to draw authority from his father, to displace his personal vulnerability in favor of the supposed stabilities of an imagined past.

And, even as in the *Monk's Tale*, there is only one fate for those who place their hopes upon paternity. The fox taunts Chauntecleer: "Lat see; konne ye youre fader

---

[11] And perhaps Chauntecleer also has been born from unclean, sinful sperm; as Lynn Staley observes, following Bernard S. Levy and George R. Adams, Chauntecleer "has a number of characteristics that show him to be Adam's heir in folly, if not in kinde." Lynn Staley Johnson, "To Make in Som Comedye': Chauntecleer, Son of Troy," *The Chaucer Review* 19.3 (Winter, 1985): 225–44, at 226.

countrefete?" (NPT 3321) and Chauntecleer does his best, flapping his wings and singing with all his heart, in the likeness of his father.[12] The result is of course predictable; the fox grabs Chauntecleer, who only escapes by likewise playing to the fox's pride. Chauntecleer can indeed prove his likeness to his father, but such mimeticisms only lead the way to death. It would have been far better for Chauntecleer to denounce the call to likeness, rejecting the ambitions to claim his father's musical authority, to choose defiliation over destruction. Instead, an overreliance on the resemblances of the past causes Chauntecleer to avoid a true interpretation of his dream, and to render himself vulnerable through the simple solace of merriness and songs. To cling to a human (or rooster) father and his earthly glories is to allow the present self to be consumed, whether in a Pisan dungeon or a peasant's yard.

The Nun's Priest urges his audience to "taketh the moralite, good men" (NPT 3440) of his story, and to "taketh the fruyt, and lat the chaf be stille" (NPT 3443). He has told a fruitful story, fecund with ethical implication. The Priest urges his audience to cast off the worldly ambitions of human parentage, of the supposed lines of human descent stretching from father to son across the generations. And, as Lawrence Warner argues, the Priest himself is caught up within this anxiety of generation and filial imitation, when he "lament[s] his failure to live up to the high rhetorical standards of Geoffrey of Vinsauf."[13] They have the chance to take the spiritual fruit he offers to them, and to eat it in the moment, redirecting their focus onto a future of spiritual transcendence rather than upon an exclusively human past. Surrendering their human ambitions, their lust to imitate their fathers, men can instead trust that God will "Make us alle goode men,/And brynge us to his heighe blisse! Amen" (NPT 3445–6).

The Host almost immediately misunderstands, praising the Nun's Priest for his sexual fertility and his potential as a father. "I-blessed be thy breche, and every stoon!…by my trouthe, if thou were seculer,/Thou woldest ben a trede-foul aright" (NPT 3448, 3449–50). It does not matter whether he listens to a speech by the Monk or one by the Nun's Priest; the Host wishes to find reassurance that fatherhood is a mode of establishing human authority upon the earth, and he will hear that message in any story offered to him.[14] Somewhere in the world there must be men with blessed testicles, men capable of copulating with several chickens, men capable of siring strong sons and true tales. The Host must believe in the possibility for paternity to redeem humanity, for fathers to live on forever

---

[12] Donald Yates has shown that many of the Latin analogues for the story which Chaucer may have used for his sources have a lord or other figure of authority in this passage rather than a father. Donald N. Yates, "Chanticleer's Latin Ancestors," *The Chaucer Review* 18.2 (Fall 1983): 116–26, at 119–21.

[13] Warner, "Woman is Man's Babylon," at 82.

[14] Peter Travis sees the Host's assessment of the Nun's Priest's fertility as the refiguring of a masculine Genius celebrating Nature's female procreations. Peter W. Travis, *Disseminal Chaucer; Rereading the Nun's Priest's Tale* (Notre Dame, IN: University of Notre Dame, 2010): 36.

in their sons and in their son's sons. There must be such a thing as "faders kin," for without that belief in something both human and stable, man would have to surrender and turn to God alone. And Chaucer does not yet wish to take that dream away. For once that vision of a productive authority so fully human is ended, the *Tales* will be ended as well. Better for men to tell their stories, to boast of their authorities, to create something (however flawed) within the world, as long as they have life within their flesh and more daylight to walk upon the road. The Parson and his sermon will come soon enough, to make men repent of the sons they have sired and the stories they have told.

The End (and the Beginning) of Father Chaucer

For centuries, even Chaucer's most appreciative readers imagined his death rather gleefully as a time of repentance. Between the *Retractions* and Thomas Gascoigne's fictive account of Chaucer's dramatic deathbed self-abnegation within the *Dictonarium Theologicum,* the critics took the lamenting, woeful Chaucer as their image of parting from the poet.[15] In the 1869 *Book of English Poetry*, for example, the author imagined Chaucer's final regrets as recompense for the earlier infelicities of his writings. The anonymous author writes:

> Along with many other early writers, and especially Boccacio [*sic*], who supplied so many of the tales of the poets, he is occasionally impure and indelicate; and this moral blemish on his great works occasioned himself much grief as his life drew near a close. He is said to have repeatedly cried out, when on his deathbed, 'Woe is me, that I cannot recall and annul these things."[16]

The deathbed details here are from Gascoigne, but the moral relish is pure Victorian. Chaucer becomes an exemplum for later generations (it is important to note that Gascoigne imagines Thomas Chaucer as the addressed recipient of his father's words) of regret, of a life changed too late to be certain of salvation.

But what I want to argue in these final pages of this book is that Chaucer's *Retractions*, even if we take it as a mode of deathbed (or near-deathbed) withdrawal from the world, nevertheless maintains an authority in its own productions,

---

[15] On Gascoigne's motivations for writing this passage, and the appeal of the penitent Chaucer, cf. Douglas Wurtele, "The Penitence of Geoffrey Chaucer," *Viator* 11 (1980): 335–60; James Dean, "Chaucer's Repentance: A Likely Story," *The Chaucer Review* 24.1 (Summer 1989): 64–76; Miceal F. Vaughan, "Personal Politics and Thomas Gascoigne's Account of Chaucer's Death," *Medium AEvum* 75.1 (2006): 103–22. As late as 1913, John Tatlock included Gascoigne's account of Chaucer's death as evidence for Chaucer having written the *Retraction*; the latter was considered a far more spurious attribution to Chaucer than the former. John S. P. Tatlock, "Chaucer's Retractions," *PMLA* 28.4 (1913): 521–9, at 528.

[16] *The Book of English Poetry: With Critical and Biographical Sketches of the Poets* (London: T. Nelson and Sons, 1869): 473.

straddling the line between the contrition necessary for a Christian man and that still faint hope in humanity's creative power.[17] Moreover, Chaucer has delivered us, at the very beginning of *The Canterbury Tales*, a truly non-authoritative and non-generative death scene, and it is far different from the leave taking he gives himself at the end of the *Tales*. The way that Arcite dies in the *Knight's Tale*, swollen with his own body's productions but unable to void them in any manner—that is how a man dies without authority and without a legacy. Chaucer's *Retractions* is, in contrast, not "that bad," to employ a colloquialism; he has put his offspring out into the hands of readers, and whether or not he must disown some "children" now, others will survive to bear witness to his presence in the world.

Looking now briefly at Arcite's death, we can identify the scene as an almost reminiscent echo of a childbirth tragedy. Falling off his horse, Arcite strikes his head before suffering other, more serious injuries.

> His brest tobrosten with his sadel-bowe.
> As blak he lay as any cole or crowe,
> So was the blood yronnen in his face.
> Anon he was yborn out of the place...
> And in a bed ybrought ful faire and blyve"
>
> (KnT2691–4, 97)

As Peggy McCracken has argued, to render male bloodshed symbolically heroic, medieval romance narratives had to suppress the symbolism of female (menstrual) blood, since having the male body rendered "permeable, promiscuous in its bleeding" reversed the medical assumptions of what it meant to be a male or female body.[18] The image of Arcite, his body cut open and bleeding profusely, needing to be carried to the bed in which he will die, is that of a soldier wounded in battle, but it bears feminine resonances as well, of the woman whose body begins to hemorrhage in its struggle to bring life into the world.[19]

---

[17] Despite Matthew Wolfe's argument that the *Retraction* does not necessarily come at the end of *The Canterbury Tales*, noting that it has sometimes been included at the end of a full codex of Chaucerian works, I take it here as providing closure for the *Tales*. I see a strong link with the Tales both in terms of its thematics and concerning the augmentation of the reference to *The Canterbury Tales* in his listing of secular works. The others have only their names given; the *Tales* are noted to "sowen into synne." That augmentation of the *Tales* at least speaks to a perceived relationship between it and the *Retraction*; reflecting on his works, Chaucer felt the *Retraction* most intensely needed to repent for the *Tales*. Cf. Matthew C. Wolfe, "Placing Chaucer's 'Retraction' for a Reception of Closure," *The Chaucer Review* 33.4 (1999): 427–31.

[18] Peggy McCracken, *The Curse of Eve, The Wound of the Hero: Blood, Gender, and Medieval Literature* (Philadelphia: University of Pennsylvania Press, 2003): 14.

[19] Jamie Fumo writes of Arcite's injuries as stemming from his "love wound," with an association between illness and the sight of Emelye. Jamie C. Fumo, "The Pestilential Gaze: From Epidemiology to Erotomania in the *Knight's Tale*," *Studies in the Age of Chaucer* 35 (2013): 85–136, at 97–8. That adds an interesting dimension to my reading of Arcite as dying in a parody of childbirth, since a death in parturition could also be understood as a death from love, or at least from coitus.

Arcite and Palamon have been engaged in just such a struggle, within a battle to reproduce their respective Theban lines with Emelye, the Amazonian princess now resident in Thebes. The men speak of love as a matter of beauty, but Emelye recognizes clearly that such courtliness is only a cover for a lust to procreate. When she protests her wish "noght to ben a wyf and be with childe" (KnT 2310), she articulates the purpose of marriage otherwise obscured by the Knight's own poetic turns of phrase. Yet the only person brought to bed in a grotesque parody of childbirth is Arcite himself. "Swelleth the brest of Arcite, and the soore/ Encresseth at his herte moore and moore...the pipes of his longes gonne to swelle" (KnT 2743–4, 2752).[20] Even worse than this exponential increase of his flesh, the swelling agony of his organs, however, is Arcite's inability to purge. In a passage that Piero Boitani calls "cruelly anatomical," the Knight lists the various remedies applied to help Arcite rid his body of the corruption that is poisoning him, but ultimately concludes "the vertu expulsive, or animal/Fro thilke vertu cleped natural/Ne may the venym voyden ne expelle" (KnT 2749–51).[21] Moreover, both of Arcite's corporeal orifices are fully sealed: "Him gayneth neither, for to gete his life,/Vomyt upward, ne dounward laxative" (KnT 2755–6). Arcite's body has become a generative paradox, rapidly producing an internal substance that must be evacuated from the body to save his life, yet unable to effect that evacuation. He is, in short, stuck in an image of one of the worst crises to impact a childbearing woman, when the child would not come out. The *Trotula's* extensive list of remedies to be attempted in such a situation, of potions to be drunk and herbal baths to be taken, of charms to be read and herbs tied round the stomach, attests to how frequent and perilous a situation it could be.[22]

This is the same moment of childbirth depicted earlier within the poem, as a decoration upon the walls of the temple to Diana. In that picture, Diana stands and is worshipped by a suffering woman.

> A womman travaillynge was hire biforn;
> But for her child so longe was unborn,
> Ful pitously Lucyna gan she calle
> And seyde, "Help, for thou mayst best of alle!"
>
> (KnT 2083–6)

This scene of childbirth comes as the very last of a series of depictions of humans destroyed by the gods. The unnamed woman, calling out to Diana for deliverance from death, for salvation from the new life within her womb, follows a series of grotesque tragedies: Daphne, Actaeon, Atalanta, and Meleager. Diana's temple is

---

[20] Fumo argues that these symptoms might also be symbolic of the plague, making a comparison to the symptoms described within medieval plague treatises. Fumo, "Pestilential Gaze," 133–4.
[21] Boitani, *The Tragic and the Sublime*, 18.   [22] *The Trotula*, ed. Green, 100–2.

covered with images of man's mortality, but it is this final image that invokes the greatest horror: a fate of perpetual suspension worse than death. An embodiment of both procreation and its antitype, the human being, pregnant but unable to give birth, is suffocated at once by the potentiality and the stasis of her swollen flesh.

Arcite dies like the suffering mother, unable to void, unable to stop production. The only generation that he can bring forth to the world is his final speech to Emelye and Palamon. And this speech has no authority. He complains of the unproductivity of his life and of his labors in love ("Allas the peynes stronge,/That I for yow have suffred, and so longe!" [KT 2771–2]), and bids Palamon and Emelye to marry after his decease. But even there he is ignored. It is not Arcite's death that produces the marriage, but rather Theseus's "prime mover" speech several lines later. Theseus is the one who gives forth the authoritative product of the *Tale*, preaching that "speces of thynges and progressiouns/Shullen enduren by succesiouns,/And nat eterne, withouten any lye" (KnT 3013–5). Arcite, like Palamon and Emelye who "endeth" in the poem's last line without ever having produced "no word hem bitwene/Of jalousie or any oother teene" (KnT 3105–7), exits the world without leaving a trace within it of his presence.[23]

The moral philosophy offered in these scenes is twofold: man should accept the fatalistic certainty of human succession and reproductive diminishment, yet man should also avoid living or dying like Arcite, Palamon, and Emelye. The vision of eternal progression that Theseus sketches out is the one within which men must try to live and, more importantly, must try to reproduce. D. Vance Smith has argued that Theseus's "prime mover speech" is an inadequate response in the face of death, really "a passivity, a capitulation to, not an overcoming of, 'necessitee;'" Theseus fails to acknowledge that there is no space, no human dominion, that will allow man to forget his own mortality.[24] That is true, but at the same time, within the bitter progress of that acquiescence to futility, some small things do still survive. Man becomes smaller, more partitive, with each generation, but he has not yet disappeared; we humans are the parts of an ever-shrinking whole, but for now at least we are still material enough to survive, material enough to be divided still further in the production of our children. Theseus gives us a vision of the end, of the natural diminishment of the human race, but its conclusion is still far off in a distant future, waiting in store for a distant generation.

Thus, with an acknowledgment of all that is lost at the end of a life, and in the transfer from one generation to another, Chaucer takes his poetic leave with some authority. He is no Arcite, swollen with the inconsequentialities of an

[23] Jerold Frakes has commented on this problem of ending the *Knight's Tale*, noting that there are three separate places in the poem that seem as if they could be an ending; the ending when it comes therefore feels like an arbitrary close. Jerold C. Frakes, "'Ther Nis Namoore to Seye': Closure in the 'Knight's Tale,'" *The Chaucer Review* 22.1 (Summer, 1987): 1–7.
[24] D. Vance Smith, "Plague, Panic Space, and the Tragic Medieval Household," *The South Atlantic Quarterly* 98.3 (Summer 1999): 367–414, at 404–5.

unproductive life, no Palamon or Emelye to be ended without a word. He offers us the offspring of his life within his *Retractions*:

> The book of Troilus; the book also of Fame; the book of the XXV. Ladies; the book of the Duchesse; the book of Seint Valentynes day of the Parlement of Briddes; the tales of Caunterbury, thilke that sowen into synne;/ the book of the Leoun; and many another book, if they were in my remembrance, and many a song and many a leccherous lay, that Crist for his grete mercy foryeve me the synne./ But of the translacion of Boece de Consolacione, and othere books of legends of seintes and omelies, and moralitee, and devocioun, that thanke I oure Lord Jhesu Crist and his blisful Mooder.   (Ret. 1085–8)

Readers of this passage have tended to emphasize the regret, the penitent divide between those "bad" works that Chaucer regrets, and those holy ones for which he begs (almost transactionally) for salvation. Yet these lines can also be read as a testament to productivity, a cataloguing of what his life has left within the world. Chaucer asks for God to forgive him his "giltes," but he does not disown them. He claims all his texts as the products of his flesh, knowing that not all of them will survive indefinitely after his death (as indeed the "Book of the Lion" did not), knowing that not all of them will win him favor in the eyes of Heaven (as he assumes *The Canterbury Tales* will not), but knowing as well that each is his own creation, an imperfect heir to the substance of his life.

In close, *The Canterbury Tales* is a text that emphasizes the inevitability of loss and the imminent humbling of mankind before the judgment of its God. But it is also a collection of poems about what it means to live a long, productive life with the certainty of that eventual loss, to create and sire offspring under the shadow of death and of oblivion. Whether we name Chaucer father in honor of his human children—Thomas, Lewis, Elizabeth, and perhaps Agnes—or father in honor of his poetry, we should recognize what each act of fathering and of creation would have cost a man in Chaucer's time, still reeling from catastrophic epidemics and political upheaval.[25] Even more specifically, we should reflect on what fatherhood

---

[25] The link between Geoffrey Chaucer and his potential daughters, Elizabeth and Agnes, is less definitive than that between the poet and his sons, Thomas and Lewis. An Elizabeth Chaucer took religious vows at Barking Abbey in 1381, receiving financial support from John of Gaunt, Duke of Lancaster. As Margaret Galway has noted, this Elizabeth appears to have maintained a somewhat intimate relationship with Lancaster's family, since the Duke discharged his costs associated with Elizabeth Chaucer's convent placement in the very same writ with which he discharged the costs of placing his own daughter, Katherine of Lancaster, in a noble household. Galway, "Philippa Pan," 483 n.4. Likewise, the other potential Chaucer daughter, Agnes Chaucer, emerges in the historical record in close proximity to the Lancastrian inner circle; she is named, along with Lancaster's daughter, Joan Beaufort, as one of the *damoiselle* participants in Henry IV's 1399 coronation. In addition to the coincidence of the relatively uncommon surname and close ties with John of Gaunt's family (as would befit the nieces of his long-time mistress and eventual third wife), scholars have also observed that both "Elizabeth" and "Agnes" would be logical names for Chaucer's children, in honor of Geoffrey and

meant for Geoffrey Chaucer, son of a vintner, subject of an increasingly disordered realm, author of a still new vernacular. Indeed, the last year of Chaucer's life (1399–1400) was spent in witnessing the overthrow of Richard II, the last of the Plantagenet kings whom Chaucer had served since childhood.[26] What certainty could Chaucer feel, facing his own death so soon after the violent death of his king, that sons might wield their fathers' authority with certainty or with longevity?

For a short while on the road to Canterbury, Father Chaucer forces his pilgrims and readers alike to confront the extent of their own vulnerability as human beings, the pettiness of their lives, and the imperfections of their creations. Contemptuous of human pride, he simultaneously testifies to the perseverance of man's desire to produce. Told by his society and Church alike of the limitations set by the world upon the creative scope and personal authority of its people, Chaucer accepts those restrictions while simultaneously depicting the constant struggle of human beings to seize more for themselves and their children than what they have been given. For a medieval man to reproduce something of himself in younger flesh was to know that he had hazarded almost the impossible: staking his future on the chance of certainty in his own paternity, the luck of a significant likeness with his child, and a safe future for that heir. And yet, beset with anxiety, Chaucer and his contemporaries sired anyways. Knowing that all things would fade and decay, each generation becoming more insignificant than the last, still they persisted, hoping to sire even a crumb of continuity. Chaucer creates in the hope that even if he loses all the offspring of his life, some small memory of his creations—at the very least, their names in his *Retractions*—will remain within the world. There is no authority to be derived from any form of human generation; generation is man's only source for authority upon the earth.

Philippa's original patron, Elizabeth de Burgh, Countess of Ulster, and Geoffrey's own mother, Agnes Chaucer. Cf. Edwin J. Howard, *Geoffrey Chaucer* (London and Basingstoke: MacMillan Press, 1976): 53; Howard, *Chaucer*, 93.

[26] For details on Chaucer's last year, see Pearsall, *Life of Geoffrey Chaucer*, 272–6. The final payment of his annuity was on June 5, 1400.

Bibliography

Primary Sources

Adam Usk. *The Chronicle of Adam Usk: 1377–1421*. Ed. and trans. C. Given-Wilson. Oxford: Clarendon Press, 1997.

Alan of Lille. *The Plaint of Nature*. Ed. and trans. James J. Sheridan. Toronto: Pontifical Institute of Medieval Studies, 1980.

Albertus Magnus. *Albert the Great's Questions Concerning Aristotle's "On Animals."* Trans. Irven M. Resnick and Kenneth F. Kitchell, Jr. Washington, DC: Catholic University of America Press, 2008.

Anne of France, *Lessons for My Daughter*. Ed. and trans. Sharon L. Jansen. Cambridge: D. S. Brewer, 2004.

Anselm of Canterbury. "Monologian." *The Major Works*. Ed. Brian Davies and G. R. Evans. Oxford: Oxford University Press, 1998.

Aristotle. *De Generatione et Corruptione*. Ed. and trans. C. J. F. Williams. Oxford: Clarendon Press, 1982.

Aquinas, Thomas. *Aquinas Ethicus: Or, the Moral Teaching of St. Thomas Aquinas: A Translation of the Principal Portions of the Second Part of the "Summa Theologica,"* Vol. 2. Ed. Joseph Rickaby, S. J. London: Burns and Oates, 1896.

Aquinas, Thomas. *Commentary on Aristotle's* Physics. Trans. by Richard J. Blackwell, Richard J. Spath, and W. Edmund Thirkel. Notre Dame, IN: Dumb Ox Books, 1999.

Augustine. *The City of God*. Ed. Henry Bettenson. London: Penguin, 2003.

Beamanoior, Philippe de Remi. *Le Roman de la Manekine*. Ed. and trans. Roger Middleton. Amsterdam: Rodopi Press, 1999.

Boccaccio, Giovanni. *The Decameron*. Ed. and trans. Richard Aldington. Garden City, NY: Garden City Books, 1949.

The Book of English Poetry: With Critical and Biographical Sketches of the Poets. London: T. Nelson and Sons, 1869.

Chaucer, Geoffrey. *The Riverside Chaucer*. Ed. L. D. Benson. Boston, MA: Houghton Mifflin, 1987.

Chaucer Life-Records. Ed. Martin M. Crow and Claire C. Olson from materials compiled by John M. Manly and Edith Rickert, with the assistance of Lilian J. Redstone and others. Oxford: Clarendon Press, 1966.

The Dicts and Sayings of the Philosophers. Ed. Curt F. Bühler. London: Oxford University Press for the Early English Text Society, 1941.

The Distaff Gospels: A First Modern English Translation of Les Evangiles des Quenouilles. Ed. Madeleine Jeay and Kathleen Garay. Peterborough, Ontario: Broadview Press, 2006.

Dryden, John. *Fables Ancient and Modern; Translated into Verse, from Homer, Ovid, Boccace, and Chaucer: With Original Poems*. London: Jacob Tonson, 1721.

The Earliest English Wills in the Court of Probate, A.D. 1387–1439; with a Priest's of 1454. Ed. Frederick J. Furnivall. London: Published for the Early English Text Society by Trubner and Co., 1882.

"Emare." *Six Middle English Romances*. Ed. Maldwyn Mills. London: Dent, 1973: 46–74.

English Historical Documents: 1327–1485. Vol. 4. Ed. A. R. Myers. New York: Oxford University Press, 1969.

The Good Wife's Guide (Le Menagier de Paris): A Medieval Household Book. Ed. and trans. Gina L. Greco and Christine M. Rose. Ithaca, NY: Cornell University Press, 2009.

Gower, John. *The English Works of John Gower*, Vol. 1. Ed. G. C. Macaulay. London, New York, and Toronto: Published for the Early English Text Society by the Oxford University Press, 1969.

Gower, John. *The Minor Latin Works with In Praise of Peace*. Ed. and trans. R. F. Yeager. Kalamazoo, MI: Medieval Institute Publications, 2005.

Guibert de Nogent. *The Deeds of God Through the Franks: A Translation of Guibert de Nogent's Gesta Dei Per Francos*. Ed. Robert Levine. Woodbridge, Suffolk: Boydell and Brewer, 1997.

Guillaume de Lorris and Jean de Meun. *The Romance of the Rose*. 3rd edition. Trans. Charles Dahlberg. Princeton, NJ: Princeton University Press, 1995.

Idley, Peter. *Peter Idley's Instructions to His Son*. Ed. C. D'Evelyn. The Modern Language Association of America Monograph Series, Volume 6. Boston, MA: D. C. Health and Co., 1935.

The King of Tars. Ed. John H. Chandler. Kalamazoo, MI: Medieval Institute Publications for TEAMS, 2015.

"The Knight and the Shepherd's Daughter." *The English and Scottish Popular Ballads*. Vol. 2. Part IV. Ed. Francis James Child. Boston, MA: Houghton Mifflin Co., 1886: 457–77.

The Knowing of Woman's Kind in Childing: A Middle English Version of Material Derived from the Trotula *and Other Sources*. Ed. Alexandra Barratt. Turnhout, Belgium: Brepols, 2001.

"Lay le Freine." *The Middle English Breton Lays*. Ed. Anne Laskaya and Eve Salisbury. Kalamazoo, MI: Medieval Institute Publications, 1995.

The Mirroure of the Worlde: A Middle English Translation of Le Miroir Du Monde. Ed. Robert R. Raymo and Elaine E Whitaker, assist. Ruth E. Sternglantz. Toronto: University of Toronto Press, 2003.

Morris, Richard. *Prick of Conscience*. Ed. Ralph Hanna and Sarah Wood. Oxford: Published for the Early English Text Society by the Oxford University Press, 2013.

The N-Town Play: Cotton MS Vespasian D.8, Vol. 1. Ed. Stephen Spector. Oxford: Oxford University Press for the Early English Text Society, 1991.

Peter the Venerable. *Writings Against the Saracens*. Ed. and trans. Irven M. Resnick. Washington, DC: Catholic University of America Press, 2016.

Shakespeare, William. "Richard II." *The Riverside Shakespeare*, 2nd Ed. Boston, MA: Houghton Mifflin, 1996.

"The Tale of Florent." Ed. John Withrington and P. J. C. Field. *Sources and Analogues of The Canterbury Tales*. Vol. II. Ed. Robert M. Correale and Mary Hamel. Cambridge: D. S. Brewer, 2005: 410–19.

Trevet, Nicholas. "The Life of Constance." Trans. Edmund Brock. *Originals and Analogues of Some of Chaucer's Canterbury Tales*. Ed. F. J. Furnivall, Edmund Brock, and W. A. Clouston. London: N. Trubner Press, 1872.

The Trotula: An English Translation of the Medieval Compendium of Women's Medicine. Ed. Monica H. Green. Philadelphia, PA: University of Pennsylvania, 2002.

"The Weddyng of Sir Gawen and Dame Ragnell." Ed. John Withrington and P. J. C. Field. *Sources and Analogues of The Canterbury Tales*. Vol. II. Ed. Robert M. Correale and Mary Hamel. Cambridge: D. S. Brewer, 2005: 420–41.

Women's Secrets: A Translation of Pseudo-Albertus Magnus's De Secretis Mulierum *with Commentaries.* Ed. and trans. Helen Rodnite Lemay. Albany, NY: State University of New York Press, 1992.

Vices and Virtues: Being a Soul's Confession of its Sins with Reason's Descriptions of the Virtues, A Middle English Dialogue of about 1200 A.D. Vol. 1. Ed. F. Holthausen. London: Oxford University Press for the Early English Text Society, 1888.

Secondary Sources

Adams, Marilyn McCord. "Anselm on Faith and Reason." *The Cambridge Companion to Anselm.* Ed. by Brian Davies and Brian Leftow. Cambridge: Cambridge University Press, 2004: 32–60.

Allen, David G. "Death and Staleness in the 'Son-Less' World of the *Summoner's Tale.*" *Studies in Short Fiction* 24.1 (Winter 1987): 1–8.

Akbari, Suzanne Conklin. *Seeing Through the Veil: Optical Theory and Medieval Allegory.* Toronto: University of Toronto Press, 2004.

Akbari, Suzanne Conklin. *Idols in the East: European Representations of Islam and the Orient, 1100–1450.* Ithaca, NY: Cornell University Press, 2009.

Ambrisco, Alan S. "'Now y lowve God': The Process of Conversion in *Sir Gowther.*" *Studies in the Age of Chaucer* 37 (2015): 195–225.

Aries, Philippe. *Centuries of Childhood: A Social History of Family Life.* Trans. Robert Baldick. New York: Vintage Books, 1962.

Arthur, Karen. "Equivocal Subjectivity in Chaucer's 'Second Nun's Prologue and Tale.'" *The Chaucer Review* 32.3 (1998): 217–31.

Ashton, Gail. "Patient Mimesis: Griselda and the Clerk's Tale," *The Chaucer Review* 32.3 (1998): 232.

Ashton, Gail. "Her Father's Daughter: The Realignment of Father–Daughter Kinship in Three Romance Tales." *The Chaucer Review* 34.4 (2000): 416–27.

Axton, Richard. "Gower—Chaucer's Heir?" *Chaucer Traditions: Studies in Honour of Derek Brewer.* Ed. Ruth Morse and Barry Windeatt. Cambridge: Cambridge University Press, 2006: 21–38.

Bahr, Arthur. *Fragments and Assemblages: Forming Compilations of Medieval London.* Chicago, IL: University of Chicago Press, 2013.

Bailey, Mark. "Demographic Decline in Late Medieval England: Some Thoughts on Recent Research." *The Economic History Review* 49.1 (1996): 1–19.

Baker, Donald C. "Chaucer's Clerk and the Wife of Bath on the Subject of 'Gentilesse.'" *Studies in Philology,* 59.4 (October 1962): 631–40.

Beechy, Tiffany. "Devil Take the Hindmost: Chaucer, John Gay, and the Pecuniary Ass." *The Chaucer Review* 41.1 (2006): 71–85.

Besserman, Lawrence. *Chaucer's Biblical Poetics.* Norman, OK: University of Oklahoma Press, 1998.

Biancalana, Joseph. *The Fee Tail and the Common Recovery in Medieval England: 1176–1502.* Cambridge: Cambridge University Press, 2001.

Black, Daisy. "A Man Out of Time: Joseph, Time, and Space in the N-Town Marian Plays." *Reconsidering Gender, Time, and Memory in Medieval Culture.* Ed. Elizabeth Cox, Liz Herbert McAvoy, and Roberta Magnani. Cambridge: D. S. Brewer, 2015: 147–62.

Black, Nancy B. *Medieval Narratives of Accused Queens.* Gainesville, FL: University of Florida Press, 2003.

Blamires, Alcuin. *Chaucer, Ethics, and Gender*. Oxford: Oxford University Press, 2006.

Blamires, Alcuin. "May in January's Tree: Genealogical Configuration in the *Merchant's Tale*." *The Chaucer Review* 45.1 (2010): 106–17.

Bleeth, Kenneth. "Joseph's Doubting of Mary and the Conclusion of the *Merchant's Tale*." *The Chaucer Review* 21.1 (Summer 1986): 58–66.

Bloch, R. Howard. *Etymologies and Genealogies: A Literary Anthropology of the French Middle Ages*. Chicago, IL: University of Chicago Press, 1986.

Bloch, R. Howard. *Medieval Misogyny and the Invention of Western Romantic Love*. Chicago, IL: University of Chicago Press, 1991.

Bloom, Harold. *The Anxiety of Influence: A Theory of Poetry*. 2nd Edition. Oxford: Oxford University Press, 1997.

Boitani, Piero. *The Tragic and the Sublime in Medieval Literature*. Cambridge: Cambridge University Press, 1989.

Breitenburg, Mark. *Anxious Masculinity in Early Modern England*. Cambridge: Cambridge University Press, 1996.

Brewer, Derek. *Chaucer and His World*. Cambridge: D. S. Brewer, 1978.

Brewer, Derek. *Tradition and Innovation in Chaucer*. London: MacMillan Press, 1982.

Brodie, Alexander H. "Hodge of Ware and Geber's Cook: Wordplay in the 'Manciple's Prologue,'" *Neuphilologische Mitteilungen* 72.1 (1971): 62–8.

Brown, Emerson, Jr. "'The Merchant's Tale:' January's 'Unlikely Elde.'" *Neuphilologische Mitteilungen*. Helsinki: Neuphilologische Verein, 1973: 92–106.

Browning, Don S. and John Witte, Jr. "Christianity's Mixed Contributions to Children's Rights: Traditional Teachings, Modern Doubts." *Children, Adults, and Shared Responsibilities: Jewish, Christian, and Muslim Perspectives*. Ed. Marcia J. Bunge. Cambridge: Cambridge University Press, 2012: 276–91.

Brundage, James A. *Law, Sex, and Christian Society in Medieval Europe*. Chicago, IL: University of Chicago Press, 1990.

Bruster, Douglas. "The Horn of Plenty: Cuckoldry and Capital in the Drama of the Age of Shakespeare." *Studies in English Literature, 1500–1900*, 30.2 (Spring 1990): 195–215.

Bullon-Fernandez, Maria. *Fathers and Daughters in Gower's* Confessio Amantis: *Authority, Family, State, and Writing*. Cambridge: D. S. Brewer, 2000.

Bullough, Vern. L. "On Being a Male in the Middle Ages." *Medieval Masculinities: Regarding Men in the Middle Ages*. Ed. Clare A. Lees, Thelma S. Fenster, and Jo Ann McNamara. Minneapolis and London: University of Minnesota Press, 1994: 31–46.

Bullough, Vern. L. "Medieval Concepts of Adultery." *Arthuriana* 7.4 (Winter 1997): 5–15.

Burger, Glenn. "Kissing the Pardoner." *PMLA* 107.5 (October 1992): 1143–56.

Butler, Judith. *Gender Trouble: Feminism and the Subversion of Identity*. New York: Routledge, 1990.

Butler, Judith. *Bodies That Matter: On the Discursive Limits of "Sex."* London and New York: Routledge, 1993.

Cadden, Joan. *The Meanings of Sex Difference in the Middle Ages: Medicine, Science, and Culture*. Cambridge: Cambridge University Press, 1995.

Calabrese, Michael A. "Meretricious Mixtures: Gold, Dung, and the 'Canon's Yeoman's Prologue and Tale.'" *The Chaucer Review* 27.3 (1993): 277–92.

Calin, William. *The French Tradition and the Literature of Medieval England*. Toronto: University of Toronto Press, 1994.

Campbell, Emma. "Sexual Poetics and the Politics of Translation in the Tale of Griselda." *Comparative Literature* 55.3 (Summer 2003): 191–216.

Cannon, Christopher. *The Making of Chaucer's English: A Study of Words*. Cambridge: Cambridge University Press, 1998.

Carruthers, Mary. "The Wife of Bath and the Painting of Lions." *PMLA* 94.2 (March 1979): 209–22.

Carruthers, Mary. "Clerk Jankyn: At hom to bord/With my gossib." *English Language Notes* 22.3 (Mar. 1985): 11–20.

Cartwright, Jane. "Virginity and Chastity Tests in Medieval Welsh Prose." *Medieval Virginities*. Ed. Anke Bernau, Ruth Evans, and Sarah Salih. Toronto: University of Toronto Press, 2003: 56–79.

Chance, Jane. *The Mythographic Chaucer: The Fabulation of Sexual Politics*. Minneapolis, MN: University of Minnesota Press, 1995.

Charbonneau, Joanne and Desiree Cromwell. "Gender and Identity in the Popular Romance." *A Companion to Medieval Popular Romance*. Ed. Raluca L. Radulescu and Cory James Rushton. Cambridge: D. S. Brewer, 2009: 96–110.

Chesterton, G. K. *Chaucer*. New York: Sheed and Ward, 1956.

Coffman, George R. "An Analogue for the Violation of the Maiden in the 'Wife of Bath's Tale.'" *Modern Language Notes* 59.4 (April 1944): 271–4.

Cohen, Jeffrey Jerome. "Diminishing Masculinity in Chaucer's *Tale of Sir Thopas*." *Masculinities in Chaucer: Approaches to Maleness in the* Canterbury Tales *and* Troilus and Criseyde. Ed. Peter G. Beidler. Cambridge: D. S. Brewer, 1998: 143–56.

Cohen, Jeffrey Jerome. "On Saracen Enjoyment: Some Fantasies of Race in Late Medieval France and England." *The Journal of Medieval and Early Modern Studies* 31.1 (Winter 2001): 113–46.

Cohen, Jeremy. *'Be Fertile and Increase, Fill the Earth and Master It:' The Ancient and Medieval Career of a Biblical Text*. Ithaca, NY: Cornell University Press, 1989.

Cole, Andrew and D. Vance Smith. "Outside Modernity." *The Legitimacy of the Middle Ages: On the Unwritten History of Theory*. Ed. Andrew Cole and D. Vance Smith. Durham, NC: Duke University Press, 2010: 1–38.

Coletti, Theresa. "Purity and Danger: The Paradox of Mary's Body and the En-Gendering of the Infancy Narrative in the English Mystery Cycles." *Feminist Approaches to the Body in Medieval Literature*. Ed. Linda Lomperis and Sarah Stanbury. Philadelphia, PA: University of Pennsylvania Press, 1993: 65–95.

Colish, Marcia L. *The Mirror of Language: A Study in the Medieval Theory of Knowledge*, Revised Edition. Lincoln, NE: University of Nebraska Press, 1983.

Cotter, Wendy C. S. J. "Miracle Stories: The God Asclepius, the Pythagorean Philosophers, and the Roman Rulers." *The Historical Jesus in Context*. Ed. Amy-Jill Levine, Dale C. Allison Jr., and John Dominic Crossan. Princeton, NJ: Princeton University Press, 2006: 166–78.

Cooper, Helen. "Choosing Poetic Fathers: The English Problem." *Medieval and Early Modern Authorship*. Ed. Guillemette Bolens and Lukas Erne. Tubingen: Narr, 2011: 29–50.

Cox, Catherine S. *Gender and Language in Chaucer*. Gainesville, FL: University of Florida Press, 1997.

Crane, Susan. "Alison's Incapacity and Poetic Instability in the *Wife of Bath's Tale*." *PMLA* 102.1 (January 1987): 20–8.

Daniel, Norman. *Islam and the West: The Making of an Image*. Edinburgh: Edinburgh University Press, 1962.

Daston, Lorraine and Katharine Park. "The Hermaphrodite and the Orders of Nature: Sexual Ambiguity in Early Modern France," *GLQ: A Journal of Lesbian and Gay Studies* 1.4 (1995): 419–38.

Davis, Alfred. "The Man of Law vs. Chaucer: A Case in Poetics." *PMLA* 82.2 (May 1967): 217–25.

Davis, Isabel. *Writing Masculinity in the Later Middle Ages*. Cambridge: Cambridge University Press, 2007.

Dean, James. "Chaucer's Repentance: A Likely Story." *The Chaucer Review* 24.1 (Summer 1989): 64–76.

Delaney, Sheila. "Sexual Economics, Chaucer's Wife of Bath, and the *Book of Margery Kempe*." *Minnesota Review* 5 (Fall 1975): 104–15.

Delogu, Daisy. *Theorizing the Ideal Sovereign: The Rise of the French Vernacular Royal*. Toronto: University of Toronto Press, 2008.

DeVries, David N. "Chaucer and the Idols of the Market." *The Chaucer Review* 32.4 (1998): 391–8.

DeVun, Leah. "The Jesus Hermaphrodite: Science and Sex Difference in Premodern Europe," *Journal of the History of Ideas* 69.2 (2008): 193–218.

Dinshaw, Carolyn. *Chaucer's Sexual Poetics*. Madison: University of Wisconsin Press, 1989.

Dinshaw, Carolyn. "Chaucer's Queer Touches/A Queer Touches Chaucer," *Exemplaria* 7.1 (Spring 1995): 75–92.

Dinshaw, Carolyn. *How Soon Is Now?: Medieval Texts, Amateur Readers, and the Queerness of Medieval Time*. Durham, NC: Duke University Press, 2012.

Dobbs, Elizabeth A. "The Canaanite Woman, the Second Nun, and Saint Cecilia." *Christianity & Literature* 62.2 (2013): 203–22.

Dollimore, Jonathan. *Sexual Dissidence: Augustine to Wilde, Freud to Foucault*. Oxford: Oxford University Press, 1991.

Duncan, Edgar H. "The Literature of Alchemy and Chaucer's *Canon Yeoman's Tale*: Frameworks, Theme, and Characters." *Speculum* 43.4 (October 1968): 633–56.

Dzon, Mary. "Joseph and the Amazing Christ Child of Late-Medieval Legend." *Childhood in the Middle Ages and the Renaissance: The Results of a Paradigm Shift in the History of Mentality*. Ed. Albrecht Classen. Berlin: Walter de Gruyter, 2005: 135–57.

Duby, Georges. *The Knight, the Lady and the Priest: The Making of Modern Marriage in Medieval France*. Chicago, IL: University of Chicago Press, 1981.

Duby, Georges. *Love and Marriage in the Middle Ages*. Chicago, IL: University of Chicago Press, 1996.

Dunkerten, Jill, Carol Christensen, and Luke Syson. "The Master of the Story of Griselda and Paintings for Sienese Palaces." *Technical Bulletin* 27 (2006): 4–71.

Economou, George D. "Januarie's Sin Against Nature: the *Merchant's Tale* and the *Roman de la Rose*." *Comparative Literature* 17.3 (Summer 1965): 251–7.

Edwards, A. S. G. "The *Merchant's Tale* and Moral Chaucer." *Modern Language Quarterly* 51.3 (September 1990): 409–26.

Edwards, Robert R. "Authorship, Imitation, and Refusal in Late-Medieval England." *Medieval and Early Modern Authorship*. Ed. Guillemette Bolens and Lukas Erne. Tubingen: Narr, 2011: 51–73.

Eggert, Katherine. *Disknowledge: Literature, Alchemy, and the End of Humanism in Renaissance England*. Philadelphia, PA: University of Pennsylvania Press, 2015.

Ellis, Deborah S. "Chaucer's Devilish Reeve." *The Chaucer Review* 27.2 (1992): 150–61.

Epstein, Robert. "Sacred Commerce: Chaucer, Friars, and the Spirit of Money." *Sacred and Profane in Chaucer and Late Medieval Literature: Essays in Honor of John V. Fleming*. Ed. Robert Epstein and William Robins. Toronto: University of Toronto Press, 2010: 129–45.

Epstein, Robert. "Dismal Science: Chaucer and Gower on Alchemy and Economy." *Studies in the Age of Chaucer* 36 (2014): 209–48.

Erler, Mary C. "Three Fifteenth-Century Vowesses." *Medieval London Widows, 1300–1500*. Ed. Caroline M. Barron and Anne F. Sutton. London and Rio Grande: Hambledon Press, 1994: 165–84.

Evans, Ruth. "Chaucer in Cyberspace: Medieval Technologies of Memory in *The House of Fame*." *Studies in the Age of Chaucer* 23 (2001): 43–69.

Everest, Carol A. "'Paradys or Helle:' Pleasure and Procreation in Chaucer's *Merchant's Tale*." *Sovereign Lady: Essays on Women in Middle English Literature*. Ed. Muriel Witaker. New York and London: Garland Publishing, Inc., 1995: 63–81.

Everest, Carol A. "Sex and Old Age in Chaucer's 'Reeve's Tale,' *The Chaucer Review* 31.2 (1996): 99–114.

Everest, Carol A. "Sight and Sexual Performance in the *Merchant's Tale*." *Masculinities in Chaucer:Approaches to Maleness in the Canterbury Tales and Troilus and Criseyde*. Ed. Peter G. Beidler. Cambridge: Cambridge University Press, 1998: 91–104.

Farber, Lianna. *An Anatomy of Trade in Medieval Writing: Value, Consent, and Community* Ithaca, NY: Cornell University Press, 2006.

Federici, Silvia. *Caliban and the Witch: Women, the Body, and Primitive Accumulation*. Brooklyn, NY: Autonomedia, 2004.

Finke, Laurie. "'Alle is for to selle': Breeding Capital in the Wife of Bath's *Prologue* and *Tale*." *Geoffrey Chaucer: The Wife of Bath*. Ed. Peter G. Beidler. Boston and New York: Bedford Books of St. Martin's Press, 1996: 171–88.

Finlayson, John. "The 'Povre Widwe' in the 'Nun's Priest's Tale' and Boccaccio's 'Decameron.'" *Neuphilologische Mitteilungen* 99.3 (1998): 269–73.

Finlayson, John. "Petrarch, Boccaccio, and Chaucer's 'Clerk's Tale.'" *Studies in Philology* 97.3 (Summer 2000): 255–75.

Finlayson, John. "Chaucer's 'Summoner's Tale:' Flatulence, Blasphemy, and the Emperor's Clothes." *Studies in Philology* 104.4 (Fall 2007): 455–70.

Finnegan, Robert Emmett. "The Wife's Dead Child and Friar John: Parallels and Oppositions in the 'Summoner's Tale.'" *Neuphilologische Mitteilungen* 92.4 (1991): 457–62.

Finucci, Valeria. *The Manly Masquerade: Masculinity, Paternity, and Castration in the Italian Renaissance* (Durham, NC: Duke University Press, 2003).

Florschuetz, Angela. "'A Mooder He Hath, but Fader Hath He Noon:' Constructions of Genealogy in the *Clerk's Tale* and the *Man of Law's Tale*." *The Chaucer Review* 44.1 (2009): 25–58.

Forste-Grupp, Sheryl L. "A Woman Circumvents the Laws of Primogeniture in 'The Weddynge of Sir Gawen and Dame Ragnell.'" *Studies in Philology* 99.2 (Spring 2002): 105–22.

Fowler, Elizabeth. "The Emperor and the Waif: Consent and Conflict of Laws in the *Man of Law's Tale*." *Medieval Literature and Historical Inquiry: Essays in Honour of Derek Pearsall*. Ed. David Aers. Cambridge: D. S. Brewer, 2000: 55–68.

Fradenburg, Louise O. "The Wife of Bath's Passing Fancy." *Studies in the Age of Chaucer* 8 (1986): 31–58.

Frakes, Jerold C. "'Ther Nis Namoore to Seye': Closure in the 'Knight's Tale.'" *The Chaucer Review* 22.1 (Summer 1987): 1–7.

Fulton, Helen. "Mercantile Ideology in Chaucer's *Shipman's Tale*." *The Chaucer Review* 36.4 (2002): 311–28.

Fumo, Jamie Claire. "Thinking Upon the Crow: *The Manciple's Tale* and Ovidian Mythography." *The Chaucer Review* 38.4 (2004): 355–75.

Fumo, Jamie Claire. "The Pestilential Gaze: From Epidemiology to Erotomania in the *Knight's Tale*." *Studies in the Age of Chaucer* 35 (2013): 85–136.

Furrow, Melissa M. "The Man of Law's St. Constance: Sex and the Saeculum," *The Chaucer Review* 24.3 (Winter 1990): 223–35.

Galloway, Andrew. "Authority." *A Companion to Chaucer*. Ed. Peter Brown. Oxford: Blackwell Publishers, 2000: 23–40.

Galway, Margaret. "Philippa Pan, Philippa Chaucer." *The Modern Language Review* 55.4 (October 1960): 481–7.

Gates, Barbara T. "'A Temple of False Goddis': Cupidity and Mercantile Values in Chaucer's Fruit-tree Episode." *Neuphilologische Mitteilungen* 77.3 (1976): 369–75.

Gibson, Gail McMurray. *The Theater of Devotion: East Anglian Drama and Society in the Late Middle Ages*. Chicago, IL: University of Chicago Press, 1989.

Gilmartin, Kristine. "Array in the *Clerk's Tale*." *The Chaucer Review* 13.3 (Winter 1979): 234–346.

Ginsberg, Warren. *Tellers, Tales, and Translation in Chaucer's* Canterbury Tales. Oxford: Oxford University Press, 2015.

Given-Wilson, Chris. *Henry IV*. New Haven, CT: Yale University Press, 2016.

Given-Wilson, Chris. *The English Nobility in the Late Middle Ages: The Fourteenth-Century Political Community*. New York: Routledge, 1996.

Goodall, John. *God's House at Ewelme: Life, Devotion, and Architecture in a Fifteenth-Century Almshouse*. Aldershot: Ashgate, 2001.

Gravdal, Kathryn. *Ravishing Maidens: Writing Rape in Medieval French Literature and Law*. Philadelphia, PA: University of Pennsylvania Press, 1991.

Gravdal, Kathryn. "Confessing Incests: Legal Erasures and Literary Celebrations in Medieval France." *Comparative Literature Studies* 32.2 (1995): 280–95.

Green, Donald C. "The Semantics of Power: 'Maistrie' and 'Soveraynetee' in 'The Canterbury Tales.'" *Modern Philology* 84.1 (August 1986): 18–23.

Green, Monica H. "From 'Diseases of Women' to 'Secrets of Women:' The Transformation of Gynecological Literature in the Later Middle Ages." *Journal of Medieval and Early Modern Studies* 30.1 (2000): 5–39.

Green, Richard Firth. "Chaucer's Man of Law and Collusive Recovery." *Notes and Queries* 40.3 (1993): 303–5.

Grennen, Joseph E. "Saint Cecilia's 'Chemical Wedding': The Unity of the 'Canterbury Tales,' Fragment VIII." *The Journal of English and German Philology* 65.3 (July 1966): 466–81.

Guy-Bray, Stephen. *Against Reproduction: Where Renaissance Texts Come From*. Toronto: University of Toronto Press, 2009.

Haas, Renate. "Chaucer's 'Monk's Tale': Ingenious Criticism of Early Humanist Conception of Tragedy," *Humanistica Lovaniensia* 36 (1987): 44–70.

Hahn, Cynthia. "Joseph Will Perfect, Mary Enlighten, and Jesus Save Thee: The Holy Family as Marriage Model in the Merode Triptych." *The Art Bulletin* 68.1 (1986): 54–66.

Hallissy, Margaret. "Widow-To-Be: May in Chaucer's 'The Merchant's Tale.'" *Studies in Short Fiction* (Summer 1989): 295–304.

Hamilton, Alice. "Helowys and the Burning of Jankyn's Book." *Mediaeval Studies* 34 (1972): 196–207.

Hanawalt, Barbara A. *Crime and Conflict in English Communities, 1300–1348*. Cambridge: Harvard University Press, 1979.

Hanawalt, Barbara A. *The Wealth of Wives: Women and Economy in Late Medieval London*. Oxford: Oxford University Press, 2007.

Hanning, Robert W. *Serious Play: Desire and Authority in the Poetry of Ovid, Chaucer, and Ariosto*. New York: Columbia University Press, 2010.

Hansen, Elaine Tuttle. *Chaucer and the Fictions of Gender*. Berkeley, CA: University of California Press 1992.

Harris, Karen. "Wise Wyf's Remedies of Love: Birth Control in the Wife of Bath." *Graduate Research Journal* 1 (2014): 11–18.

Harvey, Barbara. "The Aristocratic Consumer in England in the Long Thirteenth-Century." *Thirteenth-Century England* VI. Ed. M. Prestwich, R. Britnell, and R. Frame. Woodbridge, Suffolk: Boydell and Brewer, 1997: 17–37.

Harwood, Britton J. "Language and the Real: Chaucer's Manciple," *The Chaucer Review* 6.4 (Spring 1972): 268–79.

Haskell, Ann S. "St. Simon in the 'Summoner's Tale.'" *The Chaucer Review* 5.3 (Winter 1971): 218–24.

Heffernan, Carol Falvo. "A Reconsideration of the Cask Figure in the 'Reeve's Prologue.'" *The Chaucer Review* 151 (Summer 1980): 37–43.

Heffernan, Carol Falvo. "Tyranny and Commune Profit in the 'Clerk's Tale.'" *The Chaucer Review* 17.4 (Spring 1983): 332–40.

Hellwarth, Jennifer Wynne. *The Reproductive Unconscious in Late Medieval and Early Modern England*. New York and London: Routledge, 2002.

Helsinger, Elizabeth K. "Consumer Power and the Utopia of Desire: Christina Rossetti's 'Goblin Market,'" *ELH* 58.4 (Winter 1991): 903–33.

Heninger, S. K. Jr, "The Concept of Order in Chaucer's 'Clerk's Tale,'" *The Journal of English and Germanic Philology* 56.3 (July 1957): 382–95.

Herlihy, David. *The Black Death and the Transformation of the West*. Cambridge, MA: Harvard University Press, 1997.

Herman, Peter C. "Treason in the 'Manciple's Tale.'" *The Chaucer Review* 25.4 (Spring 1991): 318–28.

Hill, Susan E. "'The Ooze of Gluttony': Attitudes towards Food, Eating, and Excess in the Middle Ages." *The Seven Deadly Sins*. Ed. Richard Newhauser. Leiden: Brill, 2014: 57–72.

Hobbins, Daniel, *Authorship and Publicity Before Print: Jean Gerson and the Transformation of Late Medieval Learning*. Philadelphia, PA: University of Pennsylvania Press, 2009.

Hodges, Laura F. "Reading Griselda's Smocks in the *Clerk's Tale*." *The Chaucer Review* 44.1 (2009): 84–109.

Holmes, George. *The Estates of the Higher Nobility in Fourteenth-Century England*. Cambridge: Cambridge University Press, 1957.

Howard, Donald R. *The Idea of The Canterbury Tales*. Berkeley, CA: University of California Press, 1976.

Howard, Donald R. *Chaucer: His Life, His Works, His World*. New York: E. P. Dutton, 1987.

Howard, Edwin J. *Geoffrey Chaucer*. London and Basingstoke: MacMillan Press, 1976.

Ingham, Patricia Clare. *The Medieval New: Ambivalence in an Age of Innovation*. Philadelphia, PA: University of Pennsylvania, 2015.

Irigaray, Luce. *Speculum of the Other Woman*. Ithaca, NY: Cornell University Press, 1985.

Jacquart, Danielle and Claude Thomasset. *Sexuality and Medicine in the Middle Ages*. Trans. Matthew Adamson. Oxford: Polity Press, 1988.

Johnson, Eleanor. "English Law and the Man of Law's 'Prose' Tale," *Journal of English and Germanic Philology* 114.4 (October 2015): 504–25.

Johnson, Lynn Staley. "'To Make in Som Comedye': Chauntecleer, Son of Troy." *The Chaucer Review* 19.3 (Winter 1985): 225–44.

Kahrl, Stanley J. "Chaucer's 'Squire's Tale' and the Decline of Chivalry." *The Chaucer Review* 7.3 (Winter 1973): 194–209.

Karras, Ruth Mazo. "Women's Labors: Reproduction and Sex Work in Medieval Europe." *Journal of Women's History* 15.4 (Winter 2004): 153–8.

Karras, Ruth Mazo. *Sexuality in Medieval Europe: Doing Unto Others*. London and New York: Routledge, 2005.

Karras, Ruth Mazo. *Unmarriages: Women, Men, and Sexual Unions in the Middle Ages.* Philadelphia, PA: University of Pennsylvania Press, 2012.

Karras, Ruth Mazo. "Reproducing Medieval Christianity." *The Oxford Handbook of Theology, Sexuality, and Gender.* Ed. Adrian Thatcher. Oxford: Oxford University Press, 2014: 271–86.

Kaske, R. E. "The Knight's Interruption of the *Monk's Tale.*" *ELH* 24.4 (December 1957): 249–68.

Kisor, Yvette. "Moments of Silence, Acts of Speech: Uncovering the Incest Motif in the 'Man of Law's Tale.'" *The Chaucer Review* 40.2 (2005): 141–62.

Kittredge, G. L. "Lewis Chaucer or Lewis Clifford?" *Modern Philology* 14.9 (January 1917): 129–34.

Klassen, Norman. *Chaucer on Love, Knowledge, and Sight.* Woodbridge, Suffolk: D. S. Brewer, 1995.

Kokeritz, Helge. "The Wyf of Bathe and Al Hire Secte." *Philological Quarterly* 26 (1947): 147–51.

Kolve, V. A. *Chaucer and the Imagery of Narrative: The First Five Canterbury Tales.* Stanford, CA: Stanford University Press, 1984.

Kruger, Steven F. "Claiming the Pardoner: Toward a Gay Reading of Chaucer's *Pardoner's Tale.*" *Exemplaria* 6 (1994): 115–39.

Kruger, Steven F. "Medieval Christian (Dis)identification: Muslims and Jews in Guibert of Nogent." *New Literary History* 28.2 (Spring 1997): 185–201.

Kudlien, Fridolf. "The Seven Cells of the Uterus: The Doctrine and its Roots," *Bulletin of the History of Medicine* 39 (1965): 415–23.

Ladd, Roger A. "Selling Alys: Reading (with) the Wife of Bath." *Studies in the Age of Chaucer* 34 (2012): 141–71.

Lanborn, E. A. Greening. "The Arms on the Chaucer Tomb at Ewelme." *Oxoniensia* (1940): 1–16.

Leicester, H. Marshall "'My bed was full of verray blood:' Subject, Dream, and Rape in the Wife of Bath's *Prologue* and *Tale.*" *Geoffrey Chaucer: The Wife of Bath.* Ed. Peter G. Beidler. Boston and New York: Bedford Books of St. Martin's Press, 1996: 235–54.

Lerer, Seth. *Chaucer and His Readers: Imagining the Author in Late Medieval England.* Princeton, NJ: Princeton University Press, 1993.

Lerer, Seth. "Chaucer's Sons." *University of Toronto Quarterly* 73.3 (Summer 2004): 906–16.

Lewis, Celia M. "History, Mission, and Crusade in *The Canterbury Tales.*" *The Chaucer Review* 42.4 (2008): 353–82.

Lewis, Katherine J. "Becoming a Virgin King: Richard II and Edward the Confessor." *Gender and Holiness: Men, Women, and Saints in Late Medieval Europe.* Ed. Samantha J. E. Riches and Sarah Salih. London and New York: Routledge 2002: 86–100.

Lochrie, Karma. *Heterosyncrasies: Female Sexuality When Normal Wasn't.* Minneapolis, MN: University of Minnesota Press, 2005.

Loengard, Janet Senderowitz. "*Rationabilis Dos*: Magna Carta and the Widow's 'Faire Share' in the Earlier Thirteenth Century." *Wife and Widow in Medieval England.* Ed. Sue Sheridan Walker. Ann Arbor, MI: University of Michigan Press, 1993: 59–80.

Longsworth, Robert. "Privileged Knowledge: St. Cecilia and the Alchemist in the 'Canterbury Tales." *The Chaucer Review* 27.1 (1992): 87–96.

Lowes, John Livingston. "Chaucer and Dante's 'Convivio.'" *Modern Philology* 13.1 (May 1915): 19–33.

Lowes, John Livingston. *Geoffrey Chaucer.* Bloomington, IN: Indiana University Press, 1958.

Lynch, Kathryn L. "'Diversitee bitwene hir bothe lawes': Chaucer's Unlikely Alliance Between a Lawyer and a Merchant." *The Chaucer Review* 46.1–2 (2011): 74–92.

MacLaine, A. H. "Chaucer's Wine Cask Image: Word Play in 'The Reeve's Prologue." *Medium Aevum* 31.2 (1962): 129–31.

Mann, Jill. *Feminizing Chaucer.* Cambridge: D. S. Brewer, 2002.

Manning, James Alexander. *The Lives of the Speakers of the House of Commons.* London: E. Churton, 1850.

Margherita, Gayle. *The Romance of Origins: Language and Sexual Difference in Middle English Literature.* Philadelphia, PA: University of Pennsylvania Press, 1994.

Marvin, Corey J. " "I Will Thee Not Forsake'" The Kristevan Maternal Space in Chaucer's *Prioress's Tale* and John of Garland's *Stella maris." Exemplaria* 8.1 (1996): 35–58.

Masciandaro, Nicola. *The Voice of the Hammer: The Meaning of Work in Middle English Literature.* Notre Dame, IN: University of Notre Dame Press, 2007.

Masson, Cynthia. "Queer Copulation and the Pursuit of Divine Conjunction in Two Middle English Alchemical Poems." *Intersections of Sexuality and the Divine in Medieval Culture: The Word Made Flesh.* Ed. Susannah Mary Chewning. New York: Routledge, 2005: 37–48.

Matheson, Lister M. "Chaucer's Ancestry: Historical and Philological Re-Assessments." *The Chaucer Review* 25.3 (Winter 1991): 171–89.

Matsuda, Takami. "Death, Prudence, and Chaucer's 'Pardoner's Tale,'" *The Journal of English and Germanic Philology* 91.3 (July 1992): 313–24.

Matthews-Grieco, Sara F. (ed.). *Cuckoldry, Impotence and Adultery in Europe (15th–17th Centuries).* New York: Ashgate, 2014.

Maynadier, G. H. *The Wife of Bath's Tale: Its Sources and Analogues.* London: D. Nutt, 1901.

McAlpine, Monica E. "The Pardoner's Homosexuality and How It Matters." *PMLA* 95.1 (January 1980): 8–22.

McAvoy, Liz Herbert. " 'The Moders Service': Motherhood as Matrix in Julian of Norwich." *Mystics Quarterly* 24.4 (December 1998): 181–97.

McCracken, Peggy. *The Curse of Eve, The Wound of the Hero: Blood, Gender, and Medieval Literature.* Philadelphia, PA: University of Pennsylvania Press, 2003.

McFarlane, K. B. *The Nobility of Later Medieval England.* Oxford: Oxford University Press, 1973.

McGavin, John J. *Chaucer and Dissimilarity: Literary Comparisons in Chaucer and Other Late-Medieval Writing.* Madison and Teaneck, NJ: Fairleigh Dickinson University Press, 2000.

McIlhaney, Anne E. "Sentence and Judgment: The Role of the Fiend in Chaucer's 'Canterbury Tales.'" *The Chaucer Review* 31.2 (1996): 173–83.

Mckinley, Kathryn L. "Gower and Chaucer: Readings of Ovid in Late Medieval England." *Ovid in the Middle Ages.* Ed. James G. Clark, Frank T. Coulson, Kathryn L. McKinley. Cambridge: Cambridge University Press, 2011: 197–230.

McTavish, Lianne. *Childbirth and the Display of Authority in Early Modern France.* Aldershot, UK and Burlington, VT: Ashgate Publishing, 2005.

Miller, Jacqueline T. "The Writing on the Wall: Authority and Authorship in Chaucer's 'House of Fame.'" *The Chaucer Review* 17.2 (Fall 1982): 95–115.

Miller, Milton. "The Heir in the *Merchant's Tale." Philological Quarterly* 29 (1950): 437–40.

Minnis, A. J. *De vulgari auctoritate*: Chaucer, Gower and the Men of Great Authority." *Chaucer and Gower: Difference, Mutuality, Exchange.* Ed. R. F. Yeager. Victoria: University of Victoria, 1991: 36–74.

Minnis, A. J. "The Wisdom of Old Women: Alisoun of Bath as Auctrice." *Writings on Love in the English Middle Ages.* Ed. Helen Cooney. New York: Palgrave Macmillan, 2006: 99–114.

Minnis, A. J. *Fallible Authors: Chaucer's Pardoner and Wife of Bath.* Philadelphia, PA: University of Pennsylvania Press, 2008.

Minnis, A. J. *Medieval Theory of Authorship: Scholastic Literary Attitudes in the Late Middle Ages*. 2nd Ed. Philadelphia, PA: University of Pennsylvania Press, 2010.

Minnis, A. J. *From Eden to Eternity: Creations of Paradise in the Later Middle Ages*. Philadelphia, PA: University of Pennsylvania Press, 2016.

Mistry, Zubin. "Alienated From the Womb: Abortion in the Early Medieval West, *c*.500–900," PhD dissertation, University College London, 2011.

Moore, Roger E. "Nominalistic Perspectives on Chaucer's *The Man of Law's Tale*." *Comitatus: A Journal of Medieval and Renaissance Studies* 23.1 (1992): 80–100.

Mortimer, Ian. *Henry IV: The Righteous King*. London: Jonathan Cape, 2007.

Moss, Rachel E. *Fatherhood and its Representations in Middle English Texts*. Cambridge: D. S. Brewer, 2013.

Murray, Mary. "Primogeniture, Patrilineage, and the Displacement of Women." *Women, Property, and the Letters of the Law in Early Modern England*. Ed. Nancy E. Wright, Margaret W. Ferguson, and A. R. Buck. Toronto: University of Toronto Press, 2004: 121–36.

Myles, Robert. "Confusing Signs: The Semiotic Point of View in the *Clerk's Tale*." *Chaucer and Language: Essays in Honour of Douglas Wurtele*. Ed. Robert Myles and David Williams. Montreal and Kingston: McGill–Queen's University Press, 2001: 107–25.

Neal, Derek G. *The Masculine Self in Late Medieval England*. Chicago, IL: University of Chicago Press, 2009.

Nederman, Cary J. and Jacqui True. "The Third Sex: The Idea of the Hermaphrodite in Twelfth-Century England," *Journal of the History of Sexuality* 6.4 (1996): 497–517.

Newton, Allyson. "The Occlusion of Maternity in Chaucer's *Clerk's Tale*." *Medieval Mothering*. Ed. John Carmi Parsons and Bonnie Wheeler. New York and London: Garland Publishing, 1996: 63–75.

Niebrzydowski, Sue. "Monstrous (M)othering: The Representation of the Sowdanesse in Chaucer's *Man of Law's Tale*." *Consuming Narratives: Gender and Monstrous Appetite in the Middle Ages and the Renaissance*. Ed. Liz Herbert McAvoy and Teresa Walters. Cardiff: University of Wales Press, 2002: 196–208.

Nolan, Maura. "'Acquiteth yow now': Textual Contradiction and Legal Discourse in the Man of Law's Introduction." *The Letter of the Law: Legal Practice and Literary Production in Medieval England*. Ed. Emily Steiner and Candace Barrington. Ithaca, NY: Cornell University Press, 2002: 136–53.

Oberembt, Kenneth J. "Chaucer's Anti-Misogynist Wife of Bath." *The Chaucer Review* 10.4 (Spring 1976): 287–302.

Olson, Glending. "Author, Scribe, and Curse: The Genre of *Adam Scriveyn*." *The Chaucer Review* 42.3 (2008): 284–97.

Olson, Glending. "Measuring the Immeasurable: Farting, Geometry, and Theology in the *Summoner's Tale*." *The Chaucer Review* 43.4 (2009): 414–27.

Olson, Paul A. "Chaucer's Merchant and January's 'Hevene in Erthe Heere.'" *ELH* 28.3 (September 1961): 203–14.

Orme, Nicolas. *Medieval Children*. New Haven, CT: Yale University Press, 2001.

Palmer, Robert C. "Contexts of Marriage in Medieval England: Evidence from the King's Court circa 1300." *Speculum* 59.1 (January 1984): 42–67.

Park, Katharine. *Secrets of Women: Gender, Generation, and the Origins of Human Dissection*. New York: Zone Books, 2006.

Parry, Joseph D. "Interpreting Female Agency and Responsibility in the *Miller's Tale* and the *Merchant's Tale*." *Philological Quarterly* 80.2 (Spring 2001): 133–67.

Patterson, Lee. *Chaucer and the Subject of History*. Madison: University of Wisconsin Press, 1991.

Patterson, Lee. *Temporal Circumstances: Form and History in the* Canterbury Tales. New York: Palgrave MacMillan, 2006.

Paull, Michael R. "The Influence of the Saint's Legend Genre in the 'Man of Law's Tale,'" *The Chaucer Review* 5.3 (Winter 1971): 179–94.

Payan, Paul. *Joseph: Une image de la paternite dans l'Occident medieval* (Paris: Aubier, Collection Historique, 2006.

Payer, Pierre J. *Sex and the New Medieval Literature of Confession, 1100–1300*. Toronto: Pontifical Institute of Mediaeval Studies, 2009.

Payling, S. J. "Social Mobility, Demographic Change, and Landed Society in Late Medieval England." *The Economic History Review* 45.1 (1992): 51–73.

Pearman, Tory Vandeventer. "Oh Sweete Venym Queynte!': Pregnancy and the Disabled Female Body in the *Merchant's Tale.*" *Disability in the Middle Ages: Reconsiderations and Reverberations.* Ed. Joshua R. Eyler. London and New York: Routledge, 2016: 25–38.

Pearsall, Derek. *The Canterbury Tales.* New York: Routledge, 1985.

Pearsall, Derek. *The Life of Geoffrey Chaucer: A Critical Biography.* Oxford: Blackwell, 1992.

Peck, Russell A. "Chaucer and the Nominalist Questions." *Speculum* 53.4 (October 1978): 745–60.

Peters, Edward M. "Transgressing the Limits Set by the Fathers: Authority and Impious Exegesis in Medieval Thought," *Christendom and its Discontents: Exclusion, Persecution, and Rebellion, 1000–1500,* ed. Scott L. Waugh and Peter Diehl (Cambridge: Cambridge University Press, 2002): 338–360.

Plummer, John F. "Hooly Chirches Blood: Simony and Patrimony in Chaucer's 'Reeve's Tale.'" *The Chaucer Review* 18.1 (Summer 1983): 49–60.

Poos, L. R. "Plague Mortality and Demographic Depression in Later Medieval England." *Yale Journal of Biology and Medicine* 54.3 (1981): 227–34.

Pratt, Robert A. "The Order of *The Canterbury Tales.*" *PMLA* 66.6 (Dec. 1951): 1141–67.

Principe, Lawrence M. *The Secrets of Alchemy.* Chicago, IL: University of Chicago Press, 2013.

Pugh, Tison. "Queeering Genres, Battering Males: The Wife of Bath's Narrative Violence." *Journal of Narrative Theory* 33.2 (Summer 2003): 115–42.

Ramsey, Roger. "Clothing Makes a Queen in the *Clerk's Tale.*" *The Journal of Narrative Technique* 7.2 (Spring 1977): 104–15.

Randall, Michael. *Building Resemblance: Analogical Imagery in the Early French Renaissance.* Baltimore and London: Johns Hopkins University Press, 1996.

Raybin, David. "The Death of a Silent Woman: Voice and Power in Chaucer's *Manciple's Tale.*" *The Chaucer Review* 95.1 (January 1996): 19–37.

Raybin, David. "Chaucer's Creation and Recreation of the 'Lyf of Seynt Cecile.'" *The Chaucer Review* 32.2(1997): 196–212.

Raybin, David. "Goddes Instrumentz': Devils and Free Will in the *Friar's* and *Summoner's* Tales." *The Chaucer Review* 46.1–2 (2011): 93–110.

Reichman, Edward. "Anatomy and the Doctrine of the Seven-Chamber Uterus in Rabbinic Literature," *Hakirah: The Flatbush Journal of Jewish Law and Thought* 9 (Winter 2010): 245–65.

Reyerson, Kathryn and Thomas Kuehn, "Women and Law in France and Italy," *Women in Medieval Western European Culture,* ed. Linda Mitchell (Taylor and Francis, 1999): 136–8.

Rice, Nicole R. *Lay Piety and Religious Discipline in Middle English Literature.* Cambridge: Cambridge University Press, 2008.

Riddle, John M. *Eve's Herbs: A History of Contraception and Abortion in the West.* Cambridge, MA and London: Harvard University Press, 1997.

Rigby, S. H. "The Wife of Bath, Christine de Pizan, and the Medieval Case for Women." *The Chaucer Review* 35.2 (2000): 133–65.

Robertson, D. W. *A Preface to Chaucer: Studies in Medieval Perspectives.* Princeton, NJ: Princeton University Press, 1962.

Robertson, D. W. "'And for My Land Thus Hastow Mordred Me?': Land Tenure, the Cloth Industry and the Wife of Bath." *The Chaucer Review* 14.4 (Spring 1980): 403–20.

Robertson, Elizabeth. "The 'Elvyssh' Power of Constance: Christian Feminism in Geoffrey Chaucer's *The Man of Law's Tale*." *Studies in the Age of Chaucer* 23 (2001): 143–80.

Root, Jerry. "Space to Speke:' The Wife of Bath and the Discourse of Confession." *The Chaucer Review* 28.3 (1994): 252–72.

Rose, Christine M. "The Jewish Mother-In-Law: Synagoga and the *Man of Law's Tale*." *Hildegard of Bingen: A Book of Essays.* Ed. Maud Burnett McInernay. New York and London: Taylor and Francis, 1998: 191–226.

Rosenberg, Bruce A. "The Contrary Tales of the Second Nun and the Canon's Yeoman." *The Chaucer Review* 2.4 (Spring 1968): 278–91.

Rosenberg, Bruce A. The "Cherry Tree Carol" and the "Merchant's Tale." *The Chaucer Review* 5.4 (Spring 1971): 264–76.

Rosenthal, Joel T. *Patriarchy and Families of Privilege in Fifteenth-Century England.* Philadelphia, PA: University of Pennsylvania Press, 1991.

Rosenthal, Joel T. *Old Age in Late Medieval England.* Philadelphia, PA: University of Pennsylvania Press, 1996.

Roskell, John Smith. *The Impeachment of Michael de la Pole, Earl of Suffolk in 1386.* Manchester: Manchester University Press, 1984.

Roskell, J. S., Linda Clark, and Carole Rawcliffe (ed.). *The House of Commons 1386–1421.* Vol. II. Stroud: Alan Sutton Publishing, 1992.

Rossiter, William T. "Chaucer Joins the *Schiera*: The House of Fame, Italy and the Determination of Posterity." *Chaucer and Fame: Reputation and Reception.* Ed. Isabel Davis and Catherine Nall. Woodbridge, Suffolk: Boydell and Brewer, 2015: 21–42.

Rubin, Miri. *Mother of God: A History of the Virgin Mary.* New Haven, CT: Yale University Press, 2009.

Ruffolo, Lara. "Literary Authority and the Lists of Chaucer's 'House of Fame:' Destruction and Definition through Proliferation." *The Chaucer Review* 27.4 (1993): 325–41.

Ruud, Martin B. *Thomas Chaucer.* Minneapolis, MN: University of Minnesota Press, 1926.

Sadlak, Gregory M. "Otium, Negotium, and the Fear of Acedia in the Writings of England's Late Medieval Ricardian Poets." *Idleness, Indolence and Leisure in English Literature.* Ed. Monika Fludernik and Miriam Nandi. New York: Palgrave MacMillan, 2014: 17–40.

Salih, Sarah. "Idols and Simulacra: Paganity, Hybridity, and Representation in *Mandeville's Travels*." *The Monstrous Middle Ages.* Ed. Bettina Bildhauer and Robert Mills. Cardiff: University of Wales Press, 2003: 113–33.

Salisbury, Eve. "Murdering Fiction: The Case of *The Manciple's Tale*." *Studies in the Age of Chaucer* 25 (2003): 309–16.

Salter, David. "'Born to Thraldom and Penance:' Wives and Mothers in Middle English Romance." *Writing Gender and Genre in Medieval Literature: Approaches to Old and Middle English Texts.* Ed. Elaine Treharne. Cambridge: D. S. Brewer, 2002: 41–60.

Sanok, Catherine. "Performing Feminine Sanctity in Late Medieval England: Parish Guilds,Saints' Plays, and the *Second Nun's Tale*." *Journal of Medieval and Early Modern Studies* 32.2 (Spring 2002): 269–303.

Saunders, Corinne J. *Rape and Ravishment in the Literature of Medieval England.* Cambridge: D. S. Brewer, 2001.

Scanlon, Larry. *Narrative, Authority, and Power: The Medieval Exemplum and the Chaucerian Tradition*. Cambridge: Cambridge University Press, 1994.

Schibanoff, Susan. "Worlds Apart: Orientalism, Antifeminism and Heresy in Chaucer's *Man of Law's Tale*." *Exemplaria* 8.1 (1996): 59–96.

Shapiro, Gloria K. "Dame Alice as Deceptive Narrator." *The Chaucer Review* 6.2 (Fall 1971): 130–41.

Shimomura, Sachi. *Odd Bodies and Visible Ends in Medieval Literature*. New York: Palgrave MacMillan, 2006.

Schlauch, Margaret. *Chaucer's Constance and Accused Queens*. New York: New York University Press, 1927.

Seal, Samantha Katz. "Pregnant Desire: Eyes and Appetites in the *Merchant's Tale*." *The Chaucer Review* 48.3 (2014): 284–306.

Seal, Samantha Katz. "Reading Like a Jew: The *Physician's Tale* and the Letter of the Law." *The Chaucer Review* 52.3 (2017): 298–317.

Sears, Elizabeth. *The Ages of Man: Medieval Interpretations of the Life Cycle*. Princeton, NJ: Princeton University Press, 1986.

Sharp, Michael D. "Reading Chaucer's 'Manly man': The Trouble with Masculinity in the *Monk's Prologue* and *Tale*." *Masculinities in Chaucer: Approaches to Maleness in the* Canterbury Tales *and* Troilus and Criseyde. Ed. Peter G. Beidler. Cambridge: D. S. Brewer, 1998: 173–85.

Shephard, M. *Tradition and Re-Creation in Thirteenth Century Romance: "La Manekine" and "Jehan Et Blonde" by Philippe de Remi*. Amsterdam: Rodopi Press, 1990.

Sidhu, Nicole Nolan. *Indecent Exposure: Gender, Politics, and Obscene Comedy in Middle English Literature*. Philadelphia, PA: University of Pennsylvania Press, 2016.

Sisk, Jennifer L. "Religion, Alchemy, and Nostalgic Idealism in Fragment VIII of the *Canterbury Tales*." *Studies in the Age of Chaucer* 32 (2010): 151–77.

Skinner, Patricia. "The Pitfalls of Linear Time: Using the Medieval Female Life Cycle as an Organizing Strategy." *Reconsidering Gender, Time, and Memory in Medieval Culture*. Ed. Elizabeth Cox, Liz Herbert McAvoy, and Roberta Magnani. Cambridge: D. S. Brewer, 2015: 13–28.

Sleeth, Charles R. "'My Dames Loore' in 'The Canterbury Tales." *Neuphilologische Mitteilungen* 89.2 (1988): 174–84.

Smith, D. Vance. "Body Doubles: Producing the Masculine Corpus." *Becoming Male in the Middle Ages*. Ed. Jeffrey Jerome Cohen and Bonnie Wheeler. New York and London: Garland Publishing, 1997: 3–20.

Smith, D. Vance. "Plague, Panic Space, and the Tragic Medieval Household." *The South Atlantic Quarterly* 98.3 (Summer 1999): 367–414.

Smith, Warren S. "The Wife of Bath Debates Jerome." *Satiric Advice on Women and Marriage*. Ed. Warren S. Smith. Ann Arbor, MI: University of Michigan Press, 2005, 247–8.

Soane-Møller, Vigdis. *Philosophy Without Women: The Birth of Sexism in Western Thought*. London and New York: Continuum, 1999.

Southern, R. W. *St. Anselm: A Portrait in a Landscape*. Cambridge: Cambridge University Press, 1992.

Spearing, A. C. *Medieval to Renaissance in English Poetry*. Cambridge: Cambridge University Press, 1985.

Spring, Eileen. *Law, Land, and Family: Aristocratic Inheritance in England, 1300-1800*. Chapel Hill, NC: University of North Carolina Press, 1997.

Stanbury, Sarah. "Regimes of the Visual in Premodern England: Gaze, Body, and Chaucer's 'Clerk's Tale.'" *New Literary History* 28.2 (Spring 1997): 261–89.

Stanbury, Sarah. *The Visual Object of Desire in Late Medieval England*. Philadelphia, PA: University of Pennsylvania Press, 2008.

Steadman, John M. "The Book-Burning Episode in the Wife of Bath's Prologue: Some Additional Analogues." *PMLA* 74.5 (December 1959): 521–5.

Stone, Lawrence. *The Family, Sex and Marriage in England, 1500–1800*. New York: Harper and Row, 1977.

Sturges, Robert S. " 'The Canterbury Tales' Women Narrators: Three Traditions of Female Authority." *Modern Language Studies* 13.2 (Spring 1983): 41–51.

Strakhov, Elizaveta. " 'And kis the steppes where as thow seest pace:' Reconstructing the Spectral Canon in Statius and Chaucer." *Chaucer and Fame: Reputation and Reception*. Ed. Isabel Davis and Catherine Nall. Woodbridge, Suffolk: Boydell and Brewer, 2015: 57–74.

Strohm, Paul. *England's Empty Throne: Usurpation and the Language of Legitimation, 1399–1422*. New Haven, CT: Yale University Press, 1998.

Strohm, Paul. *Chaucer's Tale: 1386 and the Road to Canterbury*. New York: Viking Penguin, 2014.

Tatlock, John S. P. "Chaucer's Retractions." *PMLA* 28.4 (1913): 521–9.

Taylor, Joseph. "Chaucer's Uncanny Regionalism: Rereading the North in the *Reeve's Tale*." *Journal of English and Germanic Philology* 109.4 (October 2010): 468–89.

Thrupp, Sylvia L. "The Problem of Replacement-Rates in Late Medieval English Population." *The Economic History Review* 18.1 (1965): 101–19.

Tolan, John V. *Saracens: Islam in the Medieval European Imagination*. New York: Columbia University Press 2002.

Travis, Peter W. "The Manciple's Phallic Matrix." *Studies in the Age of Chaucer* 25 (2003): 317–24.

Travis, Peter W. *Disseminal Chaucer; Rereading the Nun's Priest's Tale*. Notre Dame, IN: University of Notre Dame Press, 2010.

Treharne, Elaine. "The Stereotype Confirmed? Chaucer's Wife of Bath." *Writing Gender and Genre in Medieval Literature: Approaches to Old and Middle English Texts*. Ed. Elaine Treharne. Cambridge: D. S. Brewer, 2002: 93–115.

Trigg, Stephanie. *Congenial Souls: Reading Chaucer from Medieval to Postmodern*. Minneapolis and London: University of Minnesota Press, 2002.

Tuana, Nancy. "The Weaker Seed: The Sexist Bias of Reproductive Theory." *Feminism and Science*. Ed. Nancy Tuana. Bloomington, IN: Indiana University Press, 1989: 147–71.

Turner, David M. *Fashioning Adultery: Gender, Sex, and Civility in England, 1660–1740*. Cambridge: Cambridge University, 2002.

Vaughan, Miceal F. "Personal Politics and Thomas Gascoigne's Account of Chaucer's Death." *Medium AEvum* 75.1 (2006): 103–22.

Walton, Michael T., Robert M. Fineman, and Phyllis J. Walton. "Why Can't a Woman Be More Like a Man?: A Renaissance Perspective on the Biological Basis for Female Inferiority." *Women and Health* 24.4 (1997): 87–95.

Warner, Lawrence. "Woman is Man's Babylon" Chaucer's 'Nembrot' and the Tyranny of Enclosure in the 'Nun's Priest's Tale." *The Chaucer Review* 32.1 (1997): 82–107.

Waugh, Scott L. "Women's Inheritance and the Growth of Bureaucratic Monarchy in Twelfth- and Thirteenth-Century England," *Nottingham Medieval Studies* 34 (1990): 71–92.

Waymack, Anna Fore. "Speaking through the 'Open-Ers:' How Age Feminizes Chaucer's Reeve." Master's thesis, University of Texas at Austin, 2013.

Weever, Jacqueline de. *Chaucer Name Dictionary: A Guide to the Astrological, Biblical, Historical, Literary, and Mythological Names in the Works of Geoffrey Chaucer*. London and New York: Routledge, 2013.

Weisl, Angela Jane. "'Quiting' Eve: Violence Against Women in the *Canterbury Tales*." *Violence Against Women in Medieval Texts*. Ed. Anna Roberts. Gainesville, FL: University of Florida Press, 1998: 115–36.

Wheatley, Edward. *Stumbling Blocks Before the Blind: Medieval Constructions of a Disability*. Ann Arbor, MI: University of Michigan Press, 2010.

Wheeler, Bonnie. "'The Prowess of Hands': The Psychology of Alchemy in Malory's 'Tale of Sir Gareth.'" *Culture and the King: The Social Implications of Arthurian Legend*. Ed. Martin B. Shichtman and James P. Carley. Albany, NY: State University of New York Press, 1994, 180–95.

Williams, Tara. "T'assaye in thee thy wommanheede:' Griselda, Chosen, Translated, and Tried." *Studies in the Age of Chaucer* 27 (2005): 93–127.

Wolfe, Matthew C. "Placing Chaucer's 'Retraction' for a Reception of Closure." *The Chaucer Review* 33.4 (1999): 427–31.

Wollstadt, Lynn M. "Repainting the Lion: 'The Wife of Bath's Tale' and a Traditional British Ballad." *The English 'Loathly Lady' Tales: Boundaries, Traditions, Motifs*. Ed. S. Elizabeth Passmore and Susan Carter. Kalamazoo, MI: Medieval Institute Publications, 2007: 199–212.

Wood, Charles T. "The Doctors' Dilemma: Sin, Salvation, and the Menstrual Cycle in Medieval Thought." *Speculum* 56.4 (October 1981): 710–27.

Woods, William F. "The Logic of Deprivation in the 'Reeve's Tale.'" *The Chaucer Review* 30.2 (1995): 150–63.

Wurtele, Douglas. "The Penitence of Geoffrey Chaucer." *Viator* 11 (1980): 335–60.

Yates, Donald N. "Chanticleer's Latin Ancestors." *The Chaucer Review* 18.2 (Fall 1983): 116–26.

Index